The World I Left Behind

The

WORLD
I LEFT
BEHIND

Pieces of a Past

LUBA BREZHNEVA

TRANSLATED BY GEOFFREY POLK

RANDOM HOUSE   NEW YORK

Library of Congress Cataloging-in-Publication Data

Brezhneva, Luba
The world I left behind: pieces of a past/Luba Brezhneva.
p.   cm.
ISBN 0-679-43911-0 (alk. paper)
I. Brezhneva, Luba, 1943– . 2. Brezhnev family. 3. Brezhnev,
Leonid Il'ich, 1906—Family. 4. Soviet Union—Politics and
government—1953–1985. I. Title.
DK275.B73A3   1995
947.085′3′092—dc20   94-41088
[B]

Manufactured in the United States of America on acid-free paper

2 4 6 8 9 7 5 3

First Edition

BOOK DESIGN BY LILLY LANGOTSKY

Foreword

ROBERT CONQUEST

The author is Leonid Brezhnev's niece. It must be said first of all that this work can be read for important insights into the milieu of the Soviet leadership of the period. But it should be added that this book is even more: it is the record of the life of a sensitive, intelligent woman. In fact, though the author's experiences of late socialism are valid and vivid, her book is also one of those human stories that sometimes emerge in Russia, and especially from Russian women. For Luba Brezhneva shares that ability to tell of ghastly and petty, infuriating and loathsome events in a dispassionate tone. The substance and the circumstances go together to make a moving and informative story.

The circumstances are those of the old Soviet regime in general and of her family connection with its long-serving chief in particular. It has been said that the roll of Soviet leaders from Lenin to Brezhnev is (even physically) like a pictorial chart of the evolution of mankind read backward. Brezhnev was indeed the epitome of a failed and fallacious enterprise. The mental deterioration of the leadership was well understood in Moscow, where it was attributed to "negative selection." Those leaders who rose in the 1930s had to meet criteria that eliminated all independent thinking and all standards but those of servility to the ruling party.

The author does not make Brezhnev exciting, but she does make him interesting, if only as a type. Dull though he was, he was for eighteen years the unquestioned, or never successfully questioned, leader of a huge military empire and spokesman for a deep-set ideological struggle with all other political forces and traditions, on a world scale. The characteristics of his court are here seen through the eyes not of a courtier but of a relative. We all know that under despotism, though usurpers of humble origin commonly raise family members into the higher echelon, a relative, even a brother, is not necessarily regarded with favor in the long run. And this was the case with the author's father, Leonid Brezhnev's brother, who was uneasy with the whole situation and occasionally the victim of intrigues, sometimes undertaken by rivals, sometimes by allies, of the general secretary. In one of her many illuminating stories, she tells how such elements were able to take advantage of an opportunity and consign her father to a psychiatric hospital for a time.

As Lytton Strachey remarked on Frederick the Great's mishandling of Voltaire, the results of arbitrary government are "apt to be disgraceful and absurd." The late Soviet experience might have taken this as a defining text. It was in fact a rare combination of insanity and stupidity. This was, at least to some degree, understood by all intelligent people under its sway. It had long since lost the respect of any but its own apparatchiks and exegetes. They saw the enforcement, and parroting, of a moribund orthodoxy as a normal and natural condition for which the question of the need for any defense hardly arose. They not only treated dissidents as psychiatric cases, but they really considered them to be such. The only question was to what degree the supposed mental abnormality in any given case was also criminal, the "offense" being against both right thinking and supernal legality.

The society that emerges follows a feudal conception. Privileges depend entirely on status: they can be revoked at the whim of anyone with enough power. The rights of individuals do not exist, and they can remain untouched, or be revived, only if they are protected by higher authority.

One of the most striking phenomena of the late Soviet period so well illustrated in this book is the apparent attitude of the ruling caste to the realities of poverty and apathy among the mass of the population. It is clear that these realities simply did not penetrate the closed minds of the apparatchiks. Enjoying the cream of material goods and services squeezed out of a deteriorating economy at the expense of unprivileged millions, they did not see themselves in any sense as an exploiting class, a parasitic extrusion on society. One is reminded of a passage in Flaubert in which a Carthaginian oligarch is unable to comprehend the idea of a slave's sadness at the death of his son. The belief of rulers that their subjects are content with their lot has usually arisen through generations of social division, hardened into habits of mind and behavior. Brezhnev and his colleagues were born into poor peasant or working-class homes. The whole stultifying stratification took place over less than an average lifetime.

The crude and repressive reality, as one sees it here, was transformed into a fantasy in the minds of the ruling group. Reading of it in these vivid and descriptive pages, we seem to be in the world of Kafka or Gogol. Doublethink is the condition of life.

Luba Brezhneva has produced one of the most valuable human documents to emerge from the late Soviet period, one that casts a light on the era's whole political and social essence. This book, in fact, is informative and moving, a richly detailed account and, at the same time, a great general view; it is a woman's individual life and a display of that primitive, pullulating organism, the Soviet state.

ROBERT CONQUEST, author of *The Great Terror* and other books, is a fellow at the Hoover Institution on War, Revolution, and Peace in Stanford, California.

Acknowledgments

I begin by thanking my parents, for granting me permission to write this book as well as for giving me priceless information and family photographs.

I wrote my story here in America, and it was in serious danger of never seeing the light, due to time limitations and my difficult emotional and material circumstances. For the fact that it was published, credit goes above all to my editor, Samuel S. Vaughan, and to my translator, Geoffrey Polk.

Sam Vaughan's supportive but unsparing remarks were of incalculable assistance. His warm and friendly letters helped me not only to work but also to survive emotionally in a country that was new and strange to me. I thank fate that I met this remarkable person, the first American to believe me and to believe in me. I would also like to thank everyone else at Random House who took part in publishing my book.

I must express a special, heartfelt gratitude to my translator and friend, Geoffrey Polk, for his truly unstinting labors and for the patience, high sense of responsibility, and exceptional scrupulousness he has displayed. His combination of professionalism, creativity, modesty, warmth, and kindness won him my complete trust and confidence, allowing for the atmosphere of complete mutual understanding that has marked our work together.

I am very grateful to Robert Conquest for having graciously agreed to write the foreword.

I cannot name all of the others whose goodwill made this moment possible. Many Americans were sympathetic to my project and to my difficult experiences in emigration; their moral support, including the valuable comments they made after reading the manuscript of this book, will always be remembered.

I am especially grateful to my lawyer, Robert Capron, for his services, his moral support, and the all-too-infrequent but always frank and warm conversations we have had. In one of my letters to him I wrote:

> It is hard to express my appreciation for your attention and your participation in my fate. Your help makes possible the resolution of vital problems. Even more important, thanks to people like you, I can now form a true picture of Americans. The two years I have spent in your hospitable country have not proved to be easy for me, and I'm glad that I have met people like you who help me bear these difficult times without losing faith in humanity.

These words apply in equal measure to everyone who gave me support during my first years in America.

Contents

CONTENTS

List of Illustrations

LIST OF ILLUSTRATIONS

Introduction

When all is said and done, the only thing any of us can call our own is our memory, and we Russians forget nothing. Or so we think. The store of memories we carry is an inescapable presence, an obsession that both nourishes and poisons our existence.

Here in America, I have gradually assembled the fragments of shattered lives into a mosaic, stories that paint a truthful if incomplete picture of my homeland. I have tried to sketch a portrait of my uncle Leonid Brezhnev, my family, and my ancestors. I have also wanted to bring to the altar of history some of the people, famous and unknown, who crossed our paths. And in my personal story, despite many distinctive features, you will find much that is common to a whole generation of Russians.

Russian by birth and language, I'm proud of my heritage. Russia has produced leading lights in the realms of science and philosophy, has enriched world culture with the work of poets, writers, composers, scientists. But I never did accept the brand of patriotism requiring a lowered head and a silent tongue. I owe Russia a debt of eternal gratitude, but I owe nothing to the state I left behind.

I have never seen my country happy. By the time of my birth, Russia had been crushed, humiliated, reviled, and pillaged. For her children, she had become a source of unending, gnawing, aching pain. But no matter how embittered we Russians became, no matter how many circles of hell we had to pass through, our memories could never be extinguished. Nothing was able—or will be able—to take the place of Russia in our hearts.

❖

Relatively little has been written about my uncle, especially in the West, though for some fifty years he was active in political life, and for eighteen years—the Brezhnev era—he stood at the head of his country. The biographical material that has come about him in post-censorship Russia has too often lacked objectivity. Observers who wrote paeans of praise to the general secretary during his lifetime are still unfounded in their statements, still distorting and falsifying, only now in the opposite direction. Conspicuously absent from virtually all accounts published to date is a truthful picture of the man—a picture of his personality and his family life.

His life story still awaits the pen of a serious biographer. Encouraged by my editor, I have written instead my own story, which attempts to suggest what it was like to grow up in the Soviet Union as a niece of Leonid Brezhnev and, along the way, to tell what I know of his life. This book does not pretend to be a work of political science; rather, it is intended to portray aspects of Soviet life from the inside and, above all, to portray the experience of one girl, then one woman.

I was fortunate in one sense, of course: though I was part of the Brezhnev clan and lived among them, my heart was often far away. I tended to identify with those subjected to humiliation and persecution, with those who had fled the Soviet Union, where human values and the rule of law had been rejected.

My decision to write this book came after long and painful deliberation. I felt obliged to reveal what I knew about the then-hidden world of Soviet life. It has not been easy to tell the inside story of my own close relatives' sorrow, of their disgrace and downfall.

I first felt the urge to emigrate to the West in the late 1960s. As the years passed, this urge became stronger. Even though close to them, I felt more and more distant from my countrymen. My thoughts of leaving the "sacred fatherland" developed into an obsession. Living in the atmosphere of a Communist country became more and more unbearable, and I left the Soviet Union at the first opportunity, not because I no longer wanted to live there but because I was no longer able to. "If your country fails to defend you," James Fenimore Cooper wrote, "if it does not respect your thoughts and your rights, then by this very failure it frees you—its citizens—from obligations."

By writing this book, I have finally stopped running away from my pursuers and have turned to look them straight in the eyes. Now that my wanderings through the minefield of memory are over, now that the writing is behind me, perhaps I can find the happiness we all pursue.

July 9, 1994

Part One

OUR ROOTS

"Did you know that purity has a smell?" my uncle asked, leaning over and seizing a handful of gleaming white snow. "It's this smell." He paused and looked beyond me into the distance. "It's the smell of freshly scoured wood, the smell of virgin birch forests.

"And what does silence sound like? . . . To me it's not this dead, frozen hush," he went on, listening intently to the woods surrounding us. "For me, silence is the chirping of crickets, the sound of mice gnawing under the floor, the ticking of a grandfather clock above a patchwork quilt. . . .

"All of these things are part of me. You, too, will carry them in your heart and hand them down to your children and grandchildren. Our roots . . .

"Never tear them out, never forget them."

Chapter One

THE HEART OF RUSSIA

*A gray sky, gray horizons filled with wandering gray
phantoms, gray birds soaring through the gray air.*

N. SHCHEDRIN

The ancestral homeland of the Brezhnevs is the Kursk region, on the great Russian plain. Among those whose lives it has nourished for generations, this monotonous, spacious, and silent land claims undying attachment: its expanses are woven into the very fabric of their souls. Here, among endless fields, deserted roads, and lazy creeks with silvery willows lining steep banks lay Brezhnevo, home of my paternal great-grandfather Yakov Maksimovich Brezhnev.

Brezhnevo was a typical impoverished Russian village in which everything bore the stamp of neglect: puddles and knee-deep mud, a few hunched-over dwellings on each side of the one street, cantankerous flocks of crows swooping over bare willow trees. . . .

My great-grandfather lived behind a long rain-blackened fence with missing posts. Through the gaps, one could see the yard, with its dirty-white chickens and a vegetable garden where tomato plants tied up with multicolored rags competed with dense weeds. As always in Russia, there was a modest bathhouse, its chimney topped with a rusting upside-down bucket.

After the stifling heat of summer, the fall soon brought to Brezhnevo a leaden sky, a warning of the impending winter and its vast, white silence. The best days came in spring, when lilacs and bird cherries bloomed brightly in the overgrown front yards and gnarled apple trees floated in a sea of white blossoms that would soon be followed by an invasion of shaggy green caterpillars.

Peasant ways had remained virtually unchanged for centuries, surviving wars, crop failures, famines, livestock epidemics, and harassment by czarist officials. Tradition was all-important: "As our parents lived," people said, "so did they bid us to carry on."

Perched on the highest hill, so that it could be seen from a distance, stood the church. On Sundays and patron saints' days, all of Brezhnevo flocked here, using the occasion to show off as well as to pray. From trunks in which they kept it neatly folded all week long, the married women fetched their finery—flowery blouses, vividly colored shawls, skirts with fluffy frills—while the maidens wove crimson ribbons into their braids.

The church was the one place where Russians could go to purify their souls, bemoan their meager lot, and quietly pray for a better life. More than a mere purveyor of spiritual teachings, the Russian Orthodox Church was a living sermon in the inimitable beauty of its art and the solemnity of its rituals. For the common folk, this was a fairy-tale world, an escape from the crudity and injustice of everyday life, a last refuge. And, above all, it was a moral force guarding them from despair and violence. The Russians brought to church their most cherished dreams and the darkest secrets of their souls.

On Christmas Day in Brezhnevo in the year 1905, a peasant girl of nineteen lingered after the service. The church was deserted except for the priest and one old woman with a basket, silently gathering candle ends. The early night was falling outside; the only light came from the dim candles burning in front of the crucifix on the lectern. The priest descended from the pulpit and blessed young Natasha as he walked by. She bent and kissed the old man's hand with its pale-blue veins.

"What do you ask for?" he inquired, smiling gently.

"Happiness, Father, and . . ." she paused, "a new shawl."

"Pray, my dear, pray. God will send a fine young man who will give you a shawl," he replied, making the sign of the cross over her.

As Natasha knelt, teary eyed, before the image of Christ on the cross and prayed passionately for happiness, the door to the church slammed. She turned around, and her eyes met those of a young man. Her face lit up. It was Ilya.

So it was told in my family.

A good son, even tempered and hardworking, Ilya Brezhnev was also sole heir of my great-grandfather Yakov Maksimovich, a respected member of the community. But it was assumed that the family of a comely young woman like Natasha—for she was a true Russian beauty—would seek to have her marry up, and talk in the village was that she and Ilya would never be able to wed.

Natasha and Ilya had been seeing each other often. On winter Sundays, the unmarried young people of the village came together to play forfeits and to exchange innocent banter. The maidens took the opportunity to work on their dowries: they embroidered towels, tablecloths, blouses, long nightshirts, and the typical Russian peasant shirts with stem and cross patterns. At one of the *posidelki*, as these gatherings were known, Ilya had sat down next to Natasha and asked for whom she was embroidering the shirt.

"For whoever I fall in love with," she had answered, without looking up from her work.

"But it looks a bit big for me."

On the day after Christmas, Ilya sent matchmakers to the home of Denis Brezhnev, Natasha's father.* Natasha had already turned down all her other local suitors, and Denis had refused to force the daughter he loved into a marriage against her wishes. He greeted Ilya's envoys warmly, placing food and a bottle of homemade vodka on the table. After a few

---

*Though almost half the families of Brezhnevo had the last name Brezhnev, not all were related.

drinks, his tongue loosened: "I want to see my daughter happy, don't I? If that's what she wants, then why not?" The day of the betrothal party was set.

At nineteen, Natasha was ripe for marriage; a year or two more would bring her the label of old maid. There could be no doubt about her feelings: she blushed whenever Ilya came near. Love was never enough, however. Villagers knew their neighbors' family histories several generations back, and before giving a daughter's hand in marriage, the parents left no story unturned. Even the character and morals of the suitor's grandfather were subject to scrutiny. If he was from another village, scouts were sent to pry such tidbits as they could out of talkative neighbors. The parents of young men were equally wary. In addition to being meek and God-fearing, the brides for their sons had to be hardworking, healthy, and strong. Peasant families judged a wife above all by how well she worked.

Presumably everyone was satisfied, because both sets of parents gave their blessings at the betrothal, held at Denis Brezhnev's home. After the village priest blessed Natasha and Ilya and the bride's mother shed a few obligatory tears, the toasts began. The young couple sat together in the "beautiful corner" of the house, under the icons.

As custom dictated, Ilya and Natasha walked through the village from house to house, bowing low and inviting guests to their September wedding. "Why such haste?" village gossips wondered and came to the obvious conclusion.

As her lawful husband-to-be, Ilya had the right to visit Natasha daily and give her gifts. The young lovers began to stay in the threshing barn until dawn, causing Denis Brezhnev many restless nights.

His wife would sigh: "Will she have a little one on her hands before there's a ring on her finger?"

When Natasha appeared in the morning, Denis would say, "My dear, you needn't go so far from home. You could visit with Ilya here, near the house."

"Yes, Papa," she would answer meekly, lowering her eyes.

And the young lovers began to spend their evenings sitting on the low wattle fence that ringed the house on three sides.

When the wedding day came, Natasha crossed the threshold of the church first. "Aha," the old women whispered, "she'll keep Ilya under her thumb!" Male attendants held wreaths over the heads of the couple as they stood in front of the pulpit, which was lined with candlesticks on each side and adorned with an open Bible and a cross. In the middle of the marriage ceremony, Natasha suddenly saw colored circles floating in front of her eyes and felt her head spinning—from the incense; she would have fainted outright had Ilya not held her up. During the lengthy thanksgiving service that followed the vows, she barely managed to stay on her feet as she listened to the new life thumping persistently in her belly.

Russian weddings, especially in the countryside, were chaotic and noisy affairs, disrupting family life and leaving a huge hole in the budget. For two or three weeks, the whole village celebrated, along with relatives from far and wide. If the weather was warm, tables were set up outside in the form of a U. Neighbors lent benches, chairs, and utensils as needed. Close relatives and friends brought food, not that anyone was too fussy about what he or she ate as long as plenty of vodka was on hand. A few revelers always slid under the table, only to be revived with cold water. By the end of the third day, when few could remember what the celebration was about, someone from another village, "visiting" for free food and drink, might feel inspired to stand up and demand another toast. Other strident voices would second his call, prompting the groom to give one more kiss to his exhausted bride.

Ilya had no great skill or inclination for farmwork and was impatient to leave for the city. His father had never considered forsaking his native soil to seek a fortune elsewhere—he used to say, "Where you were born is where you belong"—but his efforts to change his son's mind failed. In 1906, Ilya took his young wife to the city of Kamenskoye, in Ukraine:* the stubbornness and ambition concealed beneath his quiet exterior had overcome his parents' resistance.

---

*Kamenskoye was named after the Russian word for stone, *kamen,* because of the quarries in the area; in 1936, it was renamed Dneprodzerzhinsk.

He was part of a human tidal wave sweeping across Russia. At the turn of the century many young people, especially those in regions with a shortage of arable land, headed to the cities, causing consternation among their parents. In the cities, some attended school or acquired valuable skills; in the end, their accomplishments often served to heal the rift between them and the older generation. A number of these young men returned to the countryside with newly acquired revolutionary ideas that they began spreading among the local youth, for which action they were labeled rebellious and destructive by the more tradition-minded villagers.

It was like a funeral when the newlyweds left: even Yakov Maksimovich could hardly hold back tears, while his wife, Stepanida, wept and wailed openly. For many years, they would not forgive their son, and periodically they chastised him for having left.

Chapter Two

❂❂❂❂❂❂❂

A WORLD TRANSFORMED

Ilya found a factory job in Kamenskoye and moved with his wife into an earthen dwelling, damp and dark, one small room and a kitchen, no plumbing or electricity—such amenities were limited to the "good" neighborhood, inhabited by engineers and technicians. The smoke that blackened the sky also turned the walls gray and continually deposited new layers of soot on the windows. Natasha worked long and hard to make the hovel a home, scrubbing the floor, washing the windows, whitewashing the big Russian stove that separated the kitchen from the room where the family slept. Only then did she unpack her dowry: fluffy feather pillows, patchwork quilts, embroidered towels, table-cloths, and colorful curtains.

The workers' wages were low, and their families barely made ends meet. After long days in front of the open-hearth furnaces, Ilya came home exhausted. But the Brezhnevs were happier than many: they had love, youth, and a child on the way.

In old Russia, it was customary for young women and girls to tell their fortunes before Christmas and Epiphany, and many do so even

Natalya Brezhneva in 1906,
the year her first son, Leonid,
was born.

The author's paternal grandfather, Ilya
Brezhnev, in 1906. " The Brezhnevs
were luckier than many: they had love,
youth, and a child on the way."

now. To learn about her marriage prospects, a girl first places a glass of water between two candles in front of a mirror and then casts a gold ring into the water. If she sees a face in the mirror, it is that of her future mate.

Natasha had done this not long before marrying. She saw nothing in the mirror, but on the gold ring appeared an image of the Virgin Mary with her baby Jesus. "This year you'll have a son," she was told by her girlfriends, who knew of what they spoke. A son whose name, for better or for worse, would one day be known around the world.

A few months after the wedding, Natasha went into a labor that would last three days and three nights. As a last resort, her women friends carried her into a bathhouse. When she began to sweat profusely, they placed her on the floor and kneaded her belly. Soon the midwife lay exhausted on the bench, praying for the Queen of Heaven to send mercy while Natasha screamed at the top of her lungs through lips caked with blood. Tears poured out of her sightless eyes. When the pain eased enough so that she could speak, she begged, "Save me, kind people." Finally belts were wrapped around her to squeeze the child out.

Ilya was in the kitchen, gaunt faced and pale. When he wasn't looking, his mother, Stepanida, who had come to Kamenskoye for the occasion, fished some sheets and a blouse out of the cupboard: she had decided that a burial was in store, not a birth.

But shrouds proved unnecessary. "He'll be a fighter," said the midwife, deftly swaddling Natasha's black-haired, blue-eyed boy. "He looks just like a little mushroom. My, how he clings to my arms. He wants everything he has coming to him!"

"As long as he doesn't take what's not his," Natasha said faintly.

It was December 19, 1906.* They named their firstborn Leonid— Leonid Ilyich Brezhnev.** Ilya would have preferred to name the boy Yakov after his own father but didn't argue with his wife. What's in a name, after all, as long as the child is healthy?

But Leonid often caught cold in the damp underground dwelling. At night, he cried endlessly. Decades later Natasha, the woman who became my grandmother, and better referred to as Natalya Denisovna, would tell me, "He sobbed like an adult, so hard that tears overflowed into his ears. Sometimes when I would pick him up to hold him, his body would be burning with fever. I would whisper, 'Protect us, oh, Lord, from the wiles of Satan.' " She had many occasions to fear that the precious son she had struggled so hard to bring into the world might be taken away from her forever.

Besides, she sorely missed the village and her friends. She somehow

---

*Until after the revolution of 1917, Russia used the Julian calendar, which was thirteen days behind the Gregorian, the calendar that had been adopted throughout Western Europe and the Americas between the sixteenth and eighteenth centuries. Due to a slipup in the 1920s, when everyone's birth date was moved forward in accordance with the new calendar, Leonid's birthday continued to be celebrated on December 19. His birth date according to the new calendar should have been January 1, 1907.

**The Russian middle name is a patronymic, formed by adding a suffix (*-ovich, -evich,* or *-ich* for males; *-ovna, -evna,* or *-inichna* for females) to the first name of the child's father. Yakov Maksimovich means Yakov, son of Maksim; Yakov Ilyich means Yakov, son of Ilya; Natalya Denisovna is Natalya, daughter of Denis. The use of the patronymic is a sign of respect and deference.

won her husband over to her point of view, and when Leonid was two years old, the family moved back to their ancestral village. But Ilya was unhappy in Brezhnevo, and they soon returned to Kamenskoye, where they had two more children, Vera and Yakov. Yakov Ilyich, my father, was born in 1913.

The workers' families in Kamenskoye could rarely afford to buy clothing, so the younger children all wore hand-me-downs from older siblings and other relatives. For the older boys, the women's hands, trained for invention by inescapable necessity, cut and sewed the men's pants and jackets. All old clothing was redyed, patched, and altered as needed.

Footwear was a greater problem; it wore out so quickly on the children's racing feet that they generally went barefoot. When the freezing weather came, the youngest stayed home: there was nothing for them to wear outside. They ran to the outhouse in their fathers' old felt boots, left by the door for that purpose. Once little Yakov, scampering across the ice-covered yard in the oversized outhouse boots, took a bad fall. He ran home and scrambled up onto the stove. (The traditional Russian stove has a special spot upon which a person can lie down and sleep or rest.) If she had seen his bloody elbows and knees, his mother—of a generation that didn't believe in pampering children—would have punished him for his clumsiness.

"Mama kept me in pants and shirts by altering Leonid's old clothes," my father told me. "Leonid was seven years older and a lot bigger, so our mother would attach suspenders to the top of his old pants and take them up in the bottom."

The courtyards and streets of Kamenskoye were the brothers' second home, a school where they learned to walk, talk, swear, fight, and smoke. Like all workers' children, Leonid and Yakov took to heart early the first rule of the street: make loyal friends or die. Perhaps this is why they had such a remarkable sense of camaraderie and personal devotion.

Growing up, Yakov disliked his name because the other children made fun of it, calling out,

Yashka, krasnaya rubashka,
Sinyaya shtana, a sam kak satana.

Yashka, red shirt, blue trousers,
And looks like the devil.

But when he whimpered to his older brother that he was being picked on, he usually found himself rebuffed as a tattletale: "Stand up and learn to fight, or I'll hit you myself."

To get to the Dnieper River, where they swam in good weather, the brothers walked through the dirtiest, roughest sections of town, sometimes stopping on the way at a Turkish sweetshop that sold the favorite luxury of the poor, "roosters on a stick" (a sort of lollipop in the shape of a rooster). Fearing attacks by local cutthroats, they usually traveled in a group of other boys, but even so there were days when Leonid came home with telltale black-and-blue marks. After tugging his hair— "You've been fighting again, boy!"—his mother would press soothing compresses on the bruises, hoping that her husband, who frowned on fights, wouldn't see. Then she would put Leonid to bed, planting a kiss on the top of his head.

In 1913, the year my father was born, Leonid was sent to a parochial school to study reading, writing, arithmetic, and divine law; two years later, after passing entrance examinations in these subjects, he was admitted to a foreign-owned high school, or *gimnaziya*. Natalya Denisovna scrimped and saved, sacrificing all else to give her eldest son an education: the tuition for one year cost her husband one month's pay.

Leonid, the only boy from a worker's family among the forty-odd pupils, was a mountain of mischief during his first school years: he loved to hop from desk to desk and race around the yard and the halls. Of all the pupils, he was the most often punished. And classroom discipline was severe. The boys sat as straight as rods during lessons. Only the teacher's steps and the rustling of pages being turned could be heard. Leonid recalled that one of his mates once threw a paper airplane onto his desk. The teacher, assuming mistakenly that it was Leonid's, gave him a whack on the hand with his pointer. By evening, his fingers had swollen, causing agonizing pain. Natalya Denisovna sprinkled some baking soda into hot water and had her son hold his hand in the vapors. She wound the hand up in a scarf before putting him to bed.

"You'll have to bear it," she said, gently kissing his head. "We can't make a complaint. We should be thankful that you were allowed into the *gimnaziya* in the first place."

When her son got into trouble, she would sometimes give him a second punishment at home, deathly afraid that he might be expelled. Leonid, in turn, seethed with anger and resentment. It was only in later grades that he quieted down noticeably, now aware that he was an oddity in his school, self-conscious about his poverty, aloof from his fellow pupils. Compensating by studying hard, he took well to the humanities, the natural sciences, and mathematics. He had more trouble with foreign languages, and there was no one in his family to coach him. He retained only one Latin phrase: *Puto fratrem dormire* ("I think my brother is sleeping"). His little brother, asleep at his side, had provided the perfect visual aid to his nightly practice.

At bedtime, Natalya Denisovna told fairy tales. Yakov and Vera listened avidly, but Leonid was not interested. Perhaps he had outgrown such childish pleasures. In any case, he was usually so tired that he fell asleep before the end.

"Who ever saw a nice czar?" Leonid asked drowsily, after hearing his mother tell of the czars' honesty and goodness. The year was 1915 or 1916. He had already heard from teachers and classmates that the monarch was a "tormentor and an exploiter of the people."

"Silly boy," Natalya said, patting her son's head. "If there were no czar, Russia would weep bitter tears indeed. People would lose their heads; they would be sheep without a shepherd. They would turn into bandits."

But Leonid was asleep.

As the 1920s began, Russia's economy fell into disarray. Industrial technicians were busy trading on the black market; workers were trudging to the countryside in search of food for their hungry families. But they demonstrated genuine devotion to their factories, working on *subbotniki* and *voskresniki,* unpaid Saturdays and Sundays. In Kamenskoye, the open-hearth and blast furnaces damaged or neglected during the civil war were restored by experienced workers who remained in the shops day and night. Casting their work clothes onto the floor, they slept right by their machines, and their children came with food for them.

Lyonya and Yasha (as the brothers Leonid and Yakov were affectionately known) used to bring their father bundles of food lovingly prepared by their mother. While Ilya ate, the boys would stare, fascinated by everything that surrounded them. The workers in the shop, who all knew and loved Ilya's sons, would give little Yasha gifts: sometimes a pile of rusty nuts and bolts, sometimes a piece of sugar, which he always divided into three parts—for himself, Vera, and Leonid. Once Yasha got so wrapped up in his games that he forgot to divide the sugar. Soon it was too late: all that remained of the treat were sticky fingers.

"What a pig," Leonid said on the way home. "Who do you take after, I wonder?" He turned away and crossed the street. In tears, wailing and apologizing, little Yasha did his best to catch up. Leonid ignored him.

My father recalled to me how he had cursed his own greed. "I sat down right on the dusty road, exhausted from crying. I stayed there until my tears dried; like all children, I soon grew tired of crying. I found some pebbles and started playing with them, forgetting all about my brother and the sugar. Suddenly Leonid came back and took me in his arms. He was skinny but strong. He hugged me and carried me home without a word. That evening when I was half asleep, I heard him saying to our mother, 'You're spoiling Yasha. He's going to grow up selfish and greedy.' Our mother disagreed, but I was falling asleep and couldn't hear her exact words."

Yakov looked so much like his brother, Leonid, that almost everyone who saw them side by side sensed that they were related. In their youth, both adopted an assertive stance, one they would never abandon. They were very Russian in character, somehow reconciling polar opposites:

The Brezhnev brothers, Leonid (left) and Yakov, in August 1944,
during World War II in the Carpathian Mountains. A few months later
Leonid would be promoted to general.

stubborn yet willing to make concessions, intelligent yet frivolous, lazy
yet having unstoppable energy, cowardly yet courageous. Even their
handwriting was almost identical.

In other ways, the brothers were very different. Leonid was always the
favorite son. In fact, Natalya Denisovna adored him so much that she
breast-fed him to the age of five. As she would say in her old age, "I'd
be sitting in the yard with neighbors, holding little Verochka in my
arms, and Lyonya would appear out of nowhere. He would run up and
suck at my breast for a little while; then it was back to play with his
friends." According to a popular Russian belief, breast-feeding for several years brings luck and success in later life.

His mother claimed the extra attention was justified by Leonid's
poor health, which continued as he grew up. In his old age, he would
joke that he had come down with every disease in the country except
syphilis. When scarlet fever broke out at the other end of Kamenskoye,

Natalya trembled with fear, sure that her favorite son would catch it. But he didn't ever catch scarlet fever, as far as we know.

Both Leonid and his brother suffered from frequent toothaches, which caused them and their mother agony and sleepless nights. Drying their tears, Natalya Denisovna would rock them to sleep in her arms, worried that they might wake their father, exhausted after his day at the mill.

The younger son, nicknamed Bychok, the Bull Calf, by the rest of the family, did indeed look like a steep-browed young bull. Except for his toothaches, he never got sick. It was said that he had inherited his good health from his peasant grandfather and namesake, Yakov Maksimovich.

Still their mother invested all her hopes in Leonid, convincing him that as intelligent and handsome as he was, he had a real future. She would say that God had given Yasha nothing but health. This favoritism, unusual in Russian families, naturally affected the brothers' personalities. Yakov was always seen as deferential and unassuming; he was less self-confident than his older brother, who was known for making demands on the people around him. Leonid definitely knew how to get his way, but he rarely made enemies. His gaze, his smile, and his gestures set one at ease instantly. Almost no one could say no to him, thanks to his mysterious ability to motivate and manipulate without causing resentment.

In the meantime, not even the will of all the workers could save the country from disaster. With the complete collapse of agriculture came an unprecedented famine. Five million people died. All of Russia was reduced to hunger, and in Ukraine the famine had taken two million lives by the spring of 1922. Every day dozens starved to death in Kamenskoye. The people of the city rose before dawn to queue up for bread. Leonid would spend hours in line before giving his place to his mother or sister and racing off to school. Cannibalism was widespread in the countryside, and rumors of it reached the city. One of the Brezhnevs' neighbors received a letter telling of a couple who had eaten their little daughter. Vera grew afraid to be around her brothers.

The winter of 1921–22 was bitter. Leonid and his fellow pupils, sitting in the unheated school with their overcoats and hats on, would breathe on numb fingers while the teacher, lecturing incongruously about the ancient glories of sunny Rome, would stamp the floor with his felt boots.

Natalya Denisovna's one great ambition was to see her elder son graduate from the *gimnaziya*, and during the famine, she exchanged food-stuffs for lessons.

Early the following spring a typhoid epidemic struck Ukraine, whose people had already been weakened by hunger. Leonid was the only one in his family to contract the disease, which left him thin and wan, barely able to stand. But he returned to school and by summer had passed his final exams.

When Leonid left Kamenskoye in 1923 to enter a land-management technical school in the city of Kursk, he took only a little clothing, a few books, and in a carefully guarded pocket that his mother had sewn shut, his birth certificate, a paper verifying that he had been vaccinated against smallpox, and his high school diploma. His mother had proudly showed this last document to her neighbors and relatives. But she never let a soul touch it. "It took so much work. What complicated things they study nowadays!" she would say.

Following his father's instructions, sixteen-year-old Leonid paid a short visit to his grandfather Yakov Maksimovich on the way to Kursk. It was a hot summer day when he arrived in Brezhnevo. He had been here many times on holiday visits, and everything he might have seen as he walked down the dusty village street would be familiar: drooping elderberry bushes lining the street sparsely, dogs lolling about in the heat, their tails between their legs, blinding light glittering on the small windows like fool's gold. . . . How he had loved coming here in the summer to trap hares and grouse, to fish with pole and net. There had always been time to swim and hike, time to forage for spurge and sorrel in the nearby woods or traipse into neighbors' gardens to pick pods full of tender peas.

Once a few years earlier Yakov Maksimovich had let him and his brother try their hands at working the fields. The plows at the time, nicknamed "drunkards," jiggled back and forth; they also rapidly went dull and acquired a layer of ingrained dirt. In this, Yesenin's "one-horse Russia," rare was the peasant with the three or four horses needed to guide the plow with ease. The plowman's arms and back had to carry almost all the weight, and only a man of tremendous strength and experience could lay down a straight, deep furrow without developing bloody blisters. Yakov Maksimovich, who went barefoot both summer and winter, had no equal on this score. Short, stocky, of long peasant stock, he was as strong as a bull. Family legend pictures him twisting an iron poker into a knot, to the neighbors' wonderment. Leonid and Yasha strained with all their might, but the plow refused to obey. . . . "What thin veins you have," said their grandfather with a chuckle. "You need to eat more porridge."

The stormy events of the fratricidal civil war of 1918–20 had not left Brezhnevo untouched: the village had been ravaged by the armies of the Whites and the Reds in turn. Yet its appearance had changed little. The main difference was that from one of the houses—reborn as the village soviet*—the victors had hung out a scrap of red cloth. As dogs mark off their territory, so had the Bolsheviks hastened to mark the cities, towns, and villages they seized.

In later years, Leonid once remarked to me how sincerely amazed his mother had been at the number of flags, banners, and pennants she saw after the Bolshevik victory. Tens of thousands of crimson rags were waving over Russian skies at a time when there was a shortage of bandages and cotton wool and the country was unable to clothe its children properly. Where were the factories that produced the endless fabric? Where had all the red dye come from?

The civil war had pitted capitalist against worker and aristocrat against commoner, but initially the peasants, the vast majority of the population, had no desire to fight on either the Red side or the White. Ultimately they sided with the Reds, since the 1917 revolution had allowed them to seize the land they worked. The Whites, uncontested landowners only a few years before, were shedding their "blue blood" to take the land back. But although the peasants saved the Communists at

---

*The Russian word *soviet* means council.

their most critical hour, they bitterly resisted the expropriation of their grain that was soon imposed. Many said, "We have nothing against the soviets, but the Bolsheviks are bastards."

While studying in Kursk, Leonid stayed in a dormitory. He would rise early, make a hasty breakfast of leftover potatoes, drink some weak tea, and run off to class. Studying came easy to him, and so did friendships.

It took a young, healthy body to digest the lunch served in the student cafeteria: gray macaroni and tired meatballs drenched in a rust-colored sauce of an origin known only to the cook. The sticky, food-stained tables held platters of sliced rye bread covered with flies. Despite the bright-colored poster on the wall requesting loudly, PLEASE DO NOT PUT FINGERS OR EGGS INTO THE SALT, the coarse salt in the old-fashioned saltcellars was lumpy from the constant dipping of wet spoons, fingers, and everything else. The greasy spoons and forks, washed but never quite clean, were heaped up on a large metal tray in one corner. Knives were not in vogue and napkins were unheard of. But no one seemed bothered by the grim, mud-colored walls, the one-dish menu, or the cockroaches so familiar to most Russians since childhood. The 1920s were hard years, but optimism was in the air. Youth hungered for activity and saw nothing beyond the call of duty in accomplishments that seemed, and were indeed, extraordinary.

The Communist Youth Union (Komsomol) was welcoming into its ranks young people of poor peasant or proletarian origin. Leonid joined in 1923—in the beginning—one of the true believers. Collectivizing agriculture, laying new roads, and building "the projects of the century," which would form the backbone of Soviet industry, the young brought their tempestuous and unrestrained energy to the altar of an unseen tomorrow. But, too, opportunists were everywhere. Komsomol officials who "hopped from bed to bed" in search of ever more golden horizons were not rare. As early as September 1923, one wrote to his friends:

My star keeps burning brighter and brighter, and I've got my eyes on high places. . . . We drink practically every day. We have girls sticking to us like flies. I'm worn out; every day it's a new one. I almost got into trouble once. I was worried that the matter would come to court, but I relaxed when I saw that no one was going to prosecute. I was already too powerful!

The Komsomol organized patrols to deal with the rowdies, who were often armed with homemade knives, congregated in the streets and parks of the city, and accosted passersby. Leonid participated in the anti-delinquency campaigns, breaking up fights, protecting young women from attacks, confiscating knives and chains.

In a recent year, after his brother's death, my father gave me a hand-crafted Finnish-style knife with an inscription on the handle: "Save us, dear Lord, from our friends, I'll save myself from my foes." Because of its story, this expertly made but homely knife means more to me than any of the jewel-encrusted silver sabers given to my uncle in later years. And its story is this: one day Leonid had helped to break up a brawl and came back to the dormitory with a huge black eye; not long thereafter, the chairman of his patrol gave him the knife as a reward for his courage and bravery.

Meeting in the dormitory, the more peaceful students would share such extra food as they had. Often their voices would break into spirited song. One lyric from a revolutionary anthem—

> Full speed ahead along the tracks!
> With rifles at the ready,
> For us there is no turning back,
> The commune's where we're headed.

Russian folk songs—"Along a Petersburg Street" and "My Darling Girl"—were also sung, as well as romantic ballads with titles like "Burn Bright, My Star," "That Cherry-Red Shawl," and "Don't Wake Her in the Morning."

Poetry was popular, especially that of Vladimir Mayakovski—"the most revolutionary of poets." Leonid liked to recite the lyrical verses of Sergey Yesenin, the self-described last poet of the village and, like Ilya Yakovlevich, a peasant's son. This was a risky proposition: Yesenin, who had traveled abroad and acquired an American wife, the dancer Isadora Duncan, wobbled at the margin of acceptability until his death, in 1925, after which his poems were banned outright.

During his summer vacations in Brezhnevo, Leonid had found a sweetheart, Naska Tolmacheva. Later, in Kursk, he was heartbroken to learn that Naska had married a boy from a well-to-do family; she hadn't dared go against her father's wishes. His grandmother Stepanida, who had once told him that he was too poor for Naska, had been right all along. I believe it was during his last year at the technical school in Kursk that Leonid met his future wife, Viktoriya, then a student at a medical school. Following the prevailing fashion, she wore her hair short. She had amazingly lovely hands, slim and tender, with pretty dimples. Leonid used to refer to them as swan's wings.

In the 1920s and '30s, new marriage rituals were introduced, and the charters of the Komsomol and the party banned church weddings for members. Leonid and Viktoriya celebrated their wedding in the technical-school dormitory, in a manner befitting members of the Komsomol. A "representative of the people" read a long, boring lecture on the new Soviet way of life, by that time well rooted in the young proletarian nation. Then came a short talk on the significance of the family cell for the building of communism, the society of the future, when there would be abundance for everyone. The newlyweds learned that sexual intercourse was not merely a physical act but a profoundly social one as well. The working class had to keep in mind, at all times, the tasks of building a new society, and only if sex did not distract from the proletarian cause could it satisfy the new ethics.

After the lecture, Russian folkways prevailed, and the young people celebrated till dawn, dancing, drinking homemade vodka, singing traditional and revolutionary songs. The local secretary of the Komsomol fell asleep with his head on his plate, and the newlyweds' friends tossed the tipsy bridegroom into the air.

Both of the mothers sent the young couple pillows, blankets, and pots from their own households. In the beginning, Viktoriya cooked their simple meals on the kerosene stove she had received as a wedding gift. Living was hard, but relatives periodically sent food from the countryside: lard, potatoes, a little butter.

Young parents were pressured to Octoberize their children instead of baptizing them. Many girls received such names as Noyabrina, Revmira (from the Russian words for "November" and "world revolution"), Lenina, and Stalina.* But when Leonid and Viktoriya had their first child, at the end of the decade, they would give her the Russian name Galina. Their son, born a few years later, would be named Yuri.

In 1926, after passing his graduation examinations, Leonid had been assigned to work in the Kursk region, where his obligations included gathering and checking soil samples in the surrounding countryside and compiling maps for the drainage of swampy areas and the irrigation of arid zones. His work took him at times to the ancestral home in Brezhnevo, where his grandparents Yakov and Stepanida still lived.

He found a place to live near Kursk's center, its Red Square, which was surrounded by churches, a palace built by the Romadanovsky boyars, and a cathedral. About a thousand years old, Kursk had served as a border fortress of the Chernigov princedom in the eleventh and twelfth centuries, suffering frequent barbarous attacks by the nomadic Polovtsians. Its people are proud descendants of the army raised by ancient Russia's national hero, Prince Igor Svyatoslavich of Novgorod-Severski. According to Brezhnev family legend, their ancestors were among those who fought with Igor and in later centuries helped defend Kursk from the Tatars and Lithuanians.

In 1927, the year after Leonid settled in Kursk, a campaign to dispossess those peasants characterized as greedy exploiters, or kulaks, was unleashed throughout Russia.** The days were numbered for countless men who had worked hard every day to increase their holdings. This mindless, bloody campaign took millions of lives and eradicated the people's ability and desire to work the land, a loss not remedied to this day.

---

*As a result of the adoption of the Gregorian calendar, the October Revolution was celebrated in November.

**The category of peasant included everyone working the land, from landless farm laborers to smallholders who used hired labor and owned livestock and a piece of land. The authorities categorized peasants as poor, middle, or kulak.

Repressive policies toward the peasantry had begun in the first year after the revolution: in June of 1918, the new government issued a decree requiring peasants to sell all their extra grain to the state at fixed prices. Lenin believed that this policy, which met ferocious resistance, was the only way to lay the foundation upon which the "mansion of communism" would eventually be built. In the early '20s, the party, still headed by Lenin, had offered a two-hundred-thousand-ruble reward for each kulak, priest, or landowner who was hanged.

Answering the party's call, factory workers—twenty-five thousand of them in 1930 alone—went to the countryside to create collective farms and "share their experience in labor discipline and the collective organization of work." In reality, they went from village to village in a frenzy of plunder. Under the guise of helping the starving children of Leningrad and other cities, they beat well-to-do peasants bloody at the village soviets, demanding to be led to concealed grain and cattle. They had been convinced that theirs was a noble cause: "uprooting capitalism in the countryside and creating a socialist agriculture."

The campaign stirred a whirlwind of passions among the villagers themselves as farmhands, egged on by the urban workers, vented their resentment against their employers. It was an excuse for neighbor to rob neighbor without shame; kulak families lost everything they had, down to the blankets torn off their sleeping children.

In later years, Leonid told his relatives about many of the things he had seen and heard during this period. A party official in Kursk wrote him a letter:

> It does my heart good to see how we are dealing with the kulaks. Everything we do follows the latest in political theory: we leave them naked, taking their livestock, meat, tools, and all other belongings.

Messages and reports coming in from different parts of the Kursk Oblast* were discussed at meetings held in Kursk. Dispatches such as the following were held up as models of action: "On the night of

---

*The oblast is an administrative unit.

November 14, the kulaks were liquidated as a class in ———— village, and the same is expected in a few days in other villages." Another, even more monstrous, read: "The kulaks were entirely liquidated as a class between the hours of 5 P.M. and 7 A.M."

Despite compulsory grain sales and expropriations, the peasants concealed their grain, sometimes with the tacit consent of local Communists, and much of it was used to produce vodka. The peasants also began to kill off their livestock to avoid losing it to the state; in 1930, the Russian peasantry, in desperation, consumed more meat than ever before.

The frenzy reached the ancestral home of the Brezhnev family. In the smoke-filled hall of the village soviet, five-person teams of poor peasants, farm laborers, Komsomol members, and party activists were created. Their purpose was to go from house to house, confiscating "luxury items."

At stormy meetings, those labeled kulaks argued with their poorer brethren: "Go ahead and join the collective farms," they would say, "if you're ready to walk around naked and hungry." Tolmachev, the prosperous father of Leonid's one time sweetheart, Naska, used to warn: "Don't listen to the Communists' propaganda. The bed they promise is soft, but wait till you have to sleep in it."

Sometimes Leonid, visiting Brezhnevo in connection with his work as a land surveyor, would argue: "You're wrong; the land should be shared. The plowing and cultivation will be done by tractor. The cows will graze on the collective-farm pastures. You'll buy your milk in the village shop, and everyone's needs will be met."

Naska's eldest brother, the same age as Leonid, would respond with obscene gestures.

"Hold on, don't get fired up," Tolmachev would tell his son. He would try his own arguments on Leonid, still a member of the Komosomol and, again, a true believer—at this stage—in the collectivization of agriculture. "Now, why do you think I'm wealthy? It's because I'm smart. So I should be the one in charge of your soviet. But look who you went and elected—Styopka! He couldn't even make his own farm prosper, and now you've handed the whole collective over to him. You'll cry bitter tears when your children have nothing to eat!"

Leonid would leave these meetings with a heavy heart. At first, Yakov Maksimovich had been happy to see his grandson working in agriculture, spending time in Brezhnevo. His attitude changed, however. Raised by the Christian commandments, he could not condone Leonid's participation in organized banditry. He would look at his grandson in silence when the young man returned from meetings. In the evenings, the arguments began: "What do you people want, anyway? You're like thieves who stop at nothing. But you're my grandson, my own flesh and blood. Let me die in peace first; then rob and plunder as much as your conscience will allow."

"We don't only take, Grandpa" was Leonid's rejoinder. "We also distribute to the poor peasants. Don't you understand?"

"I don't want to understand. All I know is that you take what doesn't belong to you and reap what you haven't sown. God will punish you."

Yakov Maksimovich had firm views on many other subjects as well, views less prophetic. He would assure Leonid that "if you start using tractors to do your plowing, you'll lose your manhood. You won't be able to make love to women!"

The evenings were long. Watching the men wave their arms and shout in each other's faces, Stepanida, feeling sorry for both, would try to play peacemaker. But gone forever was the closeness that had once joined grandfather to grandson.

In later years in Moscow, when the topic of collectivization came up, Leonid Ilyich sometimes told the story of Styopka, a peasant from a village near Brezhnevo. Before the revolution, he had been one of the poorest peasants, known as an idler, a brawler, and a drunkard. Out of pity for his small children, fellow villagers used to leave sacks of flour by his gate on their way back from the mill, but Styopka was too lazy to pick them up. Neighbors would chuckle or cluck at the sight of the children scurrying around like ants, dragging the sacks into the barn.

Styopka would sell part of the flour for drink. At home, he would wobble up to the table—his only piece of furniture—and bang it with his fist, asking "Who's boss here?" His entire brood of dirty, half-naked children would hop around him with their ready answer: "You, Papa, you!"

When collectivization began, Styopka somehow sobered up with amazing swiftness, in time to become an activist and, eventually, a collective-farm chairman. Walking from house to house, he taunted the women he saw weeping and clutching their modest possessions: "We're trying to help you. Don't worry, you'll have a blanket—a shared blanket half a kilometer in length, that is. The beds and tables will also be shared."

At the women's rebukes, Styopka's eyes would narrow into a suspicious scowl. "Anyone who is against the collective farms is an enemy of Soviet rule and a friend of Curzon's."*

Leonid remembered clearly one overcast November day when he came to Brezhnevo "to drop in on his grandfather for a minute," as he liked to say. After washing his hands, he sat down to a bowl of steaming-hot buckwheat porridge. There was also milk, in a pitcher with cream floating on the top. Yakov, considered a middle peasant, still had his cow. It was only later that the middle peasants were sent off to log the Siberian forests along with the kulaks. Leonid's grandparents, nearly eighty, were never deported, because of their age.

"Lyonya," said his grandmother, cutting thick slices of bread, "today Styopka is going to confiscate the Tolmachev family's property. Doesn't anybody care? They have grandchildren to support. It makes my skin crawl to think about it—"

Leonid stood up and bolted out the door. The gates to the Tolmachev home were wide open. Standing by the barn was the youngest son, a brother of Naska's. In a torn shirt, barefoot and pale, he was jabbing a pitchfork into the air, repeating as though delirious, "I'll kill whoever comes near!"

---

*The Englishman Lord Curzon (1859–1925), known for proposing the Curzon line to establish the eastern borders of Poland in 1919.

Tolmachev, disheveled and wild eyed, struggled to get to his son. "Let me go," he cried out, "or my boy will wind up in prison!" But the hired hands held him back.

When the young rebel had been subdued and tied up, the Reds chased the terrified women from the house and began spiriting away everything of value they could find. The patriarch stood to one side, gritting his teeth and moaning softly as though in pain; his daughter Naska stood beside him with a small child in her arms, looking at her tormentors with undisguised hatred. Leonid watched for a few minutes and then turned and left.

The following morning brought deportation orders. Tolmachev died of heart failure on the way, and his entire clan, including the small grandchildren, was sent on to Siberia, a land that was to serve as mass grave for tens of thousands of peasant families, as it had for countless Cossack families less than a decade earlier.

Before the 1917 revolution, district police officers were sometimes sent to collect unpaid taxes in the villages. Amidst tears and screams, they seized property for auction. The family cow, the source of milk for the children and the old people, might be driven away; pigs, chickens, and the last copper samovar belonging to the family might be taken. But even during those bleak days, the authorities never descended to the systematic barbarism of the collectivization years: they never seized grain, potatoes, a peasant's last horse, women's clothing, essential farming equipment, or household utensils.

A tragic irony is that much of the grain confiscated during collectivization rotted in grain elevators, clubhouses, and the by-then-empty landowners' estates. Grain had to be discarded at the same time starving children were dying like flies.

Sitting in his office in Kursk, Leonid may have given little deep thought to the information bulletins he was reading: the numbers and reports represented strangers whose lives were of no interest to him. But as his land surveying took him from village to village, he saw families like the Tolmachevs being stripped of everything from tools and tablespoons to women's skirts. During his childhood summers in Brezhnevo, he had visited the homes of men now branded kulaks, playing with their children and knowing only kindness from them.

They were described as greedy leeches, but what of Tolmachev? Despite all their disagreements, Leonid knew him as a kindly man and a good neighbor to his grandfather Yakov Maksimovich. . . .

Leonid Ilyich moved out of Kursk in late 1927, having been given surveying assignments first in Belorussia, near Orsha, and then in the central Urals. For a while, he lived in Sverdlovsk (Yekaterinburg) with the family of a former czarist general, renting a corner in the kitchen. The old man had not received a pension, and he and his wife were unable to work, not only because of their advanced age but also because they were Former People, that is, part of the upper classes under the czar. Their own room was tiny but cozy, cluttered with books and old photographs.

Leonid, considerate and outgoing by nature, rapidly became friends with the family. Evenings would find him sitting with his hosts. The general was polite but taciturn and extremely circumspect. Leonid, despite all that he had seen, tried to sway the old man to the cause of socialism, describing in glowing colors the "shining future in store for Russia." The general didn't argue but switched to the formal mode of address and reminded Leonid of his age—a hint that it was time for bed. In 1937, when the vagaries of fate brought Leonid back to Sverdlovsk, to this same tiny apartment, the general had become a victim of the same wave of terror that Leonid himself was fleeing by then. But the details of that story must wait.

It was in Sverdlovsk that Leonid's political career really began. Due to his age, he had to leave the Komsomol. The next logical step was membership in the Communist Party, whose ranks were swelling.

Even people in the arts and sciences joined the party. Men and women of culture and talent who had enriched the country with their knowledge and inventions stood trembling before barely literate ironsmiths, menial laborers, and housewives, answering questions about such weighty matters as the errors of right deviationists, the tasks of the party, and the significance of the recent plenary session of the Central Committee.

Membership did have its drawbacks: after joining, party members had to cough up monthly dues until the end of their lives, even out of meager pensions. They also had to attend deadly dull meetings. Leonid once recounted a trick that an old friend of his had come up with: before a meeting began, he would draw an alert pair of paper eyes and glue them onto the inside of his glasses; then, after asking a companion to give him a poke in the ribs if he started to snore, he felt free to fall asleep. Leonid greatly regretted not wearing glasses himself.

In later years, speaking about the interrogation he had to submit to after applying for party membership, he recalled nervously discussing his moral character, anxious to ingratiate himself with the commission. When the grilling was over, he went out into the hallway to await the decision, trembling and gulping down *validol* tablets to calm his nerves.

In 1929, he was accepted as a candidate member of the party. He was also elected people's deputy from the Bisertsky Rayon of the Sverdlovsk Okrug.* But more than a year passed before Leonid, by this time back in his native Kamenskoye, actually received his membership card.

Why did Leonid enter the party so late, given that workers' children were entitled to full membership six months after acceptance as candidate members? Russian political scientists still debate the question. A conversation I overheard in the early '60s offers an answer. I was a high school student at the time and visiting Moscow with my father. At a gathering, the men began telling one another how long they had been in the party. Someone asked Leonid why he had joined relatively late. His answer: "The way things were, I had to have second thoughts about being in the party. There were too many so-called Communists blatantly disgracing the party's good name at the time." In later years, I would hear both from Leonid himself and from other relatives how dis-

---

*Both are post-revolutionary administrative units; the *rayon* is part of the *okrug*, which in turn is part of the *oblast*.

gusted he had been by the savage brutality, lawlessness, and pigheaded-ness of those in charge of the anti-kulak campaigns, how appalled he had been that the chairmen of the village soviets were growing wealthy, using political ideology as a cover to profit from the sorrows of others. As he grew old himself, Leonid frequently recalled his peasant grandfa-ther Yakov Maksimovich, a man who had followed his own lights for ninety-five long years, and felt much anguish that he had not heeded Yakov's words.

By 1931, when Leonid Brezhnev rejoined his wife, Viktoriya, and their two-year-old Galina, Kamenskoye had grown enormously; its pop-ulation now exceeded one hundred thousand. Because housing was scarce, they moved in with Leonid's parents, to whom the government had allotted a small apartment in which they lived with their unmarried children, Vera and Yakov.

In the late 1920s and early '30s, Kamenskoye produced a great demand for engineering skills, for this was a time of large-scale industrial construction, including the building of a new chemical works, a cement factory, an electrical-equipment plant, and a railroad-car factory. And so Leonid, Vera, and Yakov all entered the same metallurgy institute.

Despite crowded quarters, the Brezhnev family—now seven peo-ple—got along well enough, at the beginning. Ilya still worked as a mill operator. His three children worked at the mill after their evening classes. The institute soon moved to Pelin Street, and the family received a one-bedroom apartment conveniently nearby, at 40 Pelin Street.

My father, Yakov, first worked at the metallurgy complex as an apprentice lathe operator; that was in 1926, when he was not yet four-teen years old, the minimum working age. To get around the law, his mother had doctored his birth certificate, changing the birth year from 1913 to 1912. He was so short that he had to stand on a special bench to reach his machine.

One of my father's tales about the '30s features Vera, older than he, whacking him for sleeping too soundly. She had begun staying out until

Dneprodzerzhinsk. The plaque, destroyed during the anti-Brezhnev campaign unleashed by Gorbachev, marked the site of the metallurgy institute that Leonid Brezhnev attended from 1931 to 1935. The inscription reads:

LEONID ILYICH BREZHNEV
OUTSTANDING FIGURE OF THE COMMUNIST PARTY AND SOVIET
GOVERNMENT [AND] THE INTERNATIONAL COMMUNIST AND
WORKERS' MOVEMENT STUDIED IN THIS BUILDING 1931–1935

dawn with her boyfriend, Zhora, and she didn't want her mother to find out. How could she wake her teenage brother, sleeping like a log after a day of work and study, to play the role of silent doorman? A pebble at the window did nothing, so she invented a more efficient method: she would tie a string to Yakov's foot—he slept in the kitchen of the family's first-floor apartment—and stretch it through the kitchen window. Coming home from her date, she would tug on the string. When even this failed, she would have to summon her courage and knock at the door, waking her mother. Natalya Denisovna would pull her daughter's braids and scold her softly before sending her off for a few hours' sleep. Later in the morning the unsuspecting Yakov would get his punishment.

The Brezhnev home was known for its openness and hospitality. As usual in Russia, there was no separate living room, and the kitchen served for everything from entertaining guests to doing homework. And so in the evening, the young members of the family would gather in the kitchen with their friends, and when they sat together late into the night, Natalya would place her best offerings on the table. Sometimes this meant pickles, sauerkraut, pies, and meat jelly, but my father remembers hard times, when all his mother could set out was dry bread tucked neatly under white napkins, one piece for each person. Sometimes the young people would dance, sometimes they would sing softly. Leonid liked to sing "The Bell Chimes On and On," a Russian folk song. His sister and wife joined in while Yakov kept the beat, tapping a spoon on the table.

Years later I heard from Natalya Denisovna about those evenings. She knew all her children's friends and liked to tease them: "Look at you night owls! Tomorrow not even ice water will wake you!" At their invitation, she would sit down and take part in the merrymaking. Occasionally she even did a Russian dance with one of her sons or with one of Leonid's friends, most often Kostya Grushevoy, the future general secretary's closest pal at the time and in years to come as well.*

---

*Konstantin Grushevoy, the same age as Leonid, served as head of the political administration of the Moscow military district from 1965 until his death, in 1982.

Like all his peers, Leonid was an accomplished performer of midair splits, and watching him prance in a circle kicking up his legs was sheer delight. "How beautiful and carefree youth is," Natalya often thought as she watched the boys whirl their partners about at breakneck speed. Sometimes she would bring out her record player and take her well-worn records from under the bed: fox-trots or tangos evocative of far-away, sunny Argentina. They all laughed when someone told of a club leader at the mill who had presented a reformed fox-trot "free of erotic motions."

Sitting unobtrusively in the corner, Natalya would admire her children. . . . "My sons are different yet alike. One is dark and the other fair like his grandfather Yakov. . . . But in personality, they both favor their father; they're smiling, even tempered, and soft-spoken. Vera takes after her aunt physically—she's pug-nosed, has high cheekbones—and she has the same easygoing personality as her brothers. They're so trusting: they almost think more of their friends than they do of their parents. Leonid would do anything for a friend; I'm sure of it."

Not that she fully approved of his loyalty. "My boy will have a hard time in life. If only his friends were all like Kostya, then I wouldn't mind. But you've got to use your head, and my children use only their hearts. They're just like Ilya: they give in to others and have no idea how to get their own way."

Natalya Denisovna, of a generation of women who barely participated in public life, was entirely consumed by her role as housewife and mother. Her children and grandchildren were at the center of her world; she measured her own life by their successes and failures, worrying when they took exams or argued with their spouses. She took scant interest in politics, a subject utterly alien to her. Nevertheless, when Leonid's political star began rising in later years, she took a naïve pride in his career, collecting all the newspapers and magazines in which his picture appeared.

Constantly away from home, the men usually left all the problems of the household for the women to struggle with, though when they found the time, Leonid and Yakov fetched water from the well and chopped firewood. Natalya Denisovna bore the heaviest load, but like a true

Russian woman, inured to inconvenience and hardship, she never complained. Before dawn, she would wake up and go to the kitchen to light the stove, shivering and wrapping herself in an old jacket. As soon as the kindling caught fire, she would set the teakettle and the large frying pan on the stove. Sitting nearby, she peeled potatoes for lunch and dinner.

She loved these early morning hours when the house was asleep. "I have practically no time just to think," she used to tell her children. "The only time I can be alone with my soul is in the morning." Sometimes while staring into the burning wood, she would lose herself in thoughts that changed with the young people's changing lives. Viktoriya, jealous, was complaining that Leonid almost never spent any time at home. . . . Vera wasn't pregnant yet, though she'd been married to Zhora for over a year now. . . . Yakov had taken up smoking. . . . As the Russians say, when your children grow up, so do their problems.

Eventually the young people would wake, and Natalya would be ready with tea, clean shirts, and sandwiches of lard, hard-boiled eggs, onions, and cucumbers for her husband and sons. Yet even this simple fare was not always to be had. Sometimes frozen potatoes were brought from the countryside for the factory workers. Natalya would soak the dirt off and then grate them, peel and all, to make patties, which she roasted on the top of the stove without oil. These *toshnotiki*, as Leonid dubbed them (a nonce word from *toshnota*, "nausea"), were brown on top, blue inside, and rubbery in texture. Still, they were eaten readily: other families had even less. Many years later, when he and his relatives were all living in Moscow, Leonid once asked his mother for *toshnotiki*. This time she used potatoes, milk, eggs, and butter, following the best recipe she knew, but Leonid turned the patties down. He wanted real *toshnotiki*.

"What you really want," Natalya Denisovna said, "is to revisit your youth."

She took care of the laundry for the entire Brezhnev household, an all-day job reserved for Saturdays. Soap was scarce and detergent unheard of; clothes were washed by hand on an old-fashioned washboard. Once a month the men brought home their work clothes, so caked with dirt they could stand by themselves, and Natalya Denisovna would soak them first—for several days—in hot water mixed with ashes. Her daughter and daughter-in-law tried to help, but she kept them away from the washboard: "It only makes your soft hands bleed."

She herself didn't mind the work, which seemed to come naturally to her tough peasant hands. Keeping peace in the home was harder. It was nothing extraordinary that she and her daughter-in-law, Viktoriya, were failing to get along; periodic conflict among the women is an integral part of Russian family life, a direct result of crowding and poverty. Anything could start an argument: an unwashed pan, too much salt in the soup, a misplaced toy. Leonid had little idea of what was happening since the womenfolk kept their bickering hidden from male eyes.

Like every wife, Viktoriya wanted a nest of her own, no matter how small, and she asked her husband to request a separate room for them as soon as possible. Leonid, who knew how many other families in the city lived in equally desperate conditions, was reluctant. For that matter, why should they move away from his mother, who was always there to look after little Galina? Viktoriya was adamant. After she threatened to go home to her parents, Leonid asked the trade-union committee for a room, and his request was granted.

Viktoriya was overjoyed, and no one objected to their departure: the crowding had been unbearable ever since Vera had married Zhora Grechkin and brought him into the Brezhnev home.

The revolution, with its attendant plundering and butchery, had been carried out in the name of the workers. But what happened in the day-to-day existence of the workers themselves, like my grandfather Ilya Brezhnev?

In the '20s, the five-day Soviet workweek began to be supplanted by the six-day week, then the seven-day week. Vacations were cut back to twelve days a year, and work was done in three fifteen-hour shifts. Workers were at the mercy of administrators, modern-day feudal lords empowered to issue reprimands and dismissal notices, take away bonuses, and publicly disgrace subordinates for tardiness, absenteeism, or nonfulfillment of production quotas. Outstanding workers, on the other hand, could be forced to transfer to work teams whose productivity was lagging, to "pull the others up." Increases in labor productivity were achieved through the broad-scale introduction of piecework: in the 1930s, approximately one half of work time was compensated according to output.

The state responded to the widespread discontent of those years with repression in various forms. Informal "comradely trials" for the resolution of workplace conflicts, instituted after the 1917 revolution, were replaced with criminal trials. Periodic purges, leading to the execution of engineers, party members, technicians, and activists, served to maintain a general fear of authority among the population.

In the frenzied striving to increase productivity while lowering costs, numerous new factories and plants ignored elementary safeguards, and the Communists even cut back the meager amounts of money previously spent on safety. Under these conditions, the incidence of industrial accidents grew at an alarming rate, and among those affected were the Brezhnevs of Kamenskoye.

In 1933, a cable that Ilya's fellow workers were using to hook rolled steel snapped, striking Ilya in the abdomen. After an unsuccessful operation, he died a long, agonizing death at home, his entire family gathered at the deathbed. His hair strewn over the pillow, he moaned softly, drifting in and out of consciousness. Ilya, who had never been sick a day in his life . . . His facial features became as delicate as those of a young boy.

A few minutes before the end, he opened his eyes and attempted to sit up. After Leonid propped his back with a pillow, Ilya looked carefully at everyone present and asked for water. Natalya Denisovna began to object that this was against the doctor's orders, but Leonid interrupted: "Give him some, Mama—he can have whatever he wants now."

On the wall above the bed was a cuckoo clock, and Ilya Yakovlevich looked toward it. The children could not decide what his gesture meant. Years later Leonid would say to his brother, "Remember, Yasha, when our father pointed his eyes toward the clock? He was trying to tell us his time was up."

Then Ilya motioned for his younger son to come near. All that Yakov understood of the phrases whispered into his ear were the two words *synok* ("son") and *dolgo* ("a long time"). The man fell into a delirium, murmuring something about a long voyage.

"He's dead, Lyonya," said Viktoriya, clasping Leonid's shoulder. It was she who approached Ilya and closed his eyes. Natalya Denisovna fell onto his chest and remained frozen there until several old women, neighbors of the family, came to wash his body and comb his hair. They placed a glass of water on a windowsill so that his soul would be cleansed; a cup of vodka and a crust of bread provided sustenance for his final journey.

When the unpainted, unvarnished casket arrived, the bottom was lined with sawdust, and Ilya's body was placed inside, dressed in the best clothing the family could find instead of the customary new suit, new shirt, and new cloth shoes. A family photograph shows my grandfather in the gray suit he would later wear to the grave. The shirt worn was one of Leonid's. Pinning it in the back—her son had grown bigger than her husband—Natalya Denisovna couldn't help feeling regret at the sacrifice: a perfectly good shirt, and money so short . . .

Mourners came during the day to bid a final farewell. In the evening, only the relatives and the old neighbor women remained, along with the sexton, who chanted psalms for Ilya all night long. The mirrors in the house were covered with towels. (This last practice survives to this day, even among well-educated families.)

Natalya Denisovna stood like a statue during the funeral service and fainted when the first clods of earth struck the lid of the casket. Her sons carried her away from the crowd and placed her on the cool grass. Only on the following day did she begin to weep and wail, lamenting her lot at the top of her lungs just as widows had always done in her native village. For a year, no matter what, she visited her husband's grave every day, adorning it with flowers and wreaths, whispering all the words of love for which she had been too busy during his lifetime.

In his youth, Leonid was handsome and charming, a careful dresser and ladies' man. In the '30s, visiting friends with his young wife, he was always the center of attention. Spin the bottle was popular, and Saturday evenings frequently found Viktoriya sulking jealously, convinced

that Leonid was kissing the same woman too often and too enthusiastically. When they came home, they were no longer on speaking terms. In
the beginning, Leonid would apologize and protest that he "didn't give
a damn for any other women." But Viktoriya continued to pout, unable
to contain her irritation.

Aware of these conflicts, Natalya Denisovna scolded her son while at
the same time trying to educate her daughter-in-law about men: "It
won't help things to fuss over every little thing. They can't stand that.
My son will stop playing the field if you show him tenderness, but if
you push aside a handsome fellow like him, he'll be snatched up soon
enough. There's no shortage of women itching to make their move."

Viktoriya found one way to make Leonid, who was very gullible, lose
interest in other men's wives. All she had to do was tell him "Tanya is a
whore and two-times her husband with anything in pants," and Leonid,
who felt that men were entitled to certain liberties but women were not,
would drop Tanya like a hot potato.

Viktoriya in those years was preoccupied with keeping her family
together. As the years passed, she would still worry about appearances,
but she would lose interest in the moral atmosphere of her family life.
Like most women who went from poverty to affluence after marrying a
party or administrative functionary, she became obsessed with wealth.
As for Leonid, he became increasingly absorbed in a career that left little time for the sharing of affection.

Even before the war that would soon plunge the entire Soviet Union
into its greatest ordeal, Leonid confessed to his brother that he didn't
love his wife but put up with her for the children's sake.

Chapter Three

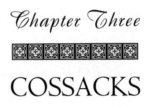

COSSACKS

And their death march was long.

ANNA AKHMATOVA

On a cold fall day in 1930 on the banks of a nameless river near the Siberian city of Salekhard, my mother's grandfather Akindin was killed by a Soviet commissar. What thoughts came to him as he lay on the steep riverbank, clutching a handful of fresh snow, staining it with his blood? Did he curse his enemies or pray for them before uttering the last words of every Cossack fighter: "Lord, I deliver my soul into thy hands"? As his lips grew numb, what was he whispering to his children, scattered to the four corners of Russia? What legacy was he leaving the grandchildren and great-grandchildren he would never see?

The memory of her grandfather Akindin, a headman of the Ural Cossacks, was revered in my mother's patriarchal, Christian family. While growing up, I also heard many stories of his kindness and bravery, though I did not learn the true story of his death until years later. We had a photograph of Akindin on the wall, and I often approached it to examine his dignified beard and smiling eyes, such a light blue that even in black and white they contrasted sharply with his ebony hair.

One morning my elementary-school teacher brought a large poster to class. On it, we saw caricatures of all those swept aside by the 1917 revolution: the czar, a governor-general, an officer of the White army, a landowner, a policeman, a kulak—and a Cossack with a fierce forelock. To make his Cossack as savage as possible, the artist had even supplied him with a ring through the nose. My feelings were hurt. Coming home from school that day, I returned to my great-grandfather's photograph. Handsome and erect, with intelligent, laughing eyes, he had nothing in common with the bowlegged monster on the poster.

That nose ring was pure invention, though some men did wear earrings, which served a purpose. A Cossack with no siblings wore two earrings, one in each ear, marking him as completely exempt from active service. Akindin had only sisters, so tradition dictated that he wear an earring in the left ear. The reason for the earrings was simple: when troops turned right in formation, the commanding officer would notice the men with earrings on the left side and spare them from the most dangerous missions.

Before the 1917 revolution, Cossack men lived at the ready, speeding off to war on horseback and in full military attire whenever central authorities called on their services. Death was never far away: every family was missing a husband, father, son, or brother. With their menfolk so often at war, the women bore the hardships of day-to-day life, and they were renowned for their toughness. The home was traditionally their undisputed realm, off limits to male interference. Only horses and weapons were seen as the personal property of the men, who never entered the kitchen or looked into the trunks holding the family's accumulated wealth and sometimes didn't even know where to find a cup to drink from.

The laws, traditions, and customs of my mother's clan can be traced to the sixteenth century. The Cossacks, a warrior caste within czarist Russia, were also something of a state within a state. The legislative power of the Ural Cossacks' internal governance was vested in a popular assembly. The assembly's leaders, called atamans, were responsible for maintaining order on all the lands belonging to their villages, they were elected, and their executive decrees approved, by a general vote. I once counted twenty-four paragraphs in a document listing the obligations of a village ataman.

When they were just beginning to talk, Cossack boys were entrusted with the care of the foals, and among the first words they learned were *harness* and *saddle belt*. And so Akindin, like other Cossack males, was an expert horseman.

In the mid-1880s, Akindin's family moved within the Ural region from Orenburg to Troitsk (a distance of about five hundred miles when traveled overland), where two Cossack regiments, the Mikhailovsky and the Nikolsky, were being consolidated. According to family legend, five-year-old Akindin rode in the saddle the entire way.

Around the turn of the century, Akindin began his own family. He had inherited blue eyes from his Russian father and curly black hair from his Greek mother, whereas his wife, Tatyana, a Karelian Finn, had blond hair, a delicate, ruddy complexion, and black eyes. Little wonder their two daughters and three sons came out in all combinations of hair and eye colors—just like thoroughbred stallions, as Akindin joked.

"We have been Cossacks for ten generations," he proudly told his children, clearly intending the Cossack tradition to be their future.

The men who had been attracted over preceding centuries by the wide-open spaces and freedom of the Urals were a motley crew: peasants, soldiers, servants from the czar's court, clergymen, and sons of the nobility—all running away for one reason or another. The historian Ivan Zheleznov put it this way: "As the bee takes a drop of nectar from each flower it visits, so did the Yaik [the old name of the Ural River] regiment take one strong young man from each estate of society." The Ural Cossacks were mainly Russian but over time incorporated individuals from nationalities native to the region—Kalmucks, Tatars, Kirghiz, Chuvashes, and Votyak—as well as escaped prisoners from Finland, Sweden, Poland, Hungary, Turkey, and Greece.

The Cossacks (from *kazak*, a Turkic root meaning "free, bold") soon acquired a well-earned reputation as pirates, ruthlessly attacking merchants, trappers, prospectors, and other travelers who ventured into the territory they claimed. In later centuries, there were no fighters more devoted to the czar: they led campaigns against successive intruders from Europe and Asia, including the Swedes, Dutch, and Turks. A Cossack song boasted,

> There's not a single land that we have not watered with blood;
> we have given the czar half his realm.

In December of 1902, Akindin and Tatyana had their third child, who was to be my grandfather. In accord with Cossack custom, the little black-haired, black-eyed boy was named Nikolay because he was born a week before Saint Nikolay's Day. Akindin dreamed of giving his sons a good education, and the boys became avid readers. Nikolay in particular was citified, not at all interested in horsemanship, military honors, or any other aspect of Cossack life; his ambition was to devote his life to the study of Russian history.

After honorably serving three three-year terms, an ataman had the right to release one of his sons from military service. Akindin, who had been elected four times, chose Nikolay for the privilege.

In the decades preceding the 1917 revolution in the prosperous merchant city of Troitsk in the southern Ural Mountains, Akindin built a large house equipped with sheds, a stable, and a bathhouse. The enormous cellars held barrels and baskets full of smoked fish of all sorts, sturgeon caviar, pickles, mushrooms, honey, and walnuts. Homemade hams and sausages hung from hooks. After Akindin's death, his impoverished widow, Tatyana, would weep softly at the memory of those cellars and the perfect order that had prevailed in her house. She had been strict with her children and servants, far more so than her husband, a lenient man with a ready laugh.

During the February revolution of 1917, the freedom-loving Cossacks, weary after three years of fighting in World War I, refused to support the czar; they also failed to support the provisional government when the Bolsheviks seized power in the fall. They wanted nothing more than to return home: according to law, each male Cossack could look forward to receiving thirty *desyatin* (about eighty-one acres) after his obligatory twenty-year military service. In the spring of 1918, however, a general rebellion against the Bolshevik government flared among the Cossacks, who were fed up with the persecution of the church, the executions of czarist officers who refused to serve in the Red Army, and the requisitioning of farm produce, according to which peasants were forced to sell grain to the state. This was the beginning of the civil war.

The Cossack general Pyotr Krasnov soon formed his anti-Bolshevik Don Army around the river of the same name; on November 18, 1918, Admiral Aleksandr Kolchak, also fighting the Reds, declared himself the "supreme commander of all the land and sea forces of Russia." In March 1919, Kolchak's army began its march toward the Volga River. By the end of April, the Bolshevik general Sergey Kamenev, a former colonel in the czarist army, had defeated Kolchak's troops, forcing them to retreat, first to the Ural Mountains, then to Siberia. It was in Siberia that the Kolchak movement was crushed forever. Those who weren't killed on the spot either fled the country or scattered throughout Russia, concealing their background.

The White Guard that fought the Reds included Siberian merchants, trappers from the Urals, well-to-do peasants, Cossacks, the petty bourgeoisie, and a significant portion of the intelligentsia. It was led by Cossack atamans as well as by generals and colonels from the czarist army. After three bitter years, the civil war ended, in November 1920, with a complete Bolshevik victory.

The Cossack code of honor was strict. Men taken prisoner were mourned as though dead and welcomed back only if they had escaped. After the defeat of Kolchak's forces in 1920, one of my mother's uncles, who had been captured by the Reds, was freed and went back to his home in the Urals. His mother, Mariya (my great-grandmother), concealed him in the bathhouse, and when he was discovered, she begged that her son not be driven in shame from the village, arguing that a severe stomach wound had prevented him from escaping. Yet when his wife, who had always adored him, learned of his return, she ran to him, fell to her knees, embraced his legs, and sobbed: "Lord, if you had only been killed. What have I done to deserve this disgrace?" He stayed alone that night in the bathhouse and shot himself.

The entire family of another one of my mother's uncles was shot by the Reds after Kolchak's defeat. Yet another uncle fought the Bolsheviks under the ataman Vladimir Tolstov. He died under unknown circumstances, and his wife was deported to Siberia along with their children. During the civil war, virtually all of the men on my mother's side of the family went off in the armies of Kolchak to take part in the heroic but doomed resistance to Bolshevism.

Before Cossack parents would sanctify their children's marriages, the subject was discussed by the whole family in great detail and at great length; after all, the decision would affect the life of the whole clan. The young couple was expected to be partners for the rest of their lives, for the clergy rarely granted permission to divorce.

My grandfather Nikolay broke with custom, however. In 1921 or 1922, he abducted Anastasiya, my grandmother-to-be, and they stayed together until he won her parents over. They had initially looked at him askance, fearing he would spoil their family line. Though impoverished by the revolution, Anastasiya's family proudly traced their roots to the illustrious Borodin and Frolov Cossack clans and saw Nikolai as a *basurmanin*, virtually a foreigner; he was, after all, one-fourth Greek and one-half Finnish, with black eyes and jet-black hair, unusual for a Russian. Anastasiya was a remarkably beautiful girl, with luxuriant, golden-blond hair, whose mother had borne her at the miraculous age of fifty-seven. During the wedding, the old woman, now approaching her eightieth birthday, felt so faint that she had to be led out of the church three times to catch her breath. Anastasiya's father had been a Cossack officer; now he was supporting himself by mending horse collars on a collective farm. Despite his woes, he never lost his pride. They say that he even wore his old, beat-up shoes with flair.

Akindin had trained young Cossack soldiers for the forces of Admiral Kolchak. In 1927, the Reds charged him with treason for this; his house in Troitsk was ransacked, and all his belongings were sold at auction. The story of the pillaging was passed down faithfully in our family, from generation to generation.

In full view of the children, who clung together in a frightened mass, sacks full of silverware, pillows, and quilts were dragged through the yard. Women's earrings were torn from their ears, their skirts were pulled off, and rings were pulled from their fingers. Akindin stood to one side, silently puffing on his short pipe. His honor would not let him show weakness. But when the hired men began to drive the horses out of the stables, he turned white. He staggered and regained his balance, pushing back the hand of his eldest son, who had reached out to steady him.

Then they let out Bucephalus—my great-grandfather's favorite, a thoroughbred who obeyed no one except his master and Timosha, the day laborer. When Bucephalus snorted, reared, and pounded his hooves, one of the soldiers barked out an order: "Bring that horse under control!" Timosha did nothing to comply—in fact, he let loose with a piercing whistle, and Bucephalus raced to the gate. He reached freedom despite the bullets sent his way by the Bolsheviks, enraged after he kicked—and nearly killed—the soldier who had given the order. Timosha almost died from the beating that his act of loyalty earned him.

The women and children were thrown into a cart and sent to faraway Siberia; the men walked. Swallowing her pride, Tatyana got onto her knees, begging the Bolsheviks to give her a blanket for her grandchildren, but they refused: "Let them die like dogs!"—which is just what happened. On the way to Siberia, Akindin's twin grandchildren, his pride and joy, died and were buried by the road, as was their mother a few days later.

Only my great-grandfather's Cossack spirit and discipline kept him alive. He began to create a new home in his Siberian exile. Given work at a stud farm near Salekhard, on the Arctic Circle, he put to good use his knowledge of horses. But, as we say, he lacked a "fence post, a yard, an icon to pray to, bread to choke on, a knife to slit his throat with."

One fateful autumn day in 1930, he went to the river to check his traps. He was overjoyed to find there a fish about two feet long—food for his little grandchildren. After tying his boat to the shore, he began climbing the steep bank with the fish flung over his shoulder. It was here that a drunken commissar shot him and left him to die on the cold earth, covered with a thin blanket of snow, after grabbing for himself the still-writhing fish. According to family stories, during his youth, a Gypsy woman had predicted Akindin's death at the hands of a madman. And what was Bolshevism, if not an attack of madness to which the Russian people had succumbed? Tatyana, heartbroken by Akindin's death, never came out of mourning.

For rejecting the new Russia, the Cossacks had been driven from their homes, killed, or sent to rot or die in Siberia. It was demanded of these downtrodden, humiliated men and women that they accept social-ism or face execution, exile, or prison walls. They held on to the past as best they could, but at serious risk: possession of thirty pairs of Cossack epaulets brought a sentence of as many years in prison.

I grew up among these people and their descendants. So, unlike the grandchildren of those who had stormed the czar's Winter Palace, I had reason to question the Soviet government from an early age. I believed that my ancestors would one day be vindicated.

My great-grandfather did leave us his uniform, consisting of a white tunic and deep-blue trousers with crimson stripes. My great-grand-mother Tatyana kept this treasured heirloom intact for many years, and from time to time she would air it out in our yard in Magnitogorsk. Once during a game of hide-and-seek, I hid behind my great-grandfa-ther's tunic. I stood quietly. How old it smelled: a mixture of mothballs and candle wax. I grew sad. Suddenly I felt Akindin's presence so strongly that I forgot about the other children. I grasped the tunic firmly with both arms and began to cry.

Akindin never accepted Russia's rejection of the monarchy. To him, it was no more and no less than treason. As a youth, he had sworn to defend the land that his ancestors had paid for with their lives. Aware of the criminal nature of Bolshevism, he refused to participate with the new authorities, finding the courage to follow his own conscience. For centuries, the Cossacks had lived for the glory of czar and motherland,

and the new Russia was alien to them, with its bursts of revolutionary change and its semiliterate, demagogic political leaders. I believe that history will honor the names of those who resisted, those who acted not to save their own lives so much as to defend their human dignity. The time will come when history will give the Cossacks their due.

Chapter Four

THE CITY OF THE FUTURE

O city of mine, since I can remember,
I've loved the hush of your streets in December
But what remains of that glory today?
Only my birthright, squandered away.

ANNA AKHMATOVA

As the saying goes, the Ural Mountains, which separate European Russia from Siberia and Kazakhstan, are "golden underneath and silver on top," for the region has always been known as a treasure chest of minerals. Interspersed among the rolling hills and mountains are vast steppes, barren in winter and alive with swaying silver grass in summer.

Around Mount Magnitnaya in the southern Urals lie rich iron deposits whose magnetic effects were first noticed by Kirghiz nomads. In later centuries, the vicinity became a battleground where Cossacks fought and died for the Russian Empire, building fortress towns that made the original nomadic masters of the steppes retreat ever farther. In the nineteenth century, as the mineral riches began to be exploited, the same lands were bought and sold, gambled away in card games, used as dowries for wealthy heiresses. After the revolution, the entire Ural region became a key source of metals vital to the country's industrialization.

In 1929, railroad cars brought to the vicinity of Mount Magnitnaya became the first homes of Magnitogorsk.* The age-old silence of the

---

*The city's name is from the Russian name for the iron-rich mountain Magnitnaya Gora.

steppes gave way to the din of bulldozers, tractors, and trucks as factories and dwellings—dugouts and tents as well as houses—were rapidly thrown up. The country's rulers had bold plans: this was to be a socialist city, "the city of the future."

All was part of the First Five-Year Plan, announced by Stalin at the Fourteenth Party Congress in 1928. Calling for a "great leap forward" into the industrial age commensurate with the country's resources, the dictator didn't mention the human costs. Grigory Zinovyev, one of his principal henchmen, was more candid, urging workers to "pull industry forward at the expense of the peasants: skin them three times." Results were rapid. By the end of the First Five-Year Plan, more than fifteen hundred plants and factories had been built, with many towns and cities springing up alongside. In the Ural region and in Ukraine, the Soviet Union created powerful metallurgical and petroleum industries. In late 1931, Magnitogorsk produced its first ore; in 1932, its first coke and pig iron; in 1933, its first steel and rolled metal.

In the late 1920s, my grandfather Nikolay managed to escape Salekhard, the Siberian city to which he, along with his father, had been banished. He then lived in hiding for a few years, moving from place to place with his wife, Anastasiya, and their four children. He settled in Magnitogorsk in 1931. In the abandoned, unheated dugout shack that became the family's first home, there was no running water or electricity; the windows had to be boarded up with plywood, since their panes were all broken or missing. The city of the future was still a dream, and the burgeoning population made do with tents, dugouts, and railroad cars.

Some were starry-eyed enthusiasts from all over the Soviet Union, even from other countries. Blinded by propaganda and showered by the government with diplomas, medals, pins, and other decorations, they built the future with little thought of their own well-being. After all, they were leading the country toward the triumph of communism. Others came with arrogance in their gaze and obscenity on their lips: this was a criminal class of repeat offenders and petty crooks in search of adventure and the relative freedom afforded by the new cities. Peasants driven from the land by collectivization were a third large group. Finally, there were those who, like my grandfather, were fleeing Siberian exile. They all could write whatever they wanted on their work applications. It was impossible to check the references of the thousands of workers streaming into the city.

Nikolay's first job was as an unskilled construction laborer, and the family had to supplement his meager earnings by selling or exchanging for food some of their last trinkets: earrings, bracelets, and rings. Only one family ring, which I would eventually inherit, survived from those years. I loved it dearly—until it was taken during a raid of my dormitory room. . . .

One day Anastasiya took to the open-air market a red satin blanket that had been her grandmother's dowry. In the evening, she chastised her husband. She regretted the loss of the blanket; even more, she feared for her children's future. "Didn't I tell you it would come to this, Nika? We should flee."

"My dear, you know I can never leave Russia."

"Russia is dead and gone!" Anastasiya answered. "Let's at least save the children."

Nikolay said nothing.

In 1932, the Soviet Union instituted a mandatory system of internal passports—documents listing their bearers' birthplace, social status, and nationality. They were required for marriage and divorce, for obtaining work, medical service, and housing. Like all others in his situation, my grandfather Nikolay concealed his true origin—the Cossack nobility*—and hoped for the best.

In the early years, Magnitogorsk had a continuous labor shortage, due in part to the high rate of turnover. One solution was to put women to work. Posters were put up all over town reading COMRADE HOUSE-WIVES! PARTICIPATE IN *SUBBOTNIKI!* [Again, the word for unpaid Saturdays.] THE FIRST COUNTRY IN THE WORLD TO LIBERATE WOMEN

---

*As of the nineteenth century, Cossack atamans such as Nikolay's father were part of the noble estate in Russia.

DEMANDS THIS OF YOU. The "liberated" women responded, flocking to construction sites. Alongside the men, they dragged heavy logs and wheelbarrows loaded with sand and cement, straining their abdomens, ruining their health, and in many cases losing forever the possibility of bearing children. Those who had worked especially well won prizes: long winter coats, wash pans, a few pieces of soap.

Once in 1933, Anastasiya was asked to come to a *subbotnik*. When she said she couldn't, the young women at her door, Komsomol activists in red scarves, threatened to throw her and her children onto the street.

"I'm four months pregnant," she replied. "You're women yourselves; don't you understand I can't lift anything heavy?"

"We'll find light work for you," one woman offered.

Anastasiya didn't go. After all, how could she leave her four small children—three girls and a boy—alone at home? She took such joy in them, giving them all she had; perhaps she sensed how little time was left. She made sure to teach good manners to her eldest daughters, Marina and Yelena, and she read them Pushkin and Tolstoy. There was no piano in the home, but she taught them to read and write music. At night, she would snip cloth from her old dresses and shawls to sew them dress clothes: red for dark-complexioned Marina, light blue for Yelena.

Admiring her beautiful daughters, she would often say to her husband, "How fine they are! Oh, how I hope to see them grow into young ladies."

"It won't be long now," her husband would laugh. "Look how they preen themselves in front of the mirror in the morning." But Anastasiya never would see them grow up.

Later in 1933, the metallurgical plant where Nikolay was working received a letter with detailed information about his Cossack background. Its author, a woman whose devotion to ferreting out enemies of the state was fierce, demanded appropriate measures with regard to the "bourgeois scum." The case was immediately handed over to the state security organs for investigation; Nikolay, classified as an alien element, was forced to leave his job.

That year, 1933, was the hungriest in the entire history of Russia, but the newspapers were triumphantly hailing the completion of the

First Five-Year Plan in four years and three months. City squares, offices, village streets, factory mess halls, and schools sprouted black loudspeakers, installed so that the masses could be reminded how happy they were at the "great economic achievements without precedent in all of human history." The whole country woke up in the morning to rousing marches. After all, it's no mean task to convince people who live like cattle that they should be confident of the future. Turning off one of these loudspeakers could result in a ten-year prison sentence.

When it became obvious that the Five-Year Plan had been disastrous for the economy, it was necessary to find scapegoats. A wave of show trials against "enemies of the people" swept through the land. Peasants were deported to Siberia for "allowing weeds to grow in the fields"; equally mindless accusations led to the execution of engineers, construction workers, party functionaries, and many others. In his speeches, Stalin called upon all workers to "bolster their revolutionary vigilance and Bolshevik sharp-sightedness" in order to "eradicate all enemies through combined efforts." Every day people woke up only to find that a new group of yesterday's friends had somehow become today's saboteurs, traitors, and spies.

Charged with subverting socialist ideology or deviating from the party line—in other words, refusing to act as servants of the party and of Stalin—many of the country's leading intellectuals were executed. Others were sent to Siberia, to earn hard currency for their rulers in prison camps from which gold and lumber were exported to the West. Their replacements were only too glad to write whatever was asked of them in return for decorations, bonuses, and above all, the chance to survive. The entire society had become permeated with lies, accusations, counteraccusations, blackmail, counterblackmail, idol worship, and hatred.

As the Russian philosopher Vladimir Rozanov had warned prophetically, speaking of the men who made the revolution of 1917: "Just wait, they will sit down and then demand that whoever keeps them from putting their feet on the table be carried off to the dungeons."

In the 1930s, the employees of the military prosecutor's office of Magnitogorsk made a commitment to complete at least 80 percent of their pre-trial investigations in three days or less. The means used to achieve such efficiency were humiliation, deprivation of sleep and food, exposure to cold, and torture.

Controlling an entire people costs money. In 1936, the Soviet legal system received twenty-five million rubles in additional appropriations. Every member of the "emergency squads" charged with keeping citizens in line received an additional two days off a month for "study and recreation."

Continual official calls for crackdowns on the "enemies of the people" had awakened the basest instincts, and searching out enemies evolved as part of the national psychology. In the frenzy of those years, the Soviet people informed on one another with or without cause, openly or anonymously. Informers were praised and held up as role models for the youth; they were also given financial rewards and promotions. Every word spoken around young children had to be watched: youngsters were trained to run straight to their teachers and report anything suspicious. A law adopted on July 8, 1934, introduced the collective responsibility of the whole family (excepting only children under twelve) for any wrong done by another family member. Ignorance of the fact that one of the members of your family was a spy or saboteur was punishable by five years of prison or exile. This last provision was repealed only in 1960, seven years after Stalin's death.

Fearing further "appropriate measures," Nikolay fled, loading his wife, children, and modest household belongings onto a cart borrowed from a neighbor. In Belovka, a village near Troitsk, my great-grandfather Akindin had built a summer house, which had been ransacked but still stood. The family started in that direction, but in the middle of the night Anastasiya went into her labor, perhaps due to the bumpy ride, perhaps due to anxiety. They had no alternative but to head back to Magnitogorsk.

Nikolay almost drove the horse to death. Dawn was breaking when they arrived at the hospital. Anastasiya kissed the sleeping children good-bye and barely dragged herself to the entrance room, supported by her husband. That morning she gave birth, but her baby was born dead.

By evening, she herself was dead, from blood poisoning: kept well supplied with government pamphlets—used mainly for cigarette paper, toilet paper, and kindling—the hospitals lacked sterile dressings. According to family legend, Anastasiya had dropped her ring during the wedding: a bad omen, foreboding an early death. She died when she was not quite thirty-two years old.

After his hasty return and his wife's death, Nikolay found the accusations against him miraculously dropped. His older daughters, eleven-year-old Marina and nine-year-old Yelena, ran the household, standing for hours in food lines, lighting the stove, cooking, and looking after their younger siblings, six-year-old Vasily and three-year-old Polina, who often stayed home alone, locked indoors. Their father's hours at the flour mill, where he now worked, were long; they were all asleep when he left in the morning and were asleep again when he came home.

The next autumn, the autumn of 1934, brought heavy rains, which streamed through the cracks in the ceiling and gathered in ankle-deep puddles, forcing the children to huddle underneath a large washtub.

When Marina and Yelena learned that their father wanted to remarry—he hoped that having a woman around would help the household—they protested: "No, don't bring a stranger into our home." Soon enough a woman did come, but no stranger: when Akindin's widow, Tatyana, learned of her daughter-in-law's death, she began asking for permission to leave Salekhard, and she settled in with her son soon after hearing, totally unexpectedly, that she was free to move.

The sight of her four grandchildren in the damp, tiny room brought tears to her eyes. During the sixteen years of Soviet rule, she had seen and gone through every form of misery and humiliation imaginable, but these innocent children, her flesh and blood—she was ready to fight for them with all her remaining strength. She set out to obtain a place to live that at least had heat. There was so much nobility and power in her gait, in her bearing, in her intelligent, angry black eyes, and even in the Karelian accent, which she never lost, that some housing official finally assigned the family a decent room, in the first residential building on

Pionerskaya Street; its foundations had been laid in the summer of 1930. With electric lights, steam heat, and twenty square meters (more than two hundred square feet) of floor space, the room was like a palace for the children, who huddled by the radiator for hours.

With Tatyana came a woman's touch: a white tablecloth, regular meals, and family expeditions to the bathhouse on Saturdays. Hiring a horse-drawn cab, she brought home a rosebush from the market and placed it in a corner of the room to "bring joy to the eyes," as she said.

But her widow's hands, heavy and harsh, could not replace those of Anastasiya. She seldom touched her grandchildren and spoke little. Once while laying her silver forks and monogrammed knives on the table, she dropped her head and began sobbing, her thoughts with Akindin and those of her children who had been killed or were still languishing in Siberian exile.

During all her years in Magnitogorsk, she only once mentioned her late husband directly. Admiring Vasily one day, she said, "We have ourselves a true Cossack, slender and quick on his feet; a steed and a sword are all he needs. What a shame his grandfather will never see him. Oh, how his eyes would have shone to see our Vasenka!"

Tatyana's arrival in Magnitogorsk was timely in other ways. A few years later, in 1937, another anonymous letter was written about my grandfather. Again Tatyana made the bureaucratic rounds, this time to point out to aloof officials that her son Nikolay had been a mere child of fifteen when the 1917 revolution overthrew the czar. Was it any fault of his that his father had been a Cossack ataman? But Nikolay was taken in for interrogation and put under arrest, and Tatyana was left alone with her four grandchildren.

The practice of deliberately exterminating noble families and distinguished individuals began in Russia as early as the rule of Ivan the Terrible, who forbade certain men to marry (to doom the family line to extinction) and exiled others to Siberia. Russia's autocrats always feared the aristocracy and the intelligentsia—freethinkers and potential rivals for their monopoly on power. Following the example of the czars, Stalin sent the most honored, celebrated, talented, energetic, and eloquent to the gallows first.

How many nameless victims of Stalinism were there? Thousands, millions? The only consolation is that the terror of the 1930s destroyed the people's last remaining faith in Marxism.

My grandfather Nikolay had tried to avoid any participation in public life and to stay as far away from politics as possible. The motto he lived by was "Let everyone else take part if they will, but not me." Once invited to join the Communist Party, he had declined with a modest "Thank you, I don't consider myself worthy." He was not one of the well-known victims; he had done nothing to incur Stalin's wrath. His origin alone sufficed to make him an outcast in the land of socialism.

Chapter Five

✦✦✦✦✦✦✦✦✦

TALES OF LOVE AND WAR

And one mad linden tree dared bloom
During that mournful May.

ANNA AKHMATOVA

Friends in Berlin once gave me a letter dated June 22, 1941. What follows is an excerpt from it that describes, better than anything else I have encountered, how a German soldier saw the initial attack on the Soviet Union:

> It was the night of the summer solstice, the shortest, most memorable night of the year. In the distance gleamed the starry sky of a foreign country. But how can the sky be divided with borders?
> Then came the dawn. The nocturnal frogs grew quiet; the bats made their final flight, bumping sleepily into soldiers and trucks. Everything around us was in a foreign country now: the vast green young fields merging into the sky at the horizon; the shiny, strangely placid river; the dogs barking in the distance; the alarmed call of a rooster. In a few minutes the order was given, and we marched, crushing dandelions and daisies with our heavy soldier's boots. For me this was the beginning of war.

A few hours later—it was still early morning—Leonid Brezhnev drove up to the building in Dnepropetrovsk where he now lived. His best friend, Kostya Grushevoy, was waiting for him. "Come in," he said. From Kostya, Leonid learned of the German invasion.

During Germany's Great Depression, some twenty years earlier, Russian women had donated their own children's gold and silver crosses, at the urging of the Soviet government, to help feed hungry German children. Did the soldiers marching east to burn, rape, pillage, and murder remember the free bowls of soup that had warmed their childhood?

In 1939, the Soviet Union and Germany had signed a pact forbidding aggressive actions by either side for ten years, and during the two years that followed, Stalin cooperated fully with the Nazis. Trainloads of Soviet petroleum, coal, iron, and grain went west, to be sold to Germany at rock-bottom prices, while in Russia hungry old women received five- to ten-year prison sentences for stealing an ear of wheat from the fields. Stalin ordered German Communists (who after Hitler's rise to power thought they had found sanctuary in Moscow) sent back to their homeland, where they were tortured and killed.

The Soviet Union was still reeling from Stalin's purges: at the Eighteenth Party Congress, held on March 10, 1939, only fifty-five of the nearly two thousand delegates that had attended the previous congress, in 1934, were present. As the Russian people put it, under Stalin they were all passengers on a streetcar: some stood, others sat, but everyone was shaking.* The '30s were years when the choice Russians faced was simple and brutal: parrot the ideology of the madmen in charge, or perish.

Informing on one's fellows had become so universal that it even flourished in the army. A popular joke had officers saluting with the words *razreshite zalozhit* ("permit me to turn you in") instead of the requisite *razreshite dolozhit* ("permit me to report").

In 1940, Leonid Ilyich was secretary for military industry of the Dnepropetrovsk Oblast party committee. Ukrainian factories were gradually being converted from civilian to military production, and near

---

*In colloquial Russian, "to sit" also means "to be in prison."

Dnepropetrovsk construction of a military airport began. Leonid, responsible for ensuring its timely completion, had his hands full: conferring with specialists, meeting with party activists, flying back and forth to Moscow. He knew no rest, day or night.

These nearly hysterical attempts to bolster the defense industry came too late, and when German troops invaded, the country was still grossly unprepared. Soviet military technology was very poor by international standards. Before being sent to the dungeons of the Lubyanka, headquarters of the secret police in Moscow, Commissar of Armaments B. L. Vannikov told Stalin outright that his policies were undermining the country's military might at the very moment when war with Germany was imminent. Indulging in wishful thinking, Stalin trusted Hitler over his own countrymen. Despite information pouring in from all quarters, he played down the likelihood of a German attack. Many of the best Soviet military and technical minds—metallurgists, engineers, military experts—were in Siberian labor camps, victims of the purges. The army was largely led by incompetent, inexperienced officers.

During the first months after the June 22 invasion, many Russians naïvely thought Hitler would save them from Stalin's tyranny. Instead, the state once more resorted to terror. In short order, it created special squads with the ominous name of SMERSH (from the Russian *smert shpionam*, "death to spies") as well as NKVD (the Soviet secret police) squads with orders to shoot anyone who retreated, deserted, or surrendered. Execution by hanging was introduced.

As my father told me, it was on July 4, 1941, that Leonid Ilyich was sent to the front, as a political instructor. This title may need explanation. During the civil war, after drafting former czarist officers into the Red Army, the Bolsheviks charged political commissars with the task of closely monitoring the officers' activity. Despite their incompetence—at the beginning, most were barely literate—the commissars had far-reaching powers. They could have a commander relieved of his duties, brought before a military tribunal, or arrested. In 1925, Mikhail Frunze, then commissar for war, succeeded in having the post abolished. Similar functions were then taken on by commanders' aides responsible for political propaganda; still later, political instructors took their place.

Charged with inspiring and organizing the soldiers, political instructors did not have the right to intervene in matters of military command. In his book *Little Land*, Leonid wrote of how he saw his task: ". . . great credit is due to the political workers, who armed the soldiers ideologically and strengthened their feeling of great love for their motherland, giving them confidence in their strength and inspiring them."

Elsewhere in the same book he wrote, "History has known quite a few feats of valor carried out by individuals, but only in our great country, only under the guidance of our party, have people demonstrated a capacity for mass heroism." The Russian people did display extraordinary courage, defending every inch of soil with exemplary tenacity, though with all due respect to my uncle, the party had nothing to do with it. The soldiers were defending their homes, their children, their loved ones, their parents and grandparents—in a word, their motherland.

In the fall of 1941, after four years of being arrested and released, arrested again and released again, Nikolay, my mother's father, was sent from Magnitogorsk to the front. I remember seeing a photograph of him taken before his departure: his hair cut short, his lips puffy, bitterness etched in the lines on his face. By some miracle, he was given three days to prepare and to see his children and his mother one last time.

It was late evening when he set off with his two older daughters to the train station from which fresh reinforcements were being shipped out daily. Marina was now nineteen, and Yelena, who would become my mother in two years, was seventeen. A little later the order would come to black out Magnitogorsk, but on that night the streetlamps still shone dimly. Finally the three arrived at the outskirts of the city, where little one-story houses were surrounded by stunted apple and cherry trees. As the sisters walked, holding their father tight on either side, they heard the muffled sound of apples falling in the fenced gardens.

Nika spoke softly, his voice choked. "Spend the winter without me," he said. "By spring the war may be over, God willing."

Remembering how his old mother had wept and hugged him when they parted, he reminded his daughters to take care of her. He also admonished Marina not to abandon her younger siblings or give them to relatives to raise. Could he have known that Marina—dark, laughing Marina—would soon be arrested on the basis of a false accusation and would perish in the camps of Mordovia, leaving a year-old daughter of her own?

During the war, Yelena, then a student at a medical institute, did night duty in a Magnitogorsk hospital for wounded soldiers. Her astigmatism kept her from being sent to the front, but in the winter of 1942 the rest of her class, men and women alike, went to the inferno of the Battle of Stalingrad, a legendary, decisive battle of World War II. Almost all were killed.

So many of the young women who took off their silk dresses to don field shirts and heavy boots never returned. One of my mother's friends, with the lovely name of Anna and lovely long braids, wrote her:

> My dear Lenochka, the fighting has stopped for a little while. In a moment they'll start bringing in the wounded, so I'm in a hurry. My braids have lost all their color, partly because I'm going gray, partly because of nits, which we drive out the old-fashioned way—with kerosene. I had to cut my hair, so that now I differ little from our men: I wear the same imitation-leather boots, the same military shirts. I have become hard and mean, my voice has become gruff. My one dream is to get a good night's sleep.

Women were not spared from hazardous missions during the war. In another letter, Anna wrote about a girlfriend who had been captured by the Germans while on guard duty:

> The most terrifying thing is not death but ending up in the hands of the Germans, who use our women as prostitutes. Lenochka, I've learned to smoke and to drink the alcohol they give us before attacks and guard duty so we won't be so cold and afraid. But I'm afraid anyway. I've learned to swear.

Below there was a postscript: "Don't tell Mama that I cut off my braids. She would miss them so much."

Anna was killed near Stalingrad. Her mother never learned that she had cut her beautiful hair.

Yelena was intent on going to the front. Unrelenting, she returned to the enlistment office to prove that despite her astigmatism, she could see perfectly well. The officer who received her, an elderly colonel with bloodshot eyes, spoke from the heart. "My dear," he said, "go to church, light a candle, and thank God you were spared. You'd be lucky if you got killed. What if you come back crippled or maimed—with no eyes or no legs, with your face torn apart?" With that, he drove her from the office. He was taking his life into his hands: if reported, his traitorous words could have put him in front of a firing squad.

The whole country was at war, not just the regions under German fire. At the Magnitogorsk complex, far from the front lines, powerful new blast furnaces, new open-hearth furnaces, and rolling mills were started up shortly after the German invasion. New workshops were built here for entire factories that had been relocated in the east. Subzero cold, blizzards, and time itself were no match for the builders, who completed two factory buildings in twelve days. The workers who ran the production lines were largely old people, women, and children; they stayed in the factories day and night, once more sleeping, eating, and drinking by machines that never stopped.

My father, Yakov Ilyich Brezhnev, came to Magnitogorsk in the spring of 1942, evacuated from Dneprodzerzhinsk (as Kamenskoye was by then known) along with the technical school where he was now an instructor of metallurgy. That year some of Yelena's friends who happened to be studying at this school invited her to the school's May Day celebrations. First came a concert, then a dance. When the student orchestra struck up its first waltz, Yakov, a short, broad-shouldered, blue-eyed twenty-nine-year-old, walked up to Yelena. Smiling, bowing, and clicking his heels gallantly, he invited her to dance. This was their first meeting. He was at her side the whole evening.

My parents' love blossomed slowly. Yelena, not yet eighteen and very pretty, had other suitors, so Yakov bided his time, considering himself an unworthy competitor.

One day during the following winter, Yelena went to the skating rink with some school friends. As they were skating, one of the young men called out, "Look, Lena! There's that old man of yours, hovering like a hawk."

Yakov, who had indeed been standing nearby watching the young people, turned around sharply and walked away. Yelena hurriedly tossed aside her skates, along with the boots to which the blades were attached, and ran after Yakov in the snow, barefoot. Her heart was decided.

It was easy for them to marry since after the war's beginning, marriage procedures had been simplified. Many used the opportunity for a quick wedding: men, to receive letters at the front and for the comfort of knowing that someone was waiting for their return; women, for love or to receive the allowance due a military wife.

In the spring of 1943, during their first year together, Yakov Ilyich was invited to work in the NKVD. His background made him a prime candidate for the state security organs: he came from the working class, he belonged to the Communist Party, and his brother was a party functionary. He came home in a gloomy mood and asked Yelena for her advice.

"Tell them no," she replied. "They sent my father from prison to prison, they killed my grandfather and all my uncles, and now they want you to work for them? They'll have you interrogating, torturing, plundering, sending innocent people to their death. You couldn't do that kind of work, Yasha."

Yakov agreed.

That evening he told Yelena the story of his own brother's narrow escape from the NKVD, in the fall of 1937. At that time, Leonid was assistant secretary of the executive committee of the Dneprodzerzhinsk soviet. Late one night a friend and neighbor, an NKVD officer, came running to their home and warned him: on that Wednesday, a black raven (as the black government vehicles used to haul victims away for interrogation and imprisonment were known) would be coming after him.

Wasting no time on reflection, Leonid drove to nearby Dnepropetrovsk, where he used his party connections to catch a plane to

Sverdlovsk. There he hid out in the apartment of the widow of the general with whom he had stayed once before, at the beginning of the decade. The general had himself been arrested and shot by the NKVD in the interim, and the widow gave him refuge at great risk to her own life.

During the long autumn evenings, they sat together in the tiny kitchen, the general's widow and the future general secretary of the Communist Party of the Soviet Union. Their conversations were slow and strained. Each tried to change the thinking of the other, to no avail. Leonid defended the party, claiming that despite the temporary "excesses," there were some good Communists.

"For some reason, Lyonya, I've never met any of those," the woman would answer.

Two or three months later the friend who had warned Leonid of his imminent arrest sent a telegram: "RETURN ALL IS CALM." Just before Leonid left, the woman who had saved his life gave him a keepsake: her late husband's personal, inscribed pistol.

One evening, in the late 1930s, Leonid was toying with the weapon while Yakov sat reading a book at a desk nearby. Accidentally Leonid pressed the trigger, releasing a bullet that hit Yakov between his thumb and index finger and left an even, round mark that is visible to this day. By a stroke of luck, Yakov had been holding his hand to his forehead, as though saluting. Had the bullet traveled one centimeter to the left or the right, he would have been killed.

The year after he returned from Sverdlovsk, Leonid was appointed propaganda secretary of the Dnepropetrovsk Oblast party committee, a post whose previous occupant, Mendel Khatayevich, had been executed. Once I asked my father how his brother could have agreed to take over for an innocent victim of the same purges he had fled. He answered, "The times were like that, Lubushka. We were all doing the same thing."

In December 1943, when Yelena was eight months pregnant, she happened to read a letter from the city of Alma-Ata that was addressed to her husband. In it, a certain Anna Vladimirovna told Yakov that their little girl had spilled boiling water on herself, causing a serious burn. Then came a detailed description of the child's pain and Anna's sleepless nights. The letter ended with a postscript:

> Yasha, I know that you never loved me, but don't forget that we have a daughter and that she is waiting for you.

This was the first Yelena had heard of Yakov's other wife, and she was devastated. In those days, almost all men had families by the age of thirty, so it would have been natural for her to suspect something from the start. But Yelena, consumed by happiness, had never thought to ask questions.

Yakov had married Anna in 1939. The first few months of the marriage convinced him that he had made an unfortunate choice. But in February 1940, they had a daughter, and so divorce was virtually ruled out. They did separate when Dneprodzerzhinsk was evacuated on account of the war: Yakov went to Magnitogorsk to teach; Anna, together with their daughter, her mother-in-law, and Leonid's family, went to Alma-Ata, the capital of Kazakhstan.

Yakov was candid about the reason for his silence: "I didn't mention it, Lena, because I was afraid of losing you." He tried to convince her that he had been planning to divorce his first wife. He pointed out that he could have brought Anna to Magnitogorsk with him, since German troops were not near that city, nor were air attacks anticipated there. Instead, he had sent her off to Alma-Ata.

Silently Yelena began to pack her bags. Yakov urged her to think at least of their unborn child's future. But her mind was made up to move in with relatives, and his pleas were in vain. Before leaving, she sat down with Yakov, as Russian tradition dictates before any parting of company.

Years later my father described this scene to me: "Unhappy, beautiful, her lips sealed, she sat on the bed among her things, with her grandmother's old fur coat and a fluffy shawl over her shoulders. Outside a blizzard was beginning to rage. I was on my hands and knees, crying and hugging her legs, when suddenly she lurched backward and went into labor."

THE WORLD I LEFT BEHIND

About eight months earlier, in April of 1943, Leonid had been appointed head of the political department of the Eighteenth Army. By April 17, he was on his way to the front lines at Little Land (Malaya Zemlya), a small beachhead located on a spit of land in the Black Sea in the vicinity of Novorossisk. He started to cross the bay on a fishing boat, but the boat ran into a mine, and he was thrown into the water by the explosion. He had known how to swim since his childhood on the shores of the Dnieper. So with the help of the soldiers, he swam to safety.

By October 9, 1943, the Taman Peninsula, of which Malaya Zemlya is a part, had been liberated. On orders of Commander in Chief Stalin, the troops of the Eighteenth Army were transferred to the first Ukrainian front under General Nikolay Vatutin.

In November, Leonid's family returned home from Alma-Ata, and his mother wrote him with the news from Dneprodzerzhinsk. He would not see Natalya Denisovna until after the war. But on one December night, he did glimpse the lights of his hometown. As we determined later, this was the same night I was born.

It was already dark when Leonid arrived at Gostomel Station. As the trains were unloaded, he ran from car to car, watching the lights of Dneprodzerzhinsk in the distance. The enemy was near and haste was essential. Leonid, suffering from a severe head cold, barked his orders hoarsely through the glacial chill.

Meanwhile, in Magnitogorsk, Yakov was helping Yelena to the hospital. Arm in arm, they plodded forward, battling a blizzard. When the gusts became too powerful for them to walk, Yakov turned to Yelena, held her close, kissed her dry lips, and softly tried to reassure her: "Be patient, Lenochka. We're almost there." And on they went, wending their way cautiously around the deepening snowdrifts. Streetcars, buses, and cars stood abandoned, immobilized by the blankets of ice.

It was around midnight when Yelena gave birth. Detecting no heartbeat, a weary doctor decided the infant had no place among the living, which is how it happened that I began life in a mortuary. A young orderly curled me into a ball, put me into a bucket, and set off for the basement, tripping over his long smock and banging the bucket on the steps.

Soon I was visited by my first emissary of grace in this world. The mortuary door squeaked open, and a large, ragged shadow hung over me: the drunken night watchman, coming down to turn out the light. He wobbled up to the zinc table and examined closely the little corpse lying on it. Seeing that I was breathing, he wrapped me in a blood-stained blanket and carried me up to the maternity ward. My mother was struggling through a fever that almost killed her, and so the other mothers welcomed me, offering their milk. But I refused, wanting no part of this unfriendly world.

My first day on Earth began with the sun breaking through the clouds to shine cold and bright. A few fluffy snowflakes were still falling, but the wind had spent its fury after a long night of wailing eerily in the chimneys and hurling handfuls of snow at the frost-caked windows.

A few days before I was born, my grandfather Nikolay was killed in battle near Bryansk, ceding me his place on Earth. His last letter arrived from the front just before his death. It was a short, almost incoherent farewell:

> During the long nights, lying in the stinking, damp trenches and look-ing at the sky, lit with festive stars, I have been wondering: will I disap-pear this way, having drunk my fill of human blood and cried out all my tears under this uncaring sky? Around me there is only pitch-darkness. I am calm and indifferent. There is no past, no present, no future. I no longer exist either. There are only the stars. Will God ever forgive even one of those who are condemned to kill and die? Farewell, my children. May you be happy.

Chapter Six

MY FIRST LESSONS

*The universities have never nurtured the Russian
soul; kindly, illiterate nannies have been the true
source of Russian education.*

VLADIMIR ROZANOV

The winter of my birth, the winter when the war's tide turned, was amazingly snowy. Snow, snow, everywhere white, glistening snow. But this was not a Russian winter of troikas festooned with bells and ribbons. No one was listening to Gypsy songs or soaking up vodka; nowhere were gay peasant women in colorful shawls and felt boots to be seen. The horses had been driven to the front lines, the women had been mobilized to dig trenches and build missiles, and vodka was something carefully and purposefully dispensed before battle.

The snow covered the bleeding earth, which had been torn apart by bombs. Gently it dusted the wide-open, frost-covered eyes of fallen soldiers and their sunken gray cheeks, brushing their lips like a kiss of death. Millions of souls flew to glory to the strains of the Soviet national anthem. And still the snow fell. . . .

Every family was touched. In ours, the death notices from the front, watered with widows' tears, tied with the black ribbons of mourning, were stored in my great-grandmother's old jewelry box.

Some of my most vivid memories are the earliest. The first thing that stands out is my baptism. I remember that when the priest immersed me in the font, I was afraid. As he was lifting me up for a second dip, I grabbed his luxuriant beard with both hands, pulling so hard that my great-grandmother Tatyana found some tufts of it in my tiny clenched fist when we got home. "That's a good sign," she said.

I was baptized right after my father left to see his brother. I was about eight months old.

Tatyana sat on a chair in the middle of our room, looking ancient and very feeble. I had to crawl around her chair, trying to stay as far away as possible: for some reason, I was a bit afraid of my great-granny. Once when I was big enough to speak my mind pretty well, the old woman, bored I suppose, invited me onto her lap.

"Come up here, little one," she said, "and I'll tell you a tale."

"No," I said. "I don't like your face."

She laughed. "What don't you like about it?"

"It looks like an accordion."

"Just you wait, my dear; some day your face will be the same."

"Never," I shot back confidently.

My great-grandmother laughed again. "Well, you've surely got the Cossack spirit."

There she sat, with her crown of white hair and her cane and, at her feet, her faithful friend Pushikha, just as old and faded, looking frail enough to shed a tear at any moment. Pushikha was a stray cat with long fluffy fur that Tatyana had brought home after Nikolay's arrest in 1937: something to keep the children distracted.

I often noticed my great-grandmother crying as she looked at me. Resting my head on her knees, I would stand patiently while she stroked my flaxen hair with trembling hands. Once I felt tears fall onto my cheeks. I looked up in surprise. "What is it, Granny?"

But she never answered.

Tatyana died almost imperceptibly, causing no trouble to anyone. She turned to the wall, sighed, and left this world. A few days later her cat joined her. I wept for both of them.

THE WORLD I LEFT BEHIND

How I would love to bring back the days when those dear to me were still alive. My thoughts return again and again to Aunt Pasha, my first instructor in faith, kindness, and truth. All my childhood memories are colored by images of this woman. I loved her more than I loved my mother, who was so often away, working as a nurse and studying to become a doctor. With simple faith and a rough-hewn kindness that in no way kept her from being a strict, no-nonsense woman, Pasha sowed many good seeds in my fragile young soul. Her affectionate gaze, her encouraging words, the gentle touch of her hand on my hair—nothing was wasted. All these I still carry with me in that treasure chest of my soul that will never die.

Aunt Pasha was really my great-aunt, one of Grandpa Nikolay's sisters. During the '20s, when Pasha and her husband, Fyodor, were deported to Siberia, their seven-year-old daughter, Arina, died during the arduous journey. Looking back at my childhood, I wonder now what made my Pasha so unswerving in her dedication to service: she helped others throughout her whole life, never feeling that she had done any great deeds. Was she moved by an innate nobility of heart or by the memory of her own little daughter's tragic death?

After leaving the maternity ward, my mother had taken me to live in Pasha's room. Pasha and Fyodor were building a house of their own. When they completed it, they invited us to live there with them.

"How could Yakov lie to you that way," Pasha said to my mother, "when you were just a wide-eyed child? You were like a little flower that could fall apart at the slightest touch. I won't stand for it. We'll raise the girl by ourselves. If you keep him, his first wife will make your life a living hell; just look how bad she wants him back even though she knows full well that he doesn't love her. To Yakov's mother, sister, and brother, she's already one of the family while you're a home wrecker. In their eyes, you'll always be a young, frivolous girl who turned the head of a married man. They'll give you nothing but abuse. He's too spineless to stand up to them."

She was hardly spineless herself. Despite subzero temperatures, she would keep me outdoors in my baby carriage most of the day. The neighbor women objected: "The child will catch her death of cold out there, Pasha. You have no heart!" But Aunt Pasha paid no heed to idle chatter. She wanted to make me strong, and that was that. After my bath, she would always douse me with cold water, saying, "As water runs off a goose, so will disease flee my Lubushka." I am grateful for her Cossack-style toughening, which undoubtedly helped me survive the trials ahead.

When first brought home from the hospital, I weighed about four and a half pounds, and like many premature babies I had jaundice. I was too weak even to cry. A three-year-old neighbor, moved to pity when he saw me, took half of his lunch—a small cutlet—and placed it on my crib. My mother, who told me years later about the boy's act, marveled at his sacrifice.

I never really cared about food and sometimes stopped eating completely, which drove adults to desperate measures: they would force me to drink milk and eat the chocolate that Fyodor bought at an exorbitant, black-market price. Pasha's dream was to make me a proper, plump little girl, but nothing anyone tried could coax baby fat onto my bones.

I grew up side by side with my cousin Tamara, who had been taken in by Aunt Pasha after her mother, Marina, my mother's older sister, was sent to the labor camps of Mordovia. We were only a half a year apart in age and very fond of each other. I was blond and she was dark, reflecting our Greek ancestry. She was in every way my opposite, sassy and mischievous whereas I was well behaved and quiet. "A real imp," Fyodor would say of her with a laugh. But she was as intelligent as she was cocky: during her school years, she was always at the head of her class.

Aunt Pasha had a Tatar friend, Musin, who would come to visit, sometimes staying with the family for a week or two. He was a neat little old man whose broken Russian we children found amusing. He had been prosperous once, with a large family of his own. After World War II, he was relocated, forced to move from his native Crimea to the Urals, part of a mass deportation in which all the Crimean Tatars were sent to the Urals or Siberia. His wife, youngest daughter, and young son were dead by the time he arrived. Musin was all alone in the world: his eldest

THE WORLD I LEFT BEHIND

The author (seated, second from left) on her eighth birthday, December 1951. Next to her (far right) is her cousin Tamara.

son survived but married and drifted away soon after their arrival in the Urals.

He was like a member of the family, and we called him Grandpa Musin. When he made the trek from his village to Magnitogorsk, the children would go to the yard to feed his horse, a gentle animal named Mukhtarka. Grandpa Musin always brought us gifts: balls of dried cottage cheese and *kumys* (fermented mare's milk), which he gave to my cousin and me with assurances that it would make us grow.

Aunt Pasha would laugh: "So why are you so short if you've been drinking *kumys* all your life?"

"I wasn't always like this," he would answer. "Life has pushed me down."

In the evening, Grandpa Musin would pray in his room. Tamara and I spied on him through the door. The old man would spread out a small velvet carpet, kneel, whisper words we couldn't understand, rub his face with his hands as if washing, and bow his head to the ground. We laughed at the sight of his pink heels protruding from his house slippers. One time Aunt Pasha caught us, and she scolded us roundly, admonishing "you girls" not to pry into other people's lives.

Dining with Pasha and Fyodor was an education. Sitting down at the large oak table, a family heirloom, Fyodor would check first to see that his silver forks and knives were clean. He had a big silver spoon, inherited from a great-great-grandfather, of whom he was fervidly proud. Though it was worn, thin, and bumpy, he never would have considered replacing it. "You can see," he would say, "how many of our ancestors licked this spoon. And so will my son and grandsons." Pouring herbal liqueur from a bottle with a colorful rooster carved onto its side, he would always say, "Honor to those whose praises we sing." Then he'd take his starched napkin out of its narrow gold-plated ring and leisurely tuck it into his collar.

"Watch how Grandpa Fyodor eats," Aunt Pasha said, "and learn." I watched and I learned.

"Are you blind? Why do you bury your face in the plate like an old lady?" Fyodor would ask across the table without looking in my direction.

Aunt Pasha would sometimes come up to my cousin and me from behind and tap us lightly between the shoulder blades. "Don't slouch," she would scold. "You're not sick, and what cares do you have to weigh you down?"

She was afraid we would ruin our posture and our girlish beauty. Tamara, who couldn't sit still for three minutes, bore the brunt of the discipline. When she was made to go without dessert, which happened often, it was up to me to see whether Aunt Pasha would let me take my portion "for later" so that I could share it with Tamara on the sly.

I felt a special fondness for Fyodor. A Cossack warrior in his youth, he had somehow escaped retribution after the 1917 revolution, but he never found his place in the world. Tall, well built, and handsome, he was, to paraphrase the Russian poet Nikolay Nekrasov, an aristocrat, a reveler, and a layabout. He seemed to float through life. He had no use for doctors, calling them all charlatans, and used home remedies for whatever ailed him. He was fond of hot and cold compresses and liked to soak his feet in a large copper tub. He never wiped his steaming red feet afterward but let them dry off on a little carpet. I wasn't old enough to have much of a sense of beauty, but for some reason I noticed how exquisitely sculpted Fyodor's small feet were. In later years, I would see similar feet on the ancient statues of the Hermitage.

"Pasha," he would call out in his husky voice while my cousin and I, leaving all the doors wide open, dragged the heavy tub to the yard, spilling water onto the floor and our feet. "Close the door, there's a draft!"

Fyodor sometimes had long, drawn-out coughing fits, which always ended in a high whistle and kept us awake nights. For relief, he would add fragrant herbs to his "foot water" and inhale the vapors. The smell filled the whole house.

I first heard about my grandfather's death when I was very little. Aunt Pasha explained it in her own way. One day she was showing me the pretty seas and mountains on a map. "And here is where your grandfather Nika died," she said, pointing to a green spot. "These are the Bryansk forests."

I understood that a forest was a place with lots of trees but not what my grandfather had been doing there.

"They sent him," said Aunt Pasha, pausing, "to a certain death. There was a war on, Lubushka."

I was too young to know the meaning of the word *die,* and so I asked for an explanation.

"In the olden days," Pasha said, sitting down on the edge of my bed, "in the forests near the city of Bryansk lived a group of *raskolniki* holding on to the old faith. To convert people to their beliefs, they gave them cranberries—monastery cranberries is what they called them. Those who ate the berries saw fire in front of them, but they also saw paradise and flying angels in the flames, so they would rush headlong into the fire . . . and die. That's what it means to die."

For years, when asked how my grandfather Nikolay had died, I answered, "The *raskolniki* poisoned him with monastery cranberries."

❖

Tamara and I had a favorite spot behind the tiled stove. There we played, talked, read, and gossiped about girlfriends. On a trunk lay a long black sheepskin coat of the kind that the Ural Cossacks traditionally wore in the winter. We would play with our dolls on it and take naps under its long flaps.

On the most important holidays, Cossack women used to wear lovely multicolored costumes with gold-embroidered muslin sleeves, and they would adorn their heads with golden lace and pearl-inlaid hairnets. My grandmother had had such a costume and wanted to leave it for her daughters. Kept in a trunk at Aunt Pasha's home, it was lost after Pasha's death, to my great regret.

Near the entrance to Pasha's house, in a corner, stood another trunk. In its depths were treasures from the past: my great-grandmother's shawls, buttons from my great-grandfather's uniform, an old silver mirror, women's moth-eaten overcoats, handmade lace, miniature portraits. . . . A small box held treats for the children: gumdrops, crystallized marmalade, rooster-shaped cookies, and mint cough drops.

"Everything in this trunk will be for you," Aunt Pasha told us. Sometimes she would have us try on long dresses and high-heeled boots with a seemingly endless number of buttons and buckles. Getting trapped in the ruffles and twisting our legs, my cousin and I would push and shove each other as we ran, thrilled, to the mirror. Perhaps our laughter and chatter were just the music Pasha wanted to hear.

The Cossack custom was to send gifts—tea, sugar, and cloth—to needy Cossack children at Christmas and Easter. The offerings were always slipped to the families in such a way that no one would know the giver's identity. Following the custom, Aunt Pasha used to send Tamara and me with packets of foodstuffs for the poorest families on our street. She always added, "Just make sure no one sees you." This chagrined us greatly: we wanted so much for people to know of our good deeds and to praise us.

Naturally Tamara and I liked to skip rope and play out of doors, especially our favorite games: hopscotch, streetcar, and school. We looked forward to our first day of school from an early age. Tamara, who always insisted on the role of teacher, gave me Ds, of course, and ordered me to have my parents appear in person. I searched out Aunt Pasha, who would come hear how lazy I had been in class. I was frustrated at having to be an eternal student, but there was no one else to play with, so I endured.

The Magnitogorsk of my youth was full of farm animals. Once Uncle Fyodor brought home two little goat kids, and I named them Sashka and Mashka. We had much fun with them, but our friendship ended all too soon, when they were banished to the barn, off limits to children.

Pasha and Fyodor kept an aged setter, Polkan, that had once helped in the hunt but, after years of being chained up in the yard, had gone soft, or so we thought: he ran up and kissed anyone who came near. Once while Aunt Pasha was off at the store, my cousin and I took pity on old Polkan and set him free, after which he killed all Pasha's chicks in short order. We were stunned by such ingratitude and paid dearly for his crime. Not only did we have to sit in different corners for two hours, until Fyodor came home and let us go, but for a long time after this Pasha would scold us: "They were so healthy and getting so plump!" We listened in contrite silence.

Aunt Anna, as we called our next-door neighbor, Fyodor's sister-in-law, would drop by our house several times a day. Jerking her hand and blinking constantly, she recounted the latest neighborhood gossip, then borrowed a packet of flour or a pot in which to make meat jelly, and ran back home. I once asked why Aunt Anna blinked so often.

"That's a nervous tic," Pasha answered. "The Bolsheviks beat her father to death with fence posts in front of her very eyes just because he was wearing the epaulets of a czarist officer."

So the Bolsheviks were murderers who killed their victims with fence posts. . . .

Aunt Anna loved bathing Russian style and sometimes took us to the bathhouse, where she would steam us and try to whip us with birch twigs so we would, as she put it, "be shapely when you grow up; otherwise no one will marry you." Marriage was the last thing on our minds, and we resisted her twigs as best we could. The worst part of the trip to the bath was the scrubbing down of our backs, a test of endurance we often failed, breaking into tears. I cried softly while my cousin wailed at the top of her lungs.

I also remember Aunt Anna for her green thumb: her vegetable garden and orchard were the grandest on the whole street. And she sold begonias and geraniums at the farmers' market, growing them in clay pots that she picked up in the graveyard. Pasha sometimes scolded her: "How can you take the last thing mourners bring for their loved ones?"

"Don't be silly," Anna answered, blinking. "What do dead people need flowerpots for? They're somewhere else anyway."

"Aren't you scared to walk around the graveyard at night?" Fyodor would ask.

"In my life, I've seen it all, and I know what's what. I'm no longer afraid of anything or anyone."

At this time, though, my attitude was quite different from Aunt Anna's. For our First Communion, my cousin and I prepared ourselves physically and morally by fasting and trying to think about God. I feared that I might commit some sin and tried to renounce all earthly temptations. Imagining myself a prim and proper little old lady, I stopped running and playing; I even started walking in short steps, hunched over. But my mother disapproved and made me resume my normal walk, saying I was beginning to look like Baba Yaga, a thoroughly detestable fairy-tale character.

As I grew up, I enjoyed attending church for Communion and confession. The priest looked to me like a holy image drifting through the smoke and the golden glow of slanting sunbeams; I loved his white beard, his light-blue eyes, his sumptuous robe, his large, ruby-encrusted cross. My disillusionment began when I detected vodka and onions beneath the sweet smell of incense. I began to notice that the priest chanted his prayers without feeling. And he always dispensed absolution a bit too readily, I thought. I decided that he must not really be listening to my confessions.

While Aunt Pasha prayed, all my attention went to the altar and, in particular, to the gate: two gold-plated doors, behind which Christ himself floated among white clouds in a heavenly glow. For me, this was the gateway to paradise.

Many societies have put forth an ideal against which everyone is measured. Nazi Germany placed a premium on Aryan blood and its supposed attributes: blue eyes, blond hair, the "correct" skull shape, and a Nordic character. Old Russia prized nobility, a cachet conferred less by coats of arms and family trees than by a fine education, good manners, and knowledge of French. But Soviet Russia held up a new ideal. To prove the proletarian pedigree demanded by the regime, it helped to have broad cheekbones, hard fists, a callous heart, boorish manners, a mother who was a cook, and a grandfather who was a farmhand. To prove their class purity, Russians started digging through their family histories, concealing any ancestors who had glorified the family name by feats of valor and distinguished service to the motherland.

Magnitogorsk had become home to many of the Former People, as the survivors of the ruling classes of czarist times were known. Quite a few of my mother's girlfriends were from fine old Russian families. Concealing their origins, they entered medical schools, trade schools, factory schools—anything to survive in the land of socialism. If found out, the children of the intelligentsia and the nobility had no chance of being admitted to an institution of higher learning: Komsomol membership, the key to advancement, was limited to young people from the working class and the poor peasantry. My mother, like her brother and her sisters, was forced to conceal her background.

I learned from my mother's tales how desperately the Former People feared exposure and its consequences—ranging from the sidelong glances of neighbors and the scorn of society to deportation, prison, hard labor, and death. Sometimes when my mother saw an aristocratic-looking face, she would ask, very softly, if the person was of noble ancestry. But the answer would always be a fearful attempt to convince her that she was talking to the grandchild of a blacksmith or a factory worker. She often gave the same answers herself.

Nadya Lopukhina, who came from the old aristocratic line of the Lopukhins, revealed her origin to my mother only after a friendship of

Leonid (right) and Yakov Brezhnev, August 1944, picking apples.
"My father went to the Carpathians, planning to meet his brother
for the first time in three years."

many years. When they both knew the truth, they would tell each other
in whispers, at night, about the lives of their heroic grandfathers and
great-grandfathers.

Like my grandfather Nikolay, Nadya's father had been exiled to
Siberia. Later he received permission to settle in Magnitogorsk. I can
still see, in my mind's eye, this tall, truly princely old man, in whose
presence we children never dared to misbehave.

As I learned from Aunt Pasha when I was grown up, my father came
by regularly during my first months, without my mother's knowledge.
He would sit by my bed, gaze at me, play with me, caress me, and sometimes cry.

In August of 1944, he left Magnitogorsk. When he said to Pasha,
"Now I'm going away, leaving the two people dearest to my heart," she
was not impressed.

"You should have thought about that before," she replied.

Leonid was in correspondence with his brother, my father, and knew
of his love affair. He counseled my parents to think things over carefully

but did not try to influence their decision. He understood my father as well as anyone could: estranged from his own family, he was himself involved romantically with a military doctor and was even planning to start a second family with her.

From Magnitogorsk, my father went to the Carpathian Mountains, where he met Leonid and, for the first time, Leonid's lover, Tamara. Here, in the mountains marking the westward borders of the Soviet Union, the Germans had built a powerful line of defense, and when it was broken, the Soviet Army was able to begin its march toward Germany. Leonid went from the Carpathians to Hungary, Czechoslovakia, and finally Berlin, while my father went to rebuild the devastated industrial complex of his hometown, Dneprodzerzhinsk, which had been liberated from the Nazis in October of 1943. At the entrance to one of its factories, in front of a modest monument, a sign announces THE FIRST INGOT CAST ON NOVEMBER 21, 1943, IN OPEN-HEARTH FURNACE #5, ON THE TWENTY-SIXTH DAY AFTER THE GERMANS WERE DRIVEN FROM THE CITY.

At age four, I discovered a major fact: I had two fathers.

This happened when I was in the countryside with the rest of my kindergarten class. On that day, the mothers and fathers could freely visit. Suddenly I noticed my mother among all the adults. She was standing by a tree with two men. One of her companions was my father, Yakov; the other was my stepfather-to-be, Pavel (he married my mother that fall). As I learned later, she was asking them, "Who would you choose out of all those girls playing in the meadow?"

Pavel pointed to me immediately: "I'd choose that little girl. She's blue eyed and fair, just like me."

Yakov answered, "There's no need for me to choose. That's my daughter," and started walking toward me.

My mother ran after him: "Yasha, I implore you. She must not know."

I liked both of the men seeking to be my father. I was willing to love either of them with all my heart. But, I thought to myself, my real father will be the one who stays with Mama.

This first family gathering has remained in my memory. When evening came, Yakov crouched in front of me for a good-bye hug. "Tomorrow I have to leave town," he said, tears welling up in his eyes. "We won't see each other for a long time. Enjoy your vacation."

Looking deep into his eyes, I stroked his cheeks and said, "I love you."

"The victors leave the vanquished nothing but their eyes, so that they may weep," as Bismarck said. And the Germans, defeated in 1945, wept. But misery and death triumphed over victory, and the victors also wept, from cold, hunger, destitution, and fatigue. World War II had taken over twenty million Soviet lives.

Magnitogorsk, untouched during the war, fared better than many other cities. But there was universal poverty. For some reason, the Communists, with their habitual enthusiasm, had begun before the war to demolish the dugout shacks that had at least kept the workingman out of the weather, providing his cat with a cozy corner and his dog with a place to curl up. Panic set in as the militia sought out those who built new dugouts or sold existing ones.

After the war, the housing situation intensified to the critical point as the city's resources were used to help restore other regions. Many six-person families were settled in rooms measuring ten square meters (about one hundred square feet). Still, those who had been evacuated to Magnitogorsk during the war were in no hurry to return to the cities of their birth, which in many cases had been reduced to rubble.

Pasha's room, to which my mother and I returned for a few years after moving out of her house, was in a communal apartment, something like a dormitory, with shared kitchen, toilet, and bathtub. After my mother's remarriage, Pavel moved in with us. We were lucky to have access to a bathtub, a cherished rarity at a time when most people made do with the traditional Russian bathhouse.

Communal apartments provided shelter, but they deprived one of any privacy. With their conditions ideal for mutual spying, they were convenient for the secret police, except that the tenants' contradictory accusations must have led to much official head scratching. The communal apartment is the perfect symbol of a whole era in Soviet social history.

To this day, communal apartments serve as the setting for passionate melodramas that playwrights only dream of portraying, from quarrels and fistfights to whispering campaigns and backhanded settling of accounts. Secrets are impossible to keep when as many as twenty families live in proximity, rooms are separated by thin partitions, and all the female residents gather in the kitchen every morning and evening. All kinds of things best left unsaid come to light in sudden, angry bursts of candor.

The tenants get to know more about their neighbors than they know about themselves: what they eat, whom they make love to and how, who their friends are, what books they read, and how many times a day they use the toilet. What is that old Jew writing every evening? Letters? Poems? Nothing of the sort. He's busy scribbling his reminiscences of prison-camp life. And what is he always gnawing on? Dried-out rye bread: he sneaks into the kitchen every night to prepare another batch, just in case the Bolsheviks haul him in again. And what about that senile opera singer, what does she hum while putting her thinning gray hair up in rollers? Is it the Snow Maiden's aria from Rimsky-Korsakov's opera? That old hag still can't accept that she was turned down for the part twenty years ago and missed forever her chance to sing at the Bolshoi. With that nasal mezzo-soprano of hers, even the Maly Theater wouldn't hire her. . . .*

The former opera singer, who had fled Leningrad during the war, was the grandmother of the boy who had once generously shared his cutlet with me. Petya, another of our neighbors, constantly tormented her. He went on the warpath every time the old lady went near the piano. Whenever he heard her sit down to play, he would grab a copper tub and a ladle and go to her door to provide accompaniment. He was, he said, "allergic to music."

Exasperated, she would open the door and let loose with the worst insult she knew: "Petya, you're a Tartuffe." It hardly offended Petya, a

---

*The Maly is a smaller Moscow theater.

metalworker, who had never heard of Molière's character, but it scared the dickens out of her, and she would usually go to his room that evening and apologize. These scenes continued until her death.

The neighbors were amazed when Petya took charge of the arrangements for her burial and in the evening, after getting drunk at her wake, wept and said kind words in her memory. There's the Russian soul in a nutshell: that wedding of incompatibles—heroism and brutishness, kindness and indifference. As a young man, Petya had fought the Nazis and was among the troops that reached Berlin, victorious, in 1945.

To this day, I remember that sweet, unhappy woman. As I sat in the Magnit movie theater, waiting for the show to begin, she would go to the stage and sit down at the old, much-abused grand piano. My friends would look at me with envy as we listened to her romantic ballads; how proud I was to live in the same apartment as a genuine celebrity. In the mornings, I often saw her scurrying about our shared kitchen in a silk gown with a writhing dragon on the back, her hair in curlers, as she cooked breakfast for herself and her grandson. Joining her hands, as if in prayer, on her ample breast—Petya used to yell, "The food here in the Urals has done you wonders!"—she would sing "That Cherry-Red Shawl." I always thought she was singing about the worn-out old shawl with which my cousin and I covered our dolls when we went to play with her grandson on the sofa.

One day—this was in 1950, when I was six—my mother and I ran into a childhood friend of hers. Rita had just returned from the labor camps of the Kolyma River, having served ten years for the crime of having the "wrong" father. I noticed she had on rubber sandals and a light coat though it was already November. My mother brought her home, and I heard them whispering and weeping into the night, sharing the tragic stories of their parents.

Hundreds of foreign engineers and skilled workers had helped build Magnitogorsk in the '30s. From 1930 to 1937, there were over 750 of them. They lived with their families—many of the men had married Russian girls—in an attractive new neighborhood poetically named Beryozki ("birch trees"). They had come for various reasons; some, believing sincerely in the ideals of socialism, joined the Communist

Party. Yet this group was not spared during the purges. Rita's father, an American engineer, was tortured to death by the NKGB (as the secret police were then known) on the first night after his arrest. Few of the foreign specialists survived. Rita's mother and grandmother died in the camps.

The morning after Rita's return, my mother and I joined her in an expedition to recover belongings left behind on the way to Siberia. They had been entrusted to the cleaning woman her family had employed.

We left empty-handed. The woman received us graciously and served tea but claimed that she had exchanged everything for bread during the war years.

On the way home, Rita broke into tears. "Lenochka," she said, "I recognized our old tablecloth on her table. There's a seam in it. Once when I was little, I was cutting out toys to put on the New Year's tree and accidentally cut the tablecloth. When my father saw what had happened, he mended it himself so my mother wouldn't get upset. I never knew before how valuable certain objects could be. How often our family sat around that tablecloth. I remember Papa studying Russian, reading Pushkin and Tolstoy to me, and when I laughed at his accent, he would tell me, 'You silly girl, when we go to America, you will also speak with an accent, and everyone will make fun of you.' I often tried to picture this America of his. He showed me on the map of the city and state where he was born. He was planning to leave Russia in one year.

"You know, Lena, I've almost forgotten his face. I do remember that he collected butterflies. It was such a treat when he called me into his office to study English and look at his collection. He had a favorite, the Indo-Malaysian *Kallima*. When it lands on a tree, it folds up its wings and looks just like a dried-up leaf. When I think back to that butterfly, I can't help thinking of how we live. Don't we also have to take on protective coloration to blend in with those bastards that killed our fathers?"

My mother tried to console her.

About a year later, when my mother and I again met Rita on the steet, we saw a transformed woman, radiant and with the scent of expensive perfume. She embraced my mother warmly, and the two of them settled down on the nearest bench for a long talk. I was seven and a half now and getting ready to enter first grade. On that day, my mother had brought me all sorts of things: a book bag, a primer, pencils, erasers, and bookmarks.

As I examined my treasures, I heard Rita telling my mother about her new husband, a violinist. "Lenochka," she gushed, "I've decided to devote my life to him. I'll take care of the house and raise our children so nothing will get in the way of his career."

My mother tried to talk her into pursuing her own studies—no one can live someone else's life, she said, and trying to do so only leads to disappointment and separation.

"But my Lazar has a real gift. I can't let him waste it!" Rita replied.

I felt like asking Rita what it meant for someone to have a gift, but my mother never let me interrupt grown-up conversations, so I kept quiet. On our way home, I asked my mother the question.

"*Gift* is another word for *talent*," she answered, but what help was that? My mother was lost in her thoughts. I tried to think of an explanation myself, as I usually did. I decided that a gift was some kind of large lump. I pictured Lazar with a huge pink swelling on his side, which Rita sometimes helped him hold up. After telling my mother that day of my interpretation, she laughed. "Strange as it seems, you're right. Talent is a misfortune that weighs down its owners wherever they go." Even now this image—a lump, the unfortunate owner of which is stuck carrying around day and night—comes to mind whenever I hear that someone has a gift.

A few years later Rita divorced her husband and moved to another city.

Nyura, who lived with her three children in the room next to ours in the communal apartment, was proud to be from the working class. Her late husband had been run over by a streetcar while drunk, but his family preferred to say that he had died in the war. Nyura had a few favorite stories she repeated endlessly, especially the ones about her beloved piglet.

"Little Borka was so intelligent," she recalled. "He recognized me and was so devoted. My husband and I had him when we lived on the commune. . . ." I never got the chance to ask what a commune was.

One of her children, Minka, was mentally and physically retarded. He sucked his thumb so much that it became translucent. The other children liked him, and we often invited him to join in our games. When asked, he would show off his thumb, but only to friends; he was very proud. We would examine it closely, amazed and impressed that it was so tiny, so pale! When adults yelled at him to take his thumb out of his mouth, he would conceal his treasure in his pocket.

Mariya, Nyura's eldest, was a kind and considerate girl. In her teenage years, she found a job at the factory where she would work for the rest of her life. She took responsibility for her entire family: her foolish mother, her retarded brother, her little sister. It seemed that all she did in life was sleep and work, and she always looked tired. But between sleeping and working, she somehow managed to marry and bear two charming children.

Nyura's room, with eight square meters (a bit more than eight feet by ten feet), was the smallest in the building, but we loved to gather there, perhaps because it was warm and dry, perhaps because Nyura let us do what we wanted. When my parents went to a play or to a movie, they would leave me in Nyura's care. Often I would fall asleep in her room, and late at night my stepfather would carry me back to my own bed.

Our house, built during the war by German prisoners, was designed to have steam heat—along the walls there was a wooden casing, underneath which steam pipes had been driven—but steam was never provided, and the walls offered scant protection from the intense winter cold. The solution was to install tiled stoves in all the rooms.

My mother sometimes worked twenty-four-hour shifts in the hospital. Though she paid Nyura to heat the stove in our room in time for my return from school, the job usually remained undone until one of my parents was about to show up. When I came home from school in the winter, the room would be so cold that I couldn't even take my coat off. I would place my chair in the middle of the room, where my great-grandmother had liked to sit before her death. Huddled there in my winter clothes, eating my favorite sandwich—bread and butter with sugar sprinkled on top—I would read books.

One day I was sitting alone like this, coiled in the chair and lost in my reading, when Uncle Vasily, my mother's brother, walked in. Short, slim, and broad-shouldered, he had unusual eyes: green, with long eyelashes, topped by bushy black brows. When he kissed me on the cheek, as he always did, I noticed that his eyelids and the trim of his sheepskin coat were covered with frost. The room was still freezing cold, since Nyura had only just lit the stove. Vasily leaned against the stove and looked at me. I turned away from my book.

"Vasenka," I said, and stopped.

Tears were running down his cheeks. I thought at first that they might be drops of melted frost, but no, he was crying.

I still can't decide what the reason was: the sight of his little niece doubled up from cold, a premonition of his own death (he died half a year later), or a surge of recollections of his childhood, his parents, his life.

One evening when I was six, we went to visit the Bychkovsky family. I was friends with their daughter, two years my junior. The adults left us alone for a while, and I had a sudden brilliant idea. It involved cutting my friend's gorgeous long blond hair. She put up a determined fight, pleading that "children get their hair cut short only for the summer." Finally I promised to cut her hair short like Lenin's, and this won her over instantly. The day before, our kindergarten teacher had told us about Lenin and shown us his portrait.

Obediently Lyusya sat down in an armchair, covering herself with a towel as we had seen barbers' clients do, while I armed myself with a pair of large tailor's scissors. When our parents returned, the deed was done, and Lyusya looked like a worthy daughter of the proletarian leader. I was puffed with pride in my work, but for some reason my friend's mother didn't admire the Lenin-style haircut. I had to listen to a lecture in which my mother explained that long hair enhances a girl's looks. There was no need for a girl to resemble the Leader, she told me; better that she should look like her own father.

THE WORLD I LEFT BEHIND

The author (left) after giving her playmate Lyusya a Lenin-style haircut, 1950. "On my face, the pride I took in my haircutting skill is obvious, so I tend to doubt that the lecture had much effect."

After dinner, we were all friends again, and Lyusya's father photographed us.

"This will be a historic photograph of the Lenin haircut," he said.

On my face, the pride I took in my haircutting skill is obvious, so I tend to doubt that the lecture had much effect. Poor Lyusya . . . Soon thereafter she came to my birthday party, and when she took some trifle from the table, I slapped her hand and called her "little baldy." It never occurred to me to feel guilty for having made her look that way.

After the birthday breakfast, we all took one another by the hand, skipped around in a circle, and sang, in our out-of-tune voices:

> Going to Lubushka's birthday party,
> we baked her a round loaf of bread,
> this high, this low, this wide,
> choose whomever you like.

But this was decidedly not my day, and the game of choosing never took place. The party was interrupted by the arrival of the mailman. My uncle had sent me a huge doll. Crouched in front of me, my mother read the birthday greeting. At the bottom of his card my uncle had added, "I was going to buy a dress and some shoes but decided that you would like a doll better."

Hearing this I remarked, "Of course, a doll is much cheaper than a dress." For my ungrateful, bratty words, I had to suffer through a memorable talk with my mother in a corner of the room.

One year the Maksimov girls—Svetlana, Natashka, and Olya—moved in opposite our room. Svetlana, who was my age, became my close friend. We usually put up with fat Natashka because she was easygoing, but we used her shamelessly as an errand girl. Olya was too young for us even to consider human, and we picked on her for the slightest reason. Their father, Vanya, a big, strong man whom I loved very much, often took us to the skating rink and the movies and played charades with us. Our parents were the same age and often took meals together, a common practice in those days.

In the Urals and Siberia, families traditionally gathered in the fall for several days to make *pelmeni* (meat pies), which were then put in a shed, where they froze solid and kept perfectly all winter. I was taught early on the art of preparing this dish. Ideal *pelmeni* are small and succulent; the secret of a perfect texture lies in diluting the filling with just the right amount of water.

In March of 1953, we were getting ready to celebrate little Olya Maksimova's birthday, and my mother helped Olya's mother make a batch of *pelmeni* for the celebration since the winter's supply had been used up.

And then Uncle Vanya had a wonderful idea.

Coming home from his mother's village and unloading the milk and the speckled, bluish beet sugar that he had brought back, he turned to us and said, "Well, kids, we can't let a godsend like this go to waste, can we?"

Natashka licked a finger, dipped it into the sugar, and put it into her mouth. She smiled and cooed blissfully, but Svetlana and I cuffed her on the back of the head, and she began to wail.

Uncle Vanya, as always, ignored our childish squabbling. "I have a good idea," he said, winking. No one could wink quite like Vanya. "Let's make ice cream!"

Natashka, her eyes still moist with tears, soon was jumping up and down and clapping her hands.

I remember still the green pot Vanya used to stir the ice cream in. Missing both its handles, it had nicks on the inside and a lid that banged because it didn't quite fit. It had been relegated to the shelf built by Vanya above the kitchen table, where it hid, unused, behind a colorful curtain. Uncle Vanya stirred the milk and sugar for what seemed like the longest time while we watched breathlessly. Finally we took the pot to the shed, solemnly, as though we were carrying the chalice of the Holy Grail. We swept aside the accumulated snow and placed the pot in a corner.

Every five minutes we ran across the courtyard to inspect the contents, and Uncle Vanya cautioned that we had to be patient, otherwise our loving glances would prevent the ice cream from freezing and might even melt it right away.

The next day my mother and stepfather took me to Olya's birthday party. We were all seated around the table when, with no warning, an announcement came over the radio: Stalin was dead.

I noticed our parents exchange guarded glances, afraid to reveal their joy in the presence of the children. Both families had reason to rejoice. No one yet knew what had become of Olya's grandfather, a sea captain arrested by the NKVD in the early '30s. Her uncle had also disappeared, from a camp on the Kolyma River in Siberia. My mother's sister Marina was still in the camps of Mordovia, or so we thought, and her uncles were among the thousands of prisoners building the White Sea–Baltic Canal. The news of Stalin's death roused in many hearts around the Soviet Union a faint hope of seeing loved ones once more. Much later my family learned that none of ours would ever return.

I saw no massive outpouring of grief for the dead dictator; in fact, I saw not one person weeping in Magnitogorsk, perhaps because so many Former People lived there.

After the announcement, we played a prank on Natashka, pouring vinegar and pepper, both of which she hated, onto her plate. When she swallowed one of the *pelmeni* drenched in vinegar and began to cry, we teased her, saying that she was mourning Stalin's death. Feeling guilty, we ran out to fetch the ice cream that she was looking forward to so eagerly. Even now when Stalin's death is mentioned, I think back to my plate, decorated with gay cornflowers around the edges, and on it, a heavenly mound of snow-white ice cream.

Chapter Seven

THE TEACHER IS ALWAYS RIGHT

In her book *The Century of the Child,* the Swedish writer Ellen Key describes modern-day education as a factory for the mass production of standardized human beings: kindergarten is the bottom floor, where the child is molded into shape; school is the second floor, used for further polishing and smoothing. Like most Soviet children, I was plunged early into this factory: my mother put me in a nursery when I was fourteen months old, and at the age of three years I was transferred to kindergarten.

The kindergarten consisted of one large room divided by makeshift barriers into cafeteria, playroom, and sleeping room. I remember well the oatmeal without butter or sugar, the dusty courtyard with its dilapidated sandbox in the corner, the cots that the children had to take apart twice a day and bruised their legs on when they fell over. On the wall hung a large portrait of the Leader. Pointing to it, our teacher would have us repeat after her:

> *Wise Stalin, like a father,*
> *Smiles down from his portrait at you.*

Kindergarten, 1949; the author is sitting on the rug with a doll. Many of the
children had been evacuated from Leningrad during the siege, and most of their
fathers had been killed at the front lines.

I didn't join in for the simple reason that I couldn't understand what it
all meant. In the first place, Stalin wasn't smiling. To me, his cunning
face and his black, samurai-like eyes seemed angry. And in the second
place, he had nothing in common with either my father or my stepfather. Finally, I knew that children with divorced parents could have two
fathers, but where could a third come from? The teacher, red-faced with
irritation, tried to convince me that Stalin had given us children everything we had.

As I grew up, I was amazed by the number of portrayals of Lenin and
Stalin that I encountered. Sculptures, portraits, and busts were on display in every corner of the Soviet Union: from clinics to crematoriums,
from taverns to train stations, the vigilant eyes of our beloved leaders
watched over us. There was no escaping these idols of evil and destruc-
tion.

More than once we heard the director of the kindergarten scolding employees for stealing a piece of meat, a pillow, or some forks. I sometimes woke up to discover that my dresses, shorts, or shoes had been stolen during our daily nap hour.

Once our *shefy* (workers at an enterprise who "sponsor" a school or kindergarten and provide its students with material assistance) sent us a box full of new wooden toys. I especially liked the figure of a peasant wearing bast sandals and sawing firewood with the help of a bear. But to our great disappointment, these lovely toys were shortly locked up in a cupboard, and we never knew what became of them.

Gifts also arrived from America: packages of food, clothing, and toys, which were distributed by government agencies and at the workplace. The American gifts, as they were popularly known, were like treasures, and we could hardly believe they were real. For a while, it seemed as though all Magnitogorsk was sporting fashionable American clothing. In the hospital where she worked, my mother received a package from an American girl my age, who had written on the outside that the gift was for "a little blond girl that looks like me." Inside I found wonderful dresses and blouses, a heart-shaped medallion, and a miniature gold watch that fit my wrist perfectly.

One day when our kindergarten teacher had to go away for an hour, the nanny who stayed with us in the yard took off my medallion and my watch, buried them in the sand, and invited me to search for them. I soon lost interest and forgot about my gifts until the evening, when my mother asked where they were. I'm sure the nanny "found" them.

(Though the clothing, medallion, and watch are long since gone, I often think of that little American girl who sent them to me. I thank her and wish her health and happiness wherever she may be.)

My mother's busy schedule meant that frequently I had to stay overnight in the kindergarten, and I sometimes stayed there up to six days at a stretch when she was on duty in the veterans' hospital. We were living in the communal apartment then, and Aunt Pasha, busy with construction work being done on her house, had no time to watch over me.

The author and her mother, 1947. Luba has an American bow in her hair;
her mother is wearing an American dress. "Gifts . . . arrived from America: packages
with food, clothing, and toys, which were distributed by government agencies. . . ."

My mother asked God to give me perfect health, and her prayers
were answered: during my entire childhood, I never once was sick, and
the entry for "childhood diseases" in my medical records was always
blank. I can remember the whole kindergarten coming down with
measles, scarlet fever, diphtheria, and mumps while I remained healthy.
Once when everyone else had gone home sick, one of the nannies asked
angrily, "What is wrong with you that you never catch anything? If you
were sick, too, we could lock up and go home."

Thinking of myself as a child, I see a girl sitting on a chair, examining the pictures in a book of Russian fairy tales open on her lap. Beside
her a gray cat is busy grooming his fur. It didn't matter that I couldn't

THE WORLD I LEFT BEHIND

The author and her mother, 1946."During the post-war years, permanent waves
were in vogue, and many women wore their hair short,
leaving silly bangs over the forehead."

read yet: I knew all the stories by heart. My companion was a tomcat
who would sometimes come out of the kindergarten kitchen and join
me on the chair.

Someone who hadn't bothered to look closely had named him Vasilisa, yet he responded readily to his female name; perhaps his vanity had
disappeared along with his masculine equipment, removed by our cook.
He was one of those cats that wouldn't kill a mouse if you put one in
front of him. On orders from the director, he was starved a few times,
but even that did no good: Vasilisa was a vegetarian who liked to gnaw
on carrots, cucumbers, and beets.

One of my most striking memories from those early years centers on the director of our kindergarten. She was tall and dark, with a kerchief tied around her jaw to relieve a constant toothache. Her old-fashioned silk dresses, all in shades of green, must have been from her grandmother's day. During the post-war years, permanent waves were in vogue, and many women wore their hair short, leaving silly bangs over the forehead. But our director didn't follow fashion and wore her hair long and free.

We children were too emotionally involved with the teachers and nannies to think about her much. Sometimes she would come to one of our groups and stand in the corner, watching us draw, eat, or play. Once she observed us while our teacher, Nina Maksimovna, told us about the forest, showing us pictures of trees and teaching how to tell the different kinds apart. When she raised a picture and said, "Children, this is a willow; it grows along riverbanks," we all turned our heads as one to look at the director, standing in a corner. She did indeed look like a weeping willow, with her bleary eyes, long hair, and green dresses, under which her sagging flesh jiggled in a way we found amusing. She was embarrassed and walked away.

On occasion, I overheard adults talking about her. She was convinced that her husband, seized during the late '30s as an "enemy of the people," was still alive. She continued to write letters and beat at the impervious doors of Soviet officialdom, trying to prove his innocence. She continued to send him money, packages, and letters, which remained unanswered.

As it turned out, one day the director did receive a letter, from an ex-prisoner, and the news broke her heart: her husband, convinced that he had been abandoned, had died of pneumonia three years after his arrest. He hadn't received a single letter in all that time.

And then one morning she was found with her wrists slashed. In the pandemonium that followed, the children were far from anyone's mind, and curious, we ran to the office. What I saw was such a shock that I fainted and was awakened only with difficulty. From then on, I shook uncontrollably whenever I went near the office.

Our director had been kept alive for years by the slim hope that her husband would some day return. The prospect of a solitary old age was too much for her. . . . In her suicide note, she wrote, "I ask that no one be blamed for my death." But to lay blame, we needn't have looked far.

When I was five years old and in the kindergarten's middle age group, I was allowed for the first time to trim the New Year's tree and to dance at the New Year's matinée. Yet one thing that happened that day almost ruined my festive mood. I had placed the packet with my holiday dress on one of the beds at the kindergarten, but as we were hanging the decorations, Vasilisa, the tomcat, jumped up on top of it. My mother had sewn it for me specially, using some starched gauze from the hospital. I got so mad at my furry friend for crumpling my dress that I locked him in the kindergarten pantry. Not till the day was over did I remember Vasilisa, and I felt deeply ashamed of my callousness.

For the tree, there were clappers, little cardboard animals, glass beads and fruits, balls, golden walnuts, pinecones, fish, mica snow, tinsel, and fairy-tale houses. Holding our breath, we pulled the decorations out of their boxes and draped them on the branches, warning one another with "tut-tuts" not to break or mash anything.

The children's matinée was held, naturally, more for the parents' benefit than for the children's. My father, in Magnitogorsk to visit us, took a photograph of me dancing. I soon was frustrated with Vadim, my chunky, clumsy partner: he couldn't hold his hand up, so I had to prop it up myself.

We were presented with gifts later that day. One was an intriguing fruit, smallish, rumpled, and orange in color. I took my time breathing in its aroma and running my tongue across its surface. I dried the peel of my first tangerine and stored it in a box that had once held a jar of my mother's Red Moscow perfume.

The drab kindergarten fare—oatmeal, watery soup, and jelly—was seldom enlivened with fruits or vegetables. My cousin and I did eat them at home, however, thanks to Aunt Pasha's small but well-tended garden.

At kindergarten, we planted onions in long wooden boxes that resembled babies' coffins. Like many other children my age, I hoped to grow green onions on the windowsill at home.

One Sunday, soon after I had placed an onion bulb in a jar of water, my mother, short of money with which to buy groceries, went to see our neighbors. They had no money to spare but gave us a cup of sunflower oil and a chunk of black bread.

I stepped determinedly to the windowsill, took the stout onion bulb from the jar of water, and handed it to my mother. Only a few tiny green shoots were breaking through the yellow peel, and I would have liked so much to see them grow and grow. Instead, Mama poured the oil into a bowl, threw in the diced onion, and we had a small feast. We used the silver forks over which my great-grandmother Tatyana had once cried, the ones that had miraculously survived the plundering of Akindin's house, so thick and heavy that I could barely hold one with both hands. Though children usually dislike pungent foods, that day I must have eaten with an enormous appetite, for my mother took a long look at me, holding her fork halfway to her mouth, and began to cry.

My mother was reduced to tears by our poverty another time as well, once when she was carrying me home from kindergarten. On that day, the roads were barely passable, given the mud and melting snow. I was wearing the thinnest of boots, and Mama took me into her arms so that my feet would stay dry. The tears ran down her cheeks. I felt so sorry that I hugged her neck tightly and said, "Don't cry, Mommy. When I grow up, I'll buy you rubber boots and a fur coat." For some reason, a woman's happiness was linked in my mind to fur coats.

Another memory from my childhood, one that comes back to me again and again, is the image of my mother making me a dress, her head bent over a sewing machine: her chestnut-brown hair, gilded in the light from the lampshade, falling onto her smooth forehead, . . . the shadow cast by her eyelashes onto her lightly freckled cheeks, . . . the light-blue veins of her hand, where I knew every single spot; . . . then a door squeaking open, letting the scent of acacia rush in, along with the sound of an apple falling noisily into the grass and my fragile, shrill voice echoing through the corridor . . .

In kindergarten, we were taught to believe that we had been born in the best country in the world, a land of happiness and progress that our ancestors had made possible by shedding their blood in the crucible of revolution and civil war. At the age of three, we already knew that Russia had moved from darkness into light thanks to Lenin, our wise leader and teacher. Barely able to speak, we were already memorizing verses about him:

> *Who is that Bolshevik fellow*
> *Climbing onto our armored car?*
> *A tall man with a cap on his head,*
> *Who can't pronounce the letter* r.

The only thing in this jumble that struck a sympathetic chord in our hearts was Lenin's inability to pronounce the letter *r*, since this was also a problem for most of our group and for most Russian children in general.

We were spoon-fed propaganda like porridge, without knowing what we were learning.

Woe to the child who didn't fit in. Often, bright, impulsive children were labeled unbalanced, and left-handers were subjected to the worst treatment of all. They were tormented by a steady stream of rebukes in kindergarten and school, even at home. Constantly required to switch their spoons and pens from the left hand to the right, they ended up unable to use either one properly. There was a left-handed boy sitting next to me at my table in kindergarten who often wept in silent frustration. I remember times when he had to stand in the corner after being caught using his left hand. Sometimes his "shortcoming" cost him the privilege of playing or taking walks or eating dessert.

Once when our nanny Raisa said that life had been better when the czar ruled, a teacher overheard and reported her. A general assembly was called, and we were instructed to explain to Raisa that "the Soviet system is better because it takes care of children."

To help mold us into conscientious Soviet citizens, our teachers also had us write Stalin and the government collective letters, which never went any farther than the wastepaper basket. For the thirty-third anniversary of the 1917 revolution, we wrote a letter to Moscow:

> Thirty years from now, in 1980, all the capitalists will have been shot and the workers will have seized the factories. There will be a worldwide revolution. There will be no more poor people because there will be Soviet power in the whole world.

The mice were so bold that after our nap hour, we had to shake them out of our shoes; the vegetarian tomcat Vasilisa was of no help at all.

When our watchwoman, Klava, bought new felt boots and left her old ones standing in the entrance hall, the mice used them as nests. When the baby mice stirred, the boots would rock back and forth as though alive, and we children would pull back in fright.

Nina Maksimovna, a pale, slender young teacher who had survived the siege of Leningrad and lost all her relatives there, was desperately afraid of mice. Every time one ran across our play area, she would hop onto the nearest table and squeal like a piglet. Her squealing caused the mouse to run back and forth, which only made her squeal even louder. Eventually one of the boys would catch the culprit and take it out to the street. Poor Nina Maksimovna! She would climb down from the table, red with shame and regret for her childish behavior. She would then remain seated for a long time, hating herself for her cowardice while we tried to hide our condescending smiles.

During our nap hour, Nina Maksimovna once took me to the store to buy a bundle of newspapers—for some reason, I was a favorite. With winter approaching, it was time to insulate the windows. I was thrilled: what a privilege to be allowed to walk around during nap hour!

On the way back, Nina Maksimovna bought ice cream on wafers, which we took turns licking from opposite sides. Then, to my great embarrassment, I dropped the treat on the dusty road. Nina consoled me: "When you're grown up and I'm a little old lady, you'll visit me and bring ice cream."

I had laughed at the words "little old lady," so she added wisely, "Before you know it, you'll be old yourself."

The children in the oldest age group, to which I now belonged, were already accustomed to helping the teachers. On that day, our task was to cut copies of *Pravda* into long strips and cover them with a makeshift paste: kitchen starch boiled by the kindergarten cook in an old pot whose handle had fallen off.

I remember how the cook would carry the pot from the kitchen with a large, greasy rag. Setting it on the windowsill to cool, she always warned us, "Don't you go burn yourselves, or I'll really have my hands full."

She was round and rosy. When the teachers' backs were turned, she smuggled us rolls and cookies, and we took turns sitting in her arms, which we considered a privilege. But for some reason, I didn't quite trust her. There was something insincere, something false about her good cheer.

The day after the job of making the papier-mâché insulation was finished, Nina Maksimovna, who was eighteen years old, was called to the local NKGB headquarters and accused of spreading pernicious propaganda among young children. It seems that one of the strips we had cut out of the newspaper contained a picture of Stalin. We never knew who had turned her in or what finally became of her.

Because of my December birthday, I entered school at the advanced age of seven years and nine months. On the first day, a group of fleet-footed boys with shaved heads caused a ruckus outside class during recess. One small boy managed to pull himself free from the others, who were piled up in a heap, and began running gleefully down the hall. But in his way stood an imposing barrier: a beautiful gray-haired woman whose snow-white blouse I still remember. Grabbing him by his arm and the collar of his blue school jacket, she methodically banged his head against the wall. Hisses of "It's the principal! It's the principal!" flew through the air. (I grew weak with awe when the school year ended and this same woman handed me my honor certificate.)

For the most part, I was modest, quiet, obedient, and well mannered. Nevertheless, I never became one of my first-grade teacher's pets. Aleksandra Vasilevna's good graces were not earned through merit; they were purchased. Once when it was my turn to straighten up after class, I saw two mothers whose children received high grades for mediocre work: one was bringing the teacher a crystal vase and the other, a box of candy. Throughout the ten years I attended school, my mother made a point of never bringing a present to my teachers; she visited only when called in.

Doesn't everyone seek the love of a first teacher? How cheated I felt—why shouldn't she love me, as hard as I study, as well as I behave myself? Determined to curry favor, I devised a plan. At home, I chose a book at random from our library, and the next day I sneaked it into the closet where Aleksandra Vasilevna kept our notebooks. The book, which had been handed down in my mother's family after my great-grandfather was killed, was a beautiful edition of Montesquieu's *Persian Letters.* I could hardly wait for our teacher to ask the class, in a tone of delighted surprise, who had given it to her. But she never asked, and I have no idea what became of my offering.

Despite the regimentation, kindergarten—with its lunches, dinners, nap hours, strolls, and hand washing—had created at least the appearance of concern. Rigid official procedures were softened by the kindness of the nannies and the affectionate gazes of the teachers. There was also private property of a sort: the children had their own chairs, their own desks, and their own closets, with a cherry or a rabbit painted on the doors. Going home in the evening from kindergarten, I left a little piece of myself behind. Not so with school.

Lacking even a trace of democracy, the Soviet school used an elaborate system of compulsion, its goal being to manage, not educate, the defenseless child. It was a faithful copy of the society that spawned it, one room in a whole palace of crooked mirrors.

I can't say that I always made my teachers' job easy. No one could make me learn by rote something that I didn't understand. For example, somehow I refused outright to learn the song by Sergey Alymov that was used to introduce music to all Soviet children. It began

> Over the hills and valleys,
> The division marched along,

THE WORLD I LEFT BEHIND

To seize by force of arms,
The coastal White Army stronghold.

How do you explain to an eight-year-old what a stronghold or a division is? Besides, the song glorified the military feats of the Red Army, of slight interest to me.

The school was a small-scale prison, complete with warden, underlings, informers, timeservers, petty thieves, and liars. Reprimands and punishments were used to pit parents and children against each other. A virtual state of war existed between teachers and their pupils, who passed down from generation to generation a whole roster of diabolical scenarios: needles on the teacher's chair, glue smeared across a table, inkwells tipped "accidentally" onto the class attendance sheet, explosions in the classroom, dead rats left for the teacher to find, blackboards covered with wax, beloved cats gone mad from valerian drops. Many teachers couldn't stand the harassment and quit their jobs. Yet all this hatefulness was cloaked behind a cheery façade of socialist competition, stirring patriotic speeches and slogans, and Young Pioneer and Komsomol gatherings.

Sitting within the stifling four walls of the classroom, I soon yearned for an escape from this world, which was alien to me. I spent hours gazing out the window, my mind far away from Soviet literature's "positive heroes," who were dreamed up by writers with whom I felt no sympathy. The truths being drilled into my head made no sense. I was part of a generation raised on substitutes and thirsty for authenticity.

Divorced from real life, saturated with propaganda, oriented toward the least common denominator, education beat down any tendency to think creatively. No wonder children came out of school crammed with ideological rubbish: every other word was based on ideology, and all subjects were treated like social studies. Not only the school system but even that holy of holies, the Academy of Sciences, was subordinated to social science in its official interpretation. In all spheres of activity, social sciences had pushed aside pedagogy, science, history, and art.

To this day, I wince when I recall the assignment to memorize the Soviet Constitution. Unable to do so, I resorted to cheating: copying others' work, looking in my book, and writing the hardest words on the palm of my hand before going up to the blackboard. All my classmates did the same, except for those able to regurgitate anything unthinkingly.

My attempts to learn the Soviet national anthem were fruitless as well. At home, whenever I recited the first line—"An unbreakable union of free republics"—my cousin Tamara would yell at me to "stop learning that garbage." I received a D in that assignment. Somewhere in the back of my mind, I can still hear the words of Aleksandra Vasilevna, who once told the class that there wasn't a person in our country who didn't know the national anthem. Was I the only one?

How I loved my feisty cousin Tamara, an orphan who experienced all the hardships of the socialist paradise. At the age of eleven, when it was no longer possible for her to live with me and my mother or with Aunt Pasha, she was put into an orphanage. The summer after she graduated from high school—with honors—she told me in a tirade, "Supposedly our country is the best in the world. We have the happiest childhood, and we live in the happiest era. That's what we're taught in school, that's what the textbooks say. What lies! Our grandfather was sent to the front to be killed even though he had bad eyes and heart trouble and a big family to support. My mother was thrown into jail when I was still at the breast; her only fault was being born into the 'wrong' family. My father never did learn that he had a daughter; he was burned to death in a tank near Stalingrad before his twenty-fifth birthday. I was never allowed to forget how lucky I was for being placed in one of the most prestigious orphanages, a place for the children of Soviet officers, not children of 'enemies of the people.' I was made to feel guilty for every crust of bread and scrap of clothing that came my way. I was constantly reminded how grateful I should be to the party, the government, and Stalin personally. Never mind that he sent my father and grandfather to their death and my mother to the living hell of the labor camps. The authors of the poems they make us learn are senile—like Dzhambul—or venal hacks—like Mikhalkov. And they sing the praises of the party with no feeling of shame! We have so many lies about this 'happy country of prosperous socialism' pounded into our heads that we eventually begin to believe."

Not Tamara. She was always spirited, but the life of the spirit was cultivated beyond the walls of the schoolhouse, if at all.

In ancient Rome and Greece, where there were no schools, children were educated through literature. As in many families of the Soviet intelligentsia, my parents attempted to fill the gaps in their child's education with foreign languages and the Russian classics. The daily dictation provided by my stepfather—passages from *War and Peace*—developed my literary taste and a feeling for the beauty and wealth of my native language. It also instilled in me the habit of constant self-improvement.

Looking over my literature textbooks, Pavel would point out where he thought the official interpretation was off base. He added his own comments as well. I remember his idiosyncratic approach to Dostoyevsky, whom he considered a man's writer, as distinct from Ivan Bunin, a "woman's writer."

"Just as a woman can't perform hard labor, she can't read and understand a writer like Dostoyevsky," he said—which didn't stop me from reading Dostoyevsky with interest.

It was also during my school years that I learned the story of Pavel's experiences during World War II. . . .

Before the war, he had lived with his parents, brothers, and sisters in Kuzmin, a large village, once quite prosperous, in western Ukraine. When the war began, he was seventeen years old, too young to be drafted into the Soviet Army. And then in the fall of 1941, the Germans came.

Their evil deeds began with the Jews: all who were found—old people, children, and women—were herded into the synagogue and burned alive. Some local Ukrainians concealed Jewish children in their homes. Pavel's mother let two boys live in her attic until someone reported them and they fled to another village. (After the war, they came back to thank her.) By the end of the war, only two other Jews from the village were alive; they had served in the Soviet Army.

After killing the Jews, the Germans started rounding up the remaining young people to send them to Germany as slave labor. Pavel and several others were assigned to Pezingen, a village near Freiburg, to work

The author's stepfather, Pavel Vychalkovsky, 1946. "One morning American tanks drove into the camp. . . . My stepfather could have emigrated to the United States but chose not to. . . ."

on a large farm. The farmer and his family treated the workers as fairly as they could: everyone labored as equals; all ate at the same table. It so happened that Aneli, the young wife of the farmer's oldest son, became romantically involved with one of the prisoners. When neighbors informed on them, the prisoner, a Yugoslav, was hanged from a tree in the woods; Aneli was sent to a concentration camp.

When he learned what had happened, her husband, an army officer, wrote to his father, asking him to dismiss all the workers and to use only German labor in the future. The farmer's wife and her young children, who had grown attached to Pavel, wept as he was sent away.

The true meaning of bondage in a foreign land became clear to my stepfather after he was sent to work in the coal mines of Alsace-Lorraine. He narrowly escaped death more than once, and he is convinced that his fair hair and good knowledge of German helped him survive. Calm, taciturn, and self-possessed, he aroused sympathy among his captors. Individual Germans periodically handed him extra food and even invited him to their homes. He would often find a sandwich or a small bottle of milk in his jacket pocket.

One morning American tanks drove into the camp and the prisoners were treated to rum, chocolate, sausages, and biscuits. My stepfather could have emigrated to the United States but chose not to; after all, his mother and sisters were waiting for him at home.

After the war, about five million Soviet citizens were returned to their homeland, some voluntarily and some against their will. The forced repatriation of Soviet citizens by Great Britain and the United States will always remain a shameful fact of human history. Among those repatriated were captured soldiers, peasants, and workers (mainly young people) used as slave labor and other Soviet citizens who had fled west with the retreating Germans. The overwhelming majority of the returnees were accused of treason. It was only in the 1980s that I heard some of the details from Pavel himself, who in earlier years was reluctant to speak on the subject.

He told me then how happy he and his fellow prisoners had been as they headed home. The Americans had given each of them a suit, a shirt, a tie, shoes, a food ration, a shaving kit, even toilet paper. As they came off the trains with suitcases containing the American clothing and shoes along with other gifts, they were met by a Soviet patrol.

"The first thing that struck me," Pavel said, "was that not a single man among them smiled at us. They began pulling the suitcases out of our hands and pulling off our overcoats, ties, and hats. Like a fool, I had ignored the American officers' graphic description of what was in store for us. . . . Some ran back to the trains in desperation. They were caught and summarily executed."

There were mass executions of returning Soviet officers. After living through the horrors of Nazi prisons and concentration camps, after exhausting their bodies in the mines and factories of a strange land, they finally found eternal rest on Russian soil in nameless mass graves. After walking down the gangplank of a ship or jumping down from a train, many were immediately led off, undressed, and shot. They never even saw the sky above their native ground.

My stepfather was among the lucky ones. The officer who interrogated him in quarantine, no monster, was reluctant to send returnees to the camps. Besides, I don't know how he did it, but during his captivity my stepfather had managed to keep intact an identifying note from the village soviet of his native Kuzmin. Holding on to a passport or such a note was considered a feat of bravery, for it showed one's determination to return home. Pavel was sent east, not to Siberia but to Serov, a remote town in the Urals. He did not see his family again for four years, when he was finally granted the right to move about within the country. After studying by correspondence at the Sverdlovsk Mining and Metallurgy Institute and receiving a diploma, he was assigned to a job in Magnitogorsk in 1948.

Pavel had many other stories to tell about the quarantine camp where he had been held. As first secretary of the Dnepropetrovsk Oblast party committee, my uncle Leonid was in charge of the work of the NKGB and the MVD (the Ministry of Internal Affairs), the official bodies that dealt with repatriated prisoners. As an adult, I heard stories from him about the *ostarbaitery* (from the German word *Ostarbeiter*—workers from the East).* Those who had worked during the war for the Germans, whether voluntarily or not—janitors, translators, cooks, miners, and prostitutes alike—were sought out and ruthlessly punished.

In 1919, in the words of Nadezhda Krupskaya (Lenin's wife), "a fine organization, bright and shiny, was created—the Young Pioneers." By 1931, there were over four million members. Children were no longer to be just children: now they had to be organized and united by "grand ideas." Joining the Young Pioneers, they promised in grave tones to carry on their ancestors' revolutionary traditions. And many of the

---

*The *Ostarbeiter* (a Nazi term) were the Russians (and others) captured by the Germans and used for slave labor in the Reich. They were, in German eyes, from the East (not east Germany but Eastern Europe). The word was Russified and used to describe these people; "*ostarbaitery*" is the transliteration of the Russified version of *Ostarbeiter*.

The author, 1955. "My father loves this picture. He says that I look like my uncle here. I never saw Leonid Brezhnev in a hair ribbon."

eight-year-old boys who swore loyalty to the party of Lenin and Stalin, lisping and mispronouncing their *r*'s, were true to their oaths, going on to become politicians, bureaucrats, and military commanders. But the Pioneer organization, like the Komsomol, was also a breeding ground for future dissidents.

Before joining the Young Pioneers, children would first learn the solemn oath in study groups; then they would pore over the biographies of Lenin and Stalin and conduct political-information seminars.

I remember my own admission to the ranks. The senior Pioneer leader gave the order to bring in the detachment's banner. After the public oath, bandannas that had been purchased by our parents were tied around our necks, and we gave the Pioneer salute, which we had perfected at home in front of a mirror. The stern gaze of the leader and the beating of the drums had a hypnotic effect. My hand trembled, and I was breathless from excitement. The boy standing next to me was a leaf, shaking. Natasha, a slender, fragile-looking girl who was glowing like a crystal ball, fainted and had to be admitted separately.

We listened to a speech by Lazar Kaganovich, who declared: "The red bandanna on your chest is drenched with the blood of hundreds and thousands of fighting men. Wear it with honor."

In later years, I would hear my uncle Leonid refer to Kaganovich as "the Jewish vampire": he was one of Stalin's principal henchmen, responsible for the death of thousands of innocent people in Ukraine and elsewhere.

Like all children, I was sent to Pioneer camp for the summer. After learning at one of our morning assemblies that the next seven days would be a dress rehearsal for combat, we were assigned ranks and told to address one another as comrade sergeant major, comrade military commissar, and so forth. When I was appointed political instructor, my mother joked that skill for propaganda ran in our family (referring, of course, to my uncle Leonid's having held a similar title throughout World War II). As a propagandist, though, I was a flop. The political instructor was expected to conduct information sessions, including group study of the Soviet Constitution, and to do so in a stuffy tent. What a thing to assign to children during their summer vacation—and to assign to me, who had never learned the Constitution. As we plodded through the text, we longed to be somewhere else, anywhere else. I still remember the sight of a boy wiping his runny nose with the back of his hand before reciting a list of our "civil liberties."

The recitation and memorization of political verbiage were required and seen as a normal part of life. Some of us seriously studied the party charters, the rules and regulations, the laws and bylaws; unable to commit to memory a single line, I felt a grudging admiration for those who managed it. I wondered whether it was similarly heroic perseverance that had earned our late and living leaders their shining monuments.

Then there were maneuvers. For the life of me, I couldn't see how we could be sent to capture fellow Pioneers and objected that I couldn't picture my friends as enemies. One evening at the mandatory lineup by the campfire, I was accused of being uncooperative and lacking imagination. I was even labeled a deserter.

At camp, we learned a great deal more than was planned. After seeing so many adult affairs acted out before our eyes, many of us became cynical about love. We knew who was sleeping with whom, who was the latest girlfriend of our director, how often Styopa, the fireman, visited Nadya, the cook. . . . And many boys learned less about our civil liberties than about smoking cigarettes and drinking vodka.

Despite what we witnessed or knew, the official attitude suggested that sexuality did not exist, that attractiveness was somehow bad. In school, no matter how hot the weather, the girls dressed like little nuns—in thick stockings, low-heeled shoes, and long cotton smocks. The most innocent adornments were banned. Boys whose fathers had given them watches had to keep them hidden in jacket pockets. Among my schoolmates were Jewish and Tatar girls who had been wearing jewelry since early childhood. Every day one of them, Tsylya Gluzberg, had to take off the gold earrings she had worn since she was five—or she wouldn't have been allowed to enter the classroom. This absurdity continued through high school. Using lipstick or rouge was considered the sign of a tramp and could bring expulsion from the Komsomol and school.

In the late 1950s, while I was still in school, the prestige of the worker began to decline. After finishing school, the young people were no longer going eagerly to the factories or to the great building projects as they had under Stalin; they tried instead to obtain a higher education. The tradition of worker dynasties (father, sons, and grandsons working at the same plant) was seriously eroded.

Our teachers used to threaten D students with trade school—no empty threat: in the '50s, transferring failing students from ordinary schools to trade schools became a common practice. After all, each trade school had to recruit the number of students called for by the plan in addition to fulfilling its production quotas. For their labor, teenage boys worked for wages ridiculously low, diminished even further by deductions for uniforms and lodging.

We could always recognize the trade-school students in their black uniforms. They were known for drinking, smoking, and fighting. Whenever they went on a rampage in Zelenstroi, it was as though a cyclone had passed through that lovely park. Seeing a flock of boys in black, the average citizen would rush to the other side of the street in fear. Pedestrians walking alone were beaten on street corners, and murders were not uncommon. On the way home after working a night shift, one of our neighbors was beat to death by a group of drunken trade-school students.

In 1953, when I was nearly ten, a nationwide amnesty had allowed the release of thousands of criminals, many of whom came to our city, making it even more dangerous. After dark, only roaming cats and foolhardy people dared venture onto the streets. Released criminals especially liked the young, expanding cities, where labor was in great demand and blending in was easy.

After Khrushchev, "the great reformer," came to power, he decided to revamp the educational system in the hope of sparking the young people's interest in industry. So in December 1958, ten-year compulsory education was replaced; now after eight years of school, students had to go to work, though the opportunity for concurrent work and study was provided: institutes gave preference to young people with work experience and a recommendation from both the party and their workplace.

At my school, the reforms meant that everyone had to take vocational classes, which were designed to churn out metalworkers, lathe operators, repairmen, cooks, seamstresses, and bookbinders. What was the use of teaching metal shop to those who were preparing for careers in the humanities? Anyway, the classes and practical training, especially the latter, were conducted so ineptly that most students soon lost all interest in learning a trade.

Our metal shop was a damp, unheated basement where we would grip a chunk of rusty iron in a vise and mindlessly polish it into shape with an equally rusty file for the assigned two hours, all under the guidance and supervision of a metalworker who hovered behind us and watched each of us work. If he was feeling good, he would go on to the next student without making any comment. But often his mood was nasty, especially if he hadn't had a chance to cure his hangover that morning. Angry, red-faced, stammering, and swearing, he would launch into his usual harangue: "Where do you think your arms are attached? You moron! That's where your legs are. . . . Why the hell are you holding the file like that? Learn to hold it right; it's not a woman's tit, you know." His words didn't bother me as much as the unbearable odor on his breath, what was to become an all-too-familiar mixture of vodka, onions, and garlic.

There was one ten-year school remaining in our neighborhood, but the only foreign language taught was English, and I was studying French. My mother and stepfather argued with officials to have me admitted, without success. They finally called my uncle Leonid and asked him to intervene.

My mother doubted that he would help. What if he began lecturing her on the principles of the party's educational program? But at that time, on matters concerning his own family, he put his Communist principles aside. After negotiations at several levels, a compromise was reached, under which I was enrolled in the school on a trial basis for one quarter. It was too late for me to start learning English since I had been studying French from about age three. So it was decided that I would take private French lessons, from Berta Yakovlevna. Together with other teachers, she gave me and my girlfriend Olya a French exam every quarter and assigned us our grades.

My childhood memories of my uncle are few. While we lived in Magnitogorsk, he was a distant figure, a general who sent our family gifts via military plane: enormous packages of onions, apples as big as infants' heads, and liqueurs for my stepfather. In 1949, my mother took me to meet Pavel's relatives in Ukraine, and we dropped by to see Leonid briefly in Dnepropetrovsk. My mother had already sent him some pictures, but he wanted very much to have a look at me in person.

I remember that day, but only hazily. I was terribly sleepy after the long ride. Uncle Leonid struck me as handsome and affectionate, and of course he seemed gigantic to a five-year-old girl. I spent a large part of the day asleep on his shoulder. As he carried me around, I detected a characteristic aroma, a potent combination of cigarettes and cologne. I heard him teasing my mother, making compliments that left her somewhat embarrassed. I vaguely recall him asking me to look toward the shore when we took a boat ride on the Dnieper; holding tight to the rail with one hand and rubbing the sleep from my eyes with the other, I stared at the gentle green banks floating by in the mist.

In May 1954, I met Uncle Leonid again, this time in northern Kazakhstan, near Kustanai. I was ten. I remember being surrounded by orchards in bloom: we were standing under apple trees, and the shoulders of Leonid's suit were covered with white petals, as was his thick hair. He had begun putting on weight but was still well proportioned and handsome indeed. He talked to my mother for a long time, but I was just as sleepy as I had been five years earlier, so I remember only bits and pieces.

"Lenochka," he said, "when I think of my father and grandfather—that whole generation . . . what an amazing breed of men was cut down." While disparaging the drunkenness and the sloppy work of his Russian contemporaries, Leonid praised the Germans for being hardworking, neat, and disciplined. For a while, he talked to my mother about love, and for the first time I heard the name of his mistress, Tamara. He also spoke unfavorably, the hurt showing in his voice, of his wife, Viktoriya. He seemed on the verge of tears several times.

On one of these visits, Leonid explained to me that he was my father's brother; nonetheless, the two Brezhnevs, very similar in appearance, remained confused in my mind for years. I guess my constant questioning got on my mother's nerves, because once she yelled at me angrily, "Why must you be so scatterbrained? Yasha is your father and Lyonya is your uncle." I repeated this formula over and over to myself: Yasha equals father, Lyonya equals uncle. But I didn't really learn to tell them apart until I was in my teens, when I began seeing my father fairly often.

I displayed a literary bent in my high school years, and my classmates admired my compositions enough to read them out loud and share them with friends. But I received a D for the content (not the grammar!) of a composition I wrote about Dostoyevsky's novella *Poor Folk*. Under the influence of my stepfather, I had attempted to show that this work is a defense of human dignity, a concept not related to one's standard of living or the governmental system under which one lives. I used Dante's words—"I will sing of that place where the human spirit is cleansed and becomes worthy of rising to the heavens"—as an epigraph. Maybe I carried the idea too far, but I was on the right track, yet I wasn't even given the chance to argue my case.

I also wrote terrible poetry, though some of the epigrams devoted to my teachers came off pretty well. Unfortunately they always learned about these poetic masterpieces from some informer, which tended to sour our relations.

Gradually my conflicts with the authorities escalated. During my last year in high school, we were asked to write a composition on the poet Mayakovski. As usual, I wrote exactly what I believed, which earned me another D for content, along with an A for grammar. But the punishment didn't stop with a low grade. This time my subversive act set off a wave of appropriate measures. I had to appear and explain myself at teachers' councils, Komsomol meetings, and the neighborhood offices of the Education Department.

My parents were summoned and warned that if I didn't recant, I risked being expelled from the Komsomol and even from school. My mother, remembering everything that had happened to her family in the '30, was so terrified that she became physically ill. My stepfather had an argument with the principal, an old Communist who insisted that I be expelled from school and sent to a factory for "re-education."

I felt totally isolated. There was no one to turn to at school: I got along well with my *klassny rukovoditel,** but he happened to be in a veterans' hospital for the treatment of old war wounds.

The episode culminated in a general assembly at which my misdeed was discussed by the entire school. This time I was given the floor. From my triumphant and solemn bearing, someone walking into the auditorium might have assumed I was there to announce an amateur play or recite a poem about our beloved party. My heart was standing

*Each grade in high school has its *klassny rukovoditel,* a teacher who looks after discipline, attendance, relations between pupils and the administration, and so forth.

still, and everything around me seemed unreal. I could see a yawning gulf separating me from those who only the day before had been smiling. What unfairness, what treachery! I lost all sensation of my body.

"You may think that you are judging me," I said, breaking the silence. "But I'm the one judging. I want you all to remember this day as one of the most shameful of your lives. . . ."

The verdict of this kangaroo court was a reprimand. But in the halls, children of all ages stopped to shake my hand surreptitiously and encourage me to stand strong.

My mother cast about desperately for anything to get me out of my latest predicament; my morale was high, but expulsion was looming unmistakably. My father was in China on business, so my mother turned again to my uncle Leonid.

By this time Leonid Ilyich was fairly well known in the political world. Having been elected chairman of the Presidium of the Supreme Soviet, he was essentially the number-two man in the Soviet Union. Thanks to his rugged good looks and his charm, he was rapidly gaining visibility, even in the West, where he was labeled—among other things—the most elegantly dressed Soviet leader. What most impressed me about Leonid was his general's uniform and the fact that he had served during the war from beginning to end.

After getting a call from my uncle, the secretary of the Magnitogorsk party committee came to our school to look into my case. That evening Leonid called my mother and stepfather with the good news: I would be allowed to take my high school graduation exam. When he added that it wouldn't hurt to start giving me a proper upbringing, my mother replied that her daughter was perfectly well brought up.

"I don't mean that she doesn't know how to hold her knife and fork correctly," Leonid commented. "She doesn't know what can be said and what can't."

In any case, that was the end of that. Or was it? Another snare was awaiting, in the form of one of the questions on my oral exam.

"Which world-famous author," we were asked, "is nearest to your heart?" The authors I was reading enthusiastically at the time were Erich Maria Remarque, Knut Hamsun, and Ernest Hemingway. I was especially familiar with Remarque's work; I adored his heroes and considered *Three Comrades* a masterpiece of world literature.

"Aha, now it's clear," said one of the members of the commission. "You rate foreign writers higher than Mayakovski?"

"I didn't say that," I protested.

"It's implied by your answer."

It was futile to try to explain to these educated fools that comparing Mayakovski and Remarque was like comparing apples and oranges. They said I held "cosmopolitan views" and gave me a C.

I felt so hurt at this injustice that for the first time in school, I cried.

The advice that my parents got was to appeal the decision. We were faced with a dilemma. On the one hand, what are grades? Isn't knowledge the important thing? Besides, who wants more humiliation? On the other hand, the average grade from the graduation exam was of more than considerable importance for admission to an institute of higher education.

The solution came soon enough. By this time, my father had heard from his brother about what I had gone through a few months earlier, after writing my Mayakovski essay. This time it was Yakov who contacted the Chelyabinsk Oblast party committee,* which promptly ordered that all harassment cease.

I took my graduation exam over and received an A.

Most of my teachers are no longer alive, but I thank God for their lives. Much as I was allergic to school, I recall most of them with fondness and gratitude. Bound as they were by the rigid curriculum and their own intellectual limits, they did their best to share what they knew with us.

I will especially never forget Roza Shapiro, who came to the Soviet education system from the pre-revolutionary *gimnaziya*. Roza saw her charges as unique individuals. She turned average pupils into high achievers and made experts of those doing well already. She was one of the few people I met during my childhood who was able to bring out

---

*Magnitogorsk is in the Chelyabinsk Oblast.

The author (right) with Olya, her friend and
fellow French student, July 1959.

the independent thinker in me. I had never gone in for mathematics, but
in her class I earned As. She urged me to study mathematics in the university. "You're a born logician," she said.

The sturdy brick building that we lived in by this time—my stepfather had received a comfortable apartment after being promoted to
engineer—shared a common courtyard with the school I attended. In
the evenings, students of the fifth, sixth, and seventh grades would
gather to race their bicycles or to play ball, hide-and-seek, and tag. The
two-story schoolhouse was like a second home for us. If we got thirsty
playing in the yard, we would go to the first floor of the school for
water since it was closer than going home. We also used the classrooms
for hide-and-seek, and in the winter we would run inside to warm up.

Roza Shapiro would be faithfully sitting in the teachers' room, waiting for any pupil who might want to consult with her. I can't remember a single time when anyone came to ask her a question, but she remained there into the evening, like a soldier at his post or a doctor on call.

When I was through playing, I'd park my bicycle by the window of the teachers' room and climb in. Roza would greet me with a friendly laugh and make me go wash my hands. There would always be an apple, a meat pie, or a cutlet in her bag for me. I would sit curled up on the sofa, and we would talk. She was old, nearly eighty, and her hands trembled. At times, tears welled in her eyes, and her head rocked back and forth slightly. "It's been like this ever since my son's arrest," she once explained.

When we finished talking, we would leave together. She lived a few houses away from us, and I would put her briefcase on the luggage rack of my bike and ride alongside her. Sometimes she invited me to her home. She lived with her younger son, who nicknamed me Forget-Me-Not for my dark-blue eyes and used to show me a collection of old prints he was proud of.

When we later moved from Magnitogorsk to Dnepropetrovsk, I wrote Roza a farewell letter, expressing as well as I could my gratitude for our talks and for her friendship and promising never to forget her. I have kept my promise and often recall this woman, who was very kind though not often given to outward displays of affection.

Another teacher always in my thoughts is Berta Yakovlevna, ample of body and kind of heart; though I remember her patronymic, for the life of me I can't remember her last name. My fellow French student Olya and I loved her very much, as a true friend in whom we could confide our adolescent secrets.

Berta loved to talk. Her set piece was the tale of her first romance, which, despite its ending, she told as though it were the one shining spot in her life. The story began when Berta was sixteen and one of her cousins left her stranded after a night in bed—the stuff of a thousand cheap songs. . . . When the young man's family learned of his behavior, they disowned him, which didn't keep him from going on to obtain a doctorate degree, filling Berta's all-forgiving heart with pride.

This first failed love did not prevent her from marrying another cousin, who wed her on the advice of his numerous relatives. For his virtue, he was fully rewarded—with two charming children and Berta's easygoing personality, which set her apart from most Soviet wives. And then there was Berta's delicious gefilte fish. She served it to me and Olya so often that we sometimes thought this traditional delicacy was all she knew how to cook.

I remember, too, her naïve instructions on the art of seduction. The key to her system was selecting the right gloves to go with one's outfit. If Olya and I had followed her advice, we would have certainly ended up unloved. I can imagine how our numerous young beaux would have flown to the four winds if we had worn the hats and lace mittens that dear old Berta swore by.

Tamara and I adored our godfather, Nika, Pasha's son, named after our grandfather Nikolay. He came back to his parents' house after serving as a military pilot from the beginning to the end of World War II. He helped teach us to read and write, he joined in our games as an equal, and in the winter he sharpened our skates and took us skiing. No one spent as much time playing with us as Nika.

When he died, in 1957, I was in adolescence—and the news hit me hard. He was only thirty-three. This was the first time I faced the loss of someone so close to me. For several years, I couldn't bring myself to enter his room, which his parents left untouched. The book on his desk even remained open to the page he had been reading before his death. In 1961, after graduating from high school, I went to bid my godfather a final farewell.

The pain of loss had mellowed with the passage of years. I sat down at Nika's desk and picked up the book lying open to the short story "A Cold Autumn" by Ivan Bunin. The pages were yellowed and a bit faded. Spellbound, I read the story, a gem of less than five pages. In later years, I would return again and again to this tale of a Russian woman forced to leave her country.

Part Two

THE CITY OF WHITE STONE

Moscow does not believe in tears.

RUSSIAN FOLK WISDOM

Chapter Eight

AN INVITATION
TO THE BALL

After high school graduation and almost two years' preparatory work in a pharmacy, I began medical school, a dream of mine since I was in sixth grade. But when my study of anatomy began, I had the same reaction to cadavers that many would-be doctors do. Most conquer their feelings. Although I, too, attempted a second visit to the morgue, the violent fits of nausea returned. When I suggested that I could not succeed, my parents objected, saying that I would get over it—my mother was a doctor herself by now—but by the fall of 1963 I had firmly bid good-bye to this childhood dream.

We now lived in Dnepropetrovsk. I lacked friends, but then I hadn't rushed to acquire any, feeling little affinity with the teenage boys I saw trying out their fists on one another in the doorways or the pretty girls I heard chattering in a mishmash of Russian and Ukrainian about such things as canning techniques.

I withdrew into a world of books. My little room was a sanctuary stocked with theosophical literature, works of history and philosophy, Russian classics, and contemporary novels—a personal schoolroom where I could revel in my Remarque, Hemingway, Hamsun, Richard

Aldington, Osip Mandelstam, and the White Guard poems of Marina Tsvetayeva. I read everything about the Russian Cossacks that I could lay my hands on and began to reconstruct our family tree on my mother's side.

It was probably no coincidence that in the fall of 1963, my uncle Leonid began moving his relatives to the Soviet capital: in one year, he would ascend to the post of Soviet party chief, in what was later known as the palace revolt of 1964. First to go were his mother and his mother-in-law, then his sister and his brother-in-law. Next to make the move was my father, just back from a stay in Poland that had been extended a year beyond the planned two years after a fire destroyed several shops at the metallurgy complex he was helping to build in Nowa Huta.

Late one night as I was falling asleep, he unexpectedly dropped by our apartment to say good-bye to my mother, my stepfather, and me. We sat up with him until six in the morning. After a few hours of sleep, he went back to his home in Dneprodzerzhinsk; a week later he went on to Moscow, for good.

Given a choice between several apartments, he moved near the Canadian Embassy, on Starokonyushenny Lane in the Arbat neighborhood. What Muscovite doesn't dream of living in the Arbat, where even the sidewalks seem to whisper about the centuries of history they have seen?

Moscow saw a transformation and a mass relocation in the early '60s. Old buildings in the center, some of undeniable architectural value despite being run-down and crowded, were emptied. The tenants were resettled in outlying neighborhoods, in five-story apartment buildings that were soon nicknamed *khrushchevki,* after the party chief Nikita Khrushchev. The downtown sites, covered with remodeled old buildings or brand-new ones, became home to people with connections in high places.

Near the end of 1963, both my half sisters moved to Moscow from Dnepropetrovsk, where they had been studying. Yelena, fresh out of medical school, was given a downtown apartment with her husband and her small daughter, Natasha. Mila, still unmarried, moved in with her parents.

I began corresponding regularly with my father. Like Uncle Leonid and my grandmother Natalya Denisovna, he had a fixation on higher education. He used to say, "Without that scrap of paper, you're a little bug; with it, you're at least considered human." In his letters, he continually praised the translating profession and urged me to attend the Institute of Foreign Languages in Moscow. He knew I had been exposed to French all my life and that I had taken private lessons during my high school years; he even knew my tutor.

Once he wrote, "I was at a meeting with some foreigners when Aleksey Kosygin* came by with his daughter Lyusya to interpret for him. In another letter he wrote, "Yesterday some French specialists came to the Science and Technology Committee, and we discussed technical problems through an interpreter. I thought of you, my precious, and wished it had been you there interpreting for us."

It was not until March of 1964, however, that my mother and stepfather let me go to Moscow for a short stay, a trial run to help me decide what institute to attend in the fall. I had visited Moscow a few times before that, but Yelena and Pavel were apprehensive now. A telegram from my father helped sway them. Impressed by the last name, the mailman had dragged himself out of bed at 2:00 A.M. to deliver it.

It read RECEIVED YOUR LETTER, LOOK FORWARD TO YOUR ARRIVAL MOSCOW. KISSES, BREZHNEV.

My father greeted me with warm embraces, the trademark Brezhnev smile, and a parcel: a pair of beautiful sandals and a Japanese blouse that I fell in love with and would wear until it had lost its shape. In the backseat of the black state-owned Volga, he kept hugging me and kissing the top of my head as though he could hardly believe I had really come. It occurred to me that he must be lonely in Moscow.

I refused to stay in his apartment, knowing how his wife felt about

---

*At the time, Kosygin was first assistant chairman of the Council of Ministers.

his "other" daughter. After he and I argued heatedly about where I was to go, my father took me to the Taganka district to stay with Lev, an old friend of my stepfather's.

Uncle Lyova, as I had known Lev since childhood, was considerate and easygoing—no match for his plump wife, with her provincial manners and fits of hysteria. Her speech was full of genteel affectation—when she wasn't cursing like a fishwife. Each had carved out a stable niche in Moscow society: he had sports, fishing, and his university students; she had her telephone conversations, friends, gossip, and knitting.

I quickly befriended their oldest daughter, Zhenya, who was two years younger than I. She was sweet and full of laughter, with luxuriant, fine golden curls that delighted me as much as they exasperated her.

Young as we were, we loved to sleep in, but Uncle Lyova would always wake us up. "Oh, to sleep, sleep, and sleep/As the years go rushing by," he would tease us, putting *sleep* where Mayakovski had written *live*.

"Each of us has two lives," wrote Vincent Sheen; "that which is, and that which might have been." With my arrival in Moscow began the life that might have been.

I can remember Uncle Lyova telling me, "My beautiful girl, your dad has been calling all morning long, asking you and Zhenya to be home this afternoon after five so he can take you out. It's all play and no work for you two!"

In the evening, my father would indeed come by, in the now familiar black chauffeur-driven car, to take us to a restaurant or the dacha of some nationally known celebrity. I was quite impressed, at the beginning anyway.

Before 1964, I had hardly ever been inside a restaurant, so I must have been quite a sight in Moscow. My father would laugh uproariously at the gyrations of this provincial young lady, this newcomer to the ball, who fretted about which fork to use, thanked the waiter at every turn, and tried to follow her Aunt Pasha's instructions about sitting up straight while seeming relaxed. Once I casually took a cigarette out of a pack that was lying on the table and asked for a light. My father, not amused by this stab at sophistication, quietly took the cigarette, crushed it, and tossed it into an ashtray.

"Don't you ever let me see you do that again," he said. Though hardly a prude, he had some old-fashioned beliefs. In his mind, a woman who smoked was practically a loose woman.

As we sat in one of the restaurants of the Moskva Hotel, other diners would come to our table and exchange a few words or even join us for the evening. My father was on a first-name basis with most of them. Here began my acquaintance with Moscow's art world—actors, movie directors, painters, sculptors, and writers. Academicians, vice ministers, Central Committee department heads, and professors also dropped by.

One seldom saw the topmost layer of the party elite at the Moskva Hotel, which was far too public for them. Later on I would meet them at their dachas, at vacation resorts, in the loges of the Bolshoi Theater, at the Palace of Congresses, and at the embassy parties to which my father dragged me, trying, as he said, to expose me "to the cultural life of the capital." So I was amazed when we ran into the party lady herself, Soviet Minister of Culture Yekaterina Furtseva, in a very public place—the Pushkin Museum of Fine Arts, on Kropotkin Street. She chatted with my father, smiling demurely while her bodyguards stood two steps to the side. Were they afraid someone was going to toss a grenade at her elegant legs? I wondered. My father's own bodyguards watched us from the next room.

Furtseva was rather short and pleasingly plump, with a charming face, a becoming hairdo, and a smooth complexion that was a credit to her beautician. As my father told me on the way home, "She's well built and knows how to dress, that Katya."

Time disappeared as in a fairy tale. Soon the end of April arrived, and it was time for me to return to Ukraine. I went, and a few days later, a letter from my father arrived. "How our days together flew by," he wrote.

Now only emptiness remains. . . . On the first day after you left, I could not escape the feeling of having lost that which is most precious. I want

The author's father (far right) in Dneprodzerzhinsk. "My father was lonely indeed in Moscow. . . . He missed Dneprodzerzhinsk, where his many friends had loved him not as Brezhnev's brother but as Yasha, . . . where, as he put it, 'Every mutt knew me.'"

you to know that you are my only comfort and happiness. To an outside observer, this happiness might seem silly or even crazy, but it's the one thing I cherish above all. It's so rare when father and daughter are best friends as well.

How true. Over the years, circumstances would tear us apart only to bring us back together again and then separate us once more. But even when we stopped communicating, we knew that we would eventually turn to each other for the help, support, and total understanding that was certain to be there. As it turned out, there were times when my father needed me more than I needed him, despite all his power. "You are my guardian angel," he would say, only half in jest.

As the years passed, he was surrounded by people, but he could not trust any of them with his sorrows, his hurts and pains. I was the only one with whom he could feel perfectly at ease, unencumbered by the hateful role imposed on him by fate, that of being The Brother.

My father was indeed lonely in Moscow, as I had suspected. He missed Dneprodzerzhinsk, where his many friends had loved him not as Brezhnev's brother but as Yasha the engineer, the life of the party, a team player not above stopping at the refreshment stand outside the mill to have a beer with the guys, where, as he put it, "every mutt knew me." He was among his own kind there, and his brother's success didn't have much effect on his way of life. His move to Moscow had thrust him into a world for which he was utterly unprepared.

In late spring, my mother and stepfather gave me permission to leave, and I flew back to Moscow. My father had made arrangements for an old friend of Leonid's, an Aeroflot pilot named Miron Denisov, to get me to the capital in one piece. The airplane that I flew on was reserved for high-level officials, local party dignitaries, their relatives, and honored guests. Of course, my fare was complimentary.

On the plane, I couldn't help noticing my fellow passengers' curious stares. My irresistible good looks? I wondered naïvely. I didn't suspect then that strangers were interested in me only as Brezhnev's niece; it would take many painful experiences before I realized the simple truth.

This time my father put me up in the Moskva Hotel, in an eighth-floor deluxe suite reserved for members of the Central Committee and their relatives. At the time, this was the best hotel in Moscow. Showing a dedication that was totally atypical for the Soviet Union and left me overwhelmed, a maid rushed in, took charge of my suitcase, and hung up all my clothes. She nearly drove me crazy with her inexplicably constant attention. Later I learned that all the employees at Moscow hotels catering to foreigners and provincial party bosses had two jobs: one was working for the KGB.

This maid must have known the opportunity she had in Brezhnev's niece. As I recall the featureless faces of all the uniformed and plain-clothes KGB agents who passed through my life, I sometimes wonder how many gold stars, food allotments, and commendations I earned them. . . .

When my father visited me in the company of friends, the "comrade" who followed him everywhere—but remained in the lobby, discreetly out of sight, when he came alone—installed himself near the floor administrator, reading a newspaper and watching my door. Seeing a face emerge to greet the next batch of guests, he asked, "Listen, will you guys be in there long?"

"Not too long," one of the "guys" answered blithely, but our poor bodyguard had to read his paper late into the night more than once. Because of his impatience, he was soon replaced by two younger colleagues.

When a popular comedy duo, Tarapunka and Shtepsel, came to the capital that season, they also took rooms on the eighth floor of the Moskva. One of them had brought his son along. Shortly thereafter, in the middle of the night, I woke to hear Tarapunka knocking urgently on my door, pleading with me to get in touch with my father immediately: the boy was sick from something he had eaten in a restaurant. The moment the comedian walked in, I noticed two figures looming behind him: the maid and some young man in plainclothes. Learning that we were merely summoning medical assistance, my house spies yawned indifferently and left. Half an hour later the boy was taken to the hospital, and in two days' time he was back, fully recovered and riding his bicycle through the hallways—to the consternation of the staff, who found themselves jumping out of the way at every other step.

The State Committee on Science and Technology, where my father worked, was near the hotel, and he often stopped by to see me at lunchtime. Our usual spot was a table in the corner of the second-floor restaurant.

Yakov Ilyich made a point of never eating anything made out of flour. His dislike went back to childhood, when his grandmother Stepanida used to give the little children the task of pounding (in a large wooden mortar) buckwheat and millet for *blinchiki* (Russian pancakes). Yasha, who because of his young age was most often saddled with this task, found the work so unpleasant that he boycotted the end product: he would sit in a corner pouting while the others ate. Leonid, downing his *blinchiki* and cream, would laugh at his brother: "Look at you, Yasha, you're like a mouse turning up its nose at a pile of grain." Noodles were my father's great exception; he loved them, as did I. The waiters in the hotel restaurant came to know us not as Brezhnev's relatives but as enthusiastic noodle fans.

It was in this restaurant, while cutting into a portion of chicken Kiev, that I realized we were being observed. I didn't think much about it at the time; it was hard for me to imagine that the neat, well-dressed young men sitting at a neighboring table, chewing their *kulebyaka* (meat, cabbage, or fish wrapped in pastry) and looking bored represented any kind of threat. I didn't feel afraid of them. Yet I did have an eerie feeling of discomfort, a vague premonition of things to come.

As spring gave way to the long days of summer, I had already flip-flopped a few times with regard to a career. I eventually settled on the Institute of Foreign Languages, as my father had wanted, but only after flirting with the idea of attending acting school. Like many giddy young girls, I thought my success in high school plays and a drama club had left me fully prepared for stardom.

One evening that spring my father and I had dinner at the Actors' Club with his friend Nikolay Cherkassov, a popular actor. Though Cherkassov saw the provincial ways through my mask of worldliness, he never talked down to me.

My father said to him, "Tell this silly girl what she can look forward to if she chooses an acting career."

To my surprise, Cherkassov began to tell me in detail what I would have to submit to before ever appearing on stage or screen.

"For example," he said smiling, "girls like you have to sleep with old men like me."

"But I'm sure that can't be the worst thing in the world," I said naïvely. He smiled and gave me a warm embrace, surprising me a second time.

The Actor's Club was the hub of Moscow's performing-arts world, a place for both business meetings and romantic rendezvous. I liked it for its unassuming, comfortable furniture and its spirited but tranquil atmosphere. The guests lingered over their well-prepared meals: mushrooms baked in sour cream, chicken Kiev, Polish-style sturgeon. The main activity was socializing. A group of customers who had known one another for years kept a constant flow of who's-who gossip moving: who had received what role, who was sleeping with whom, what couples had broken up, who was talented, who lacked talent but had a reliable benefactor. Yet I detected no mean edge. Gossip was simply a pleasant pastime, part of a sophisticated way of life that was new to me. Ever watching for stars, I observed the diners waltz from table to table like players in a never-ending game of musical chairs.

The younger generation was represented by Mikhail Kazakov, Oleg Tabakov, and Yevgeny Yevstigneev. But most often my father and I sat with older actors, such as Mikhail Zharov, Boris Andreev, and Erast Garin. Short and slight, Garin was a first-class comic actor known for his role as an idiot king. Offscreen he was known as an expert in the art of swearing.

Andreev had a curious way of scolding Garin for his language: "F—— you, Erashka, you f——ing idiot, can't you see there's a young lady present?"

Pressing the knuckles of both hands against his teeth in a masterful imitation of fright, Erast would say, "I plead guilty, I ask your forgiveness, and f—— you, too."

Though I longed to be a part of this world, I soon realized that trying to be admitted to the State Cinematography Institute without connections was not worth the effort. Many talented young people struggled for years to get in. It was another story for the children of actors, directors, and cameramen. The school was moviemakers' turf, just as the Institute of International Relations belonged to the political-power elite. If an actor's son decided to break the mold and study international relations, his father would have to seek help from political and diplomatic figures, while if their sons were interested in movies, they would have to find sponsors from that world. Similarly, the two most prestigious Moscow medical institutes were beholden to the Health Ministry.

The only person my father could turn to for help was the attractive, powerful Yekaterina Furtseva, the culture minister. Why? After all, Father knew many actors and directors, but now that he moved at a high level in the hierarchy (thanks to his brother), he wouldn't have thought of asking a favor of a mere actor or director, no matter how famous. Members of the Moscow elite observed strict etiquette in their relations, and his position required that he deal only with the person in control of all the capital's official cultural life.

One June evening in 1964 found the cream of Moscow society gathered at a general's dacha in Barvikha. My father invited me along. By this time the huge, lordly mansions, overmodestly referred to as dachas, no longer impressed me, despite their flower gardens, greenhouses, swimming pools, and saunas. When my father and I arrived, the party was in full swing. The guests—wandering around the grounds, lounging, standing around, singing, or dancing—paid no attention to us. My father didn't want to stay long and started a vigorous search for Katya, as he called Minister Furtseva. A barefoot young man in shorts pointed uncertainly in the direction of the garden.

We set off down a path lined with spruces and evenly spaced white gingerbread benches. On one of these benches, we discovered Katya. Her appearance was so grotesque that I didn't recognize her at first: her hair had fallen to one side, and her mouth was wide open; a swarm of midges, attracted by the smell of cognac, was circling above her face.

Grimacing, my father tried to rouse her: "Katya, get up, get up!"

My dreams of an acting career were crumbling before my eyes. Oh well, I thought, at least I can watch and learn about the cultural life of the capital.

Katya opened one eye, then the other, and sat up. My father, oddly, seemed accustomed to this sight, as though he had seen the minister in worse straits. He merely adjusted her dress, which had slipped up beyond the limits of propriety.

"Wha—at?" Katya bellowed, looking at us wildly. Coming to her senses, she smoothed her hair with a strangely delicate gesture and, glancing at my father, said, "So it's you, Brezhnev?"

It was obviously impossible to have a serious conversation, so I made motions to my father: *time to go!* But he persisted, remembering his promise to make me famous, and asked Katya about helping me to enter the film institute. An answer finally filtered through her drunken haze, to the effect that she would make sure I got a role "in that film, the one

Bondarchuk is shooting tomorrow." In her own mind, she was talking to Leonid. All my father's further questions brought the same response: "Yes, certainly, Lyonya."

At one point, she slid up to my father and me to kiss us. She was wearing a pretty polka-dot dress with a schoolgirlish lace collar. (The next time I saw her she was sober, sweet, and smelled of exquisite French perfume; no one mentioned our previous encounter.)

Leaving Madame Furtseva to resume her nap, we walked back to watch the antics of Soviet society's by now somewhat soured cream.

In the backyard, I stopped in surprise. Rodion Malinovsky, marshal of the Soviet Union and Soviet defense minister, was diving into the fountain; nearby stood potbellied comrades in multicolored swimming trunks. There was one gray-haired gentleman already in the water. Another, his swimsuit decorated with big white daisies and pulled down as far as decency allowed, stood next to the marshal. Suddenly a swimmer clambered out of the fountain, a goldfish in his hand. He didn't even notice that he had left his trunks behind; he was too busy expressing, with a choice selection of obscenities, his delight at his successful catch and his disgust that others had gotten away. Marshal Malinovsky was saying, "That f——ing goldfish slipped right out of my hands." He spread wide his short, plump fingers, as if to show everyone that he hadn't caught anything.

I silently prayed to God that no one in this drunken crowd would notice us. But the fishermen recognized my father and rushed in our direction, shrieking and beckoning us to join them in the fountain. Breaking away from their wet hands and slobbering kisses with a promise to join them later for an early-morning swim, we literally ran away and leaped into the waiting car.

I never saw Rodion Malinovsky again, but I did hear him years later. One of the times when I was visiting my father in the Fourth Department Clinic, on Granovskovo Street, the terminally ill general was also being treated there, for kidney disease, I think. In terrible pain, he screamed uncontrollably whenever his anesthetic wore off.

How soon our lives end, I thought, and how often in tragedy and sorrow, all the goldfish slipping through our fingers.

❖

After work, before going home or to see his brother, my father would often stop by the hotel and bring me something from the snack bar. Later in the evening he might call from his brother's dacha, in the outskirts of Moscow, to ask about everything I was doing.

"I'm calling you from the private phone in Leonid's study," he might say. "Everyone else is watching a movie, but I can't sit still. I'm worrying about you; your entrance exams are around the corner."

"Like communism," I'd laugh.

A window in my room looked out on Red Square. I had the desk placed so that I could admire the onion domes of the Kremlin, which I spent hours doing. It was early summer, the weather was hot, and I wasn't excited about having hundreds of irregular French verbs to memorize. I had only my books to keep me company: my father monitored my every move, as well as the number of pages I covered each day. He would check to make sure that there was food in my refrigerator so that I wouldn't have to go to the store. He even ordered the television set removed from my room and the telephone switched off during the day.

At times, noticing my complete indifference to the intricacies of French grammar and knowing that more than anything else I loved travel and new surroundings, my father regaled me with accounts of his foreign experiences.

His tales of China weren't inspirational, however. In the '50s, he had worked as an engineer for five years in Shanghai, where Soviet experts were helping build a metallurgical plant. He recalled the open blisters, caused by heat and humidity, that had tormented him day and night. His encounters with Chinese cuisine were not pleasant, and he described with distaste silkworm soups, snake-meat casseroles, dog cutlets, and monkey brains. The Soviet experts in Shanghai looked forward to the steamer from home, which put in to port several times a year. Leonid regularly sent his brother packages of herring, sausage, and Russian vodka.

Some evenings Uncle Leonid would call me. He always had the same question: "Are you studying?" Then he would say, "Study hard, Lubushka; you need to get into the institute." After wishing me good luck, he would say good-bye, fully satisfied that he had done his bit to ensure that his niece was developing in the right direction.

My father also made quite a fuss about whether I would be accepted at the institute. Actually this was a nonissue; as I eventually learned, the examinations merely concealed the real contest, which was among the parents. There was a system that virtually guaranteed admission for the children of highly placed officials. Well ahead of time, all the prestigious institutes received lists—the so-called director's lists—of the names of applicants for whom entrance exams would be a simple formality. My name was on such a list; nonetheless, my parents and uncle were thrilled when I was officially accepted by the Institute of Foreign Languages.

In honor of the occasion, Leonid gave me a beautiful book on French impressionism. My father was so happy that he reached into his pocket, pulled out his own ballpoint pen, and presented it to me.

I later gave this pen, which has a gold cap and bears an inscription from Mao Tse-tung, to my stepfather. In the '50s, Chinese officials gave the Soviet specialists expensive presents, knowing how insignificant their gifts were in comparison with the factories the Soviet Union was building for them. Exquisite silk artwork from the Beijing Museum adorns the walls of my father's apartment. One piece hangs in his little den; its left-hand corner bears the dedication "To Brezhnev from Mao Tse-tung."

When I was enrolled for classes but still living in the hotel, two innocent new girlfriends from the institute tried to visit. My father was sitting in my room, drinking coffee with the first secretary of the Dnepropetrovsk Oblast party committee. I was at my desk, pretending to study while gazing absentmindedly out the window.

Meanwhile downstairs my poor friends had been stopped at the elevator by two KGB men and steered to the administrator's room, where they were interrogated—for three hours. Who were they, where were they from, why had they come, what was their relationship with me and my father? My new friends were terrified, and this was the last time they even thought about visiting.

It was clear that I could not remain in the Moskva indefinitely. Because of his wife's attitude toward me, I had rejected the idea of staying with my father, and now he had to decide where I would spend my student years.

I insisted that we have a look at my institute's dormitory, located in Moscow's Sokolniki district. It was far from the worst of its kind, but my father was shocked by what we found: broken windows, radios blaring, drunks roaming the hallways, filthy children underfoot. Some of the students were living eight to a room.

As we rode back to the hotel, Yakov Ilyich kept shaking his head, repeating, "Leonid must be told about how our children are living."

This was a phrase I would hear from him often in years to come: "Leonid must be told." Would he tell his brother? I don't know. Their relationship at this time was close, but in later years they were to see less and less of each other. In this case, though, he did tell Leonid.

My plans were changed. The best dormitories in Moscow were those on the campus of Moscow State University, in the Lenin Hills. As I was preparing to move in, I heard one of the deans mentioning that my uncle himself had ordered that I be given the best room there and that a telephone be installed for me. Was this unfair? With the advantage of hindsight, I know it was: the dormitory was supposed to serve the university's own students. At the time, though, I thought little of it.

The fall of 1964 was capricious and drawn out, clinging to sweet summer like an old widow reliving her youth. The weather was dry, sunny, and windless, and the leaves lingered on the trees until November.

One October day a phone call to my dormitory informed me that I should go to the airport: a car from the Central Committee would be waiting downstairs. I knew this meant my father would be flying into Moscow and wanted me to meet him. Shortly a black Volga arrived and took me to the airport.

Father arrived exhausted and run down; but as always, he was neat and smartly dressed. He smelled pleasantly of expensive cologne. After giving me a hug, he announced that for the first leg of the journey, he had flown by military plane. I suspected that he had flown to the Far

East at his brother's request, but I had no way of knowing for sure: he had descended from a civilian passenger plane and carried no luggage.

He added that he had had a nosebleed, and sure enough, later, while getting his lighter for him from his jacket pocket, I came across two bloodied handkerchiefs. We walked to the car, which was waiting for us right outside the lounge.

"Welcome, Yakov Ilyich," the driver said in greeting.

My father responded with a nod. He appeared under the weather. On the way to Moscow, he felt the need for some fresh air; he stopped the car, and we stood at the side of the road. The fall foliage was aglow, a patchwork of yellow, fiery crimson, and all the hues in between. Frost had already started to sprinkle the grass in the mornings, but the days were warm and summery.

"What a paradise!" my father exclaimed, swallowing the fresh air avidly.

The beauty of the woods around Moscow, with their subtle half shades and the bright blue sky suspended above, is as hard to describe as a Beethoven sonata or a Kandinsky painting.

I noticed that my father was pale. There were beads of sweat on his forehead. "Are you all right?" I asked. "Maybe we should go to the hospital."

"No, I'm not all right," he answered in a singsong, staring at me. Then: "I'm afraid for you girls." Falling silent, he added, "Lubka, let's drive to your place, where it's quiet, where I can lie down."

My dormitory room was tiny, only six square meters (about sixty-five square feet). I left my father alone there after covering him with a blanket. He slept until evening and woke up in a happier mood. We sat down to tea.

"For what I've been doing, Khrushchev could unscrew my head and never put it back in place," my father said, stirring his tea. "Do you understand? Or are you a total fool?"

I understood exactly what my father and his friends were up to.

Chapter Nine

THE PALACE REVOLT

There are two histories; an official, falsified
version, and the hidden story of real events.

HONORÉ DE BALZAC

I had been to the airport quite a few times that fall to meet my father: beginning in August, he was regularly flying back and forth to the provinces—other Soviet republics and other cities within Russia. The word *conspiracy* was not used, but my father made no secret of what he was doing—enlisting support for my uncle's plan to unseat Khrushchev. The brothers met almost daily and trusted each other implicitly.

By the summer, members and candidate members of the Presidium of the Central Committee were already in agreement with the plot to force Khrushchev to step down as head of the party and the country.* The main thing that still needed to be done was to gain the support of the secretaries of the oblast party committees. My father, one of those charged with this task, once mentioned that because of Khrushchev's popularity in the provinces, winning over the provincial party bosses required painstaking care.

*In 1952, the Politburo of the Central Committee of the Soviet Communist Party was renamed the Presidium; in 1966, the name Politburo was restored. Since 1958, Khrushchev had occupied the top posts in both party and government (as first secretary of the Central Committee and chairman of the Council of Ministers).

On one of his returns, I greeted my father in a large hall at the Vnukovo Airport, so clean that it fairly sparkled. Set aside for deputies to the Supreme Soviet and other dignitaries, it was lavishly decorated with imported furniture. Two of its features caught my attention: fresh flowers set in a crystal vase, even when no deputies were in sight, and great tranquillity. A few steps away women and children were sleeping in rows on the dirty floors of the waiting rooms for the masses.

I didn't spend a great deal of time in this deputies' den, since I only welcomed my father back from trips and never saw him off. And so it took me a long time to decipher a mysterious sign I saw on the wall, in English, for the sake of foreign diplomats. When I found out what VIP HALL meant, I felt uncomfortable; I couldn't see myself as a "very important person."

I still remember an employee who tried to set me at ease when I was there during her shift, offering me something to eat and a cup of coffee. In the invariable starched white blouse and severely cut English suit, she seemed to typify what a female functionary should look like.

During the summer and fall, party bosses came from Moldavia (now Moldova), Ukraine, and the Urals, and my father held meetings with them in restaurants, sometimes taking me along. It was sometime in September that I first noticed him switching tables for fear of being overheard.

In my room at the Moskva Hotel, he had never talked about Leonid or Leonid's activities, only about my studies. If he needed to say anything important, he would escort me outside for a walk. At that time, I hardly knew Moscow, and I am grateful for his having shown me its most beautiful spots. Only a few years later I would grow disenchanted: it is impossible to truly love a city in which you have known great unhappiness, much as it is difficult to love a person who has caused you great harm.

As I look back now, I see that this was the sunniest period of my Moscow years. Father hadn't yet started drinking to excess, nor was he being hounded by those who later became the scourge of his existence.

As for the political drama unfolding around me, it was of little interest to me at the time.

The very first time I heard about the plot to unseat Khrushchev was in 1964, during my first stay in Moscow. On April 16, my father and I were watching television with others at the apartment of his close friend the academician Aleksandr Samarin. During a news broadcast, the announcer, his well-trained voice trembling with excitement, informed us of the "extraordinary date being celebrated by the entire country": Khrushchev's birthday . . . One of Samarin's guests began to applaud; everyone else hushed him up so we could hear.

The scene shifted to an award ceremony. My uncle appeared. Smiling broadly, he presented Khrushchev with the gold star of Hero of the Soviet Union, embracing him warmly. With apparent sincerity, he declared, "Dear Nikita Sergeyevich! Your remarkable achievements have won you the respect and love of our entire party, of the entire nation. They fill our hearts with joy and pride in you, our comrade, friend, and leader!"

At that moment, I felt ashamed. . . . Then came the Judas kiss.

Even my father was somewhat shocked by his brother's duplicity. "Ye—eah," he drawled, "what a performance."

Sometime that spring I heard from my father the planned date of Khrushchev's ouster. He put it simply: "Khrushchev will be removed July 5."

In May, I received a letter in which my father wrote, "We are anticipating these events, and are worried. But right now everything is still going well."

On July 5, Khrushchev returned, as planned, from an official visit to Sweden, entering the country via the Soviet seaport city of Baltiysk. On hand to greet him were Admiral Aleksandr Orel of the Baltic Fleet and Soviet Defense Minister Rodion Malinovsky; the latter, there on vacation, had by this time joined the conspiracy against his boss.

But when Khrushchev descended from the steamer *Bashkiria*, he was still in command. Nothing had changed in his absence.

I don't know why the first plot failed. I only remember that when I asked him, my father answered succinctly: "They weren't ready."

In July, not long after his trip to Scandinavia, Khrushchev appeared before the Plenum* of the Central Committee with yet another proposal for reorganization of agriculture and reforms in the areas of science and technology. This contributed to the growing discontent in government circles: his colleagues understood that hasty and inconsistent reforms were splintering the country's internal structure. Moreover, his proposals and ideas were mutually contradictory, prohibiting their serious evaluation.

At the beginning of October, Leonid was invited to Berlin, to the fifteenth-anniversary celebration of the formation of the German Democratic Republic. When he returned, on October 11, Khrushchev was still vacationing in the Crimea, where he had been since October 2. My father met his brother at the airport.

Yakov Ilyich phoned me late that night. He had just finished a long talk with his brother, he told me, and would be spending the night at his dacha. He promised to come by for me the following day, but as far as I can remember, he didn't do so. I was too wrapped up in my own life to notice.

On the morning of October 13, a Tuesday, I made a call from a pay phone to my father at work, not yet knowing what a turning point that day would mark in my country's history and in my life. I was calling to announce that my mother and stepfather were coming to Moscow. Normally in such cases, my father and I would decide who would greet them at the airport. One of us also had to contact Leonid's aides, who would find them a hotel room.

My father was agitated and seemed not to understand what I was saying.

"What's wrong, are you ill?" I asked.

"No, strong as a bull," he answered tensely. "I'm worried. Something

---

*A plenum was an assemblage of all the hundreds of members of the Central Committee. Between plenums the Presidium of the Central Committee was in charge. See also footnote on page 141.

is starting up now, Luba. . . . You shouldn't go anywhere for the next few days. Just remain quietly at home. We might end up in Siberia together."

"What is my connection with all of this?" I said, truly amazed, though I realized he must be referring to the planned removal of Khrushchev.

"If this thing falls through, that bald-headed idiot won't spare any of us Brezhnevs."

What amazed me most was how openly my father had spoken on the telephone, given that someone was undoubtedly eavesdropping on our conversation.

At around midnight, my father rushed to my dormitory. He had dropped by late on other occasions, often for the purpose of making sure I was alone. Sometimes, furious, I would throw open all the cupboards, which hurt his feelings; he didn't want me to put him in the same category as the university's operative detachment, which liked to inspect every nook and cranny of students' rooms in search of lovers and spouses.*

"I was just at Lyonya's dacha and decided to drop by on the way home. Let's have some tea," he said, settling into a chair. His breath smelled of cognac.

"You can't hide here," I laughed. "I'm living in a goldfish bowl. I'm watched from all directions."

Not only that, but during the previous two weeks, all incoming calls on my phone had been blocked—to keep me from blurting anything out, I suppose.

My father responded: "So you think I'm not being spied on myself? They listen in on my phone calls; at work, they planted a spy across from me, and it makes me sick to look at his ugly mug. There's another fool constantly circling my apartment building, watching to see who comes and goes. Recently I talked to my neighbor Mischa. He told me, 'Listen, Yasha, was it you they assigned that pest to? He'll scare away all

---

*The *operotryad* was a sort of hybrid of the KGB and the MVD. In a fit of anger, my father once aptly dubbed it the asshole detachment (*zhoperotryad*).

my girlfriends. Let's pour kerosene on him.' We had a good laugh and went our own ways, but it's no laughing matter."

The Mischa in question was the novelist Mikhail Sholokhov. He kept an apartment in the Arbat and every now and then came to town from Vyoshenskaya, the Cossack village where he lived. I had heard from my father about his parties, which featured an abundance of booze and ballerinas.

As I listened now to my father's mention of Mischa, I was reminded of the evening in 1963 when I first met Sholokhov. To me, not yet twenty, he was only another old man. Perhaps offended by my lack of interest—he was accustomed to being showered with attention—he asked me to dance. His style of dancing was old-fashioned; he held his back as straight as a rod and kept one arm flung far to the side.

"Do you know who I am?" he asked during one of the turns of the waltz.

"No, I don't," I said. He was so stunned that he stopped in his tracks, causing my fashionably wide and fluffy skirt to fly up, almost onto our faces.

"So you don't know who I am?" he exclaimed when he had regained the gift of speech.

"No, I don't. My father called you Mischa, and that's all I know about you."

"Then you weren't taught literature very well in school."

This was unfair to my teachers: in school we had studied quite thoroughly his *Virgin Soil Upturned*, in which he praises collectivization. We resumed dancing.

"So, you're a man of letters!" I said, raising my eyebrows as if amazed. "How fascinating!"

At this, he interrupted our dance again, led me to my father, and walked off without another word.

"What's the matter with him?" my father asked, surprised. "Apparently you've been hurting people's feelings again."

"Hurting people's feelings? Me? Now, really. I'm well bred enough not to insult such a dear old man as that Mikhail."

My father waved his hand and walked theatrically to the other corner of the room, which meant, in our private language, "Let everyone think we came separately."

On the way home that night, he asked me what I could have said to upset such a well-known cynic as Sholokhov. I didn't know how to answer; I sincerely believed that nothing I had said should have offended anyone. After all, there were many celebrities I didn't know, and I often found myself at a loss when the hostesses of high-society gatherings, gushing with delight, introduced me to guests with some claim to fame. I would have to pretend that I had been hearing about these strangers and dreaming of meeting them all my life.

"Am I supposed to know the minister of the chemical industry or the director of Gastronom Number 2?" was the best answer I could find to my father's question.

"Don't try to deny it; you know Sholokhov very well," he snapped. . . .

My thoughts came back to the present, and I rose to heat some water for tea. When I returned, Yakov Ilyich was on the phone.

"Don't worry," he said to me after finishing his conversation. "Everything will be fine."

"I'm not worrying," I assured him.

I might have been worrying if I could have guessed what all this—my father's repeated visits to my dormitory, his telephone conversations with Leonid's aides on that fateful day—would mean for me a few years later.

We sat down to drink our tea. But Father was agitated; he kept jumping up, walking about the room, and stumbling over the furniture.

"This is a coffin, not a room," he would say in annoyance every time he hit himself.

He had obtained dozens of apartments for strangers, but it never occurred to him to get me a one-room apartment where I could live and study properly. As we Russians say, the mother won't understand if the baby doesn't whine—and I prided myself on not complaining.

"Khrushch flew in yesterday from Pitsunda,"* said my father, finishing his tea and sprawling on my sofa. "They raked him over the coals all

---

*Khrushch, literally, is a June beetle, an unflattering nickname for Khrushchev.

day long at the Presidium. Just look what that damn idiot brought the country to! My brother had it right when he said, 'A little fool who fancies himself a czar.' "

"Fool or no fool, the intelligentsia has had a chance to breathe more freely for a time in his day," I remarked.

"We should be thinking of the people," my father retorted, "not the intelligentsia."

I often remembered these words later, when my uncle was in power. Very close to his brother during the first decade after his move to Moscow and not understanding much about politics himself, my father often simply repeated Leonid's words, accepting them as truth handed down from on high. His blind faith was infuriating and endlessly frustrating. Sometimes when he seemed to be in the right mood, I tried to change his mind, but even then he spoke so heatedly in defense of his brother's policies that I lost heart. As my uncle consolidated his power, all the Brezhnevs became increasingly out of touch with real life, and my father and I understood each other's opinions less and less.

Leonid knew what a dangerous man Khrushchev was—he was well informed about Nikita Sergeyevich's participation in the bloody purges of the 1930s—so I often wondered why he would involve his younger brother in the conspiracy. He warned my father candidly, "Keep in mind, Yasha, if Mykyta* finds out about this, he won't spare anyone."

It was also difficult for me to see why my father told me, a girl barely out of her teens, about a political conspiracy fraught with risk. His complete faith in my ability to keep a secret was no justification and an unconvincing explanation. Indeed, I did keep quiet all these years—until writing this book. Far removed from thoughts about politics, I had my busy life to live, and I had no idea then of the conspiracy's historical significance.

My father was by nature cautious, even a bit timid, and loved me boundlessly. Why did he involve me, if only indirectly, in these events? Once I asked him.

---

*The name many in the party elite used to refer to Khrushchev.

"I knew that if the conspiracy failed, we would all be in hot water, no matter how much or how little we knew. No one would have escaped Khrushchev's vengeance, not even you. He wouldn't have bothered to investigate who was part of the plot and who wasn't."

The struggle for power was a game of winner-take-all, in which everything was up for grabs, including the lives of loved ones.

On other occasions, my father spoke to me in greater detail about the two sessions of the Central Committee—that of the Presidium, on October 13, and that of the Plenum, on October 14—at which Khrushchev was forced to resign from his official posts. He told me that as the members of the Presidium criticized Khrushchev, venting their personal dissatisfaction, none of them—including my uncle—bothered to mention his virtues or merits. My uncle had a trump card ready. "If he's stubborn," he had told my father, "we'll rub his face in his own shit—the blood he spilled during the purges." What Leonid had in mind were the lists of people to be shot that Khrushchev had approved with his own signature. As far as I know, the documents were never actually presented and may not even have been compiled. But the threat of using them had the desired effect, for Khrushchev consented to leave "voluntarily." He expressed the wish to make a final request at the upcoming Plenum.

Leonid's response was harsh: "Nikita Sergeyevich, that cannot happen."

Tears came to Khrushchev's eyes, but he took himself in hand and signed an unconditional resignation.

Why didn't they let the old man have his last word? I cannot say whether this was part of a political strategy or simply a display of ill will. At the beginning of the Presidium session, according to my father, Khrushchev had continued to conduct himself as though he were still in charge: he was unable to come to grips with what had happened and refused to express remorse for his policies.

For a long time afterward, he was defensive and would not acknowledge his own mistakes, laying blame for his failures on anybody and everybody. His protest was conducted only at the level of hallway discussions and was never officially heard. The memoir he published in the

West would remain forbidden literature to Soviet citizens until the glasnost period of the 1980s.

The report that Mikhail Suslov read at the Plenum on October 14, 1964, found fault with Khrushchev for not having carried out a single one of his reforms consistently. This was true enough; the half measures that seem to make political analysts quiver with admiration even today were just that—half measures. For example, by giving them internal passports, Khrushchev allowed collective farmers the opportunity to live where they wanted. But he didn't give them land, which was what they needed most. A flight to the cities ensued, leaving the Russian countryside underpopulated.

Another valid criticism made in Suslov's report concerned Khrushchev's cult of personality. The rapturous applause greeting the sensational 1956 speech on the cult of Stalin had barely died down before the author of that speech began to grab power for himself; as early as 1958, he was holding the two key posts of party leader and head of state, thus removing himself from criticism and control.

Khrushchev's son, Sergey, has written that on October 1, 1964, after hearing from a former bodyguard about suspicious conversations between Nikolay Ignatov (a Central Committee member) and secretaries of the oblast party committees, he quickly relayed this information to his father. The next day, before leaving for Pitsunda, Khrushchev told his party comrades, "Friends, I know you are planning something against me. Watch your step—if anything happens I'll send you running like a pack of puppies." But he apparently took no steps.

Khrushchev's lack of substantive reaction to his son's words would make sense if he were resigned to his fate, convinced that it was already too late to ward off his enemies; indeed, some political scientists have put forth this hypothesis. I favor a different explanation, based on my impressions and on descriptions of Nikita Sergeyevich by people who observed him closely. I believe Khrushchev was brought down by his own self-assurance: to put it bluntly, he had bit off more than he could chew. As often happens with the high and would-be mighty of this world, he had lost his sense of reality. Convinced in his heart that his throne was safe from all challenges, he simply ignored the warnings and went off to the Crimea as planned. This is the only way I can explain the genuine surprise and discontent he displayed when he was summoned back to Moscow on October 13 and his subsequent behavior that day at the Presidium, where he did not resign immediately and resisted until it became clear that all his colleagues had been lined up against him.

The Plenum, of course, accepted Khrushchev's resignation. It was announced that he had been removed from his post for "dangerous subjectivism" and "confused voluntarism." On October 15, at a Moscow assembly of active party members, it was announced that Khrushchev had retired "at his own request." As for the public at large, they learned only that Khrushchev had retired "due to his health."

Kosygin took Khrushchev's place as chairman of the Council of Ministers; Leonid took Khrushchev's place as first secretary; Nikolay Podgorny, a Central Committee secretary, took Leonid's place as president of the Supreme Soviet. The Plenum was a total success for those conspirators who had worked so long to prepare it.

But the de facto coup barely changed the structure of power, merely replacing one group of government lackeys with another.

The plot could not have succeeded had it not been for Khrushchev's strained relations with the three "whales" of the Soviet state: the KGB, the army, and the party. He had made too many enemies in the party by such "inexcusable" innovations as doing away with the yearly, untaxed bonuses that high officials had been receiving. The timeserving apparatchiks didn't want to let power out of their hands and felt their comfortable chairs being pulled out from under them by the June Beetle's constant personnel changes. By the time all the plans to unseat him were in place, Khrushchev was completely isolated, with no one able or willing to support him.

Nikita Sergeyevich loved to be photographed hugging production leaders and heroes of socialist labor and paternally slapping the shoulders of celebrities, like the first person to travel in outer space, Yuri Gagarin. He even met with people in letters and the arts, but in conversations with him no one could get a word in edgewise, and the intelligentsia found his boorish familiarities and his vacuous, demagogic speeches annoying. After a short-lived thaw in the '50s, he muzzled the intelligentsia. His stupid ideas, arrogance, and lack of culture made him the object of universal ridicule.

To average citizens, he was a salesman with nothing to sell. They soon tired of his hysterical appeals to "catch up with and overtake" America (which elicited condescending smiles from Americans, we thought) and to "show the imperialists Kuzya's mother," a colloquial threat. This expression was at the center of one of the endless tales that circulated about Khrushchev. Supposedly, an interpreter who didn't know its meaning once rendered Nikita Sergeyevich's ravings as "First Secretary Khrushchev has a friend named Kuzya and is anxious to introduce you to his mother."

As the party, state, and military leader, Khrushchev had not been well liked at any level of Soviet society. He lacked the most necessary attribute for leadership—respect. His contradictory and inconsistent character was everywhere apparent. He spoke out against the arms race but created a threat of nuclear war during the Caribbean crisis (the Cuban missile crisis). He was the first to lift, partially, Stalin's iron curtain, but he had the Berlin Wall put up. His only admirers were those close enough to him personally to be able to forgive his crudity.

In the early '60s, he had unleashed a campaign against "social parasites," a category that often included creative people—writers, artists, poets, and actors. Some were exiled from Moscow, others thrown into prisons or psychiatric wards. Under Khrushchev, if someone wanted to write a book, he or she could do so only by maintaining a regular job at the same time. Even world-famous authors had to teach, contribute to periodicals, or work as reviewers or censors in state publishing houses. Like their lesser-known colleagues, they had to be officially employed somewhere to avoid the label of parasite. But under my uncle, this state of affairs—idiotically wasteful of the country's talents—would not change for the better.

How did the people react to Khrushchev's removal and to his successors? As I remember, they reacted calmly. No other candidate besides Brezhnev had been nominated for the post of first secretary. My uncle was attractive, energetic, and charming; he had extensive experience in party work, though at fifty-seven he was still relatively young.

Unlike Khrushchev, Leonid believed in stability in policy and personnel: there would be no leaps, no risky experimentation, no public humiliation of officials who fell from grace—they were instead given posts a few rungs lower in the hierarchy. The apparatchiks had chosen correctly. For them, 1964 marked the beginning of two decades of unprecedented contentment.

I conclude my look at the palace revolt of 1964 by writing what I know of the historical figures involved. My information is based on what I observed and on what I heard from my uncle and my father.

Participants in the plot have stated that Leonid Brezhnev had a list of the conspirators' names. I don't know whether this is true, but I have no doubt that he started and led the effort to remove his boss, gradually gathering around him a group of men who had a grudge against Khrushchev. Support from Kosygin, the well-respected first assistant chairman of the Council of Ministers, made it possible to attract other Central Committee members to the plot. Some of the other officials who knew what was being planned were Podgorny, Suslov, Aleksandr Shelepin, Vladimir Semichastny, Pyotr Shelest, and Gennady Voronov. Brezhnev was somehow able to keep these rivals—who for the most part hated one another—from squabbling.

The first person to whom my uncle had turned was Nikolay Podgorny, a fellow member of the Central Committee. The response was favorable: Podgorny had no love for Khrushchev, whom he had worked alongside of for years in Ukraine.

On vacation with their families in the Crimea during the fall of 1963, the two men—Podgorny and Brezhnev—had come to the conclusion that "everyone has had it up to here with Nikita." They expressed their dissatisfaction with Khrushchev's intractable personality, his coarseness, his arrogance, and his intolerance. Without yet discussing his removal, they suggested that his sails be trimmed.

In July of that year, Khrushchev had recalled Podgorny from Ukraine and appointed him second secretary of the Central Committee in place of Frol Kozlov, who had been touched by scandal. Specifically, Kozlov was accused of graft and connections with organized crime, and a large cache of American dollars was found in his safe. There were apparent links between his case and that of Yan Rokotov, who had been convicted of illegal currency dealings in 1961 and executed. As if that weren't enough, Kozlov's daughter had been romantically involved with—and had supposedly given information to—a certain Oleg Penkovsky, under investigation as a spy for the West.

The story of Kozlov's fall from grace illustrates an important aspect of Khrushchev's personality. My father told me that Nikita Sergeyevich summoned Kozlov to his office and dressed him down for two hours nonstop. The result was that Kozlov suffered a stroke, which left him temporarily paralyzed; he recovered but not well enough to work again and died a few years later.

Give Khrushchev his due: he wasn't afraid of chewing out subordinates when they misbehaved. He was known for his colorful language and direct manner. In this respect, he was quite different from my uncle. Leonid was extremely reserved, partly due to his nature, partly due to his military experience and training. It would have been totally out of character for him to bang his fist on a table, hurl files at subordinates, or tear up papers; he reserved his rare outbreaks of anger for his wife and other relatives. On the job, he knew how to control himself, though he used strong language at times. Few of his associates ever harbored ill will toward him, probably because he displayed an even temperament.

One of the most active participants in the plot to oust Khrushchev was Nikolay Ignatov. As a member of the Presidium of the Central Committee, Ignatov had supported Khrushchev in 1957, when a group within that body attempted to replace him with the triumvirate of Georgy Malenkov, Lazar Kaganovich, and Vyacheslav Molotov. But for some reason, Khrushchev eventually lost faith in Ignatov, who in May of 1960 lost his position as Central Committee secretary and joined the growing ranks of the dissatisfied. He made his personal views known quite openly, hinting that the time for a change of leadership had come.

I remember listening with interest to Ignatov's tales of the partisan movement against the Nazis in the vicinity of Orel. He had three Orders of Lenin. My father used to josh him: "Kolya, what do you need all three for? Give me one!"

"It's about time you earned one of your own," Ignatov would reply laconically.

Ignatov and my father became friends as a result of evenings spent at each other's homes during the period preceding October 1964. He frequently took my father and me to his dacha outside of Moscow, where a delicacy-laden table inevitably awaited us.

Accompanying my father everywhere during those first months in the capital, I always elicited puzzled stares. My black sweater, white men's shirt, and plain gray skirt looked out of place alongside the imported outfits, shimmering with all the colors of the rainbow, that were favored by the girlfriends of high-ranking officials. My father would hasten to explain that I was his daughter.

The stares would become warmer and even more curious: "Just think! Brezhnev's niece and so modestly dressed. She must be putting on an act."

No one seemed to consider that perhaps I had no desire to emulate the courtesans, whose lovers ordered their clothes by catalog. But to be perfectly honest, my plain attire and my hairstyle—parted in the middle and pulled back—were partly a pose. Let's just say that I liked to do things my own way.

One evening in 1964 at Ignatov's dacha stands out in memory. When my father and I arrived, it was already quite late. The other guests had been drinking; some had been in the sauna and were sitting in various poses and degrees of undress, but all with at least a towel or a sheet to keep them within the bounds of decency.

Next to Ignatov sat two young women, a blonde and a brunette, both remarkable. With her dark complexion, green eyes, slender, aristocratic wrists, and emerald earrings, the brunette bore a striking resemblance to a serpent. She wore a skimpy white dress, obviously from Christian Dior. I looked her up and down—one of my bad habits, doing whatever I pleased. She was so gorgeous that I truly found it hard to take my eyes off her. Knowing that I was Yakov Brezhnev's daughter, she smiled condescendingly.

"Do you like her?" Ignatov asked across the table.

"She's lovely," I answered.

"That's what money and power can buy," he said. "You know what they say—the pretty girls go where the banknotes are. . . ."

I felt my insides churning.

But Ignatov was unstoppable. "If you like her," he went on, "then drink to her health." He poured me a glass of cognac.

"I'm not a hussar," I retorted. "I don't drink to 'the fair sex.'"

Ignatov, a bit giddy after the sauna, didn't want to take no for an answer, even when my father asked him to leave me alone. At least take a sip, my father finally suggested, for the sake of peace. But I wouldn't make an exception to my rules for some drunken bigwig.

Ignatov hit the bottle hard that evening. He danced a bit too furiously with his black and white angels, as he called them, and even invited me to waltz with him.

I didn't dance with drunks, I said. He laughed uncontrollably.

"Yasha, what a stubborn daughter you have," he said, wiping away the tears that were streaming down his cheeks. He was standing near my chair, off to one side. "She won't dance with me, a member of the Presidium! But I could have hundreds of beautiful women crawling at my feet; all I would have to do is whistle."

"Could you cope?" I asked quietly.

Now he roared with laughter. And then suddenly he turned pale, swayed, and sank to the floor. My father reacted first: jumping up from his seat, he grasped hold of the man. With the help of others, he moved him to the sofa and gave him a drink of water. The green-eyed girl with the emeralds stroked his sweat-drenched forehead with a damp towel.

On our way home that night, my father dismissed my comment—I had mentioned that Ignatov looked deathly ill—by saying that his friend would snap into shape in the morning. "As soon as he swallows some valerian, he'll be his old self."

But Ignatov didn't recover for long; in 1966, my father would be attending his funeral.

Mikhail Suslov was one of the two men toward whom my father felt a particular hostility, the other being Yuri Andropov. In 1964, I already knew from my father that during the Stalin era, Suslov had taken part in compiling lists of persons sentenced to death, lists that were taken to the dictator for final approval. And it was under Suslov's guidance that the peoples of the Caucasus were deported eastward after World War II. Somewhat later he again proved his dedication, shipping Latvians, Lithuanians, and Estonians to Siberia.

The Gray Cardinal, as the reserved Suslov was known in Western countries as well as in the Soviet Union, carried out orders efficiently under Stalin, Khrushchev, and finally Brezhnev. Once Leonid said of him, "When I look at his ashen lips and into his dull, colorless eyes, I wonder if anyone could have ever loved him. I can't conceive of a woman agreeing to kiss him."

Suslov had a loathsome habit of looking through people, out of contempt, not indifference. I should recall, too, that he was physically ill. Even as early as 1964, he had connected to him at all times an intestinal-discharge tube, which can hardly have made for a pleasant existence.

Occasionally Suslov relaxed enough to carry on a conversation, but all he spoke about were his children: he would say that they were receiving a strict upbringing and were turning out to be quite constructive, obedient, and modest. As my uncle joked, one could at least infer from these conversations that some woman had kissed Suslov after all.

Once when Suslov was praising his children, my dear uncle, ashamed as he was becoming of his own, blurted out, "Mischa, what are you hinting at? Something about my two problem children? That's just the way it happened: I didn't have much luck with them."

Suslov tried to explain his way out of the blunder he realized he had fallen into: "Not being burdened with responsibilities to the degree that you are, Leonid, I was fortunate enough to raise my children myself," and so forth. His argument had an unconvincing ring, and an awkward moment followed. Someone—perhaps Dmitry Polyansky, a Central Committee member whose children had also been a disappointment—

remarked, "All the young people nowadays are turning out rotten, and that's just the way it is."

Some political scientists lean toward the notion that the conspirators were seriously considering Aleksandr Shelepin for the post of first secretary. Shelepin, who in 1964 was assistant chairman of the Council of Ministers and chairman of the Committee for Party and State Control, had served three years as head of the KGB, from 1958 to 1961. My father, repeating the sentiments of his brother, stated that putting an ex-KGB chief in charge of the country would have been unacceptable, given the recent memories of the Stalin-era purges. Shelepin's rise to power might have led to serious international repercussions as well.

During the first years after the October 1964 Plenum, Leonid Ilyich knew that Shelepin wanted his job and was plotting against him. I don't know exactly when this was, but my father has told me that sometime during that period, the Mongolian leader Yuzhmagin Tsedenbal informed Brezhnev of Shelepin's desire to become first secretary, calling him at his dacha on the government phone line. I remember how my father indignantly called Shelepin, who was only about five years his junior, an upstart and a whippersnapper. My uncle never concealed his antipathy toward Shelepin.

Shelepin's prestige would become even more shaky later. In the mid-'60s, rumors began to circulate that he was behind an incident in which an airplane carrying a Soviet delegation lost its bearings and crashed into Avala Mountain, in the vicinity of Belgrade. Among those killed was Nikolay Romanovich Mironov, head of the Central Committee administration. He was greatly loved by the Brezhnev family, and his friendship with my uncle dated from the time during the 1940s when Leonid was secretary of the Dnepropetrovsk Oblast Party Committee and Mironov was deputy. He had volunteered for the front after five years of university studies and returned from the war seriously wounded. Yet this did not keep him from being a cheerful fellow.

Leonid was very attached to Mironov, who may have been the only person other than his old friend Kostya Grushevoy who spoke to him candidly. They would often part company in anger after stormy arguments, only to talk again the next day as though nothing had happened. Leonid always forgave Mironov's forthright, sometimes crude manner.

Mironov had sometimes invited us to his dacha near Moscow, where he gave us a hearty, traditional Russian-style welcome. This was one of the few places where I could go without fear of walking in on a drunken orgy.

Neither Leonid Ilyich nor my father had any doubt that Mironov had been killed by the KGB and that Shelepin—who, as chairman of State and Party Control, still had influence with the KGB—was involved. Mironov was one of a small number of party functionaries who openly hated and fought with the KGB; his candor and his dedication to principle made him many enemies. Shelepin, like everyone else, was fully aware that Mironov openly despised him and had spoken out against him in high places more than once.

In political circles, Shelepin was known as an active adherent of Stalin's rehabilitation. His pro-Stalin policies during Brezhnev's rule even frightened the party bureaucrats, so no one was surprised when, in late 1967, Leonid demoted him, making him head of Soviet trade unions, completely subordinated to the Communist Party and the government.

A complete analysis of the ouster of Khrushchev is beyond my competence. This chapter should be taken as the testimony of an observer and a witness: my goal has been to share my recollections with the reader, not to make the kind of far-reaching conclusions that are properly the province of political scientists and historians.

At the time, I hadn't fully come to grips with my unique situation. I was still naïve and had no idea of the significance of the events unfolding before my eyes. I saw Yakov Brezhnev as my father, not as Brezhnev's Brother, and even my uncle's titles were an abstraction, distantly related to my own life. I had little interest in politics, and my indifference became legendary at the institute. During lectures on political subjects, I would fall into a dull stupor, and all the words would dissolve into one utterly meaningless blur.

Tests on political economy and Marxist-Leninist philosophy were like torture. At times, I would turn in a blank sheet of paper, praying silently to be spared. Fortunately institutes were not permitted to give their students less than a two in the political subjects. But even a three was a serious blow, since it meant one's stipend could be taken away.

Once at an oral exam, I felt as if I were dying. I struggled feverishly to overcome my mumbling and at least put together one complete sentence, to no avail. Someone was saying something about basis and superstructure. . . .

"What's this?" The professor's friendly voice brought me out of my trance. "You're not going to be a disgrace to your uncle, now are you? If there's something you don't understand, I can take some extra time for you."

That's all I need, I thought. If he suspects I'm dense now, just wait till he works with me one-on-one. I couldn't understand the first thing about the subject he was teaching and, least of all, the purpose of making a young woman digest all this rigmarole about basis and superstructure. How was I going to explain that to him? What a relief to see, out of the corner of my eye, the professor write down the number four. Just what I wanted.

"Thank you," I said, taking back my grade book. "Next time I'll ask my uncle to go over my work with me."

I said this with a deadpan expression that left the professor guessing: was this poor political illiterate serious or joking?

In the years after Leonid Brezhnev's death, the Russian press was to condemn him for his leadership in the 1964 conspiracy against his own benefactor, Khrushchev. To all appearances, my uncle was never tormented by remorse, claiming that the plot had been carried out for the people's benefit. Once he said, as if to justify himself, "Khrushchev was a thorn in everyone's side, and the people—not just the party apparatus—were ready for him to step down."

The plot against Khrushchev was so thoroughly clandestine that the conspirators did not even trust their own chauffeurs and secretaries. To me, naïve and highly principled or oversimplifying, as young people can be, the affair seemed an incarnation of betrayal and cowardice. When I hinted at this to Leonid, in 1967 or so, he became angry and let loose

Leonid Brezhnev (front row, second from right), about 1938. My uncle belonged to the party elite that had survived the purges of the 1930s and World War II; he was an integral part of the new generation formed during the Stalin era.

with a lengthy monologue. His main points were that we young people had received everything on a silver platter and weren't even willing to study as hard as we should; it was easy for us to accuse the older generation of being wicked and not to understand that their deeds had been necessary to ensure future generations a better life.

"Besides," he added, "Khrushchev brought the conspiracy on himself."

When asked who was likely to inherit his power, Khrushchev had often answered, "Leonid Brezhnev," singling out my uncle for praise on many occasions. If only Nikita Sergeyevich could have guessed that the inoffensive, smiling Lyonya would stab him in the back. Or at least break his grip.

Once, soon after Leonid had become first secretary, he took a walk in the woods with my father. Because Yakov had played such a vital role in the revolt—winning support from the provincial party bosses whose votes (as members of the Central Committee) were essential—Leonid felt a special gratitude toward him.

"Yasha," he sighed, "I don't know how long I'll live. I don't even think about it. I only think about how I can do more for our people.

They have suffered greatly and deserve better. Our extreme poverty has always shocked me. Are Russians worse than Czechs or Germans? They should eat their fill and sleep in comfort if we want them to work well."

Was my uncle really concerned about the people's needs? Did he sincerely believe that he had been selected by fate to be their benefactor? Like any politician, he needed to feel that his actions were justified. He had often repeated the formula "The people are not here to serve us; we are here to serve the people," but this idea faded and was forgotten as the years passed. I have no intention of making excuses for him, but it would be unfair to deny that he loved his country; he did. In his own way, he wanted to make the Soviet Union more prosperous and more happy. But he did not believe, after a certain point at least, in the triumph of socialism, in Marxist-Leninist principles, or in the possibility of communism.

It was the late '60s. During another one of their frequent walks in the woods, Yakov, himself a party member who believed dogmatically in the official line, asked his brother, general secretary of the Communist Party, "What do you think, Lyonya, will communism ever come?"

Leonid laughed without mirth. "Oh, for heaven's sake, Yasha, what are you talking about? All that stuff about communism is a tall tale for popular consumption. After all, we can't leave the people with no faith. The church was taken away, the czar was shot, and something had to be substituted. So let the people build communism."

My father came away from this conversation deeply disappointed.

In the summer of 1990, a few months before I came to America, my father and I visited the cemetery at the Novodevichy Monastery. Here, under heavy marble slabs, lie the remains of celebrities and top officials, as well as those of their parents and other close relatives.

We laid a small bouquet of violets on the grave of my grandmother Natalya Denisovna. The watchman lent us his watering can, and we watered the pansies growing nearby. After several minutes of silence, we spoke grateful words of remembrance, as Russian custom requires. My father shed a few tears.

We paid our respects to Chekhov and Mikhail Bulgakov and stood for a short while by the grave of Zhenya Milaev, my cousin Galina's first husband. We walked a little farther and then came to Khrushchev's grave.

I stood for a few minutes by Ernst Neizvestny's monument, in which the sculptor captured the duality of a leader who was undeniably gifted in his own way but also shortsighted, chaotic, and unpredictable.

We recalled our visit to Khrushchev and his wife, Nina Petrovna. In the late summer of 1970, my father unexpectedly suggested a trip to the former leader's dacha at Petrovo-Dalnee, and I agreed immediately. I had heard and read a great deal about Khrushchev by then and was eager to meet him.

To avoid attention, we took a taxi instead of the government Volga we usually rode in. I was worried about how the ex-ruler would react to a visit by close relatives of the man who had taken his place. To my great surprise, Nikita Sergeyevich and his wife greeted us cordially.

"We've been waiting," said Khrushchev, embracing my father. "How you've aged, Yasha," he added sympathetically.

They had known each other for many years, at least at the level of attending receptions together and enjoying cognac in each other's company. Our visit, planned to last thirty minutes, went on for almost three hours.

Nikita Sergeyevich showed us his fruit trees and vegetable garden, even demonstrating a watering system that he had developed himself. He had real talent as a gardener. I examined with curiosity this man whose name had been on the front pages for so many years. Nothing remained of his past glory. Before me stood an old man with a round, good-natured face that featured the famous wart. He had pouches under his eyes, a flabby chin, and a trembling hand with the freckles of age.

Nina Petrovna invited us to stay for lunch. She was affectionate with me, like any other elderly Russian woman would have been. Once when she got up from the table for something, she couldn't resist patting my head and urging me: "Eat, Luba, eat." There was an old-fashioned feeling of home in her clean and cozy dining room. The lunch, prepared by a cook, was good; the atmosphere, congenial. While a relaxed conversation developed between Nikita Sergeyevich and my father, Nina Petrovna asked me about my family and my work. She in turn told me about her grandsons and complained of her health.

"Your daughter resembles you Brezhnevs," Nikita Sergeyevich suddenly said, looking at me. At a loss, I searched his face but found no hint there of hard feelings, hostility, or hidden resentment.

He noticed my stare. "Why do you look at me that way, Lubushka? I really thought back then that your uncle had broken my back. But not really . . ." After a short silence, he added, "He just broke my nose."

I didn't know what to say.

"I, too, have many sins on my conscience," he continued. "Yasha, do you remember Stalin's son, Vasily?" he asked, turning to my father. "Recently I have been seeing him in my dreams. He was so young and handsome, and his nose was so, well, so Russian, I guess. . . ."

He fell silent again. I sensed that he was looking for forgiveness.

My father had told me, of course, the story of Stalin's son, Vasily, whose well-known lack of sophistication made him the opposite of his sister, Svetlana, a woman of education and culture. Spirited, openhearted, and far too devoted to his friends, Vasily made no effort to acquire an education, and his lifestyle brought the family much grief.

Once at a party at which foreigners were present, Vasily proposed a toast to his late father, declaring drunkenly (after Stalin's death, Vasily remained in that state most of the time), "In the old days, the entire nation kissed my father's Georgian ass, and everyone—including all the members of the Politburo and Khrushchev himself—considered it an honor. But then they cornered him like an old wolf and poisoned him."

He began to cry. One of the guests—secret agents were always present at such parties—went to the nearest phone booth to file a report.

Vasily was arrested the same night and was sent to the notorious Vladimir Prison. After being held there for several years, he was banished to the city of Kazan, where he quietly lived out his days—tippled them away, to be more exact. He died in a hospital at a tragically young age, devoured by resentment and hating the world.

Partly to blame for this—Leonid once told us that Khrushchev and Nikolay Bulganin had been put in charge of "containing" Vasily— Khrushchev was evidently feeling remorse now.

Nikita Sergeyevich also recounted an anecdote about Tito. In the middle of 1948, relations between the Yugoslav Communist Party and the Soviet Communist Party were broken off. Then came an end to the economic and cultural relations between Yugoslavia and the other Communist countries. Stalin threatened to occupy Yugoslavia and "call Tito—who has got too big for his britches—back to order." The rift between Yugoslavia and the Soviet Union lasted until 1955. In 1956, Khrushchev invited Tito, labeled a "defender of fascism" in the Soviet press a few years earlier, to visit him in Moscow. The reception was lavish. After all, amends had to be made for the years of mistreatment. Official negotiations alternated with banquets.

Khrushchev's tale was new to me, so I listened with interest.

During one of the Yugoslav leader's visits to the Soviet Union in the early '60s, he was taken to the Crimea on a pleasure trip, to admire the magnificent scenery. An "imperial hunt" was arranged, standard fare for such high-ranking guests. When Tito shot a deer, Khrushchev gave a banquet in his honor. My father, on vacation in the Crimea with his brother, also attended.

At the height of the evening, Tito filled two glasses with cognac, approached Nikita Sergeyevich, and said, "Nikita, let's drink to the success of our meeting!"

Khrushchev, unable to drink much due to his age, answered, "No, I can't drink. Go ahead and drink with Yasha Brezhnev, the youngest among us."

Then Tito picked up two large glasses of vodka and replied, "I can't drink either, but my aide will drink for me. Let's watch the two of them and see who comes out on top—the Yugoslav or the Russian." My father and Tito's aide gulped down the vodka along with a bit of food.

Tito filled the glasses again. "Now we'll see who's really stronger— an Ivan or a Miloš," he exclaimed. And they drained their second glass.

And so it went.

The next morning, before returning to Belgrade, Tito phoned Leonid to ask him how his brother was doing.

"I think he's all right" came the answer.

"What is he doing right now?" Tito persisted.

After checking, Leonid answered that Yakov was swimming in the pool.

"My aide is still dead to the world; we can't wake him up," said Tito. He paused and added, before hanging up, "I guess you Russians really are tougher than us."

Nikita Sergeyevich laughed as he told the story. Then he recalled Voronov and Shelest, former associates of his who had betrayed him during the conspiracy. "You know, Yasha, no one ever comes to visit me. What can they possibly be afraid of?" he said sadly.

Well, well, I thought, is this man sitting before me really that fearsome Nikita Khrushchev, the one who banged his shoe on the table at the United Nations? Is this the man who, reveling in his omnipotence, shouted in public at Illarion Golitsyn, the well-known artist and scion of the Russian aristocracy, calling him a bespectacled agent of imperialism? Is this the same clumsy oaf who stamped his foot at a defenseless poet?

I left for home that summer day with a strange feeling of sadness, one that I have never been able to explain fully, even to myself.

Chapter Ten

LOVE KNOWS NO BORDERS

Youth there was—it came like Sunday lightning.

ANNA AKHMATOVA

In November of 1964, my father took me to the annual parade celebrating the Bolshevik Revolution. After the tanks, rockets, and armored troop carriers, rows of marchers approached. Above the street floated portraits of my uncle and other Central Committee members. From time to time, we saw Lenin's bald head, decorated with paper flowers. Shouts, laughter, and songs could be heard against the background of slogans, which were broadcast to the entire country. In the crowd of spectators far below were many children—clinging to their parents' shoulders, frightened by the noise, their faces blue from the cold after a long wait in the narrow alleys off Gorky Street. I had no love for such spectacles but welcomed the opportunity to spend a day with my father.

According to my uncle, when Stalin reviewed parades, he would pace the rostrum, look down at the ecstatic, adoring multitudes, and comment laconically, "And there are my sheep!"

As I saw the foreigners standing near us, snapping pictures, clapping, and returning the greetings of the passing throngs, I felt an urge to call out: Don't admire the technological accomplishments that could kill your children. I didn't want them to be taken in by the size of the crowd, the flags, the banners, the flowers. The spectators had been herded here by local trade-union and party committees to stand in the rain and snow.

The monotony was broken when a group of cosmonauts joined us on the guest rostrum. My father, who knew them from banquets and receptions, flirted with Valentina Tereshkova, the first woman in space, and told the men anecdotes sotto voce.

The Soviet rocket program made no sense to my father: do you try to reach the stars when you're dressed in rags? Once in the late 1950s, after the first Soviet sputniks were launched, Yakov said to his brother, "Lyonya, let's at least find something with which to cover our behinds before we go into space; now the whole world will see how naked we are."

Leonid laughed. At that time, he was responsible for the space program. "Yasha," he said, "we know that space exploration is premature when we can't even keep our people properly fed. But that's politics for you."

To my delight, Yuri Gagarin approached us after the parade. As we talked, I thought how stupid it had been of me to forget my gloves. Noticing that I had burrowed my hands—which were beginning to go numb—into the collar of my father's coat, Yuri wordlessly took them, rubbed them, and slipped them into his own gloves. He told me I looked like a crayfish that somebody had pulled out of a hole in the ice. Before he went on his way, I promised to return the gloves via my father.

I did give them to my father later that day, but he lost them. I should have expected as much: he had given up wearing gloves because he lost them so often. I next saw Yuri was at a party about a month later. I went up to him, shamefaced, to apologize.

"Your punishment," he said, "is to reserve the first dance for me."

"Oh, for heaven's sake, Yuri," I replied. "That's no punishment. How lucky I am—"

"No trite phrases, Luba," he said, and his smile vanished.

Yuri, the Soviet Union's first cosmonaut, was attractive in a down-to-earth way, with his round face and broad-set, light-blue eyes. I remember that he danced oddly, pulling in one leg for some reason.

Roman Karmen, 1964. "The day after the parade, my father decided to ignore all
other holiday invitations . . . and take me to see the well-known director
Roman Karmen. Roman and I . . . enjoyed trading jokes."

© WALTRAUD LINDNER

Fame never spoiled him: he retained his winning simplicity and positive
outlook and, except for some envious souls, was loved by everyone.

The day after the parade, my father decided to ignore all other holiday invitations, official and unofficial, and take me to see the well-
known director Roman Karmen. Roman and I were already acquainted,
and we enjoyed trading jokes.

Referring to Otiliya Raizman, a highly regarded camerawoman,
Roman had once said to me, "Listen, Lubushka, Otiliya and I had an
argument about how cards and letters should be addressed—with the
wife's name first or the husband's name first. I told her that the man
should come first if he's got anything to his name because his wife is living off him. She nearly scratched my eyes out—she's a feminist. What
do you say?"

I told him he should make it easy on himself and stop writing letters.

The answer set him laughing. From then on, when reminded that he was behind in his correspondence, he would explain with a straight face that he hadn't written various letters because he couldn't decide whom to address first, the husband or the wife.

Karmen lived in one of the seven Moscow high-rise apartment buildings put up for the elite during Stalin's day. The Father of the Peoples had sunk millions of rubles into this showpiece on Kotelnichesky Embankment, which stands to this day as a silent monument to his era.

Our host's name brought the dour, sleepy-eyed doorman to attention. He flung the oak doors wide and walked with us to the elevator.

The tenants were mainly writers and artists whose work glorified the Communist Party. Were their elegant apartments an earthly reward for selling their souls? I wondered as my gaze roamed over the oddly cold luxury: carpeted marble staircases; paintings in massive gold-plated frames. But Roman Karmen and the people around him are different, I decided, telling myself not to see villains everywhere. What can you do if you dislike, in the abstract, those who follow party guidelines in art and find yourself charmed whenever you meet them in person? With these thoughts, I approached Karmen's apartment.

The door opened as soon as we rang, as though the neat, dark-complexioned young man standing behind it had been waiting for us. His steel-blue eyes made me feel uneasy, perhaps because they were penetrating and intense, but I didn't think much about it.

Deftly removing my fur jacket, the stranger introduced himself in a stilted, accented Russian. "My name is Helmut," he said. "I am German. I am studying in Moscow."

Helmut offered his arm and guided me into the living room, which was overflowing with people. The center of attention was the host himself, short and slight, with lively, intelligent eyes. I was not yet twenty-one, at an age when one wants to be irresistible to silver-haired men, and to me Roman Karmen was the very essence of refinement and perfection.

After giving my father and me a warm welcome, he gestured expertly, seating me on the sofa beside him. He asked how I was doing with my studies and with the boys. Soon he took me in tow, planning to make introductions. But Helmut stole me away, explaining hastily to Karmen that our having already met that evening gave him the right to do so.

Helmut had been brought to the party by a relative of his, Waltraud Lindner. She was an East German photojournalist, in the Soviet Union at the time to take stills for Karmen's latest film, *The Great Patriotic War.**

My clothes that evening were perfect. I had on the light-pink sweater my father had given me for the November holiday. It was of delicate Italian wool. My smooth hair was combed back in a bun. My father and I had selected brown high-heeled shoes from the Kremlin store to go with the sweater; to match them, a dormitory neighbor, a daughter of the defense minister of one of the other socialist countries, had lent me some amazingly beautiful beads that she had brought back from the Orient. I was thrilled.

The film star Nikolay Cherkassov, with his large, aristocratic hands, his long, thoughtful face, and his exceptional height, stood out among the celebrities. He had recently soared to even greater popularity among Soviet audiences, playing a professor in *Our Legacy Is for the People*. During the party, when he offered to conduct an IQ test he had found in a magazine, I tried to worm my way out of participating: I had a low opinion of my own intellect. Cherkassov insisted. To my surprise, I received a fairly high score—the same as Helmut's.

When we sat down to eat, Helmut brought his chair and squeezed in next to me. My Soviet upbringing had the upper hand; greatly flattered and pleased, I nevertheless willed myself to appear aloof and hinted that I had countless other beaux to choose from.

My glance turned to Vadim, a young man who worked with my father at the Committee for Science and Technology and whose career promised to be bright. My relatives had been touting this government minister's son as the perfect marital prospect. I began to flirt with him.

My German was no quitter, however; continuing to maneuver adroitly, a broad smile on his face, he positioned himself between us, forcing Vadim to retreat. Joking and flashing brilliant white teeth, Hel-

*This is the Russian name for World War II. The movie was popular worldwide and in 1965 was awarded the Silver Dove.

mut extracted my telephone number and invited me to the Bolshoi the following evening. I got a good laugh—which I kept well hidden, of course—from his promise to secure the best seats in the house. The best seats in Moscow theaters were a thing I hadn't recently lacked.

All this time my father had been helpfully hovering about and periodically swooping down like a hawk. He was visibly relieved when Helmut announced that he had to leave early on urgent business.

After saying good-bye to everyone, Helmut came to me and gently squeezed my hand. No one else noticed this innocent gesture, which I took as a first declaration of love. I kept my fingers rolled up in a tight fist for the rest of the evening, trying to retain the sweet, warm sensation.

Most of the other guests drifted off, but I couldn't leave—my father was in a corner, engrossed in conversation with an old man. I talked with Cherkassov, who played with my mind as a boy plays with a kitten, delighted with my provincial naïveté and frankness.

"My pretty wallflower, read us something in French," he demanded. "What's wrong; is that too much to ask to make an old actor happy?"

Why not? The evening spent with Helmut had inspired me, and too few guests remained for me to have stage fright. I started with a few poems by Jacques Prévert, and Cherkassov especially liked "For You, My Love." Next I read two passages from *The Little Prince,* then becoming popular in Moscow. My audience, whether they knew the language or not, liked the sound of the original French, and it was with pleasure that I read Saint-Exupéry's delightful rhythmic language. Cherkassov asked me to repeat the word *apprivoiser* over and over. I explained that it was French for "to tame."

"What a beautiful word," he said with admiration. "Much nicer than our *priruchat.*"

"With your nasal voice, Kolya," Roman said to Cherkassov, "you should have studied French instead of becoming an actor. You could have read Paul Éluard's poetry and courted pretty Parisiennes."

Someone told the story of a banquet put on sometime earlier for a French theater group. The head director of a Moscow theater was in his cups and, to show how highly he thought of one of the French actresses, approached her from behind and smacked her on the derrière with all the force of his large palm. Her deafening squeal needed no translation. The other guests had looked on in shocked silence, fearing the worst. But scandal was avoided: seeing the famous director still grinning good-naturedly, the actress herself broke into a smile. Everyone heaved a sigh of relief.

The next day Helmut phoned; announcing that he would call for me at six in the evening, he hung up before I could say a word. I would soon learn that this military-style brevity was his normal way of speaking. A colonel in the East German army, he was in Moscow to do graduate studies at a military academy.

My face burned—just a few hours, and we would be together. I took a shower, as much to compose myself as to wash. What a relief to feel the water beating against my shoulders, streaming down my back, face, and breasts. I stepped back out of the shower, took a few hard, deep breaths, and furiously rubbed my skin red.

My entire modest wardrobe—several dresses, two suits, a few blouses, scarves, and stockings—was lying on the bed. I liked the way the red dress looked, but it was too flashy for the occasion. The black suit with the white blouse? I didn't want to look like a hotel adminis-trator. . . . I settled on a gray suit and a green blouse.

There were only a few minutes to go, and my heart was racing. My hair, combed back into a bun as usual, was no problem. I wanted to highlight my eyes somehow, but among the pitiful remnants of my great-grandmother's youth—my collection of little jewel-encrusted boxes and bottles decorated with coats of arms—there was nothing that would do. The boxes and bottles held only rice powder, settled from the passage of years, and equally ancient perfume, emitting a heady smell akin to that of old vinegar.

I sprinkled some of it on anyway and sped to the elevator, pulling on a coat. Helmut, his arms outstretched, was waiting when I emerged from the dormitory.

A surprise awaited us: we ran into my father in the lobby of the Bol-shoi. He shook hands with Helmut, greeting him courteously, but nodded dryly to me. Before I could gather my wits, he took his companion by the arm and headed toward the government loge, bodyguards trailing behind at a respectful distance.

Our seats were at the same level as my father's loge, and despite the low lights I managed to identify the woman sitting to his right—Minister of Culture Katya Furtseva.

During Boris Godunov's aria, my gaze returned to Helmut's face again and again. He was so different from anyone else I knew that he seemed like a visitor from outer space. Part of it was his distinctive accent and heartfelt smile, but there was much more. I had noticed a special spiral of spirit the previous evening. It was the outlook of those who live for today. Like the military pilot he was, he acted as though his life on Earth were a fleeting passage. He took nothing too seriously, finding joy in the instant, wherever he could, making no attachments and treasuring nothing long-term. He seemed so unreal that to make sure he really was with me, I touched his hand. In response, he clasped mine again, gently but firmly, and held it until the intermission.

How I dreaded the prospect of the boys bleeding to death in the second half, in the dream of the czar's assassin. Everything started to swim in front of my eyes—the rows of chairs, the chandelier above us, the elaborate stage set. . . .

Helmut glanced at me. "Let's go to my place," he said. My answer would have been the same if he had suggested a trip to the North Pole.

Visiting my father's loge to kiss him good-bye, I caught a familiar whiff of cognac. "I'll call you later on tonight," he said. "There's something we have to talk about."

His hint was more than transparent. I cheerfully ignored it.

I didn't return to the dormitory until three days later. Did we sense, even then, how short-lived our love might be? We drank it down in gulps, as though we feared that this crazy happiness might disappear into the void at any moment or remain only as a sweet pain near the heart. From that moment on, I dedicated myself to dismantling my life and reshaping it to fit new feelings, new desires. I cast down the gauntlet to my relatives, the authorities, and life itself.

THE WORLD I LEFT BEHIND

The author in 1965, the year she was in love. "Did we sense, even then, how short-
lived our love might be? We drank it down in gulps,
as though we feared that this crazy happiness might disappear
into the void at any moment. . . ."

Not surprisingly, my whirlwind romance, with a German colonel no
less, enraged my father. He knew with an unshakable certainty that we
would never be allowed to marry. I, on the other hand, had high hopes.
Did not love conquer all?

My uncle had not yet learned about my adventures. My father rarely
confided intimate family affairs to his brother, partly out of discretion,
partly out of concern for Leonid's health (my uncle had suffered a heart
attack in 1957). When Leonid asked about his nieces, my father's standard answer was "They're all fine, busy studying."

What he didn't mention was that I wasn't progressing as well with
my studies as my half sisters were with theirs. Love now consumed all
my time, thoughts, and feelings.

The Institute of Foreign Languages was across town from the
Moscow State dormitory where I lived, and getting up early for the long

commute required a supreme effort. My father knew about all my failures, my missed classes, and my refusals to take part in volunteer activities, since the dean called him regularly with progress reports—I should say lack-of-progress reports. From time to time, when his patience with my "improper behavior" ran thin, my father would call my mother in Dnepropetrovsk, who got so worried that she sometimes even came by plane to Moscow for Little Family Talks. She had already gone through one major disappointment, when I withdrew from medical school.

Like many young people, I found their lectures deadly boring, but I loved my parents enough to hear them out and promise to reform. They had a simple plan for my life: diploma, marriage, children.

"Dear little daughter," they told me over and over again, "you can't go on living this way."

But I could and did, though not without difficulty.

Going to see Helmut in the dormitory for foreign graduate students was a major undertaking. Every time, I had to surrender my passport or student ID at the entrance and obtain a pass. In addition, despite our attempts to win the cooperation of the head maid, she reported everything—the time of my arrival, the names of any people who arrived with me, and the length of my stay—to my father as well as to the KGB. Still she accepted our flowers and other gifts graciously.

If we had just been two young lovers on a fling, the KGB might have seen nothing wrong with our meetings. After all, the days of expelling someone to Siberia for an affair with a foreigner were long gone. But the situation was worse. We were serious about each other. And for the party chief's niece to marry a foreigner, let alone a German colonel, was beyond imagining.

Of course, during those first months, we couldn't have cared less who was spying on us. It was enough to love and be loved in return. Like two little ostriches, Helmut and I buried our heads in the sand, assuming that the outside world was equally uninterested in us.

The building I lived in was divided into two-room blocks; during my student years, I was moved from block to block, but every single time I was given a room next to the *dezhurnaya*, the combination head maid and paid informer. Her duties included everything from summoning the authorities to distributing clean linen and taking in the students' dirty linen. How symbolic. Without leaving her room, she knew everything about everyone; on each floor, there was an informer who kept her up to date.

Besides going to see Helmut at his place, I took him to my room. The *dezhurnaya*, of course, knew about his every visit. As soon as he walked in, she would leap across the corridor to join us, demonstrating a youthful lightness of foot that no one would have thought possible. Every time Helmut came back from Berlin, he would bring her a suit-case full of gifts. Like her counterpart in the foreigners' dormitory, she took our would-be bribes, but they did no good.

I began to feel surrounded by an alien world, where strangers peered around corners and through keyholes, whispering and reporting, in Gogol's words, a "collection of such hideous monsters that even now I can't bear to remember."

Surveillance, dirty tricks, and poison-pen letters were rampant at Moscow State. I would like to get my hands on the reports filed about me by informers during my first years in the capital. They would certainly tell a fascinating if twisted tale, about our lives and about Soviet mores. And with those reports, how much easier it would have been to reconstruct the events, the names, and the dates for this record.

Not only did every floor of the dorms have its resident informer, but every class had a student informer, and every academic department had an instructor with the same duties. Denunciation was one of the most productive industries, as well as one of the most painful of the Soviet Union's festering sores. Yet the institution of the organized snitch had begun in Russia with the rule of Peter the Great, when there was even a chief informer for the whole country, and has persisted regardless of the political system. In my days in Moscow, people knew pretty well who the informers were. The attitude toward them was one of resignation: "We all do what we have to do to get by."

Students who followed their own lights, rejecting the status quo, were persecuted as dissidents and subversive elements. The word of the *dezhurnaya* was enough to have you dragged through the mud at Komsomol meetings. Typical accusations were bringing a girl from the "outside" to visit; allowing an expelled student to continue living on the premises; failing to keep your room clean; neglecting shared duties, such as answering the telephone on your floor. Many young students were expelled for these offenses, a special tragedy for those from the provinces. Accustomed as they had become to life in Moscow, they did whatever was necessary to keep from going home, to keep from returning to a way of life that now was alien. Working as a night watchman, a janitor, or a loader was one solution; another, a marriage of convenience to a Muscovite. Some expelled students drowned themselves in the bottle and were heard of no more.

I was at least certain that if I were expelled, my father would help out, if necessary, with money and a place to stay. Calling me by his pet name for me, he often said, "Murzilka, if you need money, just tell me." But usually I preferred to borrow from others—one reason being that in those days, he didn't have much extra money, though he enjoyed plenty of perks. Leonid, incidentally, never gave his brother or his nieces money: he felt that the privileges we enjoyed because of his position were a sufficient gift.

Helmut's dormitory allowed visitors to remain until 9:00 P.M., but they were supposed to get special permission and a temporary pass, red tape no one wanted to bother with. The operative detachment was particularly adept at sniffing out the women brought home by male students. Caught in the act, a Don Juan might get a punch in the face or perhaps just a slap on the wrist—that is, confiscation of his student ID, which he could get back by going to the dean with a letter explaining his behavior in detail. His girlfriend would fare worse. The operatives were likely to take her to their headquarters and threaten to expose her—to her parents, to the institute where she was enrolled, to her Komsomol organization. The price of their silence was her submission.

They changed tactics when they met resistance: gallantly offering to accompany the young woman to the nearest subway station, they would rape her in a park. They might come back to headquarters with a few scratches on their faces, but, they reflected philosophically, every occupation has its hazards.

One such victim whom I knew personally was the daughter of a famous general. "I was willing to do whatever those punks wanted, anything to keep my father from finding out," she told me. "They knew, too, and felt completely free. They took turns." She had to be taken to the hospital after slashing her wrists.

Under Soviet law, the punishment for rape was from seven to twelve years of prison. But the operatives' powerful protectors in the KGB succeeded in hushing up this affair. They threatened the family with publicity, causing even the young woman's powerful father to back off. He wanted the operatives prosecuted but in closed proceedings.

My father learned of this woman's story and was both outraged and afraid for me. He would call several times a day, asking me to keep from getting involved in anything and not to open my door to anyone.

My uncle also knew of the case, from my father's stories. His reaction was "We should shoot people on the spot for those kinds of high jinks." But his words went no farther than the dacha porch where they were uttered. The high jinks continued.

Helmut and I often had to meet outdoors, and the winter of 1964–65, my first in Moscow, was especially cold. Like others who could afford it, we went to cafés and restaurants, to the theater and the movies. We also warmed our bones by the radiators in the entrance halls of apartment buildings; in Russia, at that time anyway, you didn't need a front-door key to walk in off the street. Sometimes we wandered into a museum. Late in the evening, with everything closed, we might cram ourselves into an empty phone booth.

Helmut wore a long leather military coat, the same kind that my father had worn while courting my mother, and he nearly froze in it, unaccustomed as he was to the Russian winter. "Now I understand why the Germans lost the war," he joked through chattering teeth. "I wouldn't be able to take a single step in cold like this, no matter who gave the order."

Most often we ended up seeking refuge in the apartment of a friend. In Moscow—in some ways the most informal of cities—you could drop in on friends after midnight with no prior warning and count on a warm welcome for yourself and a companion. Volumes could be written about the kitchens of the Moscow intelligentsia. Here, over a modest offering of food and potent coffee, the problems of the world were heatedly discussed and resolved: Who sold out Russia to the Bolsheviks? What if Trotsky had come to power instead of Stalin? Was the husband of the poet Marina Tsvetayeva working for the secret police? Why did she hang herself? Is it true that Brezhnev's wife is Jewish?

Of Russian kitchens, the poet Yosif Utkin wrote,

> *Tongues in the kitchen,*
> *Wagging with great flair.*
> *No rumor too wild,*
> *All topics welcome there.*

Helmut kept out of our political discussions, except for one time when we were talking about Khrushchev. Then he commented, "We East Germans live in constant fear of the Communist police apparatus, and we are given the impression that only East Germany is to blame for World War II. I remember that your Nikita Khrushchev once said, 'East Germany is a corn on the toes of the West that we can step on whenever we feel like it.' "

We were also welcome at homes where politics was an unclean woman, corrupt beyond redemption and not to be mentioned. Instead, the burning issues were the symbolism of color in the work of the philosopher Pavel Florensky, the occult philosophy of René Guenon, the theosophical teachings of Helena Blavatsky, Dostoyevsky's failed attempt to create the ideal image of the Slav. How we Russians love to talk! The arguments went on till everyone was hoarse and first red, then blue, in the face. Never again, we each would think as we hurried off to work nursing headaches. But the next evening would find us back in the kitchen. Words, words, words . . . they are a Russian addiction—and that is a dangerous confession for the author of a book.

We could always spend the night in a friend's home. When most of the guests were leaving, we would take two blankets, two pillows, and improvise a bed from some antediluvian sofa.

Unlike me, Helmut was always on time. Even after a night of drinking and conversations held in clouds of cigarette smoke, he would leap out of bed the next morning; at nine o'clock sharp, he would be in the library or classroom, fresh and full of energy.

Sometimes he would instruct our hosts to wake me and pack me off to the institute. But if the hosts turned out to be, like me, able to sleep through anything, Helmut might well find me in the kitchen of the same apartment the next evening.

My father's opinion of such carryings-on was what you might expect, especially after I told him flat out to stop calling my friends in search of his wayward daughter. Sometimes I was out of touch for several days at a stretch.

The authorities' first overt interference in our relationship came with the searches of my room. These began sometime in February 1965. They were carried out by the university's operative detachment, presumably under orders from the KGB.

Such searches might be better described as raids, resulting as they did in disappearances—of official documents, letters from my father, family memorabilia, French books. I had inherited a ring from Akindin, my Cossack great-grandfather. Fashioned by a master craftsman, it had been given to him for "impeccable service to czar and fatherland." The outside was sprinkled asymmetrically with rubies and diamonds, and the inside bore an inscription: "Honorable is the ring on the Cossack hand." Dishonorable hands stole it from my room.

According to family stories, while the Bolsheviks were robbing Akindin's home in the 1920s, his wife—my great-grandmother Tatyana—squeezed the ring in the palm of her hand so hard that the drops of blood she drew left a stain that remained visible on her ring for a long time afterward. Before the theft, I used to love to play with this ring in the evening, lying on my bed and missing my parents. I could almost feel the warmth of Tatyana's hand and would kiss the ring, stone by stone.

What hurt most was the disappearance of a simple black-and-white photograph. From the war years, it showed my parents swirling in a waltz. My mother had given it to me for my eighteenth birthday, and I had written on the back "Last forever, O moment, for you are beautiful!"

After one raid, I went to the headquarters of the operative detachment to declare officially that some articles of value had disappeared from my room. At the same time, I demanded to know the justification for the continuing searches. The head of the detachment, an ex-convict from the Usachovka district of Moscow, well known for its criminals, had a simple response. He pulled out a bundle of photographs and tossed them onto his desk: a sampling of beautiful young women, both with and without clothing, in poses ranging from suggestive to pornographic.

"Some were uncooperative, but we brought them around," he said, lighting up a cigarette and blowing the smoke in my face. "We have a method that always works. Wanna see?"

"You bastard," I burst out. "What are you hinting at? You should be put on trial, and I'll make sure you are!"

"As if you had that kind of power," he answered, staring into my eyes with calm arrogance. "Right now they're interested in you. If my turn comes, it'll be a different story."

"What do you want?"

"I'm telling you to stop running around with that Kraut boyfriend of yours. If you don't, we'll kick you out of Moscow."

Sometimes we hear the truth first from the mouths of babes, and sometimes from the scum of the earth.

"But that's not because we personally want it that way," the chief continued. "We don't care who screws who. We just follow orders. And up there"—he pointed significantly upward—"they say so." For some reason, I followed his finger with my eyes. An enormous ink spot stood out clearly right above us. Someone in my position before had lost her composure. Why, I thought, did she hurl the inkpot at the ceiling and not in the face of one of these creeps?

So now I knew—or thought I knew—the reason for the observations, the snitching, and the searches: they wanted me to stop seeing Helmut. But I still couldn't see what real purpose was achieved by raiding my room. What good to them were my photographs and letters? Or the history textbook from France? True, there was a little bit about the Soviet Union in it, but not much. Seeing nothing subversive about the book, I had kept it on my shelf and read it openly whenever I felt like doing so.

Sometime later that year they confiscated a work that must have aroused greater interest—Solzhenitsyn's *The First Circle*. I was barely halfway through it; it had just appeared in manuscript form and was passing from hand to hand among students. I was sure that I had been set up, that the same person who gave me the novel had turned around and informed to the operative detachment. But I will never have a clear picture of the behind-the-scenes maneuvering of those "friends" who drank tea with you one minute only to run to the authorities the next. My situation was complicated by the fact that they had found *two* copies of the book in my room. My crime was thus not mere possession of banned literature but its propagation as well, which could bring six years in prison.

During those years, we read forbidden authors in the underground editions known as samizdat. The works of Nikolay Gumilev, Akhmatova, Tsvetayeva, Pasternak, Mandelstam, and Solzhenitsyn were treasured and read until they were dog-eared and falling apart. Sometimes they were given to you only for a day or for several hours.

"I hear you're reading all kinds of trash now!" my father snapped at me, rushing to the dormitory after learning that I was "harboring subversive literature" in my room.

"What should I read then? The party charter?"

"Read the classics."

"Solzhenitsyn *is* a classic."

My father spat on the floor in disgust. Then, seeing how adamant I was, he changed tactics and tried to appeal to my instinct for self-preservation.

"You little fool, . . . don't you realize that the KGB doesn't care who your uncle is? You don't even have the same last name as Leonid. They'll take full advantage of that. What if they throw you in jail?"

"Don't worry; they won't dare do that." I was trying to convince myself more than him.

Years later, in the early '70s, I asked my uncle Leonid whether he had ever read anything by Solzhenitsyn. Highly offended, he answered with pride that he never read anti-Soviet trash.

"But even Lenin read all the bourgeois literature. He said that we must know the enemy's face."

"I receive reports, I know all about his writings," he answered.

I found his attitude dismaying. During one of our meetings, which I referred to as the "talks of Saint Serafim of Sarov" (a favorite author of mine), I asked him why I had to defend the right to read, why reading sounded like such a subversive idea to him.

"Because," he said, "if everyone starts doing what they feel like, there won't be any order in our country."

For Leonid Brezhnev and his colleagues, the ideal country was one in which everyone marched in step, where discipline and order reigned supreme.

The fall of 1965 brought me another privilege: invitations to the KGB headquarters, at the Lubyanka, for little talks. At the beginning, the men with whom I spoke merely chastised me mildly, still hoping that I could be re-educated. Noting that my parents were "decent people," they sighed. In every family, it seemed, there was at least one misfit. Was I so dense that I really couldn't understand my family's perfectly understandable opposition to a romance with a German colonel?

"What ingratitude! Your forefathers built and created unsparingly. Your uncle never leaves his office, sacrificing his health for the welfare of the country. Your father is an honored metallurgist, your stepfather is well regarded as an engineer, and the kindergarten run by your mother is the best in her city. You have all these examples to emulate, and look at you!" There were stares and glares. "Don't forget that you're a Soviet woman."

One time I couldn't stand it any more. "No, I'm a Russian born in Soviet Russia," I said.

Ignoring this, my interrogator added, "Not only that; you're the niece of the first secretary as well."

I jumped up. "Yes, when my behavior is disgracing his name, I'm Brezhnev's niece! To make me feel guilty, you remind me of something that has brought me nothing but problems and shame—the fact that my uncle is first secretary. But when the topic of my civil and legal rights comes up, suddenly I'm eliminated from the Brezhnev clan. Then you claim I'm unrelated to him, since my stepfather adopted me when I was fourteen and I have *his* last name." Sometimes they even went to the point of telling me not to refer to Yakov Ilyich as my father—was it to underscore that I had no one to run to?

The more they demanded that I abandon Helmut, the more stubborn I became. I once noted that in any case, Law 47 (banning marriage to foreigners) had been repealed. "It hasn't been repealed as far as you're concerned," my interrogator said, rolling up a file of papers.

Am I really all alone? I prayed that God would make me strong enough to defend my love.

My student years coincided with the birth of a new movement of "people who think differently." And I felt a spiritual kinship with these dissidents, a word that began to be used widely to describe those who strove to break down the rigid barriers of ideological control.

In late 1965, rumors began circulating in Moscow about the arrest of two writers, Andrey Sinyavsky and Yuli Daniel. I asked my father about them. He knew nothing about their case but promised to find out. Several days later I brought up their names again, and my father began to berate them both, his opinion clearly based on his brother's. After hearing him out, I asked him whether either he or Leonid had ever read anything by the controversial pair.

He gave me the stock answer: "We haven't read any of it, nor do we plan to."

I had read some of Sinyavsky's criticism; I liked his style and his original approach to contemporary literature. I couldn't see anything criminal in what he had written and didn't know then that he and Daniel had published work abroad.

There was an open trial, but the real trial went on behind closed doors. I asked my father to take me to the courtroom, but he wouldn't hear of it.

The press pounced on the two dissidents like a pack of jackals. They were labeled renegades, slanderers, and unbridled enemies. The hackneyed clichés from smear campaigns against Mikhail Zoshchenko, Akhmatova, and Pasternak were resurrected: "I haven't read it myself, but I know that . . ." "Popular anger" against the two critics, in the form of denunciations by workers and peasants, was quick to surface.

My onetime dancing partner, Mikhail Sholokhov—a drunken anti-Semite and burned-out novelist who spent his time uttering diatribes against his colleagues—joined the onslaught. He called for the "scoundrels" to be "shot without investigation or trial."

It was in the early winter that both were given long sentences. I was stunned. What for? For writing? For having talent?

My uncle reddened with anger when the names of the writers came up. He referred to them as "those hacks, those pitiful little writers." My father, who totally shared his brother's opinions and quarreled with me because of my support for the dissidents, could hardly have suspected that some years later he would find himself in a situation not too different from that of the men he found so contemptible.

Helmut gave me an engagement ring in January 1966, a little over a year after we met.

In December, he had flown home to visit his mother and buy clothing. He wanted to stock up on warm clothing—he knew all the charms of the Russian winter by then—and find some fashionable things for me to wear. His departure had been delayed, so I spent a few hours at the airport. Finally the plane left and I headed home, looking forward to a hot shower and a night's rest.

I was depressed. Helmut was going to be gone for two weeks, and things at the institute were going from bad to worse. My absenteeism had raised the possibility that I would not be allowed to take the winter final exams. And I was expecting Helmut's child. I didn't want to ask my father for help. I had thrown down the gauntlet to my family, hadn't I? Shouldn't I try to solve my messes on my own? Something in my character and in my upbringing made me seek my own way of doing everything. But what can a twenty-one-year-old do, faced with a world that seems to be conspiring against her?

Arriving at the dormitory, I discovered to my surprise that the door to my room was unlocked. Usually the woman on floor duty would lock my door after a search. The door swung wide, and I heard a male voice: "Come in, come in."

In the doorway loomed a man with a powerful build, the broken nose of an ex-boxer, and a scarf pulled around his bull neck.

I walked in and saw, on the bed, a second man, square faced and a bit shorter, in a raincoat and hat.

"So," said the man on the bed, "when will we be leaving?"

"Where to, if I may ask?" I noticed that I was caught between the two of them. I was terrified.

"Wherever you like. We'll send you off in twenty-four hours. You've had your little Moscow fling, but enough is enough. Your neighbors have been complaining that the noise from all your rowdy guests keeps them from sleeping and studying."

"That's not true, and you know it perfectly well."

"Just remember, little girl, that everything *we* say is true."

"You don't want to end up in a psych ward, do you now?" added the tall one, trying to sound concerned.

"No, I don't."

"So that's that. Get your things together, and we'll take you to the airport," he said, using the familiar form of address.

"You can address your mistresses as *ty*," I said of the familiar "you."

My fear had given way momentarily to indignation and contempt. What a pitiful excuse for a man. I felt myself beginning to tremble but made a supreme effort to stay still. I couldn't help raising my right eyebrow, as I always do when angry.

"Please don't forget your place," I said. "In my eyes, you're just a flunky."

As I said this last word, my trembling ceased. Calmly I looked into his well-fed face. I told him in an even voice how loathsome he was. Only impotents like him, I began to say, agree to go through women's personal belongings, since that's all they're good for.

I didn't have time to finish—with the rapidity of a cobra, he thrust his hand forward and struck at my left kidney. I was thrown backward, and the pain took my breath away. Everything swirled and grew dark, and I lost consciousness.

It was late night and pitch-black when I came to. From my first sensation, a salty taste on my lips, I realized that I had a bloody nose. Clinging to the wall, I turned on the light, and the sight of the floor, drenched in red and maroon, scared me more than anything I had ever before seen in my life. I had been bleeding heavily from the mouth, and would easily have choked on the blood had I not been lying facedown. I could tell that my visitors had kicked me at least once while I was unconscious. Later, vast continents of bruises would appear up and down my sides.

Morning came, and with it nausea. I dragged myself to the sink and looked up; in the mirror I saw blood and muck pouring from my nose. Black-and-blue marks surrounded my puffy eyes, from which streamed tears of anger and powerlessness. And I knew the worst: I had lost my child. . . .

For the first time in my life, I felt the desire to be big and strong; how I wanted, at that moment, to knock my attackers down and grind them into a pulp. My face swelled up even more from the tears. I felt small, unhappy, and abandoned. Above all else, I felt an unbearable self-pity, which drained every ounce of remaining energy. I sat down on the cold floor and began heaving with uncontrollable sobs.

I don't know the names of the two men who cornered me in my own dormitory room, nor do I know the name of the man who issued their orders, but I've never forgotten my attacker's face: his puffy, gray-blue eyes, his boxer's nose, the white silk scarf around his thick neck. I even remember the gold signet ring on the hand that he used to give me—and who knows how many other young women—an expert beating.

Two weeks later the swelling had disappeared, and I could once more attend classes, though I still had black eyes, which I concealed behind sunglasses. And my sides still ached. I was afraid to walk the streets in the evening, and at night I trembled at the slightest noise. Before entering my room, I would listen carefully to make sure no one was behind the door.

It was in this state that I welcomed Helmut back from Germany. I cried when I saw the ring, a plain but beautiful gold band. But would the marriage it promised ever be allowed?

After the attack, I swallowed my pride and went to my father. His outrage knew no bounds, and he put all his heart and soul into getting to the bottom of the incident. But none of his efforts bore fruit; when he was informed by the militia that petty hooligans had attacked me and that similar cases had been reported recently, he accepted this story. I, however, was convinced that my nocturnal visitors had been sent on someone's orders. They were professionals, not juvenile delinquents.

Helmut was frustrated by his inability to protect me, and for a long time he gritted his teeth, itching for a fight.

The opportunity came one night that winter. He dropped by to see me with two Iraqi officers, one of whom, Hussein, was a close friend of his. We were spending an enjoyable evening when, at eleven o'clock, a group of operatives barged into the room and told our friends to get out. The Iraqis, unaware of the way things were run in our country and feeling friendly after a couple of glasses of cognac, invited the operatives to join us at the table. They couldn't imagine that it was acceptable for strangers to invade your room and escort your guests out.

Helmut asked the intruders to leave, but they were persistent. When one announced that he was going to pull the chairs out from under our guests, Helmut began scuffling with them. With the Iraqis' help, he ejected the operatives, leaving them in the corridor.

We were never able to explain adequately to our guests what an operative detachment was: they returned to their homeland convinced that the operatives had been personal enemies of ours.

The following morning I woke up to the ringing of my telephone, followed by a familiar voice demanding an explanation. I brusquely told my father to leave me alone; I was still half asleep and had nothing to explain.

He said, "I'll be with you in a half hour."

He arrived as promised. Calmly I told him everything that had happened.

"You could have shown a bit more restraint."

I got angry and declared, for show, that I was going to leave that lousy dormitory. If I had done so, maybe I could have escaped the next attack.

A medical note was required of those who missed more than two or three classes, and admittedly I was often absent that year. I had been called to the dean's office several times; I was also reprimanded at public meetings.

After my beating, I could easily have obtained a note from the Kremlin hospital or from the university clinic. But something in me said no, and the result was an official announcement that I was being expelled from the institute.

I didn't yet know that the continuing pains in my side were a sign of serious kidney damage. Had I gone to any urologist, he or she would have given me a note without my pulling any strings—and then hospitalized me for observation.

In fact, I was too much of a coward to see a doctor, though I was having fevers, and when the pain came, I would turn pale and find myself bathed in sweat. Like all the Brezhnevs, I worried about my health, and I had nightmares of an official-sounding voice announcing "Your kidney has been dislocated and must be removed immediately."

After news of my impending expulsion got around, the dean tried to avoid me, and my former instructors lowered their eyes when they passed. I was alone.

When my father came back to Moscow—he had been inspecting metallurgical plants in the provinces—he went directly to the rector, who assured him that his daughter could re-enroll in the evening section or be reinstated in the fall. But after that conversation, I learned that only native Muscovites and people already employed in the field they were majoring in were allowed to take evening classes.

With pains persisting in my left side, browbeaten and exhausted, I had lost all interest in my studies anyway. When I went to see my mother for the winter vacation, she was so dismayed by my haggard appearance that she immediately attempted to reach my uncle by phone. Dissatisfied with the answers given her, she went to Moscow in the spring to see him in person and ask for assistance. I learned about this trip only much later and would have been against her going to such trouble for me. And her efforts brought no results in any case. To her shock and dismay, Leonid, after hearing her out and offering the usual coffee and fruit, said, "Lenochka, it's all her own fault. She was doing poorly in school, got involved with a German, and reads forbidden literature. It's not so bad. She'll be able to go back to her studies in the fall."

In February 1966 came a second attack, a repetition of the beating I had suffered two months earlier.

After the pair—faces new but personalities the same—left me unconscious on the floor, the telephone woke me.

My father's voice was agitated: "Stay where you are. I'll be right over."

Battling an excruciating headache, I got up, washed, smeared my face with liquid makeup, and put on dark glasses. I examined myself in the mirror. I had done the best I could, but swelling was still visible on my face. Would my father notice? I didn't want to tell him anything this time. What good had it done me in December? He might say I could solve everything simply: *just tell your German to get lost!* Though my father loved me boundlessly, it was only years later that he really understood how much I loved Helmut.

He arrived half an hour later. As usual, he brought food; this time it was a big box of pastries.

"Why so many?" I asked. "I can't eat them all, and I don't have a refrigerator."

"Just give the extra ones to your neighbors. Students are always hungry."

I noted with relief that he hadn't seen any of the marks on my face.

He must be excited about something, I thought. Catching his breath and wiping his brow with his handkerchief in a typical gesture, he sat down on my only chair. To my surprise, he began to cry.

I got the full story only after he regained his composure. But between tears, he let me know that my half sister's husband had just beat her up.

Mila had married a student at the Institute of International Relations. I had once hinted cautiously that he had a bad reputation; it was said that he led a dissolute life and was fond of drink. My father, who approved of the marriage and even held it up as a model to me, had brushed aside my comments at the time but now was forced to agree.

At the same time that my uninvited guests were with me, Mila's future diplomat came home drunk and demanded beer. Hearing that there was none in the house, he called his wife a country bumpkin, adding that if she hadn't been Brezhnev's niece, he would never have sat next to her in a toilet stall, let alone married her. Mila insulted him in return, and he hit her in the face with a bottle, knocking her unconscious. When she came to and crawled to the telephone, planning to call an ambulance, her husband struck her a second time.

Her nose was shattered, and she was operated on that night.

Listening intently to my father, I couldn't help wondering, Was this coincidence or divine will?

The only difference between us was that she had been taken to the Kremlin hospital while I was afraid even to go to the university clinic. What would I have told the doctor? That I was just beat up by the KGB, a second time? After all, how could those charged with protecting our country commit such a heinous crime? If I had insisted, would I have been diagnosed as having delusions of persecution? Psychiatric treatment was what I feared above all else.

I endured while the operative detachment kept trying new ways to wear down my patience. One night when I came home, I found that the contents of my suitcases and my cupboards had been thrown onto the floor. My sugar and instant coffee had been dumped out and mixed together thoroughly; my sheets were tied in a knot; my bras and panties were methodically scattered around the bed.

You have to hand it to them: my adversaries were professionals who knew their craft well, whether it was beating kidneys or wearing down nerves. They had calculated correctly. The latest escalation left me feeling totally violated.

Once, at the brink of desperation, I flew into the office of the operative detachment, in the main building of the university. Furious, white, and trembling, I asked between clenched jaws, "How much longer?"

They were obviously pleased. Now they knew just what to do. In a vicious cycle, their harassment had fueled a protest, and this in turn brought on further harassment. The new formula of sugar, coffee, bras, panties, and sheets was used again and again. In retrospect, I can see that my hot temper only made me more vulnerable: righteous indignation, desperation, and hysteria played into their hands.

Once my father called me and said that in fifteen minutes a car would be waiting for me by the central dormitory entrance and that we were going to be received by Leonid Ilyich. The word *received* was a surprise to me. We always referred to our visits to his party offices as simply "going to see Uncle Lyonya."

A few days before this phone call my room had been raided, and this time I had come home to find on my bed shredded photographs of Helmut—a new twist, which cut my heart like a knife. But what good is my hotheadedness? I asked myself. Why do I try to argue with them? They just come back more viciously every time. I had sat long into the night with the heap of trash, fighting back an urge to build a bonfire.

Now I wondered whether there was any connection between the latest raid and the invitation to a "reception." Not likely, I thought.

Knowing my personality and how exhausted I was, I was afraid I would probably start an argument with my uncle. I simply didn't want to go, and since for me the first secretary was no monarch, let alone a moral authority, I was tempted to decline the invitation. But when my father added curtly, "Leonid wants to have a chat with you," a hope suddenly welled up in my breast. Maybe, just maybe, my uncle will be so impressed by our love that he'll let me and Helmut leave the country. He knows what love is, I thought; hadn't he loved Tamara once?

The building that housed the Central Committee of the Communist

Party was impeccably clean. To create a comfortable, cheery atmosphere for the officials who worked there, a small army of janitors scrubbed it thoroughly every night. The yellow hardwood floor, covered with walkways of pink-and-green carpet, was a pleasure to the eyes. As usual, a young male secretary sat in the large reception hall. My uncle occupied suite six.

I murmured to my father that it should be called ward number six, after Chekhov's story about an insane asylum.

"That joke had better stay between the two of us," my father cautioned, glancing at me significantly.

There was nothing extraneous in the office: only a long conference table at which the first secretary presided regally, a small table behind the big one, and a portrait of Lenin on the wall.

"Hello there," my uncle said, kissing me and pressing me heartily to his broad chest, as was his habit. He was still fairly young then, with showy good looks. His most attractive features were his deep-blue eyes, his agility, and his broad smile. His hearty manner, which many fell for, no longer impressed me, not consciously, at least. But he was still my uncle: I loved him and even then felt sorry for him. And no matter how angry I might be, when we were together, I couldn't help being swayed by his charm. In fact, though my problems over the years would lead to more than one of his lectures, I never felt anger toward him personally. I found him an outgoing, optimistic man. He loved to gesticulate and was a born performer with a gift for imitations.

His easy laugh was one of his most appealing characteristics. Sometimes after hearing his pronouncements, I'd say with great solemnity: "I thank you for this talk. It has been an incredibly important and interesting experience for me." He would burst into such hearty laughter that I had to laugh, too. But I hadn't come to the Kremlin that day for the pleasure of my uncle's company.

"You keep getting prettier and prettier," he said, looking at me. "Look, Yasha, how much she resembles our late father."

I sat in the armchair. My father, seated opposite, timidly glanced at me and Leonid in turn. What next?

"How have you been doing?" asked my uncle in a fairly friendly tone.

I was wondering how much he knew. He looked at me questioningly. I remained silent, staring him straight in the eyes.

"What's the matter?" he asked. "Are you ill?" I was still silent.

"What's wrong? You were asked a question. Didn't you hear?" my father interjected.

I exploded. No, I hadn't planned to give my uncle any details about what had been done to me—only to ask him to show generosity of spirit and give me special permission to emigrate with Helmut. But the memories were too fresh: of Helmut's pictures torn on my bed, of the two attacks. I began to tell my uncle, in a confused and meandering fashion, about the operatives and KGB thugs who had pawed through his niece's bed and pried into her soul. I didn't mention that I had been beat up. Again I was afraid of being called crazy. . . .

I paused: what would the man in charge of millions of Soviet Communists do to defend me from the KGB and the militia, presumably subordinate to him?

"Would you be capable," I asked him, "of picking someone's pocket or breaking into someone's apartment?"

My uncle's eyes bulged. The surprise he had registered during my tirade seemed genuine.

"Yasha, is it true what she's saying?"

"I've never been there during a search," my father said, lowering his eyes.

"So you think I'm lying," I jumped on him.

"I believe you, my dear, but I really wasn't there."

"A lot of help you are," I shot back.

While we were talking, a meal was served, along with cognac in a small carafe. I was too upset to think about food and said I didn't want anything. I couldn't refuse, however, when my uncle started feeding me morsels from his plate.

The brothers began to talk about their children. My thoughts were elsewhere. I had already begun to suspect the worst. I had no real protection, no understanding. Could my own uncle be behind the harassment? My father? When such thoughts came to me, as I must confess they occasionally did, I chased them from my mind in order to maintain my sanity, which I would have lost if I had learned of their involvement. Yes, they were against my plans to marry Helmut; I could even understand that. But they were both decent, caring men, and they could never condone cruelty or attacks against me.

Then I thought, What does it matter *who* is behind all this? I could see now that if it came down to it, those closest to me, including my father and my uncle, wouldn't save me. As I watched the two brothers as they conversed in measured tones about the problems of Leonid's daughter, Galina—she was leading a free life, coming home late at night or not at all—my blood ran cold. What about me, a young woman whose only crime was wanting the happiness that all human beings strive for?

I prayed for the visit to end. Why had I even been invited?

Unexpectedly my uncle turned to me and began lecturing. "You people hide behind our backs and decide you don't like the way things are run," he said. "You don't have the intelligence or the strength of character to look at yourselves objectively. You're used to having other people do your thinking while you live for your feelings." My father was looking on approvingly. "You put your own interests first, and then, when society puts the slightest constraints on you, you become dissidents. You change boyfriends and husbands; you stop loving your motherland; you disrespect your parents. . . ."

He went on to cite examples of women he had known during the war, women who for him "epitomized the Soviet woman."

Only Communists and fascists made women bear arms, I retorted, and it's nothing to be proud of. To me, it was a disgrace.

At the word *fascist*, my uncle was reminded of Helmut. "You had to go and fall in love with a blond Kraut when there's no shortage of fine Russian boys. For all we know, it was his father who killed your grandfather at the front."

"For your information, Helmut has dark hair and dark-blue eyes."

Leonid Ilyich grunted.

Before I left, he told me, "I'll order that you not be bothered."
But the KGB would continue to bother me—to put it mildly.

An evening at the end of spring . . . Helmut, radiant, threw my door wide open and stood on the threshold. Using his pet name for me, he said, "Sonya, my dissertation was accepted!"

Tears of joy and apprehension came to my eyes.

"Aren't you happy for me?" he said.

"Oh, what does your dissertation matter?"

He took no offense, for he understood. He approached and embraced me.

The next day Helmut came to call, less sunny this time, and admitted that he had been called to the special section of the Defense Ministry for a talk. I sensed that whatever had happened involved me, but we continued to meet.

On June 22, 1966, the twenty-fifth anniversary of the German invasion of Russia, Helmut phoned to say that we should meet at noon. He asked me to wear his favorite dress, one he had given me. I did, though it seemed almost indecent to wear a long evening gown, made of crimped brown chiffon, in broad daylight.

It was a sad and subdued Helmut whom I found waiting on the campus, sitting opposite a long row of busts portraying some of the great scientists of history. His bench was across from that of Mendeleyev.

"We need to talk," he said as I sat down and before planting his customary kiss on my eyes.

After a few feeble attempts at small talk, he came to the point. He had invested too much time and energy in the army to leave it. During his most recent talk at the special section, he had been presented with an ultimatum: leave Brezhnev's niece alone, or leave the military.

I motioned for him to stop. The sun and the sky and every green, living thing went dark, and I felt a sudden chill, as though the cold caress of death were weighing heavy on my skin. Covering my face with my hands, I somehow found the strength to whisper a favorite prayer, "Lord have mercy. . . ."

In a short time, it was as if the sunshine had returned; the sky had regained its bright blue. The chiming of children's voices resumed, but something was lost forever.

I went back to my room, a sad and silly figure in my gown. Later that evening, set apart from the world by four smooth, white walls, I found myself locked in a quiet struggle between hope and desperate longing. Sweat streamed down my face, leaving bitter salt on my lips. I could see the reflection of a streetlamp in the murky contents of the tumbler standing before me. When I touched the cool glass, my hand quivered.

Beyond the window, there was life, full of noise and churning passions. The silver feather grass was still shimmering on the steppes of my childhood. All over the world new ideas and new children were being born. Somewhere a solitary lark was gliding through the midsummer sky.

The insistent ringing of the telephone wrenched my thoughts back to a world that would soon be without Helmut.

In the spring, I sometimes still see him, running through the trickles of snow water in his shiny-clean boots, his arms flung apart to embrace me. And so handsome! And I remember the smell of melted snow, the bare earth, free of its frozen mantle, the faint aroma of cologne on his freshly shaved cheeks. What joy we had during our final spring together! But why do I think of a time that will never return?

Why, in spite of all obstacles, do we seek the intoxication of love? Love, helpless and all powerful. Love, filled with beauty and ugliness, strength and weakness, lies and truth. Love, the immortal. Why do we continue to strive against all odds for happiness? Is it that we hope to overcome the ultimate indifference of fate? With gratitude for all these wonders, O love, I embrace thy holy name.

Memories of Helmut would bring back that ache that comes when reading old love letters. But life moves on. I was reinstated at the institute in the fall, and the study of language restored order in my world.

Half a year after Helmut's departure, mutual friends in East Germany sent me a clipping from a local newspaper. There was Helmut's portrait alongside a long article calling him the "youngest, most talented, and most handsome German general." Doubtless this was true. I was happy for him.

I still have the engagement ring Helmut gave me. It bears a nick that has a story behind it. . . .

One day about a year after Helmut's departure, my faithful friend Veta and I found that we had no money left from our stipends. We spent hours trying to figure out how in the world we could earn or borrow some money to get by on. Nothing promising came to mind, so in the end we decided to put something in pawn until stipend time.

As usual, the pawnshop we went to was packed with matrons of indeterminate age, puffy-faced drunks, and elderly women in vintage hats. With the impatience of youth, we left and went to a store that bought used silver and gold jewelry. The buyers often paid a pittance for museum-quality pieces they knew would fetch a fancy price from collectors.

A mild-looking old man sat at the counter, his glasses perched sedately on the tip on his nose. His small gray eyes lit up with cunning when he saw us: aha, two young students, this should be good! But his interest waned when he learned that I had nothing but the modest ring on my finger. When I took it off and showed it to him, he said that since it was foreign, he would have to test it for gold content.

"Go ahead," I said.

Watching as he grabbed a file, which seemed to me enormous, and scratched "the merchandise," I felt as though he was dragging sharp little teeth over my heart. I snatched my ring from his hand and stalked out of the shop without another word. I was ready to break into tears.

"You're crazy, Luba." Veta ran after me. "We have nothing to eat!"

"Don't you understand, Veta? This is all I have left of him."

One evening after class during my last year at the institute, I went downtown and walked around, gazing at the shop windows, which were becoming more and more colorful from year to year. With my back to the street, I watched the reflections of the passersby.

All of a sudden, my heart seemed to be beating out of control. A

The author in 1966, after her lover left Moscow. "I remembered his voice, his smile,
his profile, the special warmth of his eyes,
which even at moments of happiness held a trace of sadness,
and I struggled to keep the tears from coming."

painfully familiar silhouette, head lowered in Helmut's usual way, was
floating by. Could it . . . be? It was his height, his build, his walk. I
rushed after him, oblivious to everything.

"Helmut!" I cried out.

When the man turned, the brown eyes of a stranger looked at me
inquiringly. Stunned, I stood with a foolish, frozen smile on my face as
the crowd streamed around us.

Helmut's face, which had become distant and hazy in my memory,
suddenly came to life. Standing there, infinitely alone amid the clamor

of the busy streets, I remembered his voice, his smile, his profile, the special warmth of his eyes, which even at moments of happiness held a trace of sadness, and I struggled to keep the tears from coming.

I kept walking, turning down the poorly lit side streets, trying to escape my own thoughts. I finally emerged onto a small square I had never seen before. A fine, cold rain was pouring down, and water was churning angrily in the gutters. It seemed to me again, as it had a few years before, that all life had vanished from the face of the earth. And I was alone with the furious, wet wind, lost in a dark place beyond time and memory.

Numb from the cold, I leaned on a lamppost, staring long and hard at the yellow disk of light above. Memories came rushing back. I remembered evenings when we would sit opposite each other, drinking tea or studying. I would be working on grammar exercises, he on his dissertation. The little dormitory room on the seventh floor of zone E was warm and cozy. Those were nights when nothing but human happiness existed in the world, nights when it seemed that even the KGB would leave us in peace.

I've never forgotten the pool of light on the white tablecloth where our fingers would meet in bursts of emotion, that place of happiness that we shared like brother and sister, that divine peace we felt.

I carry the memory of that pool of light as a talisman, as an unfulfilled dream, as the sole absolute truth I have known in this life. I guard it as a symbol of everything beautiful that life has to offer. I will take it with me when I leave this world.

Others have not even had that much. As my favorite Russian philosopher, Vladimir Rozanov, wrote, "Defend your love with your feet and your teeth! Defend it against reason, against power!"

Chapter Eleven

NO ONE TO TURN TO

*Yes, I see the unclean beasts roaming around and
sniffing at my feet. . . . But they will not devour me,
God will never allow such injustice. I answer their
repulsive snorts by crying out boldly;
I live, and my soul lives!*

N. SHCHEDRIN

My war with the authorities continued after Helmut's departure in June 1966.

In the fall, I received a letter from the chief militia officer in charge of Moscow State University, instructing me in no polite terms to come to his office. When I arrived, Zaitsev—for some reason, I still remember his name—didn't so much as say hello; I think he was uncomfortable dealing with those he perceived as his intellectual superiors. The lecture he gave ended with a demand that I leave Moscow; otherwise, I could be expelled from the city for violating the law requiring citizens to have their internal passports with them at all times.

I explained angrily that during raids of my room, I had been robbed eight times of my documents, including the all-important passport.

"No, you lost them through your own carelessness," Zaitsev countered.

I responded with silence. Why reason with someone laboring under a life sentence of dishonesty? Fortunately his threats turned out to be hollow.

Later that fall the phone rang, and a pleasant baritone invited me to a well-known address on Dzerzhinsky Square—the KGB headquarters at the Lubyanka.

The night before, some friends had gathered in my room. Among them were French and Danish students. Everyone praised the Soviet system and proposed toasts, both to the government and to Leonid Brezhnev personally. By this time, no one believed these ritual incantations. My guests were simply being prudent: there was always at least one informer accompanying any group of foreigners.

One Soviet student—the idiot—had asked the Dane sitting next to him, "Why don't you get rid of your kings?"

Before the nonplussed student could answer, I replied for him: "Because they don't want to live as poorly as we do."

When I arrived at the KGB office, I was scolded for "going too far." When I asked my inquisitors to be more specific, they said, "You talk too much."

"So I talk a lot in my own home. Who can tell me not to?"

The answer was simple: they could, and they did.

"Do you know what all of this anti-Soviet talk of yours reeks of?"

I had no idea, but the questioner appeared to detect an unbearable stench. His claim that I had made anti-Soviet statements was not entirely groundless. I had often spoken freely in fairly public circles and hardly made a secret of my dislike of the Soviet system.

One evening after that encounter I got home from studying in the library only to discover a stranger sprawled on my chair, the picture of young male arrogance. Spewing obscenities, he began to rail against me for the crime of having relatives in positions of power. His wild eyes told me that he was mentally unbalanced, and I feared that he might be moved to immediate heroics. I was right: he grabbed my neck with both hands, assuring me that in the not too distant future the Brezhnevs would all be hanging from the lampposts and that he would be happy to tighten the noose around my neck personally. Fortunately neighbors came home at that moment and slammed their door; the noise made my attacker shudder and release me, and he slipped out the open window (I was living on the first floor then). Judging by his eyes and trembling hands, I guessed that he was a drug addict, recruited by the KGB for one night. But I never found out for sure.

Sometimes a period of calm would set in, something like an unspoken truce. Periods like that were more frightening than the interrogations. What new tricks were being concocted?

During conversations with the KGB, my mind would wander. Who are these men, who are their parents? What do they do in their spare time? What are their thoughts, what kinds of dreams do they have? The appearance of most was strikingly uniform. They reminded me of pointers, their ears perked up and their noses to the wind. Constantly on the lookout for anything seditious, they were cautious yet capable of tearing you apart if ordered to do so.

I came to realize that I didn't have a single secret from them. They knew my character like a map and seemed even to know my thoughts. It was impossible to hide from their enormous full-time and part-time staff. Informers were not fully trusted, so there were those who informed on the informers—their wives, brothers, friends, and co-workers. An informer found to have lied or concealed information might disappear without a trace.

Most informers were amateurs who did their work unpaid, though not uncompensated. I got to know one who spied on me, a man who taught Russian to foreigners at the Pushkin Russian Language Institute. He worked for the KGB in exchange for perks, periodically meeting with his handler in a special apartment to hand over information he had gathered about colleagues and foreign students. In exchange for impeccable service, he was allowed to go abroad, with all the financial benefits that such trips entailed. He was typical of the informers from the intelligentsia: an outgoing, sincere-sounding fellow, the life of the party. Well read and charming in his own way, he knew two foreign langauges; an anti-Semite, he had no regrets about reporting the "misdeeds" of his Jewish colleagues.

In addition to my firsthand experience, I knew quite a bit about the techniques of the political police from reading Solzhenitsyn and listening to my parents' tales: in elite circles, much was known of the KGB, which was frequently the subject of informal conversations. My father used to tell me what he had learned about the fate of well-known people. In particular, I learned from him the truth about the academician Nikolay Vavilov: he was thrown to his death into a pit of lime in a prison yard. But my father's inconsistent attitude toward the KGB was frequently cause for frustration.

In 1969 or 1970, I heard that Pyotr Yakir had suffered an attack by the KGB similar to mine: thugs had beaten his kidneys, one of the surest ways of intimidating without killing outright. No external marks remain, and the victim can die slowly for years.

In June of 1972, Pyotr was arrested for "anti-Soviet activity." Soon thereafter I was visiting my father's home, where the top military brass of Moscow had assembled for a social gathering, and at one point the talk turned to this case. Someone said, "Stalin is accused of killing a lot of innocent people. But I say there's no smoke without fire. Take for example that Yakir fellow:* his son Pyotr turned out to be viciously anti-Soviet. Wasn't he just following the father's footsteps?" To my surprise, my father chimed in: "The people Stalin punished were probably up to something."

I was furious: "So then the NKVD had legitimate justification for pursuing your brother Leonid in 1937. And . . ." I went on and on in the same vein. Showing condescending smiles, everyone listened politely, without interrupting.

When I finished, the polar explorer Ivan Papanin remarked, "Yes, indeed, Yakov Ilyich, you do have your hands full with that one." He smiled indulgently. "Oh, well, I guess she's still wet behind the ears. She'll come round."

I got up and left. What would those imbeciles say, I thought, if Yuri Andropov's KGB heroes dragged one of them in to crack a few ribs—if they could find any under the layers of lard.

"If you don't know how to act in decent company," my father said the next day, "then stay home."

---

*The reference is to Pyotr Yakir's father, arrested in the '30s.

In fact, my understanding of power relations in the Soviet Union came gradually. There was not a single soul in the whole country with whom I could be entirely candid. I began to see the KGB as a universe unto itself. The party, the army, the government—to a certain degree, these were all under the KGB, and their members stepped gingerly around its long tentacles just as mere mortals did.

Even my uncle had reason to fear the political police, which he had fled in 1937. I remember one time when my father and I went to see him in his office. When Leonid remarked, "You know, Yasha, Andropov was sitting there a few minutes ago," my father pulled back from the chair as though he had seen a poisonous snake curled up on its leather upholstery. My uncle laughed. "You know," he said, "I'm a bit wary of him myself."

One of the things about the KGB that most shocked me became clear during a visit to the Lubyanka, back in the days when the KGB was trying to separate me from Helmut. I was greeted near the entrance by a handsome young man, about thirty-five years old, I guessed. He had an attractive smile on his full lips. Would someone like him be capable of beating people up, breaking their fingers, putting out lit cigarettes on their bodies? I wondered. He looked nothing like the vacant-eyed bully-boys who had been sent to my room. I was handed a pass, and we set off down seemingly endless corridors.

To the left were evenly spaced upholstered doors; to the right, windows. As I walked to my interrogation, I couldn't help thinking of the desperate people who had walked this way before me. Thinking of those who had jumped out onto the pavement below, to a death they preferred to continued torture, I slowed down in spite of myself, suddenly seized with terror.

"Feeling ill?" my companion asked in a concerned voice.

"No, fine," I answered. "As well as someone can in this dungeon."

Out of the blue, he asked if I liked sports.

"Yes," I answered.

"I can see that from the way you walk."

I remarked, "The soul and the gait are the body's silent song," to which he added, "Heine."

My amazement that this person would know the words of Heine left me unable to say a further word. Yes, the KGB was indeed a world unto its own—and that meant, though I had never really understood this before, that it included every category of human being, from the bone crushers sent to do its dirty work to highly literate and presentable young men who knew the classics of German poetry by heart.

As the months passed and the KGB continued to "invite" me to its headquarters, I even found, to my dismay, that I felt a certain rapport with some of my interrogators.

In the '60s, I attended hundreds of parties with my father, more than I can remember. But I never accepted an invitation from the people in his circle to go anywhere without him, though they asked me to concerts, receptions, barbecues, organ recitals in Lithuanian Catholic churches, and sauna parties.

An event I attended with my father in 1967 stands out in my memory. The invitation to spend a Saturday at a vice minister's Barvikha dacha led us to expect a Russian idyll: a boat ride down the river, still-warm fresh milk, tea from a samovar—which is what we found, more or less.

When we arrived, the tables were set with oysters, caviar, white sturgeon, and champagne. Guests wandered around the grounds. Some headed to the swimming pool to cool off while others took partners to upstairs bedrooms or amused themselves by fanning the coals in the samovar with an old felt boot. Those with energy to burn tried their hand at mowing the meadow with a scythe or rowing on the river.

As evening approached, the party moved indoors. By some unwritten law, the dachas of Moscow's elite were sumptuous but never comfortable; none of those I saw had any individuality, any atmosphere conducive to creativity, love, or reflection. The interiors were a jumble of carpets, crystal, Gobelin tapestries, paintings, and photographs.

One of the officials, an embroidered towel wrapped around his head, was imitating the best man at a traditional Russian wedding. Known for being tightfisted as well as tempestuous, this man was fond of bragging: "Yes, I'm greedy and proud of it. When I'm old and gray, I'll have money and girls galore while you all go begging." (He never did enjoy his golden years; he died not long after this gathering.)

After dinner, a certain Kolya Kovalev sat down next to me. To keep him from noticing me, I tried to be as quiet as a mouse under a broom: we were already acquainted, and I remembered his annoying habit of pressing candy on me with assurances that "sweets are good for kids." He was short and stocky, with a handsome face; past middle age, he could have easily been my grandfather. For years, he introduced himself as a Central Committee department head, but, as I would soon find out, he had another occupation.

True to form, he picked up a box of candy from the table and offered it to me. "Unfortunately, Soviet officials never hand pretty women bonbons wrapped in banknotes, as was done at the court of Louis XIV."

There was a sudden outburst. One of the prosecutors of Moscow, who had been prosecuting the vodka too hard, had got into a heated argument. As other guests stepped in to calm things down, Kovalev offered to have me driven home.

There was nothing to hold me at the party; I was disgusted, bored, and eager to leave. I had even asked for my father's permission to leave, but he had cut me short, saying that I should be grateful for the sincere hospitality being lavished on us.

With very little convincing and without saying good-bye to my father, I walked off. I didn't expect to be driven home in a Zim, so I hesitated when I saw the door of one of these luxury cars being opened for me. I abandoned common sense and sat in the backseat. Kovalev, who wore the usual scent of cognac and cologne, sat next to me.

When we stopped, the door was opened for me to get out, as courteously as it had been opened for me to enter. As I had begun to suspect during the drive, the car's destination was KGB headquarters.

I was taken gently by the arm and escorted down the now familiar corridors to an interrogation room.

After being warmed up with a number of fairly innocent questions, which I answered truthfully, I was asked about my father: what people are associating with him, what do they talk about, where do they meet? I said nothing. Why did they have to involve me in all this? Why, I wondered, don't they assign an agent to float around among his associates and in that way find whatever dirt they need? After two hours, I was taken home.

One thing was becoming clear to me: the real cause of the KGB's interest in my humble person was not Helmut (by now out of the picture), Solzhenitsyn, or my outspokenness. The KGB was trying to use me as a conduit for information about the Brezhnevs—and not only about my father, but about my uncle as well.

Once—also in 1967—a blank sheet of paper was put in front of me at KGB headquarters. I was instructed to write. The following exchange ensued:

"What should I write?"

"Everything you know, everything you've seen or heard."

"Absolutely *everything*?"

"Yes, everything," the man answered, almost cheerfully.

"Are you serious?"

"Completely."

I made it clear that I wasn't going to inform on my relatives. Pavlik Morozov, the Young Pioneer who was held up to several generations as a role model, had never been my childhood hero.

I sat alone in the room for four hours without writing a line. When the interrogator finally lost patience, he said, "All right, then, write that you refuse to testify."

"Testify?" I was outraged. "What kind of testimony did you have in mind, and against whom? Against my own father? Against my uncle, the general secretary?"

Before leaving, I asked why my work record had been stolen from my room. I had worked almost two years before enrolling in the institute; for that reason, upon graduation, I would have my five student years counted as work—but only if I had the necessary documentation. What good my work record was to the KGB, I have no idea.

"I never stole a thing from you," one of the comrades answered in an injured tone.

"You know," I said, "when the Gestapo beat a fellow German to death, they would at least return the victim's belongings to his relatives along with his remains. They explained, 'We are honorable. We don't need to steal.' "

The comrade lifted the glass of water that I had earlier refused and emptied it in my face.

Good. The cold water brought me to my senses. Gone were the hallucinations that I had started to see after sitting so long, locked in that stuffy room. I was back in fighting form, ready to defend myself if necessary. But, unexpectedly, I was hastily escorted out of the building.

I stood by the entrance, trying to control the circles swimming in front of my face. I was overjoyed to be free, but at the same time I felt almost offended that they would throw me out so abruptly after holding me for so long. Why did they? Because of my interrogator's unplanned anger? I doubted it. I was dealing with professionals who knew their adversaries' psychology well. My efforts to answer my tormentors with defiance, and at times even humor, may have kept me sane, but that's about all they did.

Now that I can look back at those years dispassionately, I have given serious thought to the question, What motives lay behind the actions taken with regard to me by the KGB in the 1960s? Perhaps someday an impartial investigator, sifting through the KGB archives, will find records of what was done to me, why, and on whose direct orders. Until then, I can only draw conclusions based on the information at my disposal.

During the first stage, in the spring and summer of 1964, I was followed and observed simply as the relative of an important official: even before the palace revolt of October, all members of the Brezhnev family were under surveillance (Leonid was then chairman of the Presidium of the Supreme Soviet). From this close surveillance, I believe, the KGB must have become well aware that I was my father's closest confidante: he spoke with me freely, and we were closer than he was to any of his friends or other family members. This access to information on my part would acquire significance later.

The next stage began when it was noticed that I was involved romantically with a German colonel and that ours was not a passing fling—we were planning to marry. In the fall of 1965, a few months before the beating that cost me Helmut's child, the KGB had let me know during interrogations that they had learned of my pregnancy. Nothing related to Helmut, however, was likely to be of any intrinsic interest to the KGB. He was simply a perfect gift to them, a tool to use against me that saved them the trouble of cooking up phony pictures of me in the arms of a lover or planting narcotics in my room. During the early "re-education sessions" in the fall of 1965, I was told that "it is the Brezhnev family that opposes your involvement with a German." Years later, in the 1970s, a KGB colonel, a friend of my father's who is also the uncle of a girlfriend of mine, told me that Leonid's wife, Viktoriya Petrovna, had been most adamantly opposed to my liaison with Helmut. I find this version plausible, given her antipathy toward my father and me, but have heard no other statements to confirm it.

Another gift I inadvertently gave the KGB was the presence in my room of two copies of Solzhenitsyn's *The First Circle*, an offense that, as I mentioned, was punishable by six years in prison.

My travails occurred against a backdrop of political maneuvering of which I was little aware at the time. During the first two or three years after the palace revolt, my uncle had not yet consolidated his power; many saw him as an interim figure. Thus my most brutal treatment at the hands of the KGB (in the winter of 1965–66) coincided with the period when my uncle was still relatively weak. Semichastny, then chairman of the KGB, was a friend and ally of Aleksandr Shelepin, who coveted Brezhnev's post and was scheming to take it over.* Indeed, some historians consider this association to be a factor in the removal of Semichastny in 1967 and his replacement by Andropov. Were the harassment and beatings directed against me part of a larger political game?

After Andropov took over the KGB, I noticed that there were new faces in the halls at the Lubyanka, and some of the more primitive thugs had been replaced by educated men. I think it likely that soon after the change, someone bright looked over my files and, in particular, the tran-

*As discussed in Chapter 9.

scripts of my interrogation sessions and decided that I could be of great use to the KGB as an informer. The KGB was always eager for information about party officials that could be used as circumstances warranted, and I was able to enter into contact with any level of society, my access to family information about the Brezhnevs being almost unique. And the resilience and stubbornness evident from my responses to their previous actions were qualities the KGB looked for in potential recruits.

Of course, I never agreed to work with them.

Chapter Twelve

❂❂❂❂❂❂❂❂❂❂

"BREZHNEV'S BROTHER"

A feast was called to honor me, and on my brow was placed
A laurel wreath with emeralds bejeweled.

IVAN BUNIN

In pre-revolutionary Russia, it was customary among the rising merchant class to invite a general to the wedding of one's offspring. The role of the "candy generals," as they became known, was that of a living status symbol. My father was used in a similar way. Paraphrasing Turgenev, I once told him hotly, "They keep you around, for you are kin to Brezhnev."

My father's feelings were hurt, understandably, but the fact remained: people he barely knew swarmed around him like sharks attracted by the smell of blood. I had many chances to observe my father's "friends" entertaining guests who were important to them for career advancement or favors. Their tables were lavish: this world saw money spent on food and drink as an investment to be recouped a hundredfold. And in this world, my father served two purposes. First, his presence would impress upon the assembled guests the status of the home they were in; after all, Brezhnev's brother himself was a casual visitor. . . . (Often, though, my father had visited this home only once before. Sometimes he didn't even know who the host was.) Second, he would be asked directly to grant favors. A telephone would miraculously appear on the table where he was seated, and someone's obliging hand would dial the necessary number. All that was required of my father was to identify himself and explain coherently the favor he wanted, whether it was having someone's son given a desirable work assignment after graduate school or seeing that the host's daughter was admitted to the institute of her choice.

My father was always outgoing and popular, but after his move to Moscow, in 1963, he began attracting a special type of companion: spongers of all stripes would ride his coattails. In the Soviet Union, *kupit*, "to buy," was hopelessly out of date; more to the point was *dostat*, "to get ahold of," a fitting word in a country where there was always a shortage of something. And Brezhnev's Brother could get ahold of just about anything. In virtually every sphere of the service sector, he had buddies willing to do his bidding, men he addressed by their diminutives: Kolya, Sasha, Lyosha . . .

Favor seekers pestered him for help in obtaining high-quality eyeglasses, spare parts for automobiles, imported medicines, rugs, apartments, private hospital rooms, boots and fur coats for mistresses, dachas, trips abroad, academic department chairs. He didn't know how to say no. I tried to convince him—with no success—that decent men wouldn't need lingerie for a mistress.

Ordinary people with complaints commonly wrote to the Central Committee, the Supreme Soviet, the press, the prosecutor's office, and the Health Ministry. They wrote to cosmonauts, workers whose names were well known, heroes of socialist labor, authors, and ballerinas. And to Brezhnev's Brother.

Hundreds of letters came every month to his office and his home. Later, when he acquired a dacha, they arrived there as well. Sometimes *Brezhnev's Brother* were the only words on the envelope. Not everyone knew his first name, so the letter might begin "Honorable Ilyich." Ruefully my father would joke: "They must think they're writing to Lenin."

His name bounced off the hallways of the Supreme Soviet, the prosecutor's office, and the central committee of the OBKhSS.* *Brezhnev's Brother is the guy to get things done; he never says no; he can do practically anything.*

---

*Organs of Economic Security of the Soviet Union, which was responsible for code enforcement, inspection, and so forth.

Raised to believe in the wisdom and infallibility of central authority, the entire Soviet Union dispatched messengers to the capital to seek redress of grievances—just as in czarist times. Alone and in groups—before work, during lunch hour, after work—the favor seekers waited outside the Ministry of Ferrous Metallurgy, hoping to catch my father on his way in or out. Some even began their vigil at night, hoping to be first in line the next morning.

Gennady Gulyaev, a close friend of my father's, once quipped,

Like so many flunkies,
The dwellers of the city,
Flock round the gates
Of their rulers, seeking pity,

breathing new life into a stanza from one of Nekrasov's best-known works. For some reason, my father didn't appear to be amused.

At times, he tried "to go underground." As he told me once, "I'm living the life of a secret agent with the alias of Ilyich; I duck in and out of this place like a prowling tomcat." I understood his position better than anyone else he knew since I constantly had to dodge hordes of favor seekers myself: at home, at the institute, and with him. More than once he and I had to run to avoid them. My father eventually requested that his official car, sent every day to take him home from work, be driven into the ministry's interior courtyard so he wouldn't have to walk out the front entrance. But this was only a slight improvement: many of the favor seekers had enough pull to get the pass required for entry into the building.

He used to tell me, when I visited him at work, "There were more again today. How the hell do they get into my office, I wonder? They sit here smoking my cigarettes, stealing my time, and telling me their hard-luck stories. What can I do? There are thousands or millions of them, and Brezhnev has only one brother to go around."

My father's office was a madhouse. There were endless phone calls and meetings, a steady stream of visitors to be received, documents to be signed. On top of everything else, there were the favor seekers who managed mysteriously to filter in.

Once I was in my father's office at six, about to walk out the door with him, when the secretary announced, "Yakov Ilyich, Vladimir Ivanovich Dolgikh is on the phone."

After a brief talk with Dolgikh, one of the men in charge of Soviet metallurgy, my father shrugged: "We'll have to run over there. I don't see any way out of it."

The secretary rapidly located a file that Dolgikh needed, and we headed across Nogin Square (now Slavyanskaya Square) to his office. The delivery made, we returned to put some papers in the safe in my father's office. Before we could leave, the phone rang again. "Tell them I'm sick, tell them I'm dead, tell them I've disappeared without a trace. . . ."

I often heard the same thing myself when I called the office: disguising his voice, my father would say that Yakov Ilyich was not available. After an abrupt click, I would call his other number and ask his secretary to put me through. My father would scold: "Why didn't you say it was you? You know I was expecting your call."

Another afternoon I was visiting the office when Aleksandr Pokryshkin arrived. He was a well-known military aviator, honored three times with the Hero of the Soviet Union award, and he felt the fact that he had taken part in the air battles above Little Land (Malaya Zemlya), the Black Sea peninsula where my uncle had served, gave him a particular right to ask favors of my father.

Going to the office refrigerator, filled with delicacies from his Kremlin allotment, my father set about making us something to eat. He washed two crystal ashtrays thoroughly—before leaving for the day, the secretary had locked the dishes in a cupboard—and served sandwiches on one and a tomato-cucumber salad on the other. With a smile on my face, I observed Pokryshkin. His eyes bulging, he explained that he had already eaten. As he left, after receiving assurances of help in finding tires for his Volga, he was still visibly shocked that my father, a man who could "get ahold of" things no one else could, would stoop to eating out of an ashtray.

Soviet officials rarely went straight home after work, preferring first to attend a play or a concert or pay a social call; if it was summer, they often retired to someone's dacha. It was also common to go restaurant hopping with girlfriends, and it was in this nocturnal world that my father began meeting the underworld types who eventually became known as the mafia of Brezhnev's Brother.

My father's associates wore various hats and titles: factory manager, academician, architect, writer, specialty-store manager, party secretary, Komsomol leader, resort manager, Central Committee official, popular singer. To me, they were a motley crew of money-grubbers, losers, black-market businessmen, and outright criminals. Once I had seen through them, I never changed my opinion.

Those who benefited from my father's largesse felt indebted to him, but in the '60s they didn't give him bribes; their way of saying thank-you was to pick up the tab for the endless drinking bouts in Moscow restaurants. I watched with deepening sadness as my father sank into alcoholism. Unable to fulfill all the requests made of him, he usually ended up helping the most pushy and the least deserving, those he should have just chucked out the door. I resented that he was so easily swayed by strangers who would abandon him in a second if circumstances changed. My own relations with him during the '60s and '70s were a roller-coaster course from periods of warmth and tenderness to times marked by little communication. The den of thieves around my father drove me to despair. How could I make him see that he should eliminate these people from his life?

One thing I understood quite well was that a no-holds-barred fight for a place in the Moscow sun was raging all around me. I came to the conclusion that the state and political elite was made up of people who held nothing sacred. To retain power, which meant above all having access to the good life, they were willing to betray friends and relations, act as anyone's flunky, and forsake the pleasure or the duty of saying what they really thought. The men ruling the country included criminally insane monsters who used a patina of official purpose to cover their drunkenness, gluttony, and banal games. I expected at least one of them to get fed up and end it all with a bullet through the head. But most went on to die natural deaths, leaving their heirs to divide up—and battle over—their property.

I do have certain fond memories from the social whirl of those early Moscow days, and not all of my father's friends were scoundrels. The World War II hero Marshal Georgy Zhukov was one of the pleasant exceptions. I met him several times, at the Bolshoi Theater and at private parties. My father, who had many celebrity friends, was very proud of this one. By coincidence, they both had three daughters, two by one wife, one by another. And my uncle had restored the great military commander, out of favor with the Kremlin under Stalin and Khrushchev, to his rightful stature.

One evening I was seated next to Zhukov. "Eat, eat, you're so skinny," he said, piling everything within reach onto my plate.

He chided my father: "You don't feed your daughter, Yakov. My Masha is the picture of health!"

Zhukov swirled me around the dance floor firmly but gently, and very precisely, as though carrying out a strategic plan. Affectionate one moment, the marshal's peasant eyes could be coldly military the next. Most of all, he possessed a kind of inner strength that women can't help admiring.

During my uncle's tenure as general secretary, theft flourished as never before. It became so much a part of our life that no stigma was attached to it. After all, when you're stealing public property, there is no clear victim; for most people, the state is an abstraction.

There were periodic crackdowns against petty embezzlement and pilfering, but the big fish were usually left unhooked. Of course, when one of them fell into political disfavor for some reason, the authorities might decide to set an example, and there were trials of major embezzlers and bribe takers. But "the little thief runs while the big one rests," as the saying goes. For one thing, many of the biggest thieves could not be prosecuted, for fear that they would implicate a chain of crooks leading higher and higher, eventually reaching the highest echelons of

The writer Konstantin Simonov, whom the author and her father
often visited for heart-to heart talks.

© WALTRAUD LINDNER

power. And amazingly, despite theft as a way of life, the country did not collapse. The economy even continued to grow.

Once in the early '60s, a group of employees at a diamond-processing factory was put on trial. My father found nothing surprising in the fact that the workers had been stealing—"What shocks me," he said, "is that only forty-eight members of the collective were involved. A few worked honestly for their salary and bonuses. I can't figure out for the life of me how they did it!"

Hotheaded, I often argued with my father about politics in general and my uncle's policies in particular. Yakov Ilyich had a low opinion of my intellect and usually smiled condescendingly. Sometimes—it all depended on his mood—he interrupted me rudely, forbidding me to speak my mind when others were present. He didn't want people to think that he had failed to bring me up properly.

Once when we were visiting Konstantin Simonov, the writer asked me what Soviet writers I read.

"I don't read any contemporary literature," I confessed.

"Why?" asked Simonov, genuinely surprised.

"Leave her alone, Kostya," interjected my father hurriedly. "She's a holy terror. Give her half a chance, and she'll prove to you that you're not even a writer."

"Well, well," said Simonov—one of the most well known and honored names in Soviet literature—with a smile. "Let's see how she floors me."

"She may not floor you," my father advised, "but she will ruin your whole evening."

Thus began a conversation that degenerated into a shouting match complete with arm waving, red faces, and mutual contempt. I attempted to demonstrate to Simonov, very concretely and not very tactfully, that aside from a handful of exceptions, a few authors whom I named, Soviet writers were doing their best to sow immorality among the Soviet people.

"Do they believe their own panegyrics, or do they secretly curse the men whose praises they're paid to sing?" I asked. I was startled to see Simonov blush slightly. I couldn't decide whether he was embarrassed or angry.

"But one can't read only the classics," he noted, modestly implying that he was not in that category himself.

"Yes, one can," I retorted.

This marked the end of our debate. My father and I walked to the entrance hall of the apartment. Simonov had regained his usual aplomb and smiled good-naturedly, trying to turn our whole conversation into a joke. But tension still permeated the air.

"I warned you she was a terror," my father reminded him as we left. "She even tries to tell Leonid how to run the government, the silly thing."

This last was unfair. True, I had tried to explain to my uncle that someone in charge of other people's lives should display a high level of virtue and that only by following moral principles would he enjoy popular love and respect and be sincerely mourned after his death. And from time to time, I did discuss specific political issues with him.

Barvikha, in the Moscow area, was a favorite spot for weekend gatherings among the political elite who had their dachas there. No wives, thank you; as men of immense responsibility, they had earned the right to have fun. To see the sedate, middle-aged men with their natty suits and widening midriffs, you would never have guessed what they were capable of. The picnics began innocently enough. After a few drinks, all inhibitions flew to the wind.

At the beginning, of course, the parties my father took me to seemed like a dream come true. Ah, to drink coffee from Dresden china, listen to Svyatoslav Richter play, dance with Yuri Gagarin or the film star Slava Tikhonov, and sip champagne with Konstantin Simonov. There were plenty of tales to be shared with girlfriends: the time Sergey Mikhalkov, who wrote the words to the Soviet national anthem, tried to get under my blouse, the time a government minister cornered me and proposed a weekend outing "at my dacha or at a party resort, whatever you like. . . ."

The spell wore off when I began wondering just who I was to the Moscow elite. Another girl from the provinces? Or Leonid Brezhnev's niece?

Once I put on a grave expression and said to a very well known person, "The most interesting and the most creative people in the country pass through your living room, and you can't have failed to notice how backward I am. Why do you entertain me? Because I'm 'a niece'?"

He looked at me intently. "No, because you're smart," he said with a perfectly straight face.

I didn't believe him.

Well-known performers were frequently brought in to amuse the jaded "aristocrats," and I often wished I could disappear into thin air, ashamed to be seen among the drunken audience. I remember one time when a phenomenal virtuoso—he knew how to play all the instruments

of the orchestra—was invited for the evening to "play something light
and cheery." With his beat-up trousers and sleepless face, he stood out
like a sore thumb among the guests, who were rosy cheeked and dressed
in the finest. I later learned that the man's wife had given birth with
great difficulty the night before. No one paid attention as he wandered
around, and eventually he went home without having played a note.

One day in 1967 in my father's office, I finally let out all the indignation that had been building up over the three years I had been in
Moscow. I let him know what I thought of his entourage, that pack of
nonentities and social climbers. For his part, he accused me of having
brought disgrace to Leonid with my love for Helmut. This infuriated
me even more, and I lost all restraint: the Brezhnev family was already
so disgrace ridden that one more scandal would make no difference in
public opinion. I went on to describe, in the most vivid language I knew,
the moral depravity of his so-called friends. I ticked off the names of
drinking buddies of his who had tried to get under my skirt, who had
offered to keep me, and who had whispered obscenities in my ear. My
father stared at me speechless.

When he finally spoke, he said, "So are they any worse than Helmut?"

I walked silently out of his office.

That evening, unable to get through to me by phone, he came in person to my room to apologize. He cursed the men who surrounded him,
vowing to break off all relations with them. He would need some time to
bring his affairs into order. No more than a month, I said, and he agreed.

But nothing changed. All that my efforts to lure my father from the
spongers won for me was their hostility. They, of course, took care not
to demonstrate their feelings too openly. I began to see less of my father
and even less of his family. No royal court is fond of those whose
thoughts are unorthodox, and I was bound to find myself beyond the
pale sooner or later.

Not surprisingly, the maneuvers of my father and his shady friends
attracted the attention of the KGB. At first, it was almost comical: my

father would be hiding from the favor seekers, and they in turn would be hiding from the KGB agents who lay in wait on Nogin Square, hiding near my father's home. Some of his acquaintances were even picked up at their own workplaces.

I often saw a KGB stakeout car waiting to the left of the main entrance to the ministry building: the agents tracking their prey. This campaign noticeably thinned the ranks of obvious favor seekers, who were sometimes grabbed and taken back to the car for little talks.

One day I was astonished to see the section of the square in front of the ministry deserted. My God, I wondered, where are all the people I used to see crowding around here, coming to see my father?

About those times, my father later told me, "I remember what a pleasure it was to actually walk out the main exit, like any other honest citizen, and stroll down Razin or Solyanka Street, knowing that no one would grab me by the arm, look into my eyes like a beaten dog, and begin pleading for assistance."

The lull lasted over a month, and my father began to feel like a normal human being again. But before long, the black Volgas quietly returned, and my father's "well-wishers" renewed the cycle of drunken escapades and orgies. Again the KGB made numerous sweeps, but none of them solved the problem of Brezhnev's Brother for very long.

There was another, even more effective KGB tactic. Imagine some Ivan Ivanovich, a typical Soviet bureaucrat: he fears his wife, goes to work every day, and likes to fish, chase after pretty women, tell dirty jokes, and curse the system under his breath. This upstanding member of society attends party meetings faithfully, though, busy dozing in a corner, he never gets up to speak. But, oppressed and stepped on by those above him in the pecking order, he's unhappy and seething with resentment.

One day he decides to cozy up to someone who might have enough power to help him out of his rut—how about Brezhnev's Brother? And he joins the brotherhood of my father's drinking buddies. One evening, however, our Ivan oversteps the bounds: trying to impress Yakov, he says a few slightly unflattering things about the Soviet regime. A perfect opportunity for the KGB.

The orderlies sent to haul him in land a few blows to his jaw, knocking teeth out in the bargain. When he comes to, Ivan Ivanovich discovers that being mentally ill is no fun, and soon he recants, telling everything the KGB wants to know and more: what he drank, what he ate, who went to bed with him, and, of course, what conversations he overheard.

Soon enough our friend finds himself back on the street relatively unharmed. What are a few teeth compared with freedom? He will never be tormented by doubts again. He knows that he lives in the best country in the world, no matter what he might see or hear to the contrary. And the KGB can be sure that there will be one fewer favor seeker prowling Nogin Square.

Among my father's associates there were quite a few Ivan Ivanoviches who learned their lesson the hard way.

Chapter Thirteen

THE PRIVILEGED LIFE

Power means you can do whatever you want.

N. SHCHEDRIN

What was the lifestyle of those who could answer Nekrasov's proverbial question, "Who in Russia lives well?" with a resounding *"We do"*? During my life in Moscow from 1964 until the end of 1990, I had access to many privileges myself, though I rebelled against the conformity that was demanded of me in return. Before returning to my own story, I feel obliged to tell what I can about the way of life of the Soviet rulers—and the moral price paid for such a life.

About the Russia of the early nineteenth century, the French novelist Madame de Staël wrote: "Nothing there is made public, but everyone knows everything." Though Soviet dictionaries, textbooks, and newspapers never spoke of a new elite, its existence was an open secret, but mainly at the level of rumor; only in recent years have the details of its life been chronicled in print with any real accuracy.

The word *nomenklatura* refers to a list of those key positions, in every sphere of Soviet life from economics to culture, that were deemed so important that aspirants could be appointed to them only with special party approval; the same word refers to the men and women who held these positions.

Those in the middle level of the *nomenklatura* and above were guaranteed a personal car, an apartment, a dacha, a special food allotment, access to special restaurants, and the special medical care provided by the Ministry of Health's Fourth Department.

The system of privileges shrank somewhat under Khrushchev, but in my uncle's era it grew even larger. The new rulers—light-years ahead of the revolutionaries who had overthrown the czar in everything but their manner, which was marked by an unmistakable crudity—came to see their comforts as a birthright.

The elite and the common people scarcely crossed paths. After all, the members of the elite had their exclusive food stores, medical clinics, and pharmacies, their own motor pools, gas stations, and telephone booths, their own schools, institutions of higher learning, and graduate fellowships, their own dressmakers and tailors. They even had their own cemeteries.

Each member of the party elite was surrounded by an ever-expanding octopus: his own family, the relatives of his wife and his girlfriends, his illegitimate children, the friends of his children and grandchildren. All stood at the government trough like so many grunting hogs, engaged in constant backbiting and jockeying for position, endless spying, whispering campaigns, and dirty tricks. Nothing was sacred, and nothing was of any interest besides career and power. All this was not surprising.

What was surprising was that at first blush, most of the sons of party bigwigs did not appear to be scoundrels. Quite the opposite. They read Mandelstam and loved the ballet, pets, and "the fair sex." They discussed international affairs and attended theater premières. They might even give you a friendly slap on the shoulder and ask you how things were going, not that they cared. Gathered among their own kind, they told jokes and even political anecdotes. Thanks to doting mamas eager to impart culture to their progeny, they could usually sing a few tunes or toss something off on the piano. They were masters in the art of being gracious guests and passengers; after all, they had been chauffeured for as long as they could remember. Expert riders on skates and horseback, they also knew all the latest dances. Many spoke fluent English. In a word, they had mastered the finer social graces. Yet what they really knew how to do was steal, consume, and destroy. Their ideals were power and acquisition. For some, the key to happiness was diamonds; for others, Mercedes-Benzes. Some went in for clothes: leather coats, sheepskin jackets, imitation astrakhan coats, designer boots. Some craved pressed caviar or smoked sausage, some had a yen for limited-edition books. This new young guard of the elite, with its coating of fine silk and silken manners concealing a spiritual wasteland, was one hideous result of the Soviet system.

At the restaurants closed to commoners, the vegetables gracing the tables had been grown in raised beds, fertilized with manure instead of nitrates, with soil and water carefully analyzed for radiation and for its chemical and bacterial content. Such beds were also protected by special security guards, from both vegetable-deprived commoners and journalistic curiosity.

Our party bosses certainly loved to eat, and their tastes were aristocratic in every way. As Mayakovski wrote before the 1917 revolution,

> Chew your grouse and your pineapple now,
> Your days are numbered, you capitalist swine.

Soon enough the Bolsheviks took the place of the capitalists and acquired their tastes. It should surprise no one that the top officials and their families seldom went abroad and that, if they did, they always returned. In the Communist heaven they had built for themselves, they had all the comforts the West could offer.

The three-story building housing one of the exclusive cafeterias stood in an alley off Dzerzhinsky Square, opposite the KGB headquarters. Someone was always checking passes at the door, though my father was able to whisk me through without one.

To my surprise, what I saw was nothing special. I had expected greater abundance, a greater variety of dishes. Still, a nice lunch was quite cheap, about the same price that an average Soviet citizen might have paid in a more humble eatery. But the commoner would get something quite different for the money—a portion of sticky macaroni, sausage made of a dubious mixture of cardboard, starch, and intestines, and a fruit compote in which a single raisin and one quarter of a worm-eaten pear kept each other company.

The special grocery allotment my father received would have been enough for three families. Every Friday, he was driven to Granovskovo Street, to an inconspicuous building with a modest memorial plaque stating that Lenin had given a speech there in 1919. Now there were no crowds waiting for the Leader, just men and women with sleek faces, stepping into black Volgas with packages of delicacies to take home. It was closed to the uninitiated, of course: no one was allowed in without a pass.

There were numerous such outlets in Moscow. I went to the one on Granovskovo Street to observe goods being distributed. My father also picked up groceries in the Central Committee buffet and at his ministry, where at reasonable prices Soviet aristocrats ordered rare foods, both Russian and imported, presumably as a reward for working their fingers to the bone in government service.

My father had his fingers in three pots, receiving one allotment as a ministry employee, another (with the help of Marshal Dmitry Ustinov, defense minister of the Soviet Union) from military supplies, and another (through his brother) from Kremlin supplies. At my request, he sketched the entire system of food outlets, with their hierarchical structure. The higher your post, the greater your presumed danger of developing bony fingers, so the greater your share. Only members and candidate members of the Politburo, members of the Central Committee, ministers, and members of the Supreme Soviet were eligible for the complimentary Kremlin allotment, whose size and quality were also determined by strict hierarchical principles.

My uncle received an unlimited amount, enough for himself and all the locusts building their nests around him. Plagued by excess weight, he regularly took medically recommended walks in the park attached to his dacha. Those entrusted with monitoring his health even had a toilet installed on the path where he usually walked. No respecter of rank and title, nature will eventually punish anyone's overindulgence in caviar and *pelmeni.*

For Communists lucky enough to have joined the party before 1930, there was a system of special food outlets. Too bad for the Johnny-come-latelies: to no avail, they filled out forms and beat bureaucratic doorsteps for years, pleading for an exception. Those who joined even a month late, say in February 1930, were denied access to this particular gravy train. I once read a letter from one who wanted my father's help. What is a month, after all?

During those halcyon days when it seemed as if I were accompanying my father wherever he went, I frequently encountered the directors of Moscow's largest stores. The most successful shoppers, I noticed, were those who knew the directors well enough to obtain the goods set aside in basement storerooms. Working in commerce brought godlike status during my uncle's time. Muscovites liked to quip, "That fellow has delusions of grandeur; he claims he's director of the Yeliseev.*"

The topic of medical service is perhaps the most painful of all. Some had the best, of course. Beginning in the mid-'60s, my father was periodically treated, mainly for alcoholism, in the Kremlin clinic on Granovskovo Street, in a private room with telephone and television. On my first visit, I brought a large sack of food: oranges, my mother's apricot jam, apples, cottage cheese, and cheese from the farmers' market. My father picked up the menu lying on his nightstand and silently handed it to me. I might as well have brought my offerings to the famous Arbat restaurant: the breakfast menu included red and black caviar, cold boiled pork with fresh cucumbers, and on and on. Not a bad place to sit and wait for the end of the world, as I once told him.

"By the way," he told me during another visit, "they don't give just anyone color TV. Just think of it: somewhere a paper pusher is being paid a hundred rubles a month to decide who gets what—'Let's see now, Brezhnev's Brother gets color—after all, they were born to the same mother—but if his cousin is admitted, he'll get black-and-white.' "

Sometimes we went for walks in the clinic's fenced inner courtyard. When circumstances permitted, he was assigned the same room, a

*This is the pre-revolutionary name, still popularly used, for one of Moscow's largest food stores.

twelve-square-meter (about 130-square-foot) rectangle with a bed on wheels to the left and next to it a television stand. To the right stood a small sofa, a dinner table for two, a sink, and a closet with two dressing gowns, one of terrycloth, one of silk. Nothing too spectacular, no great luxury, you may say. But a room like this, let alone the food and the nursing care, was beyond the wildest dreams of the ordinary Soviet citizen. The Kremlin clinic was worlds apart from the hospitals that I would see as a journalist in the 1980s.

Then, at the height of the Afghan war, I took my mother for tests at the neurosurgery department of the Burdenko Clinic. The corridors were packed with beds and stretchers holding wounded soldiers and officers. Moans, delirious cries, the smell of blood . . . it was more like a wartime field hospital than anything else. My mother, who had worked in military hospitals throughout World War II, left the clinic in tears.

By contrast, the *nomenklatura* convalesced in a lovely wooded park not far from my uncle's dacha. The medical profession kept close track of their health; after all, if the rulers died off, who would be left to tend the duties of state and assure the well-being of the citizenry? Regular checkups were mandatory.

In the Kremlyovka, as the Moscow *nomenklatura* fondly referred to the Kremlin clinic, everything was imported, from equipment to medicine. Ironically many of the staff physicians were unqualified and corrupt, since hiring was based more on party membership and connections than on medical skills. Frequently more competent doctors from other clinics and scientific institutes had to be brought in to treat the patients. The *nomenklatura*'s doctors were likely to do permanent damage, as in the case of my stepmother, Anna Vladimirovna, whose operation for an enlarged thyroid was botched by the Kremlin clinic's doctors.

My aunt Vera was once scheduled for an operation at the Kremlyovka, and she prepared a packet with a substantial sum of money for the surgeon. Unfortunately, Viktoriya Petrovna called before the operation to tell her not to give the doctor any money. "Vera," she said, "he already has all he needs from us. Galina just fixed him up with an apartment. Let him at least treat you for free." Vera followed her sister-in-law's advice. The operation was a failure, resulting in a long stay in intensive care.

Yes, despite the widely held view that those in power got all their special services free, sometimes even they had to pay, in the form of cash, apartments, cars, or favors. As for commoners, they frequently had to bribe everyone from the attending physician to orderlies, nurses, and lab assistants.

In the late '60s, when he was being treated on the same floor of the Kremlin clinic as my father, I sometimes saw the celebrated Kliment Voroshilov. A short man with snow-white hair and a soft blush on his cheeks, he looked something like a gnome out of a fairy tale. His life-long habit of dousing himself with cold water was the secret of his health and longevity, or so he told me.

As far as I know, the civil war hero General Voroshilov owed his high-flying military and political career completely to Stalin's patronage. Obedient and industrious, he was convenient to the dictator, who would humiliate or praise him as he saw fit. Yet Voroshilov was amazingly lucky: even after his benefactor's death, fate preserved him, and to the end of his days he played the role of a decorative army dog.

As I got to know him, I realized he wasn't quite as simpleminded as he had seemed at first. He had a fairly good grasp of the Russian classics and a long, complex life behind him—years in which glory and disgrace ran parallel, in which good and evil walked hand in hand. He had sent his comrades to the firing squad but loved animals; he had obtained bread for the starving children of Petrograd but kept his refrigerator locked and inaccessible to his own grandchildren. He went to the most fashionable parties, saw the most beautiful women, and ate the most sophisticated food but still loved Russian cabbage soup and vodka.

I listened with interest to his stories but never felt any affinity of spirit with him. He seemed a dried-up mushroom in the forest. His glory had faded, and nothing remained in his life but the miserliness, sickness, whims, and suspiciousness of age.

One day he shuffled softly up to my father and asked him to go with him for a walk in the hallways: "Yasha, you promised, let's go."

My father used my visit as an excuse to say no. Klim sat down at the window, looked out vacantly, and began to drum his fingers quietly on the pane.

When he was finally led away by the alarmed nurses, my father spat on the floor and said, "Listen, Luba, Voroshilov swept aside those people who could hinder his career. He had his own comrades shot. He set himself up for life and then saw to it that his children and their children for ten generations down the line would live easy. But he's a complete imbecile. He led the troops for a few years, waving his saber, but he's a paper general. Now he can come here, where the nurses even scrub his butt for him, all because he's the great commander."

I couldn't resist saying to my father that though he had never seen combat, he was here, too, being treated at public expense.

"Stop it, Luba!" he said in reply. "In the first place, I'm not being treated; I was put here to be kept under wraps. Second, no one asked whether I wanted to be a straw man: I had the role of Brezhnev's Brother imposed on me. Now let those who put me here take care of me. If I sold my soul to Satan, I should get some benefits in this life. I'll have to answer on the other side."

"Watch out, you might end up answering for everything in this life," I warned.

"For what?" My father was sincerely surprised. "I didn't move to Moscow of my free will, and no one asked me whether I wanted to be hospitalized. Let my captors serve me."

I never saw any of the elite wearing Soviet-made clothes. They bought their foreign fashions at Section 100, an emporium located partly on the third floor of the GUM building,* partly on the Red Square side of the first floor of the same building, and partly in the famous apartment building known as the House on the Embankment.

During my first years in Moscow, my father did most of my shopping, buying me boots, warm scarves, blouses, and jeans. Everything in Section 100 was well made and in fashion, and getting the right size was

---

*GUM is the acronym for State Universal Store, the Soviet Union's largest department store.

no problem, since the saleswomen, bending over backward to please Brezhnev's Brother, all knew my size.

Sometimes my father asked me to come to the store and give my advice, but I'm not much for spending time in stores, so I didn't go often. Anyway, my father, unlike most men, knew his way around women's clothing: he knew well that Austria made better women's boots than Greece and that perfume from France was the dream of every Soviet woman. He would never buy his daughters any but Italian fur coats for the winters—those from Yugoslavia were too bulky.

Unlike most Soviet stores, which specialized in a single type of goods, Section 100 had everything: tobacco, purses, perfume, footwear, furs, cognac, handkerchiefs, lingerie. The smiling saleswomen, unobtrusive but helpful, had the military bearing of KGB agents; they were presided over by a matron whose face bore traces of the hard fight she had surely waged on the upward climb to her cozy spot. With a pleasant appearance tastefully enhanced by French cosmetics, she greeted her clients at the door by name and patronymic, ensuring that only the right people entered. Around the corner in the same building, there were stores for the masses: workers in tattered pants, peasants with sacks slung over their shoulders, intellectuals in beat-up shoes and shabby, coarse woolen coats. As they shopped, few suspected they were a stone's throw away from a fount of consumer plenty.

The story of privileges in the Soviet Union could fill an entire book, so numerous were the levels and categories. I should add that there were also private stores reserved for a number of narrowly defined groups: the military, cosmonauts, prominent scientists, movie and ballet stars, Heroes of Labor, newspaper editors . . .

In the mid-'70s, my uncle unexpectedly helped out World War II veterans. "Even today," he wrote, "many years after the battles, we are always duty bound to remember those who took part, no matter how busy we may be. It is the moral duty of government bodies and all citizens to give them attention and concern, to help them with their everyday problems. This is the law of our entire life." But he went overboard, creating a new privileged class.

This concern for veterans ultimately pitted the rest of the Soviet people against them. Yet what of the survivors of the millions whose bodies lay on the fields of battle?

Many of the surviving veterans—some of whom had risked death during the Spanish civil war, the Finnish war of 1939, and World War II—were ashamed to go with their booklets to a store closed to everyone else. "All for the sake of some damn sticks of sausage," they told me. They found it even more humiliating to buy something out of turn at a regular store, ahead of old women who had lost husbands and sons. Others, mainly "rear-supply drivers" who hadn't fired a single shot, felt no shame and even used their privileges for profiteering.

Ultimately, with a veterans' booklet, you could buy anything: crystal, Austrian boots, imported running shoes, jeans, mink coats, Finnish furniture, sewing machines, television sets, washing machines, and cars. Many of these goods were resold, cynically and fairly openly. Unknowingly, my uncle had bestowed privileges on the veterans' children, who, through their parents, were suddenly able to build dachas and buy cooperative apartments.

The veterans even got free gasoline. While learning how to drive, I noticed an old man among my fellow students. He told me the real motive behind his pains: free gasoline—not for himself, however, but for his son. The poor fellow sweated blood and nearly had a heart attack, but he finally got his license, though he feared the vehicle more than the devil.

I brought up the subject of veterans' benefits with my uncle, suggesting that the new privileges should be given to the *families* of all war veterans, both living and dead. As it was, the state was helping above all those whose fathers and grandfathers had returned in one piece—already a gift from heaven. If any group had a right to privileges, I argued, it was the wives, children, and grandchildren of those killed in the war.

"There's not that much money in the country. There wouldn't be enough to go around," Leonid answered. I spoke to him of the profiteering that had sprung up among the veterans, who had been quietly minding their own business before the changes.

"We will punish those involved to the fullest extent of the law," he replied.

"But that's cruel." I was indignant. "First you give people a benefit, including the opportunity to break the law; then you punish them for it."

Apartments were yet another commodity distributed according to social status and influence. No outsider ever had access to the places where the "servants of the people" lived or took their vacations.

Housing was an eternal problem, an issue close to the hearts of average citizens. The goal of providing every family with its own separate apartment, equipped with modern conveniences, was stated many times but never met. Nikita Khrushchev, declaring war on communal apartments, rushed into the construction of five-story concrete boxes with shared toilet facilities and no elevators. They were designed to last from twenty-five to thirty years. To this day, many Muscovites live in them, hoping for the "brighter tomorrow." Many still live in communal apartments, for that matter. Once in the mid-'80s, I was riding by some of the *khrushchevki*, cracked and leaning but still not torn down. I was shocked to see that they were inhabited: curtains hung from the windows; frying pans sizzled; children were crying. I saw a cat grooming itself in a wide-open window. He can leap out if the building collapses, I thought; the people won't be so lucky.

Beyond such obvious factors as the view, the number of rooms, and the floor space, an apartment's "rating" depended on the neighborhood, the street, the building—and even the floor—where it was located.

The House on the Embankment that I have mentioned is well known in Moscow. Very spacious for the Soviet Union, its apartments average from 170 to 250 square meters (about 1,830 to 2,690 square feet). I often visited this building, especially the apartment that had been inhabited by Marshal Mikhail Tukhachevsky before Stalin had him executed. At each visit, I was awed, even intimidated, by its dimensions. The entrance hall was 45 square meters (more than 480 square feet), and the three rooms were each from 45 to 50 square meters. The ceilings were four and a half meters (nearly fifteen feet) high.

In the '30s, communal apartments were the norm in Moscow, even for scientists, artists, and writers; most families of three or four persons had seven square meters (seventy-five square feet) to call home. Meanwhile an organization called the Special Construction and Assembly Administration was putting up luxury buildings reserved for the *nomenklatura,* beginning with the House on the Embankment. Virtually everyone living in this particular building was taken off to be shot during the Stalin-era purges, and only one tenant from that period still remains. Hence its other nickname: the mass grave.

Elite housing is located in areas close to the center of Moscow and abundantly supplied with greenery and serenity. There is a whole set of such buildings on Kutuzov Prospekt, where part of Leonid's family lived, and similar ones on Granovskovo and Stanislavskovo streets, Sivtsev Vrazhek, and Shevchenko Embankment. Their apartments are often custom designed, with two to eight rooms.

My uncle Leonid and aunt Viktoriya Petrovna moved into 26 Kutuzov Prospekt in the 1950s. A few years later their daughter, Galina, moved back in with them, after divorcing Zhenya Milaev. Leonid ordered his next-door neighbor moved out so that the two apartments could be consolidated. No one was evicted—perish the thought! Instead, the neighbor was given a better apartment, in the same building or somewhere nearby. In the end, the Brezhnev family occupied the entire floor.

No leader on earth worried so much about his own safety and went to such pains to hide from the populace as the Soviet head of state. The system for guarding his residence had been well thought out. At the entrance, visitors had to present their documents to an armed guard, who would call my uncle's apartment and ask him, Are you home, are you ready to entertain, do you know the guests? Even my father and his sister, Vera, were required to present their passes to visit Leonid. Access to the Brezhnev floor required the presentation of yet another special pass.

A similar but much less stringent system exists in the building on Shevchenko Embankment, where my father has lived for many years. There it is old women who sit by the entrance like watchdogs, ready to pounce on any intruder. They have a list of those who can be admitted and require additional notification before each visit. An exception is made only for the closest relatives: daughters, sons, and grandchildren.

After Leonid Brezhnev's death, plaques in his honor were installed in many locations, including the outside wall of 26 Kutuzov, which was adorned with a bas-relief depicting him in marshal's uniform. These memorial plaques were torn down during the anti-Brezhnev hysteria unleashed by Gorbachev.

The dwellings of the elite, which I visited often during my early Moscow years, were like museums, some boasting stunning collections of old Dutch masters—Rembrandts and so forth. But as in their dachas, everything was thrown together without taste, for the sake of mere display: Yusupov* cobalt tea services, Meissen china, mantelpieces expropriated from palaces, crystal chandeliers, paintings, tapestries, icons, bronzes, crystal, silver, Baccarat cut glass, Chinese vases, porcelain, inlaid chests of drawers, ancient weapons, harpsichords, and fans.

I coveted only the books. The apartments I visited as "a niece" had magnificent libraries, not inherited from aristocratic ancestors, of course, but confiscated from "enemies of the people." There were some unique treasures, volumes no used-book store could ever have carried. Bored by the chitchat, I would withdraw discreetly to a corner and bury myself in reading; in such homes, the books were not to be borrowed. It was in the writer Konstantin Simonov's study that I read Annie Besant's work on theosophy and the writings of Saint Serafim of Sarov.

My passion for books once drove my father to larceny, albeit petty. The victim was Leonid Ilyich Brezhnev himself, though I doubt that he ever noticed. In the early '70s, when a slim volume of the works of Mikhail Bulgakov was published in the Soviet Union, it sold out almost immediately. I phoned my father and asked him to please get me a copy from the Central Committee book counter. He said that he had already used up his quota, taking several for his other daughters and his friends.

"I didn't even take one for myself," he added lamely.

"That's not right!" I said and hung up. I wanted him to understand

---

*Yusupov porcelain goods, highly prized to this day as antiques, were produced before the revolution in factories owned by the aristocratic Yusupov family.

how unfair it was—how could he refuse me such a small favor, especially since, unlike the rest of the family, I almost never asked him for anything?

Two weeks later he called, told me there was a copy of the book for me in his safe, and promised to bring it along the next time he saw me. Knowing that the next visitor to his office might wheedle the book out of him, I rushed to Nogin Square.

He took Bulgakov's book out of the safe and said, "You've turned me into a thief—I swiped it from Leonid's bookshelf. But no one will notice as long as you don't report me!"

"You know I could be punished as an accomplice, don't you?" I asked, laughing.

The homes of our top officials were also well stocked with live-in servants, a mixed blessing at best. As devoted as they might be, they all had to obey the KGB and make full reports on all members of the family they were serving, all visitors to the home, and topics discussed. They delved into the most intimate details, including the frequency with which the highly-placed couple made love. It was easy enough to peek into papers and notes, gather crumpled-up, unfinished letters from wastepaper baskets, and eavesdrop at doors. Servants were considered part of the family to such a degree that their presence was ignored and little attempt made to conceal anything from them. They heard all the complaints, all the tales of peccadilloes. Yet to the KGB, they offered answers to questions: What are the weaknesses of the head of the family? Which child does he favor? How often does he visit his mistress? What are his tastes?

In addition to good pay, the servants received perks similar to those of the low-level *nomenklatura:* free room and board, free recreation and trips to the south. For their relatives, they received imported medicines, apartments, and admission to institutes. They were certainly not as unsophisticated as appearances might have suggested. They were educated, patient, helpful, and polite. Their memory was excellent, and they knew how to restrain their emotions. When subjected to humiliation, all they could do was grin and bear it. How, for example, did the maid feel when thirteen-year-old Vikusya, Leonid's granddaughter, slapped her on the cheek? (My father was outraged by this incident.)

Leonid's children and his adult grandchildren had beautiful apartments of their own. They were able to find living space in the most prestigious locations in less than a week; the Moscow City Soviet had a special supply of apartments for this purpose. The Brezhnev clan also changed apartments freely, as they desired. I'm not sure when my father moved from the Arbat, but it was Marshal Ustinov who gave him the apartment where he now lives, in a building nicknamed the Generals' House.

Once I mentioned to my uncle a conversation I'd had in East Germany. Visiting Dresden in 1975, I had seen the ruins in the middle of the city. The opera building and a church still lay in a heap of bricks.

When I asked a journalist, an acquaintance, why these historic structures, damaged in World War II, had not been restored, he answered, "Because we first want to provide housing and the other essentials. Then we will think about beauty, culture, and recreation."

I agreed and thought of Russia: why, when old people are going hungry, the hospitals lack medicine, and many, if not most, tenants have to live in communal apartments, is the construction of marble monuments the first priority? I asked my uncle what he thought.

He was taken aback. "So you think we're less concerned about our people than the Germans? Just look how much new housing I've built around Moscow. These new buildings we're putting up are nothing like the *khrushchevki*. I plan to do whatever is need to ensure that each of our families has its own separate apartment."

I commented that the new residential districts were being built haphazardly: first buildings were thrown up, then people moved in, and only then was thought given to such amenities as clinics and bread stores. "There are some mistakes," conceded my uncle, "and we are fighting against them." I didn't ask whom he meant by "we."

When I was a child, my parents took me to a resort in the Crimea for the *nomenklatura*; there I found myself in another world, a fairy-tale kingdom where wishes were granted at the wave of a wand. We were welcomed to the shade of neatly laid out groves of trees and the comfort of crisply clean sheets; we were surrounded by sweetly fragrant lilies of the valley and polite, subdued conversation. There was a pool for those who for some reason might be averse to swimming in the clear blue sea. The sand on the enclosed, protected beaches was unnaturally yellow, and I began to suspect that someone washed it at night. The tennis courts were always well stocked with slim, suntanned young people who looked strangely out of place in Russia. The menu read like a passport to gourmet heaven.

Summer vacations during my childhood had provided vivid glimpses of how the other half vacationed. Provincial train stations were marked by dirt, stench, cries, people sleeping on benches and floors, crowds at ticket offices, long lines to use the toilet, and carbonated water, tepid and cloyingly sweet, which never quenched anyone's thirst. People took the trains by storm, losing belongings and children in the process. I still remember the sight of a young woman, her cotton dress crumpled from sleeping on a station bench, calling hysterically for her small daughter. All this for the privilege of spending two weeks swimming in a polluted sea that reeked of urine and sewage, lying on the hot sand, your foot on a stranger's shoulder, and standing in a long line to eat fried mackerel or a pale, bluish chicken leg.

All vacations have hazards, I guess. When I think of the Crimea, I am reminded of a little adventure my uncle had there; my father told the story one evening. Once when the brothers were out walking together in the Crimea, they stopped in a vineyard to answer nature's call. Leonid, who had a phobia about snakes, suddenly caught sight of an adder at his feet. Feeling the warm liquid pouring down, the snake arched its head gracefully as if deciding how to react to such an indignity. But it never had a chance to get even.

"You should have seen Lyonka jump out of that vineyard!" my father told me. "He sailed over the bushes like a young antelope."

The picture was so clear in my mind's eye that recalling the story always made me giggle.

Theoretically all Soviet citizens had the right to a dacha. There were four types: garden plots, from 400 to 800 square meters (4,300 to 8,600 square feet); cooperative dachas, from 800 to 3,500 square meters (8,600 square feet to a little under an acre); private dachas, which could be mansions; and state dachas.

The shacks on garden plots, known as chicken coops, were unheated, intended for summer use only. Especially in the winter, the coops around Moscow were raided by escaped prisoners and drunken young people from nearby villages. The uninvited guests, releasing all the rage they felt for the propertied city folk, smashed dishes and furniture, splashed ink, lit fires on the floor, defecated in saucepans and teapots, blocked up stovepipes with bricks, chopped down trees, and devoured the preserved vegetables and fruits.

The first dacha cooperatives were created in Stalin's day, largely to reward those who heaped praise on him, and were reserved for use by specific ministries, agencies, and academies. Most of these dachas are now occupied by the children and grandchildren of celebrities.

In the beautiful Nikolin Hill area, a short drive from Moscow on the Rublev Highway, is one of the best-known cooperatives: RANIS, whose initials stand for Rabotniki Nauki i Iskusstv—Workers in Science and the Arts. In the late '70s, its chairman was the composer Tikhon Khrennikov. He had no power and merely added his signature to documents handed down from above before going back to his ballads.

I sometimes visited the dacha of the RANIS assistant chairman, Vladimir Ottovich Shmidt, son of Otto Shmidt, the scholar, polar explorer, academician, and world traveler. Across the road was the huge lot of the poet Sergey Mikhalkov. Also not far off was the dacha of the poet Robert Rozhdestvensky, who glorified in verse my uncle's accomplishments (the Baikal-Amur Railway in particular), and the dacha of Aleksandra Pakhmutova, who made millions of rubles creating music to such immortal lyrics such as

> *Are you in the Komsomol?*
> *Yes*
> *Let us never part!*

The death of a RANIS dacha owner always set off pitched battles among prospective heirs, other cooperative members on the waiting list, and third parties with special pull. Vladimir Shmidt once called me to say that the widow of Flyorov, a celebrated academician, had passed away. Her dacha, he explained, could be sold to another member of the cooperative at a very low price, but there was a danger of losing it to some influential person not on the list.

"We'll wage a fight to the death," warned Vladimir Ottovich, refined intellectual though he was. Fight or no fight, the dacha did indeed end up in the hands of an outsider. The new owner—in name only—was the niece of some Central Committee department head: having state dachas at their disposal, men in his position were not permitted to buy their own, and so they often did an end run around the law with the help of relatives.

Private dachas, the most expensive, could be freely sold, willed to heirs, exchanged, and given away. Certain building standards, such as a height limit, applied even to these dachas, but the leeway was greater than that for cooperative dachas. For example, the owner could place a shed or a garage anywhere. Only cutting down trees required a permit— say, if you wanted to eliminate the pines whose shade was keeping your strawberries from thriving—but such permission was a mere formality.

Barvikha, originally just a village in the Moscow region, became the main site for the dachas—both state and private—of the Moscow elite. All the conveniences could be found there: stores, a restaurant, a movie theater, a dry cleaner's, a library, a sports complex, and a clinic. Rublev Highway, which connects Moscow to both Nikolin Hill and Barvikha, was carefully monitored and manicured. Accidents were unheard of: there were none of the potholes and open manholes that usually lay in wait for the Soviet driver, even in downtown Moscow; there was no chance of a rotten branch dropping onto your car or a drunk peasant stumbling into your path. Traveling this highway was a delight, if you could ignore the militiamen watching from checkpoints at every turn.

State dachas, one of the big rewards of the *nomenklatura*, were instituted right after the revolution. The countryside was torn by civil war; thousands were dying of typhus; villages torched by roving gangs were still ablaze. Running wild like wolf cubs, ragged, hungry, homeless children roamed the land. The roadside gallows had not yet been dismantled. Meanwhile the Bolsheviks began to divvy up the expropriated or abandoned estates and dachas.

My uncle's dacha was called the Dalnyaya ("Faraway"); though it was quite near Moscow, the name had stuck with it ever since the days when Stalin had used it and the capital was much smaller. Surrounded by a high fence, it was carefully guarded—not by a whole KGB division, as under Stalin, but just as vigilantly. There was no entry without a pass, of course; even the arrival of relatives was always planned. As Pushkin wrote in the nineteenth century,

> To preserve the peace of the lords at their leisure,
> The plain folk must not be let near.

The state dachas reserved for the elite were equipped with stables, orchards, and conservatories. My uncle had pheasants and peacocks strutting about in a pen. The quiet, secluded park on the property was a place for the general secretary, believing in all sincerity that he had been chosen by his nation to express its will and its interests, to stroll in peace.

Holidays in Barvikha were never complete without light shows, fireworks, horseback riding, and picnics: scenes of the Bolsheviks' heirs at play that could have been lifted straight out of a novel about the Russian nobility.

The dacha that stands out most in my mind belonged to Semyon Mikhailovich Budenny, the legendary military commander and civil war hero. He was known to everyone for his long, curling mustache and the *budyonovka*, a cloth military helmet named for him.

Located on a vast lot in Bakovka, near Moscow, his dacha dazzled the eye with tapestries, paintings, museum-quality furniture, handmade carpets, and marble statues from Venetian palaces. Once, visiting with my father, I asked if I could stroll around on my own. As I walked off, Budenny, his celebrated whiskers swinging back and forth, began to show off his Arabian racehorses, affectionately stroking and kissing them on the muzzle.

I came upon a small river with a boat pulled up onto the bank. A young soldier was sitting there, one of many assigned to dig ditches, prune hedges, and clean the horses and stables. He approached and offered to take me across the river, and I accepted.

On the other side, I was amazed by the profusion of berries and mushrooms in the forest. To all appearances, this was land untouched by human hands, untrampled by human feet. Meanwhile, beyond a fence, the commoners were crowded together on small garden plots, fighting over every scrap of land.

Budenny begged us to stay for dinner, but we begged off. Later I ran into the marshal several times at the Bolshoi Theater. An opera lover? I wondered. Then I noticed that he was busy helping himself to cognac and sandwiches—and thus ignoring the stage. At a performance of *Aïda* in which Galina Vishnevskaya was singing the lead, I was reveling in the singer's sumptuous voice. Meanwhile from one of the government loges came sporadic noise and laughter, interfering with my enjoyment of the music. It was the marshal himself, regaling my father with tales from his epic past—mainly his victories with the fair sex. You could be back at your magnificent dacha, I thought, and was tempted to walk over and ask him why the hell he wasn't.

During the civil war, Budenny had shown he could ride his horse rather well and wave his sword like an expert. Otherwise he never distinguished himself. But he filled a need for symbolic figures and played his role splendidly. A sad need for heroes elevated him, but to those who knew him well, he was a jester, a drunkard, a womanizer, and a simpleton.

Loyalty to family has always been a hallmark of the Russian character. Viktor Gen, a Baltic German, described us well in the nineteenth century: "In Russia, the individual is submerged in the body of the family." This virtue became one of the most glaring vices of the Soviet elite.

An informal system of nepotism began in the first years after the revolution. Lenin's personal frugality was spoken of for decades after his death, but even he gave special help to his wife's relatives. So it should come as no surprise that the members of the Politburo, along with the _nomenklatura_ elite in general, were prone to pamper their children. The elite's offspring must have been blessed with exceptional talent and diligence, judging by their careers. In fact, the ascension to government service was automatic for the children, grandchildren, and great-grandchildren of our political bosses. I don't know of a single "noble" son or daughter who descended into the masses by becoming a cook, a metalworker, or even a simple engineer.

As early as the 1930s, there were special schools to separate the _nomenklatura_'s children from hoi polloi. Later—first in Moscow, then in other cities—came schools in which a number of subjects were taught in foreign languages: English, French, German, Chinese, and others. Most prestigious were the English- and French-language schools, since they paved the way for jobs in almost any country of the world.

The next stop after high school, for budding diplomats, was the Institute of International Relations in Moscow, the Institut Mezhdunarondykh Otnosheniy, or IMO. This is where Andrey, my uncle Leonid's grandson, studied in the late '70s. He graduated during the Afghan war.

Even though they lived well within the Soviet Union—their fathers saw to that—the children of the elite all dreamed of foreign travel. Hence their desire to graduate at all costs from the Foreign Trade Academy, the Higher Party School, or the Higher Diplomatic School—the springboards to a career earning hard currency for peddling to foreigners what they knew were lies about the Soviet Union.

My life, too, seemed to pull me toward foreign shores. But I wanted to travel on my own terms. I found disgusting the plebeian, savage joy with which the gilded youth descended on their foreign booty: paper napkins decorated with naked women, Touch-Tone phones, Marlboro cigarettes, undershorts with KISS ME or PLAY WITH ME printed on them. In their homes, I saw marvelous collections of model cars plus American badges, imported liquor and Coca-Cola bottles, and ashtrays from foreign restaurants and hotels.

Ladies of the evening were just another privilege in the Soviet Union, where the prevailing attitude toward women was amazingly cynical.

Government officials especially liked to have affairs with actresses, singers, and ballerinas, and so many of these women were working for the KGB that the authorities usually winked at their activities.

My father told me that once after General Kliment Voroshilov learned that an actress he had taken a fancy to had been assigned to spy on him, he went to the Lubyanka and administered a punch to the face of secret police Deputy Chairman Stanislav Messing, who promptly resigned.

I was always reminded of this when I saw Klim on my father's hospital ward. Finally—this was less than a year before Voroshilov's death, in January of 1969—curiosity got the best of me, and I asked him if it was true. Evidently it was: transformed, his eyes lit up with a righteous indignation undiminished by the years; the old man spat out a fair sampling of Russian invective.

Men become amazingly careless in the embraces of their "beloved," and some actresses built their careers on the information they provided. No wonder Andropov knew some of the innermost secrets of even the most reticent Kremlin officials: in a half hour's time, an adroit and beautiful courtesan could find out things that could never be extracted in a Lubyanka basement.

A Kremlin courtesan was seen as doubly lucky. The KGB protected her and let her have virtually whatever she wanted; on the other hand, she was showered with gifts from a man who would spare nothing for his "true love" as long as she gave him occasional, brief escape from life's troubles. "Going to bed with the party" earned her many privileges: wonderful apartments, dachas, sable coats, French cosmetics, clothes from foreign catalogs, a healthy savings account. When her official died or left her for some reason, she would be assigned by the KGB to another. Eventually she would be allowed a decent retirement, as it was called: a chance to get married and put her life in order.

I've seen some of these kept women's apartments—impeccably neat, often elegant, and always devoid of human warmth. The inhabitants could not be loved, only bought, sold, exchanged, or passed on. They served genuine Brazilian coffee in antique, translucent Yusupov porcelain cups and took me into studies where rare books, titles that intellectuals saw only in their dreams, stood unread on the shelves. Proudly they showed me around their pristine, candy-box-pretty bedrooms and had me sniff their pillows, stuffed with Japanese herbs reputed to enhance sleeping. No Japanese herb could really help, though; their nerves must be shattered, I thought, and I could not help but feel pity for their lives.

Chapter Fourteen

SWIMMING UPSTREAM

How did it feel being a niece of this man who ruled Russia for years? Everyone who knew who I was imagined me endowed with unlimited powers. Yet my uncle wasn't able to protect me from the KGB, for an example. Still I couldn't fool myself into believing that I lived like everybody else. As a student at the Institute of Foreign Languages, I had a private room in the Moscow State University dormitory, my own telephone, and free access to the Kremlin stores and medical clinic.

Not everyone knew my identity, so I was not always spared the smug arrogance that was the hallmark of Soviet public interaction, that familiar, all-knowing intonation, as likely to come from a factory executive as from the woman handing you the claim to your locker at a public bathhouse. After people learned who my uncle was, I was amused to see a transformation. Now they would spare no efforts to respond to my slightest whim—anything to please their "superior." But I rebelled against being defined as a member of the Brezhnev clan or as a superior.

There was no love lost between me and my half sisters, who saw the role of general secretary's niece as their exclusive turf and feared that I would claim part of their inheritance. They wanted their father's other daughter to disappear from the scene, the sooner the better. During my infrequent visits to my father's home, my stepmother, Anna Vladimirovna, rattled the dishes more than was called for, and her face hardened. But she made no other overt display of hostility, and my father felt satisfied that we had finally learned to get along.

Also, I had no desire for the role of a poor relation waiting in the wings. After Helmut left Russia in 1966, I began distancing myself from all my relatives on my father's side. Tired and disgusted by Moscow's upper crust, I gradually descended into the realm of ordinary Muscovites, people forced to cope with a harsh world that I, too, felt churning under my feet. These were not tired aristocrats who had to invent problems out of thin air. I was relieved to find in them a capacity for kindness and sacrifice that persisted despite illnesses, anger, and infinite frustrations.

I made a few fast friends, who went out of my life only when circumstances tore us apart; some died, and some fled westward, to send me letters, few and far between, about their bitter lives in exile.

From time to time, Eastern European Communist leaders came to the Soviet capital. They came for instructions, they came for intrigue. They came to hammer out lucrative contracts for their countries. Often they came to betray one of their comrades. And they came for rest and relaxation.

The general secretary received the bought-and-paid-for party princes gladly: after all, the state was picking up the tab for the lordly food and drink. Leonid loved parties and enjoyed any opportunity for a drink as long as his health permitted. He was known for his Russian-style hospitality; he offered his vassals hunting trips, saunas, and, for those still able to perform, a selection of women. Such visits were a time for handshakes, kisses, photographs of leaders embracing, assurances of eternal friendship, and, of course, gifts. Along with the cognac and the caviar, guests received generous contracts for the construction of factories, plants, power stations, and railroads in their countries. Brezhnev asked in return only peace and tranquillity; he insisted that no one cause trouble, disturb the world community, or "violate the integrity of the socialist camp."

When the people of Prague decided to make a number of reforms in 1968, echoing the Soviet "thaw" that had followed the long, cold winter of Stalinism, was this integrity threatened? Moscow, incidentally, knew little of what was happening in the other socialist countries and was caught off guard by the developments. Diplomats and other Soviet representatives, even though they were almost all working for the KGB, were careful to report only those "truths" that higher-ups wanted to hear from them; to express personal views or assessments was to invite recall or worse.

Alexander Dubček, the intellectual who led the Czech rebellion, should be given his due. Up until the last moment, he tried to negotiate a peaceful resolution with the Soviet party leadership, arguing that he was not, in fact, against socialism but merely wanted reforms that would help his country overcome its economic crisis.

My uncle, however, saw Dubček as an insurgent stirring up a nation that had been living peacefully up to that time. As he said, "Bad examples are contagious. What one can get away with will become law for all." Dubček became an irritation to the Politburo, then to the general secretary personally. As my father once told me, the prevailing opinion was that Dubček had lost his senses.

As the Politburo debated the situation in Czechoslovakia, the events of 1956 in Hungary were still fresh in everyone's minds. Pyotr Shelest, then first secretary of the Ukrainian Communist Party, was most furious of all; no one knew the consequences all this might have for Ukraine, where, not long before, a group of dissidents and Ukrainian nationalists had been put on trial.

Leonid Brezhnev favored a waiting game. He opposed the use of extreme methods and genuinely expected that the conflict might resolve itself. The other members of the Politburo spoke in favor of military intervention.

On the night of August 20, 1968, Soviet aircraft dropped paratroopers into Czechoslovakia in an intervention signaling the return of the Soviet Union to the brutal totalitarian stance that tolerates no ideological deviations. Soviet intellectuals understood this well; their protests were muted, however, because they lacked mass support. Citizens who picketed, demonstrated, or wrote protest letters were arrested. Some received five- to seven-year prison sentences, and others would languish in mental hospitals, all for the "insane" act of expressing an opinion. Could anyone in the corridors of power, I wondered, have any idea of what it meant to serve seven years' hard labor in a Siberian labor camp? I knew something of it from my friend Georgy.

Once when my father was retelling the harrowing tale of the NKVD hunting down his brother in 1937, he pointed out that Leonid "could have ended up in a lumber camp."

I couldn't resist saying, "Too bad he didn't. If he had, maybe he wouldn't have the heart to send young kids today to such places."

My father responded by accusing me of political immaturity and told me not to poke my nose into affairs that didn't concern me.

From what I was able to observe, the occupation of Czechoslovakia and the gross interference in its internal affairs caused Leonid no remorse. He believed that he was performing his sacred duty to the Czech and the Russian peoples. For that matter, no one I met from the older generation who had survived the war approved of the Prague Spring. They all roundly condemned Dubček and other supporters of reform.

Leonid, who had been in Czechoslovakia in May 1945, when the war ended and had buried his own comrades-in-arms there, was unable to excuse the desecration of the common graves and the monuments to Soviet soldiers that occurred shortly after the Soviet intervention. He trembled whenever he spoke of it. For him, the Russians, who had sacrificed their lives in foreign lands, were liberators and not an occupying army.

As I listened to my uncle's stories about the war, I often wondered what life at the front had taught him, what human qualities he had displayed at that supremely difficult time for the country. Leonid served for the duration of the war, helping to liberate Poland, Romania, Hungary, and Czechoslovakia from fascism. After seeing city after city fall to the Nazis in 1941, after experiencing close brushes with death, the men of his generation who survived drove the Nazis from Russia by steeling their hearts and adopting an inflexible, inhuman code of values. At the same time, they came fully of age, and beneath their hard shells they harbored deep feelings.

Leonid's attitude toward Prague may have been influenced by his friendship with the hard-line secretary of the Czechoslovak party, Klement Gottwald. Their relationship had begun in the '40s, when my uncle was first secretary of the Dnepropetrovsk Oblast party committee. During visits to Ukraine, Gottwald enjoyed the hospitality of the Brezhnev home; at the dining table drinking chilled vodka, the two leaders reminisced about the war days in Prague, the joint Soviet-Czechoslovak victory celebration, the oaths of eternal brotherhood, the shared exhilaration over the long-awaited peace.

In my presence, Leonid once said, "If we hadn't brought our troops into Czechoslovakia, all the Communists would have been killed."

"No great loss," I said. My father nudged me under the table, his way of saying, "Shut the hell up!" My uncle pretended not to have heard me, making it clear that he couldn't care less about such stupid comments. He went on, "The fascists were already at the border, so the only thing left for the Politburo to do was to vote for intervention." By fascists, he evidently meant the West Germans.

Then he made a statement that jolted me: "From now on, I'll put a muzzle on the socialist camp and keep it shut as long as I can." And he made a gesture as though he were muzzling a dog.

In the '70s, I decided to introduce my father to Georgy Malyuchenko, my close friend since 1969 and a remarkable man.

Once a professor at Moscow State University, he was the author of several books and articles about the theater. In 1937, accused of links with Trotsky, he had been sent to the labor camps of Kolyma and held there until 1956.

My father and I went to the scholar's modest quarters, a small, damp room in one of the outlying districts. He lived surrounded by books accumulated in the years after his release. I knew that during visits to the Lenin Library and perusals of private collections, he often winced with pain as he noticed books bearing his family seal. All had been confiscated from the five-room apartment in which he was living at the time of his arrest.

Malyuchenko gave us a courteous but cool reception. The only way I knew to warm him up to visitors was to steer the conversation to literature and the theater; when I did, he would always brighten and show off his books and his photographs of celebrities of the theater. But the subject I wanted to hear about was life in the camps. What would make a man who had slaved for nineteen years on trumped-up charges share his experiences with the general secretary's brother?

The day before, the old man had explained the essence of Dostoyevsky's and Vladimir Solovyev's theories of dark and light angels, citing compelling examples from his own observations. I decided to bring up this subject again. His interest aroused, Malyuchenko spoke of a world where human feelings were crushed so brutally that even rage and despair were a blessing: they showed that your soul was alive. . . . Here is the story he told us.

"In 1937, a handsome young actor who was touring in Moscow set out on a walk around the city. He ended up on Red Square. He hummed and walked briskly, thinking of his fiancée back in Riga. Suddenly someone addressed him in broken Russian—a foreigner asking directions to the Tretyakov Gallery. They both switched to German. That night three NKVD agents came to the actor's hotel, got him out of bed, and dragged him half-asleep to the Lubyanka, where he was beaten and tortured for three days and three nights. He denied any connection with German intelligence but was quickly convicted of espionage and sent to Siberia. We slept in the same barracks.

"For a few years of cold, humiliation, and hunger, he remained convinced that his arrest had been a stupid mistake and that he would eventually be released with an apology. Toward the end of the third year, he began to doubt that his fellow prisoners were really all enemies of the people. He began to observe and listen closely; his confidence in the possibility of justice shattered, he began to plot an escape.

"I did everything but get down on my knees and beg him to reconsider. My entreaties fell on deaf ears.

" 'Death is better than this injustice,' the Latvian actor told me.

"No one could get very far. . . . When the guards caught up with him, they beat him and hauled him back to the camp. The next morning he was forced to walk a gauntlet of his fellow prisoners. Guards stood behind us, watching carefully; each of us struck a blow with the sharp rods we had been given. I hit him myself. Fear never fails to awaken the dark angel.

"When the actor reached the end of the line, his heart gave out, and he died. He was so young. Twenty-five . . . as I wept for him later, I recalled how he had lamented to me night after night, 'I can't sleep, Zhora; my needs as a man won't give me a minute's peace.'

"The following morning we were ordered to stand in a large pit and then to bend over enough to bring our heads level with the ground. Whenever a guard saw a prisoner's head sticking out, he would hit it with his rifle butt. We tried to hold one another up with our elbows, but, exhausted after the previous day's ten hours of felling trees in sub-zero temperatures, we began to faint. As you can see, I'm almost two meters tall [about six feet seven inches], so it was especially hard for me to stay in the required position.

"After several blows to the head, I became enraged. I remembered my friend who had just been beaten to death. The next time one of the guards raised his rifle butt to strike me, I grabbed it and dragged him into the pit, rifle and all. Then five guards began beating me.

"During the beating, I asked, 'Why, my brothers, do you beat a fellow Russian Orthodox?' They only hit harder. I was strong and healthy, something they couldn't stand. They beat me till they were too tired to continue.

"The next morning we were taken to work in the forest. I felt that death was nearby, awaiting its appointed hour. It was forty degrees below zero, a ten-kilometer [six-mile] walk under strict guard, and no one knew whether any one of us would get back to the barracks alive. Everyone knows what skimpy rags they gave us. Enemies of the people didn't even have the right to a belt: they were allowed nothing from which they might make a noose and end the misery. They wanted us alive, to work us like dogs and, when *they* decided we were too worn out, to shoot us somewhere in the bushes. Come to think of it, they didn't like to waste bullets. Their weapons of choice were rifle butt and hunting knife. We all knew that resistance was useless. Besides, we had neither the moral nor the physical energy to try anything.

"We came to the work site; my fellow prisoners began sawing down trees. I lay down under a spruce, unable to lift a finger after my beating. Before my death, I wanted to be alone with my soul. As I was lying there, a tree crashed down, breaking a bone in my foot. That was it: if the guards noticed, they would slit my throat in the bushes. But then one of the prisoners, a doctor from Moscow, improvised a splint for my foot. Some other prisoners set me down where I could work without moving, trimming limbs off felled trees. When quitting time came, they carried me to the barracks—the whole ten kilometers. The guards, pretty drunk, didn't notice a thing—Stalin supplied them with plenty of alcohol to keep them warm, and many eventually drowned their lives in the bottle. My fellow prisoners, the same men who had beat the young actor to death, hid me under rags until I was able to walk again. They saved my life. There's the mysterious Russian soul for you."

My father was spellbound by the professor's tale.

When we rose to leave, Malyuchenko followed, to see us to the street, but I asked him not to bother. I didn't want him to see the shiny black Volga waiting outside. On the way home, my father vented outrage at the injustice visited on the old man.

"He was just the victim of what you like to call 'one of those mistakes,' " I interjected.

In a burst of charity, my father promised to help find Malyuchenko a decent apartment. I said nothing, knowing from long experience that he would forget his vow the next day, as soon as some new favor seeker needed an apartment for a mistress.

My father's drinking and debauchery fed rumors, and his authority in his own family was slipping. Feeling increasingly independent, his daughters and their husbands began avoiding him.

I eventually stopped going to his home altogether but often dropped by to see him at his office. It was still a madhouse: constant phone calls, visitors running back and forth, clerks and favor seekers coming and going, reports to be delivered. We sometimes met to see a play or to eat out. When we lost contact for a few weeks, he would call me suddenly and ask in a voice full of concern why I was acting like such a stranger.

My stock answer: "The pope is easier to reach than you are."

"You should have called me at home," I would hear him object in between giving instructions to some provincial factory engineer on another line.

"Anna Vladimirovna said you were asleep and offered to wake you, but I told her I never disturb people enjoying a well-earned rest," I explained.

My father would laugh and hang up.

In 1970, I graduated from the Institute of Foreign Languages. During my final three years, I concentrated on my studies and came close to graduating with honors. My father wanted me to continue, and I was offered the chance to do graduate work in linguistics or French literature. But the child my husband and I were expecting took precedence.

My marriage to Mischa, the son of an Armenian architect, a fine young scientist who despite his accomplishments was a commoner, had caused shock waves among my relatives. Their view was that Luba must be out of her mind, freely choosing to share the life of an ordinary citizen. Their opinion meant nothing to me by this time.

My husband had firmly decided against using my father's or my uncle's influence, and he went through all the usual hardships of a Soviet scientist. Mischa's nationality worked against him. Bearing his Armenian last name, I, too, experienced the hostility directed against non-Russians in Moscow, not by the people as a whole, but by the faceless bureaucrats who ruled us.

Beginning with Helmut's departure and until my marriage settled the point, my father sought constantly to find eligible young men for me. He loved to drag me to snooty salons so I could hear a potential husband play the piano and discuss Picasso after first chatting in French with his grandmother. . . . Out of pure malice, I would appear as dull and countrified as I could. When my father took me home, I would declare, to his immense annoyance, that I would only marry someone wise and wealthy; a sweet old man like him, after all, could do more for me than some young dolt.

Once when he invited me to the home of a government minister who had "a wonderful son," I remarked that all the charming men like himself were either already taken or dead and asked him to fix me up with a job as a maid with one of his friends, so I could support myself as a spinster. I painted a picture of myself preparing the health food then coming into vogue among the rich and powerful of Moscow.

"Your jokes turn my stomach," he said.

"Your 'wonderful young men' do the same for me."

Marriage immersed me in ordinary Soviet life; I came to know lines, food shortages, and hours-long waits in the corridors of neighborhood polyclinics to see a general practitioner or have an X ray taken.

We had to face the problem of where to live. I didn't want to go to my father or uncle for help, nor would Mischa have stood for it: he was opposed to using my family connections in any way. In January of 1970, we purchased a cooperative apartment in one of the new outlying neighborhoods of Moscow.

Cooperative apartment buildings, constructed at the tenants' expense, were not much better than state-owned buildings. The imported materials for which tenants paid extra—wallpaper, tiles, and toilets—were all sold on the black market and replaced by Soviet-made junk.

The day after we moved, my father dropped by "to spend five minutes with us," as he put it on entering. The elevator didn't work, and two thirds of the units were still vacant. Our apartment had no furniture and no electricity, but it was overflowing with guests: everyone we knew had come by to celebrate our housewarming.

I will always remember that evening, one of the happiest of my life. We piled our books in a corner, laid out two mattresses and a blanket on the floor, and covered them with sheets. The food was on a tablecloth between the mattresses, and we all drank tea straight out of a three-liter jar. My father joked that the next time he came, he'd be sure to bring his own tea service, "or you'll have me drinking out of a bucket like a camel." Everyone laughed.

The jar was like a campfire. We sat around it in a circle on the floor, united by love and sincere affection, completely at ease with one another, with nothing to hide. Someone had propped me up against the wall so I wouldn't collapse: I was still getting over a case of the flu that had lasted more than a month. My position allowed me to observe my father freely. He was sitting on a crate we had provided him, as our eldest guest, for lack of a better seat. All the others were young people with dissident tendencies, and almost all of them would emigrate to the West within a few years. None asked my father for favors; they treated him with the respect becoming his gray hair but with no trace of sycophancy, flattery, or even idle curiosity. I felt sorry as I watched him: he had gone too long without the warmth, sympathy, and understanding we were sharing.

One of our friends had his guitar with him, and we all sang. Besides Russian ballads and folk songs, there were contemporary songs, by Aleksandr Galich, Vladimir Vysotsky, and Bulat Okudzhava. These were the favorite singer-songwriters among the youth but were out of favor with the authorities, and we remarked slyly that we had nothing to worry about, with the general secretary's brother himself on our side. At this, my father bellowed with laughter and fell off his crate.

My husband and I saw Yakov Ilyich to his car at two in the morning, when he left reluctantly, giddy with an overflowing happiness. He strode jauntily, his hat cocked Russian style to one side, his hands in his pockets, whistling "Katyusha."

For years to come, he recalled this gathering, asking me from time to time about the people he had met.

Still basking in the afterglow of my housewarming, he called the next morning: "I just came from a five-minute meeting [that is, an hour-long conference], and I've been trying to figure out what work needs to be done in your apartment. I've decided to take up the matter seriously next week."

I thanked him but ignored his offer. A few minutes later, swamped with urgent business and calls asking for favors, he would forget about us. He often reproached me for not reminding him of my problems—after all, perfect strangers felt no compunction about putting their claws into him. But I didn't know how to do it and felt that it was his duty to remember his daughters without reminders.

Nineteen-seventy was a year filled with joyous events: my husband received the candidate of science degree in the spring,* and in August our second son, Andrey, was born. The day after my release from the maternity hospital, my father brought me an enormous package of things I might need for the baby. There were also presents for me—perfume from Paris and cosmetics. He stood by the baby carriage, studying my son's face intently.

As the years passed, both my uncle and my father would note with pleasure the striking similarity between themselves and Andrey, who was growing into a muscular, broad-shouldered boy with bushy eyebrows. My father frequently watched my children playing on the carpet. Glancing at Andrey, who acquired a silly way of tossing his head back like a pony and looking down at his little friends as he talked to them, he would tell me proudly, "That one favors our side of the family, the Brezhnev side."

Except for the wives of the political elite and the wives of admirals and generals, practically all Russian women work outside the home: they need the money to help support their families. Children are put into day care at a young age, allowing even new mothers to work.

I, too, joined the workforce soon after graduation, taking a job in the translation section of a scientific institute. Yet there was one thing I never did translate: to this day, I haven't the slightest idea what the institute's cryptic initials—TsNIITE—stood for.

I remember those days fondly. We faced, and always met, a heavy monthly work quota of translation and summary writing but found ample time for socializing. My new colleagues included some of Moscow's finest young intellects, most of them also dissidents. It was here that I met the wife of Yuri Mamleev, a well-known writer who spent several years in America after emigrating. And one of the other

---

*The candidate of science degree corresponds roughly to the American Ph.D.

translators was Aleks Shchedin, a fellow student at the Institute of Foreign Languages.

At work, I proudly wore tight jeans (coming into fashion then), yellow suede boots, and a black T-shirt featuring a tiny American flag: all presents my father had brought back from a trip abroad. I was the envy of my co-workers.

Aleks worked at the desk opposite mine, and one day I saw him shaking with laughter. I looked down to see what was funny. He pointed to my socks, one red, one blue: I was wearing mismatched colors for luck.

Just before his emigration, to Holland in 1976, he told me, "I fell in love with you because of those socks." Our friendship never developed into anything more, but to this day I remember Aleks with great love and gratitude and sometimes with sad thoughts of what might have been.

In 1970, a group of Jews was convicted of hijacking an airplane with the intention of leaving the country. Two of them were sentenced to death; their sentences were later commuted, and like the nine others they served long terms in prison camp. Their trial sparked the beginning of a peaceful mass movement of Jews seeking the right to emigrate. By the early '70s, many of my friends—both Jews and Russians pretending to be Jews—had already left the Soviet Union. The haste with which my uncle eventually began handing out exit visas aroused suspicions: was he letting the Jews escape or trying to "save Russia from the Jews"?

My father knew that many of the people he had dined with at my home were leaving for the West; I made no attempt to conceal the fact. He condemned their actions: "Their motherland gives them everything they have, and then they turn around and betray her."

"You talk just like a KGB man," I said but smiled.

It was no use trying to explain to him the concept of freedom to live in the country of one's choice. His views were conservative, his support for his brother's policies steadfast.

During Leonid's rule, quotas limited Jewish enrollment in universities and the number of Jews given residence permits in the major cities, and some Jews were refused positions because of their nationality. My uncle did not create these policies but never spoke out against them; the Jews had the best jobs, apartments, and dachas anyway, as he saw it. "Even the best graveyards of Moscow are filled with Jews," he would say.

I have no justification for his attitude. I was ashamed that racial and religious discrimination, that blemish on civilized society, existed in the Soviet Union, and when I saw my Jewish friends being harassed, I tried to help them as much as I could.

I was part of a generation that lived in a state of continual frustration with the bans, limits, and regulations we encountered. Alongside our conflicts with society, we were often eaten by internal conflicts, by nagging doubts about our own worth. Trying with no success to find an antidote to the spiritual emptiness all around us, many turned to alcoholism, drugs, and suicide.

Others—candidates of science, engineers, and physicians, yearning for truth and tired of their angry, gloomy thoughts—threw themselves into unskilled labor, where they at least felt free from a life of lies. A distinct type appeared: the oddball who was both intellectual and worker, a university graduate clad in overalls, covered with soot and grime. This sort of freedom was viable for some, but not everyone could afford such a drastic break: it was not so attractive if you had children you wanted to feed and perhaps even to treat to ice cream on Sundays.

Among my friends were many artists who had no choice: they had to work as janitors, watchmen, or boilermakers to avoid becoming "parasites." Before one painter who was a friend of mine could be admitted to the Union of Graphic Artists, she had taken a part-time job restoring the faded murals of saints on the inside of rural church domes. Because this was not an official job, she also worked as a stoker to satisfy the law requiring that everyone be gainfully employed. She was lucky in one way: her fellow stoker Vitya, perennially drunk and unwashed though he was, would volunteer to work her shift as well as his own while she was doing her restoration work.

Eventually friends who had gone the menial-labor route set aside their brooms and pokers and returned, like prodigal sons, to their desks, operating tables, and university chairs. Others hurried to apply for emigration and, if luck was with them, set off for foreign shores. There they adapted, with varying degrees of success.

The supervisor of the translation section where I worked was a specialist in Japanese. Also a dipsomaniac, he would come back to the institute after binges of several weeks and walk around as gingerly as if he were balancing a crystal ball on his head. He was a democrat but a coward, with a respect for freedom tempered by a greater fear of higher-ups. Realizing that ten people couldn't function in a room of twenty square meters (about twenty-four square yards), he often sent us to work at home or in the library, to our delight.

Our schedule was hardly structured. We reported to work at 9:00 A.M. promptly, since someone at the door of the institute kept track of all tardiness. But by 9:05, we sometimes had our section sealed off from the inside "for urgent work": how convenient that the office had plenty of sofas and armchairs, the better to catch up on sleep missed the previous night. Everyone's closet held a blanket and a pillow for maximum comfort.

I noticed that the telephone was a key fixture of office life, very important—for peace talks with husbands and lovers, for homework consultations with beloved offspring. Other popular pastimes among the women were touching up eyebrows and trying on the tights or blouses delivered by the in-house *spekulyant* (black-market dealer) who dropped by our section twice weekly.

One o'clock was lunchtime, and the entire section in which I worked—except for two elderly women who preferred to heat up a lunch brought from home—went to a nearby restaurant. The meal and conversation usually lasted about two hours. Some might go straight from the restaurant to the nearby GUM, and if something hard to find was being sold that day, the scouts would call back with a detailed account—sizes, colors, brand names. Sometimes they would ask for additional forces and funds, and we would negotiate with the other sections and send a delegation to the store. The shoppers would try to return in time for the final work hours, which would be spent trying on purchases.

Nonetheless, as I have mentioned, we always met our monthly quotas. This, thanks to the traditional Russian *avral* (storm work): at the end of every month, we began a frenzy that lasted until the remaining assignments had been completed.

Two years after my hiring, the nest of dissidents I worked in began emptying out as my colleagues left one by one for the capitalist countries. The director, a diminutive man with Hitleresque bangs that he was constantly shaking back—it made you want to slip him a three-ruble note and the address of the nearest barbershop—came running into our section whenever a translator made known his or her intention to emigrate. Little fists waving, he would threaten to have us fired and break up our "anti-Soviet snake pit." Before he left, handsome Tolya Buyanovsky, the pride of the section, would reassure him: "Don't worry, we'll leave by ourselves."

The director was such a fury at times that I called him the Pocketsize Lion, a nickname that stuck to him like glue.

Those who applied to emigrate were fired and wound up unemployed while awaiting action on their applications. Shchedin, who knew three foreign languages, had to find work at a streetcar station, assigning the drivers their routes; I remember that his mother also helped him out with food. After Yuri Mamleev's wife was fired, Yuri, unable to get anything published, wore flannel shirts sewn by his aunt from old bathrobes. Many made ends meet by giving private lessons.

Eventually my section dwindled to three translators—the two women near pension age and me. In 1974, I, too, gave notice.

"Where are you going?" Our director looked at me, black eyes flashing. "We were just planning to raise your salary by five rubles."

"Excuse me," I answered heatedly, "you don't mean my salary but my allowance, the pittance that the nice Bolsheviks allow us to have."

The director didn't understand but did offer to up the raise from five to fifteen rubles.

By law, I had to stay at my job for ten days after giving notice. Two days before my final one, the director ran in out of breath and offered me a forty-five-ruble raise, which would have brought my salary to 150 rubles a month.

"Don't haggle with me; we're not at a bazaar," I said. "I can't work at an institute that fires some of its best employees."

"What do you have in common with those renegades? They're leaving the country anyway. Besides, your uncle is so . . ." he began.

"Go on," I asked curiously.

"So—well, you know—so famous," he said after a pause.

"Famous for what?"

"For being general secretary."

"Oh, I thought it might be something else," I answered, my voice a study in disappointment.

On my last day at work, I was given a going-away party by the institute as a whole, in accordance with tradition. Sonya Shtern, a translator in a different section, looked at the cakes and fruit laid out before us and wept bitterly. On that day, she had been jilted by her lover. Then her only daughter, her pride and joy, had told her that she was going to marry and leave the country. Finally, when Sonya was back with her husband, both of them lying in their bedroom treating bad-news headaches with vinegar compresses, their cat, Barsik, had run away through an open door.

"Never again," she said, blowing her nose into a lace handkerchief and swearing off children, lovers, and pets.

My husband, Mischa, belonged to what he and his friends called the deceived generation. Beginning in the '50s, the Soviet mass media and other propaganda outlets had been drumming into people's heads the importance of higher education. Young people were led to believe that if they studied well, they would live well. Study they did, and very hard at that. But when they graduated, they found nepotism and corruption suffocating scholarly life.

If your father was a doctor of science, he would carefully weed out anyone who might stand in the way of your career: you were sure at the very least to become a candidate of science; if you had any brains at all, the doctorate degree was also yours.* The consequence was that many talented but unconnected young scientists were crushed. Some were driven to emigrate; others remained, slowly rotting away, their work uncompensated and unrecognized. During the perestroika period of the late '80s would come another brain drain, as the best and most enterprising flocked into the newly formed cooperatives.

Without a powerful backer, inventors stood little chance of seeing the fruits of their toil. In their patent applications, they had to list as collaborators the names of the right people—those able to get an invention past the necessary committee. Otherwise red tape would eat up so much time and energy that none would remain for inventing.

The publication of scientific articles and monographs was plagued by similar corruption. More than one hundred works—all the work my husband published—bear the names of co-authors, but only one really merited the title: Samvel Grigoryan, corresponding member of the Academy of Sciences of the Soviet Union, who not only supervised Mischa's work in the field of soil dynamics but participated in it directly. The other co-authors had only a vague idea, or none at all, of the work involved.

Mischa had been hired by the Department of Hydraulics of the Institute of Petroleum and Gas in the '60s. The department head, world-renowned professor Isaak Charny, welcomed my husband with outstretched arms, knowing that Samvel Grigoryan, under whom my husband had done his graduate work at Moscow State University, would not allow mediocre graduate students.

After Charny's sudden death, the other professors began settling old scores by taking revenge on his students and professors. Even as great a scientist as Belokon got caught up in the general hysteria, coming down unjustifiably hard on Charny's graduate students, in the name of scientific rigor, of course. The word at the institute was that Belokon was "at war with a dead man."

This type of conflict between scientists had become the norm. Often

---

*The Russian doctor of science degree is considered somewhat more advanced than the American Ph.D.

members of the commissions at candidate or doctoral defenses "dropped bombs" on a trembling graduate student, all to take revenge on his or her adviser.

In the '60s, my cousin Galina Brezhnev, Leonid's daughter, had an affair with an instructor at my husband's institute, a tall, handsome, black-haired man. I learned about this from my father, who repeatedly lent her his apartment when she learned that he and his family were going to be out of town.

"We have nowhere else to make love," Galina would explain frankly, when asking for the key.

One Monday morning Anna Vladimirovna, leaving the dacha to make an unexpected visit to the dentist, decided to use the occasion to tidy up the apartment. She was in for quite a shock: first there were the kitchen and bedrooms, in total disarray; then came the sight of the general secretary's daughter, sleeping peacefully in her lover's embrace. Galina had to make do with her girlfriends' apartments from then on.

It was about this same time—the late '60s—that Mischa and I made our first application to leave the Soviet Union, not as emigrants but to work in Algeria. But there were considerable obstacles in our way, the main one being the institute's party committee.

Then X, a likable instructor not very well versed in his subject but privy to all the backdoor goings-on at the institute, offered my husband a three-way deal, one that would supposedly win us approval from the committee in question. For a consideration (my husband's signature in the grade book of a student who had paid X to "fix things up"), X would arrange a meeting between my husband and Galina's lover, who was in a position to help us—in exchange for some other favor, of course. My husband agreed.

The favor, it turned out, was Grigoryan's evaluation of a doctoral dissertation. Galina's lover told my husband, "Mischa, convince Samvel to give me an evaluation, and you can name any favor you want."

My husband agreed to talk to his former graduate adviser, asking in exchange that Galina's lover have a talk with the secretary of the institute's party committee. They shook hands on the deal.

Grigoryan was a highly principled scientist who would give a favorable evaluation only if the work merited it, and he had no real reason even to glance at the work of some unknown. But when my husband gathered his courage and explained the situation, Grigoryan agreed to look the dissertation over.

"Keep in mind," he warned, "that if the work is a bunch of nonsense, I won't write anything. The most I can promise is that I won't make any negative comments."

He didn't ask whether the work had been done by someone other than the supposed author, but Mischa volunteered the information that Galina's lover had at the very least digested the material: he wouldn't disgrace himself or Grigoryan at the oral defense.

The dissertation was accepted, and my husband called the new doctor of science to remind him of the agreement. Grateful, Galina's lover promised to keep his part of the deal. But he never even showed up at the meeting of the party committee, nor did he have a talk with any of the committee members. The truly byzantine maneuvering had achieved nothing, and our plans for Algeria faded rapidly.

Galina's lover was a married man with children, and Leonid was opposed to their relationship, as was my father. Before too long, they broke up, and Galina moved on to Yuri Churbanov. Nevertheless, her former lover rose on the career ladder rapidly, gently sweeping every obstacle from his path. I assume he used his affair with the general secretary's daughter for all it was worth. Very affable, quite impressive looking, never at a loss for a pleasant word, he eventually became the head of a department at the Academy of Sciences.

From the moment Vladimir Vinogradov, a so-so specialist with scant interest in science, became rector of the Institute of Petroleum and Gas, he worked to keep energetic fresh talents from gaining any power. Many young people who had dedicated themselves heart and soul to science buckled under the pressure and fled to other Moscow institutes—there still were some where their contributions would be appreciated.

Meanwhile a horde of second-rate specialists rose to prominence, just as skilled as their master in the art of advancing themselves through the work of capable, well-trained young people. They knew how to keep a close rein on their protégés and, most important of all, how to keep them hidden from public view.

Vinogradov had insisted that my husband list Vladimir Biryukov— an old friend of his who had helped him displace the previous rector in the mid-'60s—as co-author of a number of his scientific articles. Biryukov was also the first Soviet contract adviser in Algeria; as such, he headed up the delegation of experts working there under a contract signed not long after the country gained independence, in 1962. Everyone knew that he was also reporting to the KGB.

Before Vinogradov's rise to power, at least ten world-class scientists had worked at the institute. In the early '70s, as these worthy veterans left this world one by one, their individual "schools"—the talents they grouped around them—fell apart; they were usually replaced by faceless, lackluster scientists. The atmosphere was poisoned by endless petty scheming, gossip, and dirty tricks. The rector put all his organizational skills and energy into the construction of new buildings and cafeterias, as well as the garages, dachas, and housing that he distributed to his hangers-on. Scientific life came to a virtual halt. Illustrative of the decline in academic standards was the fact that between 1967 and 1977, only one department head at the institute was a member of the Academy of Sciences of the Soviet Union: Yuri Ovchinnikov, the well-known mathematician.

By the mid-'70s, my husband had prepared his own doctoral dissertation for the Institute of Petroleum and Gas. The necessary experiments had been done, the rough draft was written, and all that remained was to type the final draft.

The day before Mischa was due to present his preliminary defense, Vinogradov called him in to his office. Avoiding my husband's eyes, he explained: "Biryukov is going to defend the dissertation. You're still young, you can write another," Vinogradov continued. Afraid that Biryukov wouldn't be able to answer questions about my husband's work, he added: "*You* will give the report to the scientific council."

He then assured my husband that he could use the next paper he wrote for his own doctorate. How generous. But even that was something, in their world.

Chapter Fifteen

IN SEARCH OF
MY FATHER

In March 1973, on the day before my husband's birthday, all the Communists in the country were assigned new numbers. Stepping ahead of all his predecessors except Lenin himself, my uncle, a "true Leninist" and "outstanding member of the Communist Party," received card 00000002.

The drunken celebrations of the Great Renumbering continued for days, at least among my father's associates. Late in the day after the renumbering, my father came by our home, his faithful friend Nikolay Skvortsov in tow. Accustomed to being regaled wherever they went, they were unimpressed by the dinner, lavish for us, that I had prepared for Mischa's birthday. Instead, they turned their attention to the crate of West German beer they had brought with them and the cognac some of my husband's relatives and colleagues had sent him from Yerevan for the occasion.

I was afraid that, as usual, my father would get drunk and start telling his family tales. He had come to relish making the rounds, titillating the jaded aristocracy with tidbits about his brother, his sister-in-law, Viktoriya Petrovna, and his niece, Galina. I knew that at any party I gave, there was bound to be an informer or two; that was no big deal, since they wouldn't hear anything they hadn't heard before. What bothered me was that my friends, indifferent to the stories that had won my father such popularity in high-society-Moscow gossip mills, would have to be exposed to such nonsense. I resigned myself to the prospect of a ruined evening. After all, I couldn't order my father not to talk.

He had acquired other annoying habits: dropping the names of his celebrity friends and bragging in public about his brother's accomplishments and even about how smart his little granddaughters were—all of this with a pompous expression that I couldn't stand and had never seen before his move to Moscow. Most irritating of all was when he handed out his photograph to my friends. It showed him on his sixtieth birthday, weighed down with medals and pleased as punch with himself.

I had once hinted delicately to him that his likeness was of no interest to the general public.

"You're crazy," he said. "My greeting cards and photographs get people careers and dachas!" This was sadly true.

But among my close friends, there were no such mercenary types, though I never could get my father to believe this.

When the two men were thoroughly soused, Skvortsov, the assistant to the general prosecutor of Moscow, set about trying to pick up my girlfriends; my father ended up on the floor in the children's room, helping his two-year-old grandson assemble a toy railroad. Finally the guests headed home, and I called one of Leonid's aides to send a car for my father. While we waited, Skvortsov put on his hat and coat, sat down, and promptly passed out. As he snored peacefully, oblivious to the sound of Adriano Celentano's beautiful voice—my favorite—wafting out of our tape player, my little boy, propped against his drunken grandfather, played with his train. Another of my father's visits was ending in the usual way.

By 1973, Father's home had become a battlefield. No one in his family was willing to see his side of things, to feel any compassion for him or try to give him moral support. As they saw it, he was a disgrace to the Brezhnev name, a second Galina. At family councils, he was periodically

Yakov Brezhnev, the author's father, on his sixtieth birthday. "The shirt
and tie were gifts from me, the medals were from others."

held up to shame like a misbehaving schoolboy. His daughters called
him Dog Crap, and his sons-in-law, who owed their careers to him
alone—"but you can't make a knave into a squire," he would say of
them—held him in utter contempt.

I had put so much distance between myself and the Brezhnev clan
that I was unaware at the time of these developments. I didn't even
know that the KGB chief, Yuri Andropov, was calling my father in for
personal "talks" and already knew quite well what had to be done about
his problems.

My father's wife was periodically driven to desperation by her husband's adventures; she began calling Viktoriya Petrovna to bare her soul

like a sister: "Help! He's completely out of hand this time!" Viktoriya had some experience with straying husbands, having succeeded in bringing Leonid back into the fold some years before, and she launched a vigorous campaign against my father. She feared, not without reason, that he would blurt out something embarrassing when intoxicated. But he continued to associate with black-market operators from the Caucasus, who wined and dined him, showing him off and using his services to buy Volga, build dachas, and have their buddies released from jail.

On August 8 of that year, Nikolay Skvortsov, drunk, died at the wheel of his car. He was my father's closest friend and constant drinking buddy. Four days later we were celebrating my younger son's third birthday. By the time Yakov Ilyich arrived, the other guests had left. He staggered into my apartment, unkempt, tieless, his unpressed slacks sagging like an outstretched accordion. Remembering how upset his wife had been over his most recent romantic fling, I couldn't help but smile sadly: there was nothing of the ladies' man about him.

My husband whistled quietly. He had never seen Yakov Ilyich in this condition before. "On the inside, I'm even more rotten than I look," my father warned us. Falling onto the couch, he added, "Why can't I learn to quit while I'm ahead?"

"Where were you?" I asked gently.

"Who cares?" he grunted, staring glassy-eyed at the ceiling. "Knowing too much just makes you grow old before your time."

"I still want to know."

"Oh, lay off" was his answer. Then: "A bunch of us got together. . . . The lowest of the low, some secondhand women. So what?" He looked up defiantly.

"All right," I said. "Sleep it off." I threw a blanket and a pillow to him.

I went back to clearing the table, and he lay in silence, examining his beat-up slacks. Eventually he searched his pockets, pulled out his cigarettes, and lit one. "It's true, I am a slob," he said and began coughing. "You know how I live?" I said nothing; he went on. "I live to supply things to the women in my life. I drag whatever I find back to the nest, but the only thing in that whole apartment I can call my own is my old red toothbrush, with its broken handle and half its bristles fallen off. . . . It's been with me since the beginning of the world. I sometimes think it's as old as I am."

"Why don't you buy a new one?"

"I keep waiting and waiting for my wife or one of my beloved daughters to take the time out to show some concern. I guess I'll never see the day."

I left the room and appeared a minute later with a new red toothbrush, which I placed on his chest. He fingered it and tears welled up in his eyes. "My Kolya is gone, dead four days now. . . ." (As he told me later, he himself had closely escaped death: he had been planning to ride with Skvortsov but changed his mind.) Kolya, intelligent and hardworking despite all his carousing, had sincerely loved Yakov Ilyich, as far as I could tell.

When my father dozed off, I called Anna Vladimirovna to tell her where he was. At her request, I promised not to let him drink any more.

Half an hour later he suddenly sat up, his head in his hands. I continued to tidy up the room, trying to be quiet and not disturb him. After a long silence, he asked me for a drink; I told him that the guests had polished off everything in the house. I also chided him gently for wanting to drink so late at night.

"Have you no feelings? My best friend is dead, and here you are like a heartless nag, telling your own father he can't have his hundred grams. . . ."

I tried to ignore his grumbling, but when he persisted, my temper flared. After he walked away from our argument and out of the apartment, Mischa caught up with him and managed, with great effort, to talk him into accepting a ride home.

One day that fall a young man contacted me, saying he had a note from my father. I gave him a bottle of vodka for his troubles and began reading the hastily scribbled message. Shocked, I learned why I hadn't heard from Yakov Ilyich lately: he was being held in solitary confinement in a psychiatric ward. In his note, he threatened to commit suicide if he wasn't released in three days.

Periodically he had been placed in the Kremlin clinic against his will, beginning in 1967, the year Andropov took over as head of the KGB. During my numerous visits, the physicians had usually explained, somewhat evasively, that he had liver trouble. Once he had asked me whether I knew the reason for his hospitalization and then went on to answer his own question: "So I'll remember that I should stay in line."

But never before had he been held in isolation, and his note was a cry for help. Naturally the first person I turned to was his wife. But when I asked Anna Vladimirovna where Yakov was, she calmly answered that he was on a business trip. "Are you sure?" I asked.

"Absolutely," she said. "He called me."

I was at a loss. Very familiar with my father's writing, which only Leonid Ilyich knew how to copy, I had no doubt that the note was authentic.

Not finding Galina Brezhneva where she worked, I left a note for her. I never got a response.

I finally called Viktoriya Petrovna and asked her if she had seen my father recently. She said that she had, but something in her voice was suspicious, and I told her point-blank that I knew what was going on: Yakov was being held in solitary confinement, and *she* was behind it. I added that if he was not immediately released, I would be obliged to bring the matter to the personal attention of Leonid. And if that failed, I would talk to American reporters.

"You'd best keep your nose out of other people's business," she advised before hanging up.

My father, other people's business?

Some friends of mine who were psychiatrists once lent me a copy of the regulations governing involuntary hospitalization. They stated that "in cases where a mentally ill person is clearly a danger to those around him or to himself, the public health authorities have the right, without consent from his relatives or guardians, to place him in a psychiatric ward as an inpatient for emergency psychiatric treatment."

My father was no threat to society, and no documentation was ever produced to show that he was. We had met the day before his hospitalization, and I had noted nothing abnormal. He was sad, as he had been for some time, and he was complaining about his wife, his brother, his sister-in-law Viktoriya, and his life as a whole. Perhaps some psychiatrists might have judged these complaints symptomatic of something pathological—manic depression or "an improper, aggressive attitude on the part of the patient toward specific people." But couldn't many of us be committed for the same reasons?

My circle of friends included doctors from the Serbsky Institute for Forensic Psychiatry, and I had even dined with its director, Georgy M. The head of treatment for alcoholism and drug addiction in Moscow, M. periodically treated my father for alcoholism and knew him well enough to have his home phone number.

M. took a keen interest in antiques, the history of Russian church architecture, and iconography, especially that of Byzantium. He knew a great deal about literature and art. The courteous demeanor of this erudite man, who had given his career a boost early on by marrying the daughter of a well-known Soviet psychiatrist and Health Ministry official, did not seem in the slightest like that of a villain. But under his control, the Serbsky Institute had acquired an ominous reputation, and many dissidents feared it more than prison. Rumor had it that M. once told some top officials, "What do we need political trials for when we have psychiatric clinics?" He headed a commission that determined the "mental illnesses" of political dissenters.

From the stories of close friends, I knew about the hideous crimes that took place at the Serbsky Institute: doctors falsified medical reports; sane men and women were given injections that left them mentally scarred for the rest of their lives; it was not rare for the medieval method of smothering with a pillow to be used to eliminate the most recalcitrant "patients." The physicians certainly never bloodied their own hands, heaven forbid. The actual murderers were usually psychotics who wouldn't have hesitated to kill their own mothers.

I decided to have a talk with Professor Daniil L., administrator of the Special-Evaluations Division of the institute. Based on his diagnoses, thousands of perfectly sane people were sent to rot in mental hospitals. L., like M., had previously been involved in treating my father and knew of Yakov's most recent hospitalization but maintained that it was justified. He declared that my father suffered from a "negative attitude toward his position in society as Brezhnev's brother."

"But that's the normal attitude of any sane person," I said. "I would have preferred being the niece of Lev Tolstoy or Mstislav Rostropovich. Would you put me down as suffering from delusions of grandeur?"

He made no comment. Looking through his thick glasses to the space above my head—I twice glanced backward, wondering what had attracted his attention up there—he tried to convince me that psychological abnormalities "occurring in the context of alcoholism" had been observed in my father. He made what sounded like a good case, citing facts and tests, resorting only occasionally to gestures to make his points. Arguing with him was useless.

My next step was to contact the relatives of M. They asked that I help them obtain a copy of the hard-to-find two-volume history of iconography by M. A. Alpatov as a holiday gift for him; the November 7 celebrations were approaching. It was a perfect opportunity for an audience with M. himself, and I got the book from one of the special stands in the Central Committee building, to which I had access.

M. repeated in full what I had heard from L. and started to tell me about a recent scandal involving Yakov Ilyich. I asked him not to go into detail since I already knew about the incident. A few months before, my father had come home with his niece, Galina, both of them stinking drunk. He collapsed while walking up the stairs to his apartment, and Galina fell down when she tried to lift him up. The woman in charge of watching the entrance soon came by. Finding the two of them sprawled on the floor, she called Yakov's daughter Lena and her husband. My father had suffered a concussion and subsequently experienced headaches. Galina was only slightly bruised.

Again I had made no headway. M. and I parted on cool terms.

I decided on a last resort. I wrote a letter, addressed it to Leonid Ilyich Brezhnev, and mailed it from the secretariat of the Central Committee building on Nogin Square. I circled my name broadly in red, hoping that this would expedite matters—letters to my uncle were usually answered after a long wait, if ever. The secretariat kept special lists of relatives, friends, wartime comrades, and others with whom Leonid had personal ties.

The next morning brought a response. At nine o'clock, I was speaking on the phone to a pleasant, unfamiliar baritone who identified himself as one of Brezhnev's aides. We could meet and have a talk in two hours, he said. After a moment's hesitation, he added, "Please bring your passport along."

About Leonid's aides. For several years after 1964, my father could call Leonid at work through a special direct phone system—I had used the system myself—but by the early '70s, he could contact Leonid only through the general secretary's aides. I often heard him asking for one of them by name, usually Viktor Golikov, an acquaintance of his from the old days in Dnepropetrovsk.

The aides of the Central Committee secretaries were handpicked, those of the general secretary in particular. Besides having impeccable biographies and having proved their devotion to the party, they had to be able to think on their feet. They conducted negotiations, scheduled meetings, handled correspondence, and wrote up reports. They called for cars, ordered special planes, and maintained telephone contact with the secretaries of the republic and the oblast central committees of the party. They were also authorized to communicate by phone with family members of the general secretary, upon his request.

At eleven sharp, I was back at the Central Committee building. When I approached the young, armed officer standing by the staircase that led to the inner sanctum, he took some lists out of a desk, rapidly scanned them, and checked my passport. Saluting gloomily, he said, "Second floor."

As I ascended the pink-and-green walkways leading to the second floor, I thought about how absurd it was: who would believe that I had to come plead for the general secretary's own brother?

The offices were filled with pencil pushers promoted from the rank and file; the corridors, with bodies in suits and ties filing back and forth. There was a constant influx of party officials from the provinces, who would sit for hours waiting to get approval for a directive that might well be canceled the next day. Some men rose to dizzying heights here, others met their downfall, but none knew how to govern a country, the best of them knowing only how to cope with it. Everywhere typewriters were rattling, telephones were ringing, and officials were striding pompously out of their offices; aides, clerks, and maintenance workers scurried about. This whole anthill was under the surveillance of the KGB and the vigilant guard of young army officers.

The office I entered was small, with new, light-colored furniture; in the late '60s, under orders from my uncle, the somber chairs, desks, and tables of earlier years had been removed from the building—at night—and modern, elegant pieces installed in their place. On the desk stood a green lamp of the type made infamous by Stalin-era movies and the KGB's interrogation rooms.

I was greeted by an assistant of the aide I had spoken to earlier. He was wearing a white shirt and a tie; his jacket perched on the back of his chair. In front of him lay my typewritten, signed letter.

Nodding toward the chair opposite him, he took my passport, examined it at length, and studied my face. He appeared to be about forty-five. "Are you Yakov Ilyich's daughter?"

"Yes."

"Have your parents been divorced long?"

I answered.

"Who raised you?"

"My mother and stepfather, but after high school I moved to Moscow, so my father watched over me from then on."

"Well?"

"What do you mean, well?" What he was getting at?

"Did he do a good job of completing your upbringing?" Something like a smile appeared on his official countenance.

"My stepfather did a better job. Fortunately for me, I lived with him as a child—"

He interrupted. "This is no place to discuss your family problems." I realized that our conversation was being bugged.

It was time to get down to the business at hand. Taking notes rapidly and professionally, the assistant listened courteously without interrupting again. When I had finished, he promised to put together a report about my visit and relay the information to the general secretary.

I didn't believe him.

Before leaving, I told him that to my way of thinking, putting a sane man in a mental hospital was a heinous crime and that I protested it. The next moment I imagined how amused he must be by such a childish notion. After taking a few steps toward the door, I was seized with rage: can't I even protect my father? He has no one else. . . .

"Listen," I said, turning to look the assistant in the eye. "I don't know who you are, so I would like to speak to my uncle personally. I want to show him a few things and tell *him* what's being done to his brother behind his back."

He was unruffled. "I'm afraid that's impossible. Leonid Ilyich is extremely busy. All I can promise is that tomorrow morning I'll report to his aide about what you've told me." He hesitated. "I think that the matter will be dealt with."

"My uncle is busy all right, shooting at wild boars in Zavidovo," I retorted. "But that's unimportant. I warn you: if my father doesn't call me within three days to say that he's been released, I'll be forced to speak to foreign reporters. I'm serious."

His features hardened. "I wouldn't recommend that."

On my way home, I decided to go to the Marx Prospekt subway station on foot: it was about a twenty-minute walk, enough time for me to review the conversation while my memory was fresh. I had not been asked for any details of the mental hospital or the source of my information. . . . "How naïve of me," I thought, "hoping to find wisdom and justice from that army of paper shufflers. . . . With a life full of orders, decrees, instructions, directives, conferences, and meetings, who has time or room in his heart for feelings?"

When I was finally called back to the Central Committee building, I met with the same man. A tragic expression on his face, his voice oozing sympathy as though I had known him for years, he explained: my father, a chronic alcoholic, had been placed in a psychiatric clinic after an attack of delirium tremens. I was shocked a second time: even the Central Committee believed the doctors' lies and would do nothing to free Yakov Ilyich.

Many Soviet dissenters were labeled mentally ill for political rather than medical reasons, but my father was no dissident. Why isolate him? Because his wife and sister-in-law were scandalized by his behavior? Because affairs of state required that he be kept out of sight? All I knew was that he was being held in solitary confinement illegally.

Several more conversations with relatives produced no results. In my desperation, I decided to contact Roman Rudenko, chief prosecutor of the Soviet Union and the man who had represented the Soviet Union at the Nuremberg trials. I knew the inside story of this trial well enough to have few illusions about Rudenko or his work, but I was grabbing at straws by this point. I went to his offices, tore a piece of paper from my notepad, found a place to sit in the crowded reception room, and wrote.

As well as I can remember, my letter went:

> I am Luba M., née Brezhnev. As a member of the Brezhnev family, I feel obliged to protest the unlawful placement of my father, Y. I. Brezhnev, in the Kremlin hospital, where he is being held at the present time. No signs of mental illness have been observed in his behavior. I demand both his immediate release and legal proceedings against the perpetrators of this unlawful act.

I never received a reply.

I knew that even if I attempted to bring suit against the illegal isolation of my father, no attorney in the country would take my case. All my attempts to bring my father's plight to the attention of officials had ended in utter failure.

I decided to send a second, more forceful letter to the general secretary. It began:

> Dear Uncle Lyonya,
> Only the present dire circumstances, which cannot fail to interest you as well as me, have forced me to write this letter. I am aware of your never-ending work schedule but request that you read carefully and take

immediate action concerning the events described below. I am absolutely convinced that for many reasons, which may be perfectly well intentioned, you have not been informed that Yakov Brezhnev, your brother and my father, is at present in a psychiatric ward, as a result of the efforts of Viktoriya Petrovna and Anna Vladimirovna. Through third parties, I have received a note in which he requests immediate help and asks that you be informed personally of what has happened. He also threatens to commit suicide and gives us three days to have him released. I hope you can imagine how despondent he must be.

Underlining the seriousness of the matter and registering a protest, I addressed my uncle with the formal _vy_ instead of the familiar _ty_ I had always used with him in conversation. I rushed to the Central Committee and sent the letter from the secretariat just before the building closed for the day.

The next day at 11:00 A.M. my phone rang, and I was connected to the general secretary himself.

"Hello, Lubushka," he began cordially. "I'm sorry, my dear, but I can't see you. I'm going away on a trip shortly. Tell me what happened."

I had prepared myself for this moment. After concisely relating the main facts, I read my father's note. My uncle listened without interrupting, coughing in his characteristic manner and heaving an occasional sigh. In less than two minutes, I had finished.

He paused, then said: "The man I'm going to connect you with in a minute or two will take care of things. Just tell him what you told me."

Next came a few questions about my sons and my health. He always seemed genuinely interested in my children. Like Yakov Ilyich, Uncle Leonid took pride in seeing how much Andrey looked like "a Brezhnev." And yet once more he asked me what I was doing and where I was working. I tried to answer in monosyllables. I didn't want to waste my uncle's time, and I was in a hurry to see my father free. I didn't take the suicide threat seriously, since the Brezhnevs tend to be skittish, but I wasn't sure. . . .

On the following day, my father called and said that he had been released.

About a month had passed since I had received his note. One of my first questions was whether he had been given any medication; I had heard a great deal about the side effects of psychiatric drugs and was afraid that he had actually been "treated." He answered that they had given him something that made him dizzy and caused a cottony sensation in his feet and hands. I thought it was probably just a mild sedative. But in the days that followed, he often seemed depressed and listless, and since I had never seen him like that before, I decided that he had been given some strong mood-altering drugs. I was shocked to see him getting worse in front of my eyes. His latest experience had convinced him that there was no one to protect him, that he was doomed to a life of playing the role of Brezhnev's Brother.

It was some time before Yakov Ilyich could speak of what had happened. He began by describing his first day. . . .

After showing that he could touch the tip of his nose with eyes closed, he was given the classic knee-reflex test. "I made a point of kicking my foot up; it would have landed square in the doctor's face if he hadn't jumped aside," he added with a laugh. I was relieved. At least his sense of humor was intact.

After the physical, the doctor began taking his family history and inquired as to whether there were any schizophrenics or alcoholics among his relatives.

He answered, "My brother, Leonid Brezhnev. Everyone thinks he's the general secretary, but he's just a schizophrenic."

Speechless, the doctor walked out hastily and returned with a colleague. They asked my father what he did for a living.

My father answered, "My occupation is being Brezhnev's Brother. And that's it." He added that he was completely sane: those needing psychiatric treatment were his relatives Viktoriya Petrovna and Galina, who suffered from pathological greed and nymphomania, respectively.

That was it indeed; before he could finish, he was tied up and taken to the ward where he would languish for about two months.

"I panicked at the start," he told me. "I'd heard plenty about how people are treated in mental hospitals. The worst of all was that the room I was trapped in had practically no sunlight. Both window frames had thick crossbars and were locked firmly. Food came through a slot in the door. There was no fresh air except for a small vent in the window, which was made of unbreakable glass and had been covered with a layer of white paint. There were bars on the outside. The silence was deadening.

"The one thing they weren't able to take away from me was a little piece of the sky. There was an old tree standing opposite the window. Of course, I couldn't see it clearly because of the paint. At times a sparrow would land on one of the upper branches. Maybe each one was really different, but I wanted to think that the same little bird returned every time. We were almost like friends. He would fly down, sit for a while pecking at something, look at me sympathetically, and then fly off. I was so envious. . . . There was no question of visitors, and the staff never conversed with me. Sometimes a doctor would come in, always one of those people whose faces you forget quickly: as soon as he left, I couldn't remember what color eyes or hair he had or what his nose looked like. They probably pick people like that deliberately. I once asked one of them, 'Why are you holding me here? It's a crime.'

"He smiled and said, 'We're treating you.'

" 'Treating me for what?' I asked.

" 'Your liver's not well.'

" 'Why don't you check your own liver? We have millions of people in the country with bad livers. Are you going to put them all into psych wards?'

" 'How did you figure out that's where you are?'

" 'I guessed.'

" 'Aren't you clever.'

"Two weeks after that conversation I went on a rampage, demanding to be released. I was suffocating; I felt like I wouldn't survive one more day in that cage. In came this woman doctor in a white, starched smock. 'Yakov Ilyich, we're responsible for you! What have you been up to?' she asked, knitting her clipped eyebrows together.

" 'Who put me in here?' I asked.

"She didn't answer, and a nurse gave me an injection. A few minutes later I fell asleep. When I woke, I took stock: the more I acted up, the worse things were going to be. I was afraid that they would use torture to make me genuinely insane.

"The only solution was to get word of my plight to someone on the outside. But who could be my messenger? It was useless to talk to the doctors, who were carrying out orders from higher up.

"About a month and a half later I heard a noise underneath my window. I stood on the windowsill and saw a young man outside fixing the pipes. He was alone. It was now or never.

"So I opened the air vent. 'Listen, young fellow,' I said. 'I'm here for alcoholism. My daughter is about to give birth. Could you take her a message? I want her to call the head physician and let me know how she's doing.' I could see he was hesitating.

" 'Don't worry, she'll meet you personally to pick up the note, and she'll give you a good tip.'

" 'But she's pregnant, isn't she?' The young man was skeptical.

" 'She can still walk, though.'

" 'All right," he said, "go ahead and write.'

"I starting scribbling without getting down from the windowsill. I couldn't believe my good fortune. I threw him the note through the vent, but the damn thing fell into the ditch where pipes were being laid. I nearly cried from sheer disappointment. I was shaking like a leaf, afraid that the doctors might barge in. I would have been done for, not to mention my benefactor.

"I wrote out another note and wrapped it in a piece of bread, and this time it landed right in his hands. 'Good throw,' he said. 'Do you play basketball by any chance?'

"I stepped down from the sill and lay on the bed. My whole body was quivering. Right then the door swung open, and in came two of my inquisitors.

" 'What's wrong, Yakov Ilyich? You seem agitated today,' one of them said. They took my pulse and listened to my heart. Then I had another idea.

" 'Doctor,' I said, 'as of today I'm going on a hunger strike.'

"They laughed. 'How long will you hold out?' one asked.

" 'As long as you keep me here.'

" 'You'll go hungry a long time, then,' he said. 'Besides, with all due respect, Yakov Ilyich, we'll force-feed you.'

"We'll see about that,' I said defiantly. I kept my word. On the third day of my fast, the door swung all the way open, and some equipment was wheeled in. At first, I didn't even realize what it was for. Then they explained. I began tearing the tubes off and yelling. My doctor said, 'If you don't want to cooperate, we'll call in some help.' Then he pressed a button, and two burly young men with huge fists appeared; they subdued me in a few seconds.

"The doctor inserted a needle into my arm while the two men held me so I wouldn't be able to tear it out. Realizing that resistance was futile, I began to cry. It hurt me deeply that Lyonya would allow such things. What is he trying to do to me? I thought. But another part of me was trying to find excuses for him, trying to believe that he couldn't know anything about what was being done to me. I guess it was the same way in the thirties, when prisoners in the basements of the Lubyanka tried to convince themselves that Stalin was uninvolved, even though he had personally signed the order sending them there.

"That was the end of my hunger strike. That evening my tormentors returned, bringing a basin, some oilskin, and a mug. They tied me up, put the oilskin on my chest and a tube down my throat, and started pumping in some foul-tasting liquid. To this day when I walk into a bathroom and see a basin, I want to throw up. When I got home, I ordered all basins and mugs removed from the apartment."

When I asked my father why he hadn't phoned me from the ward, he said, "Are you crazy? The room was the size of your dormitory room: six square meters. I walked around like a caged animal for days at a time, to keep my legs from withering away. The door was locked, the bars on the window were two inches thick, there was no telephone, no television. . . . They gave me food through a slot in the door, and to add insult to injury they gave me copies of *Pravda* and *Izvestiya* so I could read about what my brother was doing. I concluded that I hadn't been put there because of mental illness, and not even because they wanted to make me insane. For some reason, they had decided to isolate me from the outside world. God only knows how long it would have gone on if I hadn't been able to get that note to you."

It was clear even then that the operation to neutralize Brezhnev's Brother had been planned and executed by some powerful person.

A few years later my father named the man who had ordered him put away: KGB chief Yuri Andropov. He had used the complaints of my father's wife and sister-in-law as an excuse.

It was under Khrushchev that the Soviet government began the policy of labeling dissidents mentally ill, a new weapon in its arsenal of repressive techniques. But as Aleksandr Herzen wrote in the nineteenth century, "You can't put a collar around an idea," and the dissidents' words and thoughts leaped over the walls of the totalitarian state to the world community. This airing of Soviet dirty linen, as they saw it, infuriated our leaders.

Brezhnev looked upon dissidents as though they had the plague. In one of his speeches, he said of them, "Our people demand that these persons be treated as the adversaries of socialism, as people acting against their own country, as accomplices or even direct agents of imperialism. Naturally we are taking measures against them as provided for by law and will continue doing so."

The part about agents and accomplices could have been lifted straight out of a speech by Stalin. The measures taken against dissidents were not, in fact, in accord with any Soviet laws. During Brezhnev's rule, as before, psychiatric hospitals were giving involuntary treatment to hundreds of perfectly sane citizens, mostly intellectuals who disagreed in varying degrees with the way the country was being run. Psychiatric repression was stepped up in 1968, after the protests against Soviet intervention in Czechoslovakia. The center of "political psychiatry" was the infamous Serbsky Institute.

Some dissidents, well-known figures like Pyotr Grigorenko, Roy A. Medvedev, Viktor Khaustov, and Leonid Pliusch, were able to muster support from leading Soviet scientists, writers, and artists. Their plight was known abroad as well, and some were able to have letters of protest published in the West. But most were unknowns who rotted away with no support, no publicity. If not for my intervention, my father might have shared their fate.

Of course, none of the letters I sent to the prosecutors and the Central Committee concerning my father were ever publicized. I told only my closest relatives about them. Even my father knew nothing of them until one of the Moscow prosecutors told him.

Most people still assumed that Brezhnev's Brother, as well as his nieces and others, lived a life of luxury and unlimited wealth. My father, as noted, did receive special goods, had access to the Kremlin shops, used all the special services, and received a special food allotment. But his privileges gave him no money, and he had none to spare. The 420 rubles that he earned in the ministry were not a fortune. His wife didn't work, and my half sisters, feeling the need to maintain a certain façade as the general secretary's nieces, demanded fur coats, furniture, cars, and dachas.

My father's solitary confinement had given him a chance to put his thoughts together and catch his breath. But his ordeal led not to a spiritual rebirth but to a simple conclusion: from then on, he would reap all the personal benefits his position as Brezhnev's Brother could offer, since he had already tasted its bitterest fruits.

He continued doing favors but began taking bribes in exchange. The temptation of money has seduced greater men than he.

At first, I chased away suspicions that my father might be taking bribes, preferring to think that such charges were just part of the malicious gossip that constantly circulated about the Brezhnev clan. But as time went on, I kept running into people who had evidence.

When things settled down, I tried to make sense of what I had gone through trying to free my father. What was the difference between our lives and the lives of madmen? I wondered. In the kitchens of Moscow intellectuals, there was always someone talking about mental hospitals and their abuse. As I listened, I sometimes wanted to cry out that our country was one big madhouse anyway, headed up by the number-one crazy, my uncle, who was convinced that the official line was correct, that he was infallible, that the people adored him.

The only question was, Would we all go completely insane, or would some of us at least maintain a modicum of sanity?

🬀🬀🬀🬀🬀🬀🬀🬀🬀

Chapter Sixteen

A PLACE IN
THE COUNTRY

At times, my father and I used to walk in the woods outside Moscow, where everything—the pure, crackling air, the soft shades of green, the bright colors and pungent smells, the birdsong—combined to create a festive mood that would last for days after the return home. "Why is the world so miserable, restless, and wicked?" I would wonder out loud. "Why can't we be happy with our birthright: a sun bringing warmth, a blue sky, clouds of snow-white cotton! What sins must Russia redeem before we, too, receive divine grace, before we break out of the madhouse of our daily lives?"

My father remembered his own childhood, when the forest was a great big fairy-tale world inhabited by talking animals, beautiful but treacherous water nymphs, and sprites both good and evil. Unfamiliar with oceans and mountains, Russians love their native woods, which have always served them practically as well—as a storehouse for everything from furs and firewood to mushrooms, nuts, strawberries, raspberries, currants, blueberries, and cranberries.

In 1974, my father suggested that Mischa and I buy a large country house, a place for us to go with our children in the summer. We expressed interest, and through his friends he soon found us something promising in Korovino, a village in the Moscow area.

One day the three of us went to look the house over. Built of timber and dominating the entire village, it had three bedrooms and a kitchen. In the courtyard were a stable, a shed, and a barn. We liked it.

While we and the great-grandson of the original owner signed papers, my father negotiated the official registration, which ran into a snag when it turned out that city dwellers were not usually allowed to buy houses in the village. Rather than sign up to weed cucumbers and tomatoes at the local collective farm—one way to obtain an exception—my husband, who had attended a special art school as a child, volunteered to help design and draw posters to advertise movies and concerts for the village club. We rolled up our sleeves and had the house fully livable within a week, painting the smallest room white and installing a white bed there, along with a white desk for my translation work.

A dacha craze was beginning; it seemed as though all of Moscow was rushing to buy up abandoned houses in the countryside. Plenty were available in the moribund and underpopulated villages: after receiving internal passports (and the attendant freedom to move) under Khrushchev, many collective farmers had left for factory jobs. As the old died off, their houses lay empty and neglected.

We were seduced by Korovino's quaintness, tranquillity, and proximity to unspoiled wild areas. It was far enough from Moscow that other city dwellers were rarely seen there. The surrounding woods and meadows were full of mushrooms and berries.

As we expected, friends and relations began dropping by, especially on Sundays. We hosted some interesting encounters, since we welcomed everyone—dissidents, refuseniks, and the general secretary's brother alike. Children used the huge stove that dominated the center of the house as a bed; other guests slept in the hayloft or in the barn, both of which were clean and cozy.

In the nineteenth century, there was a world-famous porcelain factory near Korovino, and our house had been built by the merchant who supplied it with dye. Prominent among the icons and photographs lining the walls was a portrait showing one of the previous owners in an arm-chair, angry and self-important. It must have taken the photographer a long time to aim and focus: his subject, sweating profusely in an enormous, beaver-lined coat, looked as though he had come straight from the bathhouse. Neighbors told us that during the summer of 1973, a hot, dry season when fires were common throughout the region, all of Korovino had burned except our house, known in the village from then on as the Burning Bush.

Once I stayed there alone with my little son, Andrey. Evening brought with it an inexplicable uneasiness: I felt as though I were being watched. Unable to fall asleep, I decided to reread Bulgakov's *Master and Margarita*. As I turned the pages, I began hearing halting steps. Listening closely, I heard someone walking about and coughing. The floorboards creaked and I froze.

My son woke up and slid down from the stove where we were both lying. He ran outside to use the potty on the porch and then ran back. After climbing up on the stove, he whispered, putting his arms around my neck as though afraid of being overheard, "Mama, an old man with a gray beard and a white nightgown is standing on the porch."

"Go back to sleep," I said. "Stop imagining things."

He was soon dozing away, but I didn't sleep a wink all night. I remembered how we had scoffed at rumors that the house was haunted by the first owner's ghost, whose footsteps could be heard at night. The next day I called my husband and asked him to come, but he was busy giving exams. In the evening, my father, chauffeured in a government Volga, came by for us.

In the beginning when my father came to visit, he and I would go, milk can in hand, to a dairy at the edge of the village. Everyone would pour out onto the street to gawk at Brezhnev's Brother dressed in shorts and a T-shirt. Embarrassed by the attention, he began wearing long pants and a long-sleeved shirt in public.

Trips to Korovino always reminded him of Brezhnevo, where his ancestors had lived. His father had moved to the city but never got the village out of his heart and soul and would return periodically to help the old men fix roofs, chop wood for the winter, mend fences, or bring in the cattle's winter hay supply.

To please my father, Mischa and I also helped make hay in the Korovino collective farm. For city folks like us, this was recreation and a chance to learn about life from the peasants' point of view. I liked to converse with the old people and listen to their unhurried tales. We met some remarkable characters, including a tough bundle of a woman who had served ten years' hard labor for a political crime and was respected even by the overbearing collective-farm chairman, or so we were told.

When Katya overcame her initial distrust, she began to share home-made wine with the general secretary's brother during the lunch break. "Except for God," she told us once, "I fear nothing and nobody. I yield only to him."

During the war, when the Germans were on the outskirts of Moscow, Katya's niece bore the child of a German officer. When someone reported her after the return of Soviet troops, two drunken soldiers broke into her house and killed her little boy in a burst of submachine-gun fire. By morning, she had hanged herself.

The commander to whom Katya went to complain was indignant: "You should be ashamed, feeling sorry for a fascist mongrel at a time when the country is still in such danger!"

Katya's answer—"Now I'm completely convinced that you Bolsheviks are worse than the fascists"—earned her ten years in the Kolyma labor camps.

The entire village took part in haymaking, leaving only the very old and frail to rest their creaking, weary bones on top of the stoves. One summer dawn when my father and I were walking to the fields to join the haymakers, he recalled the times Leonid had gone to Brezhnevo to make hay with his grandfather Yakov. At the time, hay was cut with scythes tempered for three weeks in cold well water. Yakov Maksimovich had an Austrian scythe, handed down in his family since the nineteenth century. He would warn Leonid, "Take your time, don't press too hard. The blade has to feel the grass." Leonid was eager to keep up with the village boys, but he had to curse his haste when, yanking the scythe up after a too-broad swing had left it stuck in the ground, he hit his leg with the blade and fell to the earth, white as a sheet. He was taken home on a cart after fresh earth was applied to the bloody wound and wrapped with a rag to hold it in place.

Also reminiscent of Brezhnevo was a luxurious Russian bath in the garden of our Korovino house. We scrubbed it clean and every Saturday heated it so that it would be ready for our guests.

The steam bath has always been essential to Russian life. When beginning the construction of a new home, peasants would lay the foundation for a small bathhouse alongside it. While cleansing and healing the body, the bath also "washed sins away." On Saturdays, all of Russia would bathe.

My father liked to reminisce about Brezhnevo while cooling off in the dressing room. On Trinity Sunday, when everything was covered in green, young birch trees were felled and their branches stripped off to be used to decorate yard, house, and church. But Yakov Maksimovich would have none of this ancient Russian custom.

"Why cut down trees for no good use?" he would say.

For the holiday, his wife made do with fresh grass, which she sprinkled on the floor of the house, and wildflowers, which she placed in earthenware pots on the windowsills.

The steam bath, on the other hand, was indeed a good use of trees: bathers always needed bundles of twigs with which to whip one another. In the fall, Yakov Maksimovich put in a supply of green birch twigs for the winter, often taking his grandchildren into the woods to help. The boys feared their grandfather and followed his instructions, panting and hating every minute. How the supple branches resisted being snapped in two! And not all were suitable; the tree had to be the right variety of birch and exactly the right age.

"Grandpa," Leonid once said, "why are you breaking them? They're still so young."

"So you're sorry for branches, are you?" Yakov snorted, stuffing some into a sack. "But this winter you'll be the first to hop into the steam bath, you wait and see."

During the ride back to the village, as young Yasha was dozing off to the clickety-clack of the cartwheels, he heard his grandfather's words:

"This very road was once traveled by hordes of Polovtsians and Tartars. When the troops of Igor Svyatoslavich passed this way, the peasants, including your ancestors, joined up with him." Yasha looked around, momentarily terrified as he imagined the whistling and whoops of Polovtsian raiders, the snorts and thundering hooves of stampeding horses, the cracking of whips, the moans of wounded men. . . .

In my great-grandfather's day, many bathhouses were still heated up "black"—that is, with no chimney: the smoke went out the door. Connoisseurs claim that this method produces the most beneficial and most enjoyable steam bath. A washtub in one corner of the bathhouse was used to steep fragrant herbs: chamomile, Saint-John's-wort, nettles, mint, and fireweed. On a wooden bench in the dressing room stood an earthenware pot with the chilled kvass esteemed by Russians for as long as can be remembered.

The bath, with its steam and heat, was a true haven for body and soul: as the saying went (among men), the sole pleasures of life are tobacco, a tavern, a woman, and a bath. Yakov Maksimovich and his son, Ilya, would whip each other with hot birch twigs (to open the pores) and raise volleys of steam by sprinkling herbal broth on the stove. Climbing in turn to the top bunk, where it was hottest—"so the heat will enter the bones"—they stayed in the steam room till they were woozy and as red as lobsters. Then they would run to the pond—"to cast off the heat." And then they would begin again. Finally came an unhurried conversation as they lay on benches in the dressing room. "You've gotten mighty thin, Ilya," Yakov once said as he examined his son's slim body. "The city is eating you up."

On Saturdays, while the men heated the stove, brought water, and bathed, the women would be in the house hastily finishing their domestic chores, baking pies, and cleaning. The Brezhnev men used the bathhouse before the women. "That way, no female smell can get mixed in with the smell of the birch twigs," Yakov Maksimovich would explain helpfully.

Saturdays also meant scrubbing the wooden floor of the house, a time-consuming ritual that began in the morning. It would first be swept, then doused with hot water and ashes. While still warm, it would be scraped with a knife until the wood glowed a tawny yellow brown. Then it would be rinsed. Finally patchwork rugs would be laid down. The furniture was washed in the same way, since it was made of unpainted wood.

Illness in the family also meant it was time to heat the bath. The patient was steamed in the bath and whipped with birch twigs, then smeared with goat fat and forced to drink a hot broth of bitter herbs. Finally he or she was wrapped in an old sheepskin coat and laid out on the stove to sleep, assured that "you'll be fit as a fiddle by morning."

Korovino began as a settlement of Old Believers expelled from Moscow by the czar. Schismatics dedicated to preserving the rites and canons of the old Russian Orthodox Church, they are a stern and uncompromising folk, their character molded by a long experience of scorn, intimidation, and persecution. They consider those who don't share their beliefs traitors to God and often met new arrivals in the village with hostility.

But they tolerated us for our usefulness. They adored Mischa, who once a week filled his car up with these people of God and drove them ten kilometers to their house of prayer. Also, making use of my father and my connections in the medical world, I was able to obtain medicine for the old people and children and arrange hospitalization for those who needed it. When doctor friends from Moscow visited me, the first thing I did was take them around to the sick people of the village.

An artist couple, friends of ours, fell in love with the local color they saw on their Sunday visits. When they asked us to find them a house in Korovino, we did so gladly. Soon the villagers—some of whom cloaked their own promiscuity and drunkenness in a false modesty intolerant of low necklines, short skirts, and dramatic makeup—found they had a new neighbor, an otherworldly emancipated woman who wore sundresses, smoked cigarettes in public, and flaunted the strange-looking pendants her husband made. She refused to have anything to do with the natives, considering them less than human. Not surprisingly, the villagers gave her a cold welcome. I sensed that trouble was brewing.

One sunny summer day when my husband and I happened to be in

Moscow, our friends went to the creek for some sketching. When they returned, they found their house burned to the ground. No one had lifted a finger to save the artists' property from what was obviously arson. Our friends went from house to house, asking for a five-ruble loan to get them back to Moscow on the next electric train. No one was willing to help, not even when the woman, in tears, took off her wedding ring and offered it as collateral. Our friends understood quite well that they were being hounded from the village and left for good as soon as possible.

Rural Russians tend to treat Muscovites—to them a strange and special caste of parasite—with an illogical mixture of mistrust, servility, and ill will. Their attitude toward foreigners is similar.

When the summer harvest festival came, Korovino would go on a collective binge. Drunken men and women of all ages were strewed like corpses on benches, under fences, on the road. . . . Some of the inevitable brawls were stopped by passersby; others escalated into free-for-alls. I was coming back from the dairy with my four-year-old when we passed a big, burly man lying on the road, his shirt in shreds, his face covered with blood. I recognized him as a local stable worker. My son hung on to me for dear life until we got home, then climbed onto the stove and wouldn't say a word for the rest of the day.

Russians are not inclined to bear a grudge; their hard lives and lack of culture can make them crude and brutal, but they are capable of an empathy few others can match. As Metropolitan Filaret, head of the Kiev Orthodox Church, wrote of the Russian people, "There is little light there, but much warmth." Morning would see the enemies of the previous day's battles, wounds not yet healed, walking arm in arm down the main street.

We found that the villagers often acted as though their only purpose in life was to drink their allotted share of vodka. Some parents gave their young children alcohol: some did so "for fun," some, so they would "sleep better." There were four-year-old boys who could down a shot glass of homemade vodka without flinching.

A neighbor of ours worked in the hothouses, where I would often go to buy vegetables or simply to sit outside in the sun and chat with the women who worked there. I met a representative sampling of Russian womanhood: one with a beautiful voice, one who loved to gossip, one who loved to flirt, one who was always laughing. But I couldn't help seeing that their harsh daily lives were grinding them into a coarse, lumpy mass.

Sometimes they asked me to stay for lunch. When they did, I tried to explain how drinking damages women's health, but they merely laughed and continued to wash down their meals with the homemade vodka. Finally they accepted that I was not a drinker (though they thought I was crazy) and at least stopped offering me alcohol. It was from them that I heard the tale of the drunken rat. . . .

Once one of the numerous hothouse rats came out during the day and ate the crust of bread soaked in homemade vodka that someone had tossed in its direction. The next day the rat returned to beg for the same treat and was not disappointed. It then showed up faithfully every day for several months; if no vodka-soaked bread was waiting, it would stand on its hind paws to beg or start running back and forth. The women's alcoholic offerings got bigger and bigger till one day they poured out some vodka and sprinkled bread crumbs on top. Sometimes the poor rat would lie down by the entrance to its nest, singing and squeaking softly, its paws up in the air, until sober relatives crawled from their holes to drag it home by the tail. Its binge didn't last long, however: soon its hair turned white, its teeth fell out, and it became blind. Finally its skin turned blue and could be seen through its thinning hair. One day the alcoholic rat failed to appear and was never seen again.

The women also made drunkards of the hothouse cats. I saw one lap up some alcohol from a saucer before taking a bite from a cucumber.

Drunken people are no more pleasant a sight than drunken rats. Peasants began coming to our house uninvited, with bottle in hand, wanting to get to know us or just to find someone with whom to shoot the breeze. They even got my father to join in—still not hard to do.

One winter day, after learning that I was the general secretary's niece and that my father often dropped by on Sundays, the local forest warden rode up behind a dashing troika to have a look at us for himself. He was short, with a thin nose and close-set, cunning eyes. The sight of the icons on our walls inspired an antireligious tirade: "Listen, professor," he said to my husband. "Do you know how many icons like these I've chopped up in my day? My stupid brother used them to pave his yard. Imagine having to walk over junk like that! When I had the chance, I just took my ax and chopped away!" As he settled into his troika, he assured us he would be back again to meet Brezhnev's Brother. The prospect hardly filled us with delight.

The more we came to know about the village, the more disillusioned we became. If Soviet women in general had few rights, the peasant woman, with her backbreaking load of work and family obligations, had even fewer. There were cows to milk and hay to mow, clothes to wash and children to tend, elderly to care for and a husband to humor. Receiving his fleeting caresses, she was happy if he didn't beat her and took as a declaration of love his gift of rubber boots, which gave her the luxury of dry feet as she plowed through the slush to the cowshed or the hothouse. She faced and overcame her trials with a sunny outlook based on total ignorance of any other life.

By forty, she was already old, with deep wrinkles, rough hands, a sagging belly, and varicose veins. Hauling water in two buckets joined by a yoke, lifting heavy objects, she eventually ended up with a prolapsed uterus and went about for the rest of her life tying her midriff with a scrap of cloth. The local midwife would set her uterus right from time to time, but as soon as she lifted some hay with a pitchfork, picked up a milk pail, or shoveled some manure, the same sad story was repeated.

Once I remarked to my uncle that with the large amount of heavy lifting that their work required, Soviet women were straining their abdomens, sometimes causing themselves permanent damage.

"Yes, it is deplorable that they have to do men's work," he responded, "but our Russian women are robust, capable of withstanding worse trials than hard labor."

I asked how he would have felt if his own daughter, Galina, had become a manual laborer.

"If necessary, I would have sent her to do that kind of work."

I persisted: "Why didn't you?"

"She went on to the university after high school."

"So the way you see it, the Brezhnev's are blue bloods who get to study, while the common folk carry cement?"

This finally got to him, and he answered, "What's gotten into you? Have you come here to preach? As usual, you want to remind me that you know more than anyone else. Don't worry, I remember. Only if you're so smart, tell me why you don't work at a factory?"

"I don't have the build for it," I answered a bit lamely, adding, "Why are we arguing when you could simply decree that women aren't allowed to do that kind of work? After all, you're the all-powerful one around here."

My uncle said nothing.

In Korovino, medicinal herbs were the main treatment for gynecological complaints. Every woman had a supply of "blood stopper," a plant whose use is described by its name, hanging in bunches in the pantry along with a whole pharmacopoeia of other herbs: nettle was used "to make the blood stronger," Saint-John's-wort, "to stop aging." Visiting one young woman's home, I pointed to some slender roots tied to a nail and asked what they were for. Laughing and blushing, she answered, "To make my husband's dick harder!"

Women were known to return to their household chores two hours after having an abortion, the principal method of birth control. One old woman told me that in her youth, she had once gone to collect firewood in the forest right after an abortion. "The blood was really gushing out," she said, laughing, "so much of it that some poured into my boots, enough to fill them up. How those boots squished as I walked along!"

Village women rarely saw the doctor until it was too late. One young woman, sharing her intimate secrets with me, complained that she was often unable to have intercourse with her husband. I asked her why she didn't seek medical help.

She looked at me in amazement: "What are you talking about? It's a long trip. The cows would go without being milked or fed for a whole day. Besides, our doctor is a man." She spat in disgust. "Can you believe some men are so perverted that they like to look at other men's wives? My husband would kill me if I pulled up my skirt for a man."

She was unshakable. When a female gynecologist, a friend of mine from Moscow, visited me, I took her to see this young woman, who, as it turned out, had a two-kilogram (four-and-a-half-pound) cyst, which the doctor removed immediately.

One summer day my father went with us and some friends of ours to a delightful little creek near the village, where Mischa and I would go swimming. We were just about to lie down on the grass after a dip when a tractor-drawn trailer passed by, loaded with women on their way to work at the nearby livestock farm. The sauciest among them, standing with her sturdy legs akimbo and her chest thrust forward, cried out: "Yakov Ilyich! What are you doing with those elegant ladies? They don't even know what to do. You won't be sorry if you come with us. We'll take care of you right away!"

The other women nodded, indicating their complete willingness to join in. My father blushed, though he was hardly a modest man.

Herzen said it well more than a hundred years ago: "Debauchery in Russia is rarely subtle; most often it is savage, lusty, noisy, crude, disheveled, and shameless." Promiscuity, one of the few pleasures available in the village, was not a matter of romantic intrigue, full of deep sentiments and soulful laments: it meant a night in the hay—often literally—with whoever could be found. There were no hotels or motels, so villagers made do with abandoned houses, lofts, barns, bathhouses, fields, and vegetable gardens. We used to hesitate to go to the woods or fields with friends for fear of stumbling across a couple making love.

Local authorities generally "tried out" all the best-looking young women in the vicinity. This was not condemned in the community since it brought tangible benefits: when a collective-farm chairman took a sweetheart, he bought her new clothing, arranged to have her home repaired, provided her family with a winter supply of cattle feed and fuel. He was, after all, part of the new rural gentry. Previously it had been the kulaks who lived noticeably better than others, but after they were eliminated, in the '30s, their place was taken by local party officials, the collective-farm chairman and head accountant, the village-school principal and chairman of the local soviet.

Whenever a new chairman of a collective farm or village soviet was elected, he began his time in office by taking care of himself, writing off as a collective-farm expense the construction costs for a two- or three-story house with adjoining shed and barn. If he failed to live up to the expectations of the peasants, he could be voted out at the next election, and a new cycle would begin: his successor would build himself a house, buy a car at state expense, and otherwise use his position for personal gain. The Korovino collective farm had been getting rid of its chairmen every year, but finally they decided to keep the one they had. As we were told, an old man, one of our neighbors, left the collective-farm meeting one evening after giving the winning argument: "A new chairman won't be any better, and if we re-elect the one we have now, at least we won't have to empty our pockets for a new house every year."

Many peasants use obscenity constantly, not just in moments of anger or desperation, but simply out of a habit born of a harsh life. My simple questions would sometimes leave them unable to find substitutes for the "plain Russian" that met all the needs of everyday discourse. Of course, there are exceptions: the contemporary countryside has many fine and witty storytellers, and quite a few people with higher education.

The Russian peasant learns to swear in diapers. Once a two-year-old boy, barely able to stand on his feet, chased some chickens that were in front of me, shouting, "Shoo, you f——ing feathers!" The local mail-man told me that when he asked a three-year-old boy to carry a letter to his grandfather, the boy, dangling his legs from the windowsill, calmly answered, "F—— off! I can't walk yet."

Before the 1917 revolution, villagers were more careful to observe certain proprieties; if they swore, they at least thought about who might be listening. A man always avoided obscenity in the presence of his mother, and children were punished harshly for using "bad language." My grandmother Natalya Denisovna told me that using even the mildest terms of abuse, such as *reptile, fool,* and *swine,* was considered a sin in her day.

I should add that obscenities had become fashionable among urban intellectuals as well. Once my husband and I were visiting a well-known movie director, and the man's five-year-old grandson was sitting in an armchair, whittling with a penknife. When the telephone rang in the other room, the director excused himself, leaving us alone with the boy. Seconds later the man reappeared and asked us not to talk to his grandson till he got back.

Many awkward minutes passed. Finally, overcome with curiosity about the strange warning, my husband asked the obvious question: "What are you carving, boy?"

Without looking up from his work, the child answered, "A prick for your father."

The director came back. Sensing our embarrassment, he guessed immediately what had happened.

He scolded us: "I asked you not to talk to this prick."

Once, back in my high school days, I was with my father in Dnepropetrovsk one day, and he took me for a walk around the city to show me where his brother had worked before the war. Suddenly a well-dressed man shouted to us from the other side of the street, "Yashka! Brezhnev! You f———er! What the f——— are you doing here? Is this your daughter? She looks a whole f———ing lot like you. So where's Lyonka, huh? Yeah, I've heard, I've heard. That motherf———er's gone pretty high. He's so f———ing stuck up that he's forgotten his friends." The entire conversation was in this exalted vein.

When my father finally stopped laughing, I asked him who this colorful character was. "Used to be one of Lyonya's deputies," he replied.

We kept the house in Korovino for only a year. In the late '70s, my husband and I applied for membership in RANIS, the dacha cooperative at Nikolin Hill for workers in the arts and sciences. I spoke to Kostya Nikulin, head of the cooperative board in Moscow, and he agreed to help but added that democratic proprieties had to be observed, "to keep the masses happy," as he put it while we were speeding down the Rublev Highway on our way to Nikolin Hill to have a chat with Tikhon Khrennikov, the RANIS chairman. The "masses" in this case were the other dacha holders.

Kostya, who also had to discuss with Khrennikov the problem of Christina Onassis, described in vivid and amusing detail the visit to his office by one of the world's wealthiest women. Surprised by her offer to purchase outright the land occupied by all the RANIS dachas for a tidy sum of money, in dollars, he had explained at length that such a deal was out of the question since under socialism the land belongs to the people as a whole and cannot be sold. Onassis, who was living at the time in Moscow with her Russian husband, had such a hard time understanding what this meant that even the interpreter was laughing.

"As you can imagine, not many things surprise me," said Kostya. "I've seen it all in that office. But no one has ever exhausted me like that prima donna. On top of everything else, she was wearing an enormous cross with inlaid jewels. As I listened to her, I was thinking to myself, 'My dear, you won't make it very far with that around here. Someone will relieve you of it in the nearest doorway.'"

When we arrived at the dacha colony, Khrennikov's wife greeted us courteously and pointed to the back: "Look for him there." We walked through overgrown weeds, and Kostya cursed softly a few times as we tripped over stumps and snags. With burs clinging to our legs, spiderwebs on our faces, and a swarm of midges at our heels, we finally made it to a wooden hut, where the composer, famous in the Soviet Union, greeted us in a cowboy shirt and an ancient, frayed pair of jeans. From his absent look, it was obvious that he was engrossed in melodies he alone could hear. He assented with a nod to everything we said about my application, hoping we would leave as soon as possible.

Meanwhile my father was using his influence to have us accepted on the RANIS list without the usual idiotic questions: How long did you serve in the army? Did you serve during the war (this, in the '80s)? Over cognac, he enlisted the support of the retired general Stepan Shutov, head of the commission of the Moscow City Soviet overseeing cooperative affairs.

We were given fourth place on the list, but we were still waiting when I left the country in 1990. Clever souls were able to get a RANIS dacha out of turn; even cleverer ones, nearby plots of land in that gorgeous region, to build on by themselves.

Once in the early '80s, my father called and suggested that we take a look at a private dacha in Vnukovo that had belonged to a well-known composer. It was being sold for fifty thousand rubles, a fairly low price. "If you're short, I'll help out," he promised. Mischa and I got in our car, picked up Yakov Ilyich, and went to have a look.

The dacha, a magnificent, if run-down, structure, looked something like an abandoned castle. I began to wonder why the price was not higher. While the men toured the numerous rooms, I examined the beautiful, spacious lot and found a white horse grazing in a clearing, pink and mysterious in the rays of the setting sun.

"Whose horse is this?" I asked the watchman standing nearby.

"I don't know; it's a stray that turned up one day. I've asked around, but no one knows."

My father joined me. "Do you know the story connected to this dacha?" he asked as we walked the grounds. "I just heard it myself. . . . The composer's son and a friend of his once invited the daughter of a famous actor here. After getting drunk and raping her, they dragged her half dead out onto the road, buried her up to her neck in the ground, and held a car race around her. I don't know if it was from heart failure or from being run over, but she died. The bastards who caused her death were sent to prison. Her father died from a heart attack before long, and then the composer died as well."

It was clear why there were no buyers. We walked over to the glade, where the pink horse was peacefully grazing. Catching sight of us, it approached and stretched its head toward my hand. Instinctively I pulled back and could not help wondering whether I was seeing the spirit of the dead girl.

Large hazel eyes stared down at me. I stroked the horse's neck, and it brushed its velvety lips against my cheek.

"Get back!" the watchman cried, running toward me. "She's wild; she won't let anyone get near her. She could bite or kick."

After touching my cheek again, the horse moved off toward the middle of the glade. The watchman was still standing next to me, out of breath.

We decided against buying the dacha.

My father never gave up his efforts to find me a place in the country. When his wife died, in 1989, he called and said, "As you know very well, I have a dacha in Barvikha. I'm old now and don't need anything. I want to have it legally transferred to you and your half sister now, so that there won't be any legal battles when I leave this world. Mila could then buy out your share, or vice versa."

My refusal—I explained that I was planning to emigrate in any case—set rumors flying. To some, I was a fool; to others, I was putting on an act. But what I knew was that no money could compensate for the psychological and moral toll exacted by arrangements like the one my father had in mind. I had never had a close relationships with my half sisters and dreaded entering into any arrangement that might lead to conflicts. They were never able to forgive me for having been born; as for me, I didn't want to have to justify my existence to them.

Chapter Seventeen

THE BITTERSWEET
FRUITS OF POWER

One day in 1976 when my mother was visiting me in Moscow, my father came by. "I'm just back from Leonid's dacha," he announced. "We strolled around the park. His doctors are all advising him to walk more, and each is pushing his own treatment; they won't let my poor brother alone. . . . He's started putting together his memoirs; he's so caught up in it that he writes from morning to night. He talked me into staying for dinner one evening, and at the table he extracted information from me nonstop. I was hoping to take another walk with him, but after the meal he charged into his study. I can see why: he just didn't want to have to see anybody. When he's writing, no one dares intrude on him."

This was the first time I heard that Leonid was writing his memoirs. About two years later his trilogy—*Little Land, Rebirth,* and *The Virgin Lands*—would be published amid much fanfare.

My father visited his brother many times during those days. Strolling about the grounds, they would discuss various chapters, reviewing facts related to their August 1944 meetings in the Carpathian Mountains, for example.

After my arrival in the United States, I managed to wade through the books, feeling obliged to judge them for myself. As the Soviet novelist Leonid Leonov wrote, "the worst kinds of lies are built from half-truths." Full of preconceived notions and the usual rehashed claims about "our socialist paradise," the trilogy offers no insight into the true nature of the relations among the people it describes, even if the obvious facts are not distorted and the dates are accurate.

Like my father, my uncle was not without some literary ability. He enjoyed sitting before a piece of paper and writing; he even composed passable verses. He knew the works of many Russian poets by heart and had a feeling for literary style. In everyday life, his language was lively, colorful, and expressive, nothing like his books or the ghostwritten speeches in which he seldom believed.

I saw nothing wrong with my uncle's idea of recording his experiences. If he had not been so prominent, his memoirs still would have been read with interest by those who had fought in the war or worked on the virgin lands, and that would have been the end of it. I must say that the trilogy would have been much more interesting—readers would at least have seen the living human being who wrote it—if my uncle's work had not been so thoroughly sanitized by the team of editors who "helped" him. But the weaknesses of the books also stem from his desire to produce works "suitable for the edification of Soviet young people."

The trilogy's social value and literary merits were discussed at party conferences and scholarly symposia, by the press and by the Writers' Union.

Once while visiting the home of a movie director, I heard some of the other guests praising the work of Vitaly Korotich, chief editor of *Ogonyok,* the most popular Soviet magazine at the time. I concurred, adding that Korotich seemed an honorable and decent man as well as a good editor. The host then picked up a copy of the magazine *Kommunist,* opened it to the first page, and, keeping the author's name covered with his hand, invited me to read the article about my uncle's trilogy. The article contained such shameless flattery that I was beside myself.

"What do you think? Who could have written such a heap of lies?" the director asked me.

"Chakovsky," I answered quickly. When he shook his head, I ticked off the names of all the writers and critics I suspected of being toadies.

"Forget it, you'll never guess," said my host, lifting his hand. The by-line read "Vitaly Korotich."

I sometimes wonder whether men like Korotich violated their professional ethics because they had no choice. I think not. Many of their colleagues preferred to say nothing about the trilogy. Of course, they did not criticize the work publicly—no one wanted to be sent to a psychiatric ward for such nonsense—but at least they kept silent. Why this slavish urge to please those in power?

Brezhnev's trilogy, declared by the sycophants a paragon of contemporary literature, the acme of pedagogical perfection, and an example of model Russian style, soon flooded the shelves of Soviet bookstores in innumerable shapes and sizes. The best printing facilities were used; tons of top-quality white paper were sacrificed. Did my uncle expect that his writings would be held up as masterpieces of Soviet literature? I don't know. But a well-orchestrated propaganda campaign was launched with precisely that goal.

At one point, my father called me and hinted that it wouldn't hurt for me to congratulate my uncle on his success. I broke into laughter.

"What a difficult personality you have," he said. "Whom do you take after, anyway?"

I must admit that even then, past the age of thirty, I still relished the role of enfant terrible.

A war movie about Brezhnev was guaranteed to be a real plum, and as soon as *Little Land* was published, alert and calculating moviemakers began to dream of a film version. Soon the project was under way. The director, the lead actor, and everyone else involved with the filming knew that it would win a prize, which in turn meant fame, money, and new, financially rewarding offers.

According to my father, Leonid Ilyich personally selected Yevgeny Matveev from among the many actors who auditioned for the lead. Their physical resemblance was striking.

The general secretary's dacha had a special room where Soviet and foreign films were shown. Once I watched *Little Land* there. Afterward everyone rushed to congratulate my uncle. My father was about to stand up and do the same, but he suddenly sat back down, as though he had remembered something.

On April 21, 1979, my uncle received the Lenin Prize for literature, "in accordance with the demands of the working people," who, we are to assume, were agog with delight at reading his memoirs. At the ceremony, a teary-eyed Georgy Markov, secretary of the Writers' Union, declared Brezhnev's trilogy "part of our literary heritage, an aid in the education of young people." From that day on, he announced, Soviet authors would hone their craft by emulating the general secretary, a prediction that mercifully was never realized. Markov concluded with the claim that "Leonid Ilyich's trilogy is unequaled in popularity and influence on the masses of readers."

The literature prize was only one in an ever-growing shower of awards received by my uncle. During his last years, when his health no longer allowed him to chase after pigeons or drive luxury cars, the collection of awards became his sole passion.

A newsreel of the Victory Parade of June 24, 1945, shows the thirty-eight-year-old Brezhnev among the generals casting Nazi banners onto Red Square. Of this moment, he wrote, "It was with pride and joy that I read the order by which General Brezhnev, chief of the political department of the fourth Ukrainian front, was appointed commissar of the composite regiment of that front. To this day, I keep as a treasured memento the saber with which I marched."

Leonid had only four orders and two medals by the end of the war. His mother, very proud, used to shine them with a piece of chalk and a velvet cloth. In the 1950s, he received his first Order of Lenin—for the production of a billion poods (a pood is slightly more than thirty-six pounds) of grain on the newly cultivated lands of Kazakhstan, instead of the planned-for six hundred million.

Many were outraged when Leonid received the Order of Victory, reserved for the greatest military commanders, men whose talent and feats of courage had played a decisive role in the outcome of World War II. (It was taken from him posthumously, in 1990.)

The fight for Little Land (Malaya Zemlya), an important beachhead that our soldiers held courageously for 225 days, was blown out of proportion as compared with other, more decisive battles—all because my uncle had taken part in it. A memorial museum was opened in nearby Novorossisk, honored with the title of Hero City.

My uncle had earned the rank of major general by the end of the war, and he deserves only praise and honor for the courage he displayed. But it would be absurd to compare him with such war heroes as Zhukov, Konstantin Rokossovsky, and Ivan Konev. He was a political instructor, never a professional military man.

As early as 1970, he had 60 orders, 14 more than the great Marshal Zhukov. After Leonid's death, thirty-three identical stars marked HERO OF THE SOVIET UNION were discovered (each had been sewn by his tailor onto a different suit or uniform so that he would never have to remove the award when changing clothing). Eventually he received the highest awards of the other socialist countries and several from the nonsocialist countries as well; counting his marshal's baton, his honorary arms, and the badges corresponding to his other honorary ranks, the number of his awards came to 112.

The sight of my uncle adorned with his rattling medals and orders reminded me of an image created by Yosif Utkin:

> *Across the governor's blue frock coat,*
> *March the medals on parade.*

Awards were just one part of a generalized, official worship of my uncle that reached grotesque proportions, all the more absurd since few believed the propaganda. He was the subject of books, pamphlets, articles, movies, and documentaries; his likeness was displayed everywhere—on posters, in paintings, and, in sculpture. To his suggestions that we meet, I would sometimes retort that I met with him every day—driving or walking through Moscow inevitably meant seeing his portrait at some street corner or other.

If Natalaya Denisovna took great pride in her son's war medals, she looked askance at his family's way of life. She periodically visited him at

the Dalnyaya dacha during her last years, when she lived in Moscow
with her daughter, Vera. But after a few days, she would often call her
Yakov and ask to be taken home.

"Isn't *this* your home?" Leonid would counter, his feelings hurt.

Natalya, a simple, unpretentious woman, was unaccustomed to luxury. She scolded Leonid, reminding him of how they had all lived in
Kamenskoye before the war, saying that his grandsons had "never
known a normal human existence," that his children, Galina and Yuri,
were good-for-nothings. Never able to buy toys for her own children,
she had made a rag doll for Vera, tracing eyes and eyebrows with soot
from the stove, lips and cheeks with beet juice. Yakov Maksimovich
made wooden blocks for his favorite grandson, Yasha. One of Ilya
Yakovlevich's friends gave Leonid a homemade pocketknife, which the
boy kept by his side or concealed from Yasha in a niche between the
stove and the wall. After he carved a design on the kitchen table one day,
his mother took his treasure away, first tugging at his bushy hair. That
night Yasha could hear his brother crying. The certain knowledge that
he had earned his punishment was slight consolation.

At the sight of Leonid's grandsons tossing around chunks of chocolate, Natalya Denisovna would begin relating painful memories to whoever would listen: "On his deathbed, Ilya had a terrific craving for meat,
thinking back to the time his father slaughtered a hog and fried a whole
panful of fresh pork for everyone to share. None was to be had. . . ."
Now Ilya's great-grandchildren had anything their hearts desired but
appreciated nothing, taking all of it for granted. "My soul still aches
when I think of how Ilya suffered, and we couldn't satisfy his last
request," said Natalya. "But you devils don't care about a thing."

No one in Leonid's home paid any attention to her by this time anyway; they thought her a bit daft.

"Your children and grandchildren will bring you grief, wait and see,"
she used to say. Time proved her right.

The wives of top officials, for the most part, were as lacking in culture as the masses, but they had tasted the fruits of leisure, which gave

them an incredibly smug sense of superiority. They had no financial worries and were free from the burden of working outside the home. They didn't know what it meant to stand in line. They had their manicures, massages, and hair done at home, and the only clothing problem they had was *l'embarras du choix.* They did of course worry about how to get rid of the blubber easily accumulated at state expense. Their narrow minds were, by and large, curious only about other people's lives, and their special joy was gathering in small groups to sip tea and dish out the latest dirt.

It was traditional for them to take an interest in their husband's business and even participate in it. The little beehive buzzing around the Kremlin, with its passionate intrigues, included former wives, present wives, and future wives along with legitimate and illegitimate children alike.

One of the central figures in this female shadow government was Leonid's wife, Viktoriya Petrovna. She certainly ran the Brezhnev household efficiently, not too difficult a task for a woman in her position. Leonid had risen rapidly, and his family had as rapidly lost touch with the realities of ordinary Soviet life. Viktoriya never did have to use her medical training, her only contact with the world of medicine being treatment at the Health Ministry's Fourth Department.

In his youth, when Leonid loved fine food and drink and took pleasure in elaborate parties, his wife's cooking made her difficult personality more bearable. But later even the culinary talents Leonid had once prized so highly only annoyed him. He began to feel painfully bored during the infrequent moments when circumstances forced him to be with his wife.

In Moscow, Viktoriya Petrovna had a one-room apartment of her own, where boxes containing gifts that Leonid had received over the years were stacked high. In the '70s, she often went there to air out the room and to dust off and catalog her bounty. Once she invited my father to come along. He noticed a number of sealed boxes on the floor—some of them marked *"for Vikusya," "for Andrey," "for Galina," "for Marta."* . . . She was at least thinking of posterity.

My father found the whole thing highly distasteful. After his visit to what he called the unclean apartment,* he began to refer to Viktoriya as the keeper of the treasury.

Concentrated power always attracts parasites, with their blatant or concealed servility, their intrigues and jealousy. And bloodsuckers were attracted to my uncle's court, as shown, like hyenas to a dying elephant. The competition among Kremlin hangers-on was vicious. One of the easiest ways to get a foot in the door was to make oneself useful to the wives of party officials, and so a flock of well-wishers swarmed around Viktoriya Petrovna, supplying her with information about Yakov Ilyich and his daughters, for example—including me. Viktoriya Petrovna was more than happy to pass this gossip on, selectively, to her husband. Indeed, creating hostility between Leonid and Yakov became a major project of hers, one that absorbed a lot of time and energy. She sowed the seeds of discord unobtrusively, while she and her husband were having breakfast or before they went to sleep. Her method was merely to describe, in lurid tones, what was happening with her in-laws and discuss with Leonid what should be done "to save those poor lost souls."

My father and Viktoriya had got along perfectly well in the '30s, during the first years of her marriage to Leonid. They both loved him; he as a brother, she as a wife. As the years passed, I could see the rift between them growing; by the '70s, they disliked each other so intensely that each minced no words in describing the other.

Naturally Viktoriya found nothing to excuse my father's drunken antics, which she saw as bringing disgrace to the Brezhnev family. Purely economic considerations entered into her dislike as well. There was no place for Yakov in her plans to ensure the material well-being of her blood relatives. To be sure, my father fed her malice.

In the late '70s, my father, newly out of the mental hospital, was, as he asserted, playing the role of the general secretary's brother for all it was worth. He began shopping in Section 100 and taking his buddies to the store in the Udarnik movie theater. There they bought large amounts of goods, resold them to black-market traders, and spent the proceeds on binges.

---

*The *nekhoroshaya kvartira* of Bulgakov's *Master and Margarita*.

When news of this reached Viktoriya Petrovna, she complained furiously to her husband, who called my father to his Central Committee office and dressed him down, threatening to send him to a metallurgical plant in the Urals or "somewhere else in the sticks." Yakov Ilyich was deeply hurt and made a great show of packing his bags—not that he ever went anywhere. He wanted to remain and take revenge on Viktoriya.

Opportunity came soon enough. Several times a year Viktoriya Petrovna's relatives came to Moscow from Ukraine. Viktoriya, concerned more than anything else about what might be said about her back home if she let her kinfolk down, took them to the elite store of which she was the director.

After one such delegation emptied out Section 100, my father learned about it. He called his brother and told him.

Leonid was usually mild mannered and easygoing; his wife's vulgar materialism was one of the few things capable of bringing out his terrifying side. When he came home that day, Leonid, not bothering to say hello, began searching the apartment, opening all the cupboards and closets. Then he took a pair of scissors and cut all the purchases to ribbons.

As long as his health and strength allowed, he periodically carried out similar "family purges," as he called them. And this had not been the first.

In the midst of a squabble with Viktoriya Petrovna, my father once yelled at her, "I was stupid not to let Leonid chop off your head that time." Later I asked what he had been referring to. He told me the story. . . .

Soon after the war Viktoriya decided that a general's wife should have a better wardrobe and threw a royal tantrum. Without saying a word, Leonid calmly scooped up all her dresses and shoes, found a hatchet, and chopped everything into small pieces. My father had never before seen his brother in such a state, nor would he ever see him so again—"he seemed possessed by a demon." To Leonid, the clothing symbolized a vulgar, bourgeois acquisitiveness he found repugnant, and he swung the hatchet as though each blow were bringing down an enemy soldier. Tears were running down his cheeks. The tragic siege of Leningrad was fresh in his mind, as were his memories of Little Land, where so many of his comrades-in-arms had fallen.

On the evening after the battle, the brothers sat alone in the kitchen. Yakov, unhappily married as well, shared his wisdom with Leonid: "Women are all alike, Lyonya. Your wife is no better and no worse than the rest."

In the long run, Leonid accomplished nothing by his outburst. His normal response to abuse and corruption was, sadly enough, passive acceptance. Once he began reminiscing about the teams of actors, singers, musicians, poets, and writers who had come to inspire the soldiers at war. He mentioned Pavel Kogan, a poet killed at the front soon after the Nazi invasion. Leonid was fond of these verses:

> *I never liked the oval shape; even as a kid,*
> *I always liked to draw my corners sharp.*

Perhaps he was fascinated because he tended not to draw his corners sharp himself: you could say that he was a kind man, but his kindness was oval shaped, of the variety that comes from inaction. What use is a heart that is big but not strong? My uncle often made me think of Vasilisa, the tomcat of my kindergarten days that allowed the mice to run free and fearless. Even I, Brezhnev's own niece, felt the long, punitive arm of the KGB at the same time that people totally unrelated to him were thriving thanks to a different kind of long arm, that of bribery and graft.

My uncle's personal life, at least toward the end, was the classic blend of tragedy and farce. He was terribly lonely, surrounded by family members who caused him more tears than they gave him solace. People often ask whether he ever had a true love in his life; after all, he was a sensual, romantic man who loved Yesenin and Pushkin and knew most of their verses by heart. He did; her name was Tamara.

"What a woman she was, my Toma!" my uncle once said. "I loved her so much. . . . I only survived thanks to her. When you have such a marvelous creature at your side, you really have the desire to live. She drove me crazy. Her voice alone was enough to send shivers up and down my spine. One time I had just come out of a foxhole and was walking alongside the trenches. It was pitch-dark, but the night was starry and the moon was out. It was something out of a fairy tale. I overheard Tamara, talking and laughing with one of the officers. I stopped and listened, enthralled, and felt such happiness that my heart stood still. I leaned on the wall, and tears began to fill my eyes. But later I betrayed her."

I was a young woman when I first heard the story of Tamara, the military physician who served alongside Leonid until the end of the war. At the time, I judged my uncle harshly, and though now I can sympathize, I can't help but hold this betrayal against him.

The circumstances of war and the Soviet legal code made it difficult for Tamara to have Leonid's child. Until the law was changed, in 1964, children born out of wedlock had no right to demand paternal support. The father could legally recognize the child, but to do so was asking for trouble at work, in the family, and in the party. All the father of an illegitimate child could do, if he wanted, was to help financially and make secret visits to a child who didn't dare call him Papa in public.

After the war was over, Tamara told Natalya Denisovna about several abortions she had had at the front. She had no time to recuperate afterward, with all the wounded waiting to be treated. Once while inspecting a soldier, she fell forward, her face landing right in an open wound, and fainted—she had just had an abortion.

During the war, word of General Brezhnev's love affair reached Stalin. "Well, well," said the man in charge of everything in the Soviet Union, from foreign policy to personal morals. "Let's see how he behaves in the future."

Hearing of this, Leonid, as my father once put it plainly, "shit his pants" and decided to leave Tamara. But their romance flickered on and off for years after the war. The whole process was deeply painful for both of them as well as for Leonid's family.

In the mid-'50s, when Leonid moved to Moscow, he arranged for Tamara to have an apartment in a fashionable neighborhood in the city. Viktoriya's hangers-on informed her. She was furious: not only did this little doctor want to break up Leonid's family, but she was already taking advantage of his connections! Leonid, who dreaded family scandals, told his wife that it was his brother who had used his connections to help Tamara.

When my father confirmed his brother's version at a family supper soon afterward, Viktoriya retorted, "Yasha, as Leonid's brother, I see why you would try to cover up for him, but that's going a bit too far. Maybe you'll tell me that it was you who slept with her and not him?" Leonid spat and left the table.

As his lawful wife and the mother of his two children, Viktoriya had the upper hand. She could complain to the party committees, where the dalliances of Communists were discussed and dealt with collectively, and she knew that the party disapproved of divorce. But her trump card was Leonid's mother. Having made a thorough study of the Brezhnev family structure, she knew that if any woman ever posed a serious threat to their marriage, Natalya Denisovna would come down on her side for the sake of family unity and propriety. Once when the question of my parents' romance was being discussed, Natalya had said, "In our family, marriage is forever." Aware that her son did not love his wife, she had the welfare of her grandchildren uppermost in her mind.

No one knows exactly when Tamara and Leonid said their last good-bye, and the details of their parting will forever remain their secret.

Truly, love required enormous courage. Once when we were in the study of Konstantin Simonov, the topic of love came up. Sipping his tea, the novelist confronted my father: "I suppose Leonid Ilyich did have a true love in his life?"

"Yes, he did," my father replied. "But after the war, he left her, and she was devastated."

"I can understand why he did that," Simonov said pensively. "I was once in the same kind of a jam." Looking at me, he asked, "Do you understand your uncle, Lubushka?"

"No," I answered passionately. "He lost more than she did. I would never even miss someone who treated me as he treated her."

"Never say *never*, my dear," advised Simonov. This conversation was held not long before I met Helmut.

I was with my father at a holiday gathering. He leaned over to me and said, "Look at the couple that just came in. She's Toma, Leonid's wartime girlfriend. I'm going to join them. Stay here and watch. Lyonka was head over heels in love with her."

I was not yet twenty but already knew about Tamara and was curious to see what she looked like. Standing by the door next to a man in a general's uniform was a slightly plump, still-shapely woman in an elegant evening dress, with an attractive hairdo and a self-assured but kindly face. Her smile and her eyes revealed an inimitable feminine charm. I could see why this woman had played such a special role in my uncle's life.

When she saw my father, she was radiant. Yakov shook her companion's hand and was moving to kiss hers, but instead of accepting this purely conventional greeting, she wrapped her arms around him and kissed him warmly, as if he were a long-lost relative. They did not talk long. My father returned to my side with moist eyes, visibly moved.

"Lyonka was a fool," he said.

Chapter Eighteen

UNDER THE AFRICAN SKY

A Russian explorer, propelled by the breeze,
To lands unfamiliar sailed over the seas.

MIKHAIL LOMONOSOV

My first, tentative plans to leave the Soviet Union began in the late '60s, and the KGB, which never stopped calling me in for talks, knew of my intentions. But it was not until the winter of 1974, soon after he was released from isolation, that I first talked of them to my father. He began showing greater interest in my social life than ever before. "I was told that two foreign cars were seen outside your house," he reported anxiously one day. Another time he told me, "I hear you visited a house known as a gathering place for dissidents and made some lengthy statements about how terrible our country is." Genuinely frightened, he warned that I could be thrown into a mental hospital, as he had been. "Galina and that crowd can get away with anything, but what's to stop them from burying you away?"

Knowing how rebellious and stubborn I was, the KGB agents assigned to me attacked my most vulnerable spot—my younger son. One day in 1974, I went into a store, leaving Andrey outside. When I came out, he was nowhere to be seen, and his bike was lying on the ground nearby. He had always before waited for me patiently.

I rushed to the nearest militia station. The officers wished me good luck: missing-persons reports, they explained, could not be filed until three days after a disappearance. I came home exhausted from grief and desperation and called my husband at work to tell him what had happened.

Fifteen minutes later the doorbell rang. I will never forget the happiness in my son's big, round eyes, the way he flung his little arms up in the air like a frail old woman. What can be compared with the joy of holding your child's quivering body in your arms, hearing his "Mama, Mama" ringing in your ear?

"Where were you?" I asked as we sat on the sofa, wrapped in each other's arms.

"I was waiting where you said, and all of a sudden some man came up and said that Daddy was waiting for me on the other side of the kindergarten and wanted me to come. At first, I didn't want to because you told me to wait for you, but he took my hand and made me cross the street. His hand hurt me. We got there, but Daddy wasn't there. The man said we had to wait. I played in the sandbox, and the man smoked. I wanted to go pee-pee, and I told the man. He said that I should go right there, but I said that it wasn't right to do that in the sandbox because other kids would come, and it wouldn't be nice for them. Then he looked at his watch, and we left. He took me across the street and told me that this was my home. He pointed to our entrance, and I ran."

My husband and I first submitted an application for emigration in 1975, thereby beginning a process that seemed to last forever. We received refusals from one OVIR office after the other.* While my father and uncle tried peacefully to change my mind, my KGB agents used different tactics.

In the kitchen—that was as far as I let them into the apartment—one of them had hinted that my heroism would end as soon as they got around to my children. How true. I recalled what had happened to Andrey—yet another reminder of their power. During a subsequent talk

*OVIR stands for Division of Visas and Registration, which had to approve the visas of all Soviet citizens wishing to travel abroad or emigrate.

with them, I promised to tear up my application and make no further attempts to leave the country.

"I will still be a dissident at heart," I added.

That was fine with them. "That's another matter entirely," one said and left.

But my efforts to leave the country continued.

Later in 1975, Viktor F., a well-known dissident who was refused permission to emigrate for many years but had helped the writer Yuri Mamleev leave the country, took steps to arrange an invitation for me to emigrate to Israel. He contacted Golda Meir, recently the Israeli prime minister, who responded sympathetically and offered to send my husband and me a personal invitation. Understanding what a fight my acceptance would unleash, I told Viktor that I would think it over. The next morning I called him and said no—not from fear but from anger: why should I have to leave my homeland under false pretenses instead of emigrating legally?

In 1976, when my husband and I moved to the fashionable Lenin Prospekt neighborhood in downtown Moscow, my father once again began suggesting graduate studies at Moscow State University. This time I agreed. At least it would be convenient, since the university was a ten-minute walk from my new home.

My adviser—he was "helping" me as a way of repaying my father for a favor—periodically called me in for vapid conversations, wresting me away from my domestic chores and devouring me with his lecherous eyes. I can't stand womanizers! A portly, stiff-necked man with a double chin that jiggled in a comical way whenever he laughed or got angry, he looked to me like a dissolute abbot.

Once, sick to my stomach from listening to his hackneyed come-ons—"Only sin can take us to the highest realms of art"; "the darker the sky, the brighter the stars"—I stood up and announced that I wasn't going to work with him a minute longer. I left before he could gather his wits.

As usual after one of my performances, the following day brought a phone call from my father. I felt that I had done nothing wrong. Asked to account for my "boorish behavior," I explained that I didn't wish to study under a man who didn't have my respect.

"Lubochka, everyone respects my friend but you," replied my father. "Anyway," he went on, "he doesn't seem too upset by your withdrawal."

"So much the better. By the way," I added, "how did you learn that I dropped out?"

"He told me himself today."

"I can just imagine how that ass tried to cover up for himself: 'My dear Yakov Ilyich, circumstances oblige me to notify you that your daughter has failed to live up to our shared expectations. Considering the great respect I have for you personally, I, for my part . . .' "

My portrayal was so close to the real thing that my father laughed in spite of himself. I knew that he had once pulled some strings to have charges dropped after this honorable professor tried to rape a young student.

My academic career had died in the bud, as my acting career had a decade earlier. Sometimes people would say to me, "You have the intelligence and no shortage of connections, so why don't you at least have a candidate of science degree?" I could now answer, "For two reasons: first, my sons; later, a double chin."

In 1977, the KGB contacted the First Section of Mischa's institute and asked that we be allowed to work in Algeria. And so, in 1978, we finally went to Africa, but only after some resistance from Vinogradov, the rector of the Institute of Petroleum and Gas. He first attempted to persuade my husband to stay. This failing, he resorted to petty tricks. At the beginning of his ten-month French course (after which he would be expected to teach in Algeria without an interpreter), Mischa was suddenly sent with a group of students to harvest potatoes at a collective farm. He took his French books along.

Vinogradov wanted to keep my husband around because he was so useful. Virtually all the graduate students listed as working under the rector were actually working under Mischa, who was considered one of the most talented and knowledgeable experts the institute had. Many doctoral dissertations passed through his hands. He also carried a heavy teaching load, including evening classes, which had been foisted on him against his wishes. He sometimes left home at eight in the morning and came back at midnight.

Connections and seniority generally determined who was chosen to work in Algeria. Hoping to make more money, many at my husband's institute were eager to go. Earning 270 rubles, a candidate of science could barely make ends meet, even if his wife worked. The only professors with cars were those who had traveled abroad. Many also naïvely dreamed of spending some time far away from the internal squabbles plaguing the institute; little did they know that in Algeria, things were worse. The long-awaited border crossing seemed to bring out the most unpleasant personality traits, and there was constant discord within the community of Soviet experts and their wives.

The Ministry of Education guidelines called for one expert from my husband's department to be sent to Algeria that year. Two candidates were on the list ahead of him. The first was very well qualified, but the institute's party committee rejected her when someone reported that she had one Jewish parent. A trip to Algeria was also out of the question for the second candidate, after he raped a young student in a laboratory the day before his application was to be processed. Though removed from teaching for "amoral behavior," he avoided criminal charges by buying the victim's parents a new Volga.

Losing the right to teach was considered a serious punishment. Everyone in the institutes wanted to give lectures, and the reason had nothing to do with a love of teaching or a sense of duty. Instead, it was because as an instructor, one earned a full salary along with the opportunity to make money from research on the side. It was not rare for an assistant professor giving lectures to earn more than a doctor of science doing only research. The road to a teaching position was often paved with quid pro quo deals, appeals to relatives, rumors, dirty tricks, and slanderous accusations.

My husband's application moved to the next stage. Only "the most worthy and the most reliable" were selected for foreign service. You had to belong to the party—which helps explain why there was a waiting list of intellectuals wanting to join. You also had to be able to leave relatives in the Soviet Union: the thought of their fate was sure to cool any sudden urges to defect.

After a soul-daunting interview, my husband's department issued him his "travel file," a combination résumé and character reference, and sent him to the party committee of the institute, where the same ordeal with the same idiotic questions awaited him.

Finally the oblast committee of the party reviewed my husband's file in his presence, and its foreign-travel commission approved it. Like everyone else, my husband was asked why he wanted to leave the Soviet Union: what benefits he was expecting to derive from his trip? If you were "a politically literate and ideologically firm Communist" (as your file invariably described you), you had to say that you were going because you had been dreaming all your life of helping other countries on the socialist path and you were losing sleep trying to figure out how to help your comrades shed their colonial legacy and make socialism triumph in Algeria (or whatever country you were headed for) as soon as possible. A candid answer—that the motivation was financial—would guarantee you'd never see the blue African sky.

An Uzbek woman on this commission asked, "Why are you, an Armenian, living in Moscow instead of in your native republic?" My husband explained that as a true gentleman, he had to make certain concessions to his wife, a Russian who didn't want to leave home.

The "travel files" contained a profusion of numbers and listed all the applicants' accomplishments but gave no clue as to their real character. The candidates for foreign service stood, puppies with their tails between their legs, responding politely to questions. For most of them, this was only form anyway, since they had already paid the appropriate bribes.

The commission's questionnaires were exhaustive and exhausting. We had to append photographs, copies of diplomas, a list of places we had worked, medical certificates declaring that we were "in generally good health," and a short biographical essay, handwritten (so it could analyzed by handwriting experts?). The Ministry of Education looked over all this paper and held a public hearing, at which Mischa had to answer questions—again. Then the commission went into closed session to discuss our suitability.

Like obedient schoolchildren, Mischa and I made the requisite medical visits, haunting the corridors of polyclinics for two months until we received the precious papers certifying us as free of mental illness, venereal disease, drug addiction, and alcoholism. Our efforts earned us the contemptuous laughter of those in the know—they had purchased their medical certificates, for hard cash, from the easily swayed physicians of the Ministry of Education polyclinic. There was a fixed price list: the signature of the head physician below the statement that you were "in generally good health" cost two hundred rubles; the signature of the therapist cost fifty rubles; those of the other doctors, twenty rubles apiece. Once in Algeria, I would be shocked by the number of my fellow citizens being sent abroad despite grave illnesses, including the terminal stages of cancer. It was not rare for Soviet experts to be sent home seriously ill within six months of their arrival.

The head of the foreign section of the Ministry of Education took bribes, as did the pushy, self-assured young women who were his assistants and inspectors. Teachers from non-Russian republics faced double jeopardy. They first had to pay bribes at home, then in Moscow. In Algeria, I often heard Ukrainian, Azerbaijani, and Armenian professors say that their entire salary for the first none too easy year of work in Algeria went to pay for the bribes and presents they had to give. Azerbaijan was especially notorious. Yet no one was greatly upset by this: everyone took it for granted, and many even tried to find excuses for the bribe takers: "They want to have a life, too."

On August 24, 1978, Mischa and I stepped off the plane in Algiers. We had eight-year-old Andrey with us; his older brother Teodor was in Moscow.

The guidelines for behavior that we had been instructed (by the First Section of Mischa's institute) to study and sign included a part urging us to respect the host country's economic difficulties. Who can argue with that? But we would soon learn what stood behind this perfectly humane-sounding language. The embassy used it to justify stripping

LUBA BREZHNEVA

The author's children, Andrey (left) and Teodor, 1974

traveling specialists of the benefits guaranteed under the contract: free medical treatment and medicines, reimbursement of expenses incurred on business trips within the country, private housing, and so forth. Even when the government of Algeria or foreign companies doing business there tried to treat us fairly, the embassy insisted that "our people" were used to a simple life and didn't need "to be coddled."

The Communists had exported their beloved communal living to North Africa: the contract allowed for several unmarried experts to be housed in one apartment—despite the fact that vacant apartments were available. Those bold souls who asked the Algerian administration for help in obtaining separate quarters were subject to retaliation. Why, comrades, do you want to live separately? Do you have something to hide? Communal apartments offered ideal conditions for mutual spying.

The embassy employees earned their abundant bonuses, citations of merit, and promotions by mistreating "their" experts and kowtowing to the Algerian administrators. The seven years I ended up working abroad would give me ample opportunity to observe their system at work. One example was the contract with the Algerian government that required our furniture to be changed every few years. The furniture was nonetheless left in place for twenty years while the new furniture was stolen from the warehouses and sold on the black market. We all had to bring our housewares from Moscow, including the towels, pillows, blankets, scissors, buckets, frying pans, cups, saucers, and plates that the contract guaranteed us.

The same day we got off the plane, we were assigned to a run-down villa. As we entered, we noticed a potted tree covered with clusters of what looked like brown grapes. They were cockroaches. From time to time, a few would fall and scurry off across the floor. They also flew around the room, buzzing like little airplanes. We nicknamed them Boeings.

In the bedroom, we were greeted by a huge pile of trash, including used condoms, dirty cotton wool, and a broken thermometer whose mercury had spilled onto the floor. We were told that water was available two hours every morning and two hours every evening.

When the water was turned on that evening, we discovered that there were no pipes connecting the running water to the sinks, the bathtub was full of trash, and the toilet was clogged. We battled stinking torrents for the next two hours. Finally an Algerian policeman came to our assistance after he saw water pouring from all sides of our villa. Later I lit the oven, and the gas came on with a loud bang, nearly singeing my face and hair. Then the stove went dead for good.

At 2:00 A.M., we finally put our boy to bed and lay down, exhausted and miserable. Our bed had apparently been thrown together by the singularly inexpert hands of the Soviet expert who had preceded us. There were a couple of bricks under each improvised leg.

I was kept awake by a steady rustling and finally turned the light on, only to find an army of cockroaches parading up and down our sheets and blanket. I ran into my son's room and found him covered with roaches from head to toe.

There would be no sleep for me and my husband that night. Mischa waged a lone battle against the bugs while I sat under the headily fragrant shrubs in the courtyard, our child asleep in my arms.

We carried all our luggage into the yard when morning came and watched indifferently as water started to stream out of the pipes all over again. Nothing was going to persuade us to go inside. I had come to work as an interpreter, and in three days my husband was going to assume his duties as head of the Theoretical Mechanics Department of the Algerian National Institute of Chemistry, Petroleum, and Gas. We both faced a colossal workload.

In frustration and anger, I went to the embassy and told the contract adviser that unless he immediately furnished us with satisfactory housing, we would return to the Soviet Union that day. Had he not known that I was Brezhnev's niece, we would have been promptly sent back home, along with an unfavorable report. As it was, we were assigned to a villa that was reasonably clean, with adequate furniture and functioning plumbing.

We should have received it in the first place, given that my husband was a department head. But the tradition was that the best treatment was reserved for those who bribed the inspectors from the Ministry of Education, something we had neglected to do.

The first week after my arrival, I was informed that I could receive the same regular food packets as members of the diplomatic corps, an honor I declined, explaining that we would find what we needed at the farmers' market. When Ambassador Gennady Rykov visited the neighborhood in Boumerdes where we lived (along with many other teachers and students from various institutes), he dropped by and asked about our living arrangements. On his orders, the economic adviser of the embassy began to keep an eye on our well-being until I finally asked him to leave us alone: his too frequent visits were setting tongues wagging among our neighbors.

Naturally, the First Section of Mischa's institute let the party bosses in Algeria know of my identity, and the embassy even knew the name of the man assigned to report to the KGB about me. Besides, my father was careless enough to send me letters and packages by diplomatic pouch and had asked one of Leonid's aides to keep track of how I was doing, making regular phone contact with either the embassy or the consulate.

Perfect strangers sometimes informed me excitedly that the general secretary's niece was in Algeria; I tried to appear surprised. Fortunately, though the news that I was there spread rapidly, few knew what I looked like.

Rioting broke out in the country in March, a few months after President Houari Boumédienne's death in December of 1978. There were tanks patrolling the streets, the Soviet club was closed down, and a Soviet ship was stationed in the harbor, ready to evacuate us at a moment's notice. We kept two suitcases packed in one corner of our villa in case we had to flee with little notice. A three-month mourning period was being observed, and the only thing broadcast on television was a mullah who read the news along with passages from the Koran. Constantly we heard rumors about terrorists and extremists. A crowded café was blown up in nearby Algiers.

We were all obliged to have subscriptions to the official newspaper, *Pravda* (since we paid in hard currency, which the government coveted), but it began coming irregularly and anyway gave us no idea of what was really happening at home. The mail from the Soviet Union was coming so late that we received only ancient history by that route. We were completely cut off from the world.

The weather was gloomy and depressing—the rainy season was a time when members of the Soviet community, the women in particular, often went crazy, committed suicide, or had heart attacks. Other problems flared: first an epidemic of jaundice among the children, then, for the first time, interruptions in the food supply. Our women, with their experience of Soviet food shortages, haunted the stores of Boumerdes from morning to night, waiting for shipments of butter, milk, and meat. As soon as something arrived, they would begin pushing, shoving, and overturning the tables, to the shock of the employees.

Once a contingent of Soviet women went to a store to stand bravely in line, waiting for a truck full of food to be unloaded. After the lunch break—from noon to 3:00 P.M. in Algeria, as in many other Arab countries—two young Algerians sauntered out of the store and leisurely carried one box back inside. The women's patience was running thin.

One, perhaps imagining that she was back in Russia on the farm, shouted out, "What are we standing around for? Why don't we unload it ourselves?"

The women proceeded to do so: everything was on the shelves in the twinkling of an eye, to the amazement of the Algerian shoppers. As for the shop clerks, they had been so terrified by the women's onslaught that they scattered to the four winds. There was a high-level investigation, the details of which I learned while acting in my role as interpreter.

Most of the Soviet experts had come for one thing alone—to make money—and carried their penny-pinching to absurd extremes. I had to smile when I saw the sun-bleached likeness of my uncle peering down from old issues of *Pravda* covering my neighbors' windows. The papers were occasionally updated, before the holidays or during spring cleaning. Curtains would have cost only a few dinars.

Each academic department had at its disposal a supply of worn-out housewares left behind by successive generations of Soviet experts: plastic tubs used by the women to store the water that was turned on twice a day—full of holes, these tubs had to be patched periodically; blankets smelling of mold and the bodies of strangers; pillows covered with dubious spots; and for the kitchen, saucepans lacking lids, dented teapots, and frying pans sporting a thick, ingrained coat of grease.

Once a sack full of these treasures was delivered to us; as department head, Mischa was expected to help distribute them. I refused to let the sack into our villa and had it put in the garden. When the neighborhood cats knocked it over during a lively romp, I was surprised to find a good toothbrush and some well-worn but clean men's socks among all the junk.

The average age of the Soviet specialists in Algeria was forty-five to fifty. Their academic workloads were heavy; they were completely unprepared for the climate; and interpersonal relations were strained. And as noted, many were ill before they were even sent. Not surprisingly, many broke under the conditions. Every year saw the death of several Soviet experts, mainly from heart attacks.

The nearly universal efforts to skimp on food led to some sad results. One family was sent home because their five-year-old girl was afflicted with dystrophy, the result of chronic malnutrition. I heard that she died soon after arriving in the Soviet Union. I myself saw her being carried to the plane, so weak that she couldn't walk.

We always kept a platter full of fruit on our kitchen table, since that was something never in short supply in Algeria: dates, figs, oranges, grapes, peaches, loquats, pears. Once Andrey came home to pick up his ball. When the boy with him stared wide-eyed at the fruit, I took the largest bunch of grapes and offered it to him.

"For me?" he asked in amazement.

"Are you coming soon?" my son asked as he ran into the kitchen. "Let's get going. Everyone's waiting. You look like you've never eaten grapes before!"

"I never have," the boy admitted, swallowing hastily. "I sometimes ask Mom for some, but she asks me if I want to eat up the car."

The greatest dream for most of us was a Volga. On the Soviet black market, this car fetched the astronomical price of thirty-five thousand rubles—when the deal didn't end with a summons to the prosecutor's office or a Central Committee commission. Usually the "merchants" were let off with a reprimand and allowed to go abroad again, as long as they upped the amount they paid in bribes to the Education Ministry.

Theft was not uncommon among the Soviets working under contract with the Algerian government. The wives of the drillers, construction workers, geologists, and land developers had particularly itchy palms. The secretary of one of the party committees had a wife who specialized in chickens: she adroitly swept them into her bag as she strolled around the open-air market and later sold to her friends whatever she didn't need for herself. She was finally caught—by other Soviet women—and a tremendous scandal of cluck-clucking followed.

Her husband tried to excuse her behavior. "After all, what do you expect? My wife worked in stores back home, and naturally she was stealing all those years. She can't help it."

But the party committee didn't give much weight to this argument, and his wife was sent home, to steal in some Soviet store, I suppose.

One of my Algerian acquaintances was a wool merchant. Although I never bought anything from him, when I was at the market, I liked to chat with him. Having lived in Paris for many years, he spoke French beautifully.

Once he took me into his confidence: "I've been watching your women steal my wool for years. They have quite a system worked out. As they're looking over the spools, running their fingers over them, they pull the one nearest the edge onto one finger and flip it into their bag, which they have conveniently ready and open. Or they first buy a large amount of wool from me, and then come back to exchange it for a different color—after unwinding a few grams of wool from the middle of each spool."

Wool and cloth were the most popular goods for resale in Russia. Kilometers of cloth (with such defects as a strip of tiny holes, an edge where the dye hadn't taken, or a thread sticking out) were bought up at discount prices and sent to the Soviet Union to be sold for a tidy profit, either at consignment stores or directly to friends, neighbors, and relatives.

Right in the center of the market, two brothers presided over long, low tables covered with rolls of multicolored fabric; their prices—the lowest at the market—had made them the Soviet community's favorites. A story was told of two women who once dawdled so long, comparing wares and unable to decide on a purchase, that one of the brothers lost patience and called out—speaking the Russian window-shoppers' native language flawlessly—"Take what we have, you silly fool. It's better than anything you'll find in Moscow!"

I was at the farmers' market one day, buying vegetables from a friend of my son—they took karate lessons together. The boy knew French well, and as we were talking, he decided that a certain tomato was past its prime and threw it into a wooden box. Next to us stood a woman who had been waiting for just this to happen: the moment the tomato landed, she leaned over, snatched it, and slipped it into her bag. His friendly smile gone, the vendor threw out—this time with obvious malice—another tomato, which the woman, the wife of one of the Soviet experts, promptly picked up.

I wished I could disappear into thin air. Finally, his features twisted in anger and revulsion, the boy took a third tomato and flung it straight at the woman's feet. The scene was worthy of Shakespeare. I hurriedly paid for my purchase and left, without even asking Andrey's friend to give my regards to his parents, whom we occasionally encountered at karate meets.

Personal conflicts within the Soviet community in Algeria were mediated at the offices of the academic department or at general meetings held in the Soviet clubs, which I tried my best to avoid. One time when Algerian representatives were invited to observe the proceedings, I was called in to interpret. The case involved a fight among three Soviet women sharing a communal apartment, all of them assistant professors.

The hearing dragged on for two hours as witnesses discussed who had hit whom with a tub, who had hit whom with a chair, who had bruised whose head, who had scratched whose face, who had pulled out whose hair. . . . Finally two of the women joined forces to accuse the third of adultery, describing in detail the nighttime visits to their apartment by a married man. The Algerian observers were shocked—even though I deliberately left out the spicier details. The "scarlet woman" was sent back to the Soviet Union, but her nocturnal visitor stayed and could still be seen around town, walking arm in arm with his lawfully wedded wife, who had been present at the hearing.

Soviet women without powerful relatives had little defense against office tyrants. Typists and secretaries were ill advised to reject the advances of their bosses; actresses and ballerinas who said no to the Politburo were asking for trouble. Standing up for one's rights meant being dragged through the mud and driven to despair.

My relations with the contract adviser, for whom I translated, deteriorated steadily. Immediately I broke with tradition: the custom for years had been that his secretary and personal interpreter also served as his mistress. I didn't even get friendly with him. I would leave banquets as soon as the official segment was completed and declined to go with him on business trips around the country, sending another interpreter instead. I even maintained an official tone when I ran into him on the street. The more I feigned naïve ignorance, the more ardent he became.

I understood his mentality well. He had been a party member and a doctor of science (these were requirements), but otherwise he was just another unknown faculty member at the Institute of Petroleum and Gas. His newfound power went to his head like spring wine when he was suddenly made contract adviser in Algeria, and he milked the post for all it was worth, knowing that his term was limited to five years and doubtless aware that no similar opportunity would ever come his way again.

He fancied himself somewhat of a provincial lord and did his best to fit the role—in vain. Lacking the slightest refinement, he didn't even know how to eat in public or to pursue the charms of a woman in a civilized manner. With his crude manners, he was more than anything else like . . . well, like an ignorant engineer in a provincial backwater.

I looked upon the parties he held as the height of vulgarity and sheer silliness, but he persisted in inviting me. After a banquet held in the adviser's villa, one of Mischa's friends at the institute, an Algerian instructor, told me that his Muslim sensibilities had been deeply offended by the spectacle following the meal: two wives of Soviet specialists—their husbands wanted very much to be retained in Algeria for another year—had performed a belly dance for the adviser's amusement, stripping down to their panties.

The skills that most Soviet instructors working abroad needed for success had little to do with pedagogy and everything to do with bootlicking. Their wives went to the adviser's villa to scrub and tidy up, take his little girl for walks, bake him pies, even make wine for him. He never had any problems with his car, thanks to the professors from his department who kept it clean and in good repair. In Algiers, one enthusiast even came to dust the adviser's office every day before work and put fresh flowers in his vase.

The adviser for whom I translated had no shortage of women willing to share his bed. But he still wanted what he saw as something special, something exotic: Brezhnev's niece. After I finally had a frank talk with him that convinced him his fantasy would never come true, he began to have one of his people spy on us in the hopes of finding information he could use to have us kicked out of Algeria. Unable to dig up any dirt, he changed tactics and convinced the rector of the Algerian Institute of

Chemistry, Petroleum, and Gas that the department headed by my husband should be abolished.

Ironically, my husband was overjoyed to be free of a burden he had long sought to shed. A year later, when the administration realized that breaking up the department had been an idiotic idea and that it should be put together again, my husband refused to become its head. Soon, after doing something that had displeased a higher-up, the contract adviser was sent back to the Soviet Union, never to return.

We had few problems for a whole year. The only person spying on us, and making no efforts to conceal the fact, was a KGB agent, an agreeable fellow who caused us no trouble and winked at all our violations of the rules.

Major efforts were made to keep Soviet specialists busy with politics, ideology, and social life so that they wouldn't get too involved in the life of the host country. There were endless cultural activities, including a choir in which all the Soviet wives had to sing, whether or not they could carry a tune. I was spared because as a working interpreter, I was not "just a wife." The choir had its own wardrobe, from which the singers dressed for the major holidays: May 9, November 7, New Year. The white-collared gowns were in the typically harsh, Stalinist style. Handed down from one generation of wives of Soviet teachers and specialists to the next long after they went out of fashion, they had served ever since the first contract was signed with the Algerian government, in the early 1960s. The robes used for the New Year were the same except that they had golden and silver-colored threads woven into the fabric.

The choir's repertoire, scrutinized carefully by the party committee of the institute, included patriotic songs about the motherland and the party as well as sentimental standards, such as "Katyusha" and "Moscow Nights." Many of us were tired of these two, having heard them since childhood. The latter includes such deathless lines as "My darling looks at me sideways, her head bowed low."

At a social gathering, Pasha Florensky—a friend who had shared several difficult years with us in Algeria and was the grandson of the philosopher Pavel Florensky—once asked everybody present to attempt to look sideways with head bowed low. No one could. Never mind, non-Soviets went crazy for "Moscow Nights." Sometimes the tired standbys would be offset by the inclusion of locally written satirical songs, many of them very witty.

My first glimpse of the barbed wire surrounding Boumerdes, the city where we were to live, had made me think of a concentration camp built near Akmolinsk (later renamed Tselinograd) in Kazakhstan during the Stalin era. Known as the Akmolinsk Camp for the Wives of the Traitors to the Motherland, its acronym—ALZhIR—spells *Algeria* in Russian.

Boumerdes was no concentration camp, nor was it a citadel of freedom. To set foot beyond the city limits, Soviet citizens were supposed to have a permit, which required a written application submitted ten days ahead of time and approval from both the contract adviser and the embassy. This was a Soviet, not an Algerian, rule. My husband and I came and went as we pleased, however, belonging as we did to the only two groups that could flout the rules: those (such as myself) who had powerful Soviet connections and those (such as my husband) whose professional services were essential to the Algerian government.

I fell in love with Algeria's magical colors and natural beauty. Fleeing the confines of the barbed wire whenever possible, we traveled the length and breadth of the country. One of the outstanding events in my life was a trip to the Sahara. Feeling totally fulfilled in the vast land where "God is near and people are far," I decided there would be no better place on Earth from which to step into eternity.

We visited the ancient Roman ruins and virtually every Algerian city, and not merely as tourists: invited in, we entered the homes of Arabs, Berbers, and Kabyle tribesmen alike. I was given the honor of attending wedding and circumcision ceremonies. Going to the baths with the Algerian women, I won their trust and learned how they kept themselves beautiful, how they raised their children, what their relations with their in-laws were like, whether or not they loved their husbands. . . .

The Algerian attitude toward privacy is refreshing. Violating the sanctity of someone's home is a major transgression and punished accordingly. The entrance is never brightly lit, and the courtyard, where the women, children, and old people of the family spend most of their time, can be reached only by passing through the entire house. In addition to mingling with the people, I also spent hours in the main library of Algiers, fascinated by what I found out about the country's history, economy, customs, and religious life.

Fluent French opened many doors, and soon we counted journalists, physicians, lawyers, scientists, writers, singers, and musicians among our friends. Eager to learn all I could about Algerian intellectuals, I especially wanted to know what advances the country had made following the ouster of the French. With deep disappointment, I saw a typically Soviet style beginning to permeate the daily life, the economy, and, worst of all, the ethics of the country. Algeria had its own party corruption and organized crime. As in Russia, the intelligentsia was persecuted, and I knew of writers who had to publish their books, banned in Algeria, across the sea, in France. My friends repeatedly pointed out to me the opulent villas of party and military functionaries, located in the most fashionable neighborhoods.

I was heartened by one salient difference: never did I see a trace of slavelike resignation or submissiveness in any Algerian. A new generation was rising quickly, young people who knew of French colonialism only from textbooks and wanted no part of compromises or half-truths. I remember how furiously they protested the Soviet incursion into Afghanistan, calling it a gross interference in that country's internal affairs. They were outraged that the Soviet people would stand by and allow their government to commit such crimes.

Most Soviet citizens, plagued by feelings of inadequacy no matter how highly educated, agonized over every word they said to an Algerian. "Did I say the right thing; have I lost face?" they would ask one another and themselves. The Algerians, on the other hand, had a highly developed sense of their own worth and carried themselves with pride no matter what their station in life.

My husband and I, meeting with Algerians freely, were hard pressed to explain why the Soviet administration didn't allow its citizens to socialize with them. The Algerians didn't bother to conceal their displeasure with limits that for most of us were just as much a part of life as air and water.

The Afghan war is an issue that still gives my conscience no rest. When I flew from Algeria to Moscow in the summer of 1980, the war was already in full swing. We were away when the troops had been sent, so I didn't know the details of events from up close. At our first meeting, I asked my father how Leonid could expose the nation to such a disgrace. Trying to justify his brother's actions, he said that Leonid had three times refused to sign the document approving Soviet intervention but that Andropov, Suslov, Gromyko, and Ustinov had insisted, the latter having been the most adamant. When I asked which of my uncle's grandsons were fighting in Afghanistan, I learned that none was.

Our government's hypocrisy, and that of my uncle in particular, was obvious to everyone in the world: while claiming to support peace and disarmament, the Soviet Union was intervening militarily in Afghanistan, sending young men to kill and be killed. Hundreds of Soviet citizens were sent to prison or psychiatric wards for sending the general secretary letters protesting Soviet policy. At the height of the war, we were informed that my husband's cousin, a military interpreter, had been killed. The son of a friend of mine returned from Afghanistan blind, and a neighbor of my parents ended up in a mental hospital because of war-related stress; he died there not long ago.

Once I asked my father why our young men had been crippled and maimed. What noble cause had thrown them into a foreign land that hated them? What great feats will glorify their names? Who is responsible for the terrible fate of those lads, torn from their mothers' arms? What of the innocent Afghan civilians who were killed? I suggested that he advise his brother to kneel down in public, as even the czars had done, and ask forgiveness or at least acknowledge the inconsolable grief of the bereaved mothers. My questions remained unanswered and my advice unheeded.

I can now ask forgiveness in the name of my late uncle.

⊠

Along with communal apartments, the Communists brought to Algeria the unpaid Saturday work parties—*subbotniki*—all too familiar in the Soviet Union. Recognized scientists with advanced degrees, invited to help Algeria develop its infrastructure, were periodically sent to sweep the embassy courtyard, wash the windows, paint the benches, and prune the hedges. The paid staff pocketed the money allocated for this upkeep. True, if the learned "volunteers" did a good job, someone would bring them out one hundred grams of vodka apiece, as in the good old days when the beneficent lords brought a bucket of vodka to the peasants after the harvest was in.

My husband categorically refused to take part in the *subbotniki*. For this and other reasons, we were often told that we would be "booted out of the country in twenty-four hours." We took the threats seriously enough to pack our bags, but because of who my uncle was, we were never expelled.

Such threats, though rarely carried out, were widely used to intimidate "misfits" and "rebels." At one meeting, when the threat of expulsion was made, a man stood up and said, "Do you think I'm afraid of my own country?" Then he returned to the Soviet Union voluntarily. Some legitimate grounds for expulsion were disruption of order, insufficient knowledge of one's specialty, drunkenness, and thievery, including petty shoplifting.

The most monstrous case that we heard of involved a young Soviet engineer and his wife. What were they to do when she discovered she was pregnant? They already had two young children. Abortion, illegal in this Muslim country, would have cost a hefty sum. The embassy, which did not allow our women to bear children in Algeria, would send them back home to give birth. But this latter prospect did not appeal to the couple, especially since it meant they would have had to buy four plane tickets with their own hard currency. After much thought, they decided that she would bear the child. And after delivering him, the engineer promptly smothered his son. Late that night they buried him in their garden.

On the following day, the mother's temperature shot up, and her condition became critical. This time they had no choice but to call a doctor, but it was too late: she died of blood poisoning. After a thorough investigation, the husband was tried for infanticide, and his two children were put in an orphans' home.

There was always a rise in conflicts in the spring, when the time came to decide the question of questions: who would stay, and who would be sent back to the Soviet Union. It was one of those high-stress periods capable of bringing out the darkest and, very rarely, the brightest in human nature. One's stay in Algeria could last anywhere from two to five years, and ordinary experts—though not department heads—had to make strenuous efforts to be retained. The atmosphere was poisoned with anonymous letters, scheming, gossip, groveling, and feuding. Futures depended on character references, which were discussed first at the level of the academic department, then at the party bureau, then at the embassy, and finally in Moscow.

One instructor in my husband's department wanted desperately to be retained. He played on Mischa's national sentiments (they were both Armenians) and informed on his rivals, tossing anonymous letters about them onto the porch of our villa. He stayed in Algeria the full five years thanks to all this fancy footwork, which cost Mischa endless frayed nerves.

The instructor's young wife, once vibrant and still beautiful, was withering away from day to day in full view of everyone. She suffered from osteoporosis, and toward the end her legs were like sticks of spaghetti. My husband and I tried to convince them that they should go home and try to do something for her health. But our attempts merely engendered new gossip. After they finally did return to the Soviet Union, she spent two years in the hospital, unable to get out of bed, and died at the age of forty.

Sheremetevo, the Moscow airport to which thousands of Soviet experts returned from abroad every year, was the site of spectacular scenes. I once watched the customs agents unroll an Algerian carpet for inspection. They found it to be stuffed with mohair—so much of the fluffy wool, in fact, that it rose like an enormous mound of dough until one of the agents began throwing it in handfuls from the counter onto the floor.

Our reliable party members bought up gold and silver and took hundreds of fashionable scarves out of Algeria for resale. I once heard a lady proclaim proudly, "The profit margin on those scarves with horse-head patterns bought my husband a garage!" Cardboard boxes—the Soviet Union's favorite luggage—often turned out to hold rolls of fabric, kilometers of shoelaces, rivets for homemade jeans, sheepskins by the dozens, and leather jackets. Who knows what else these amateur smugglers were bringing home to the commodity-starved Soviet Union?

The smuggling was two-way; several times I watched as Soviet women leaving via Sheremetevo had sticks of sausage pulled out from under their coats (they wanted to save money on food while living abroad) or diamond rings (unavailable in Algeria) taken out of their bras. It was not rare for the customs agents to extract anodized chains and other trinkets from women's private parts.

Once when we were returning from Algeria, the customs inspector discovered to his astonishment that our fifteen suitcases contained nothing but printed matter, virtually all of it in French. At a loss, he used his walkie-talkie to summon a colleague who supposedly knew that language. The expert, who obviously had no knowledge of French, looked the books over lackadaisically and said, "Let them through."

I could hardly believe my ears. I had been worrying that we would have to turn to my father to get us out of this potential mess: we were bringing in the works of Solzhenitsyn, the Bible in several languages, several children's Bibles, which I was planning to give as gifts, and clippings from anti-Soviet newspapers and magazines. If they had been in Russian, they would have ended up in special warehouses, branded with one or two stars, depending on their level of "harmfulness."

Later people with experience taught me a sure way to get anything through customs, and I used it gladly—after a several-years-long period of calm, I didn't want to have another run-in with the KGB. Besides being out of practice, I now had children and so could ill afford to be as bold as I was during my student days. The simple secret was to find a porter with a cart and hand him twenty rubles with no explanation. At the end of his shift, he would keep ten rubles and give the rest to "his" customs inspector.

Once in the early '70s, Mischa and I went to the Moscow airport to see friends off to Israel—something we did often in those days. The family's fourteen-year-old daughter had a broken leg, and one of the customs inspectors, noticing her braces, declared that they were made of a rare metal that was not to be taken out of the country. A physician removed them on the spot, as the girl wailed and sobbed with pain.

"Never again," she wrote in a letter later, "will I set foot in the land of my birth."

The wife of a teacher in my husband's department told me her customs story when we were both in Algeria. After searching her son's knapsack and her suitcases, purse, pockets, and private parts, customs officials found nothing out of the ordinary except for fifty rubles—twenty above the limit. But this was enough for her to be taken off the flight list and all her money confiscated. Distraught, her eyes red with tears, she found herself and her seven-year-old son alone and penniless in the waiting room. She finally screwed up her courage and turned to a stranger, who gave her the two kopecks she needed to call relatives. After the coins were swallowed up in an out-of-order telephone, she asked someone else. A militiaman standing nearby, thinking that she was begging, announced that he was planning to take her in. But after her son burst into tears, he escorted her to the militia station and called her relatives. He even treated the boy to candy. Russia, land of endless contradictions.

Each year a list of positions to be filled under the contract for the next year was compiled and posted in Moscow, at the Institute of Petroleum and Gas. But the privilege of working under the Algerian sun was not awarded according to open competition. In the spirit of the times, Ministry of Education inspectors used the principle of supply and demand—there were more people eager to go to Algeria than there were positions available—for personal gain. Specialists were chosen not only for their professional abilities but also, as shown, according to who could do the most for the inspectors. Like so many others during my uncle's rule, they got away scot free, though under Soviet law all this—the misuse of authority and the acceptance of bribes—was illegal. One result, not surprisingly, was the number of truly incompetent teachers, a disgrace to their profession, who were sent abroad.

Eventually I, too, began paying off the Ministry of Education. When the inspector handling my travel file asked me to help get her into a cooperative apartment in a nice area, I complied, turning to an old acquaintance with influence in the distribution of housing.

An official investigation of bribery in the Ministry of Education was initiated under Andropov in 1983, but it was hushed up before it could be completed, and several of the inspectors were offered the option of quitting their jobs quietly. One of those whom I had dealt with chose to have herself committed to a mental hospital, where for the right price the psychiatrists determined that she was suffering from a nervous breakdown. This had long proved a successful method of escaping prosecution.

General Secretary Andropov was not able to uproot the system; in fact, during his administration people began taking even larger bribes, but more cautiously.* The Soviet nationals in Algeria who had got there by bribing the Ministry of Education stayed; to guarantee continued approval, they also brought gifts back to the Soviet Union on their yearly summer vacations. The inspectors who accepted these tributes made sure that their vassals got the best villas and the best apartments in Boumerdes and were given fewer extracurricular assignments. The most unfair part of it was that the specialists who hadn't given bribes had to do an inordinate amount of teaching to make up for the bribers' smaller academic loads.

We were all supposed to attend political seminars and briefings once a week. The main dish served up was always the same, "We are ahead of everyone on the planet, and the foundations of communism are growing stronger day by day," with side orders consisting of pitiful mumblings about economic gains and harvest statistics.

---

*Andropov served as general secretary from November 1982 until his death in February 1984.

Sometimes I was asked to prepare a news report based on information in French newspapers. The party organizer and the contract adviser usually wanted to go over my material ahead of time so that there would be no unpleasant surprises. As soon as my uncle's name came up in one of these reports, as it did constantly, every head in the room would turn in my direction, as though Leonid were standing somewhere behind my back. I hated this: I'd had my fill of cheap fame after my first arrival in Moscow. Just as I avoided the general meetings at the Soviet clubs, I disliked, and almost never attended, the political seminars.

I was not alone in noticing that the higher a specialist's level of social involvement in the Soviet-sponsored events, the lower his professional qualifications tended to be. Second-rate instructors tried to grab positions of power from which they could silence anyone who might discover and mention their shortcomings. A secretary of the party committee or the trade union could get away with giving mediocre lectures. Party bosses were often given work requiring no more skill than that of a lab assistant.

Once when the contract adviser was ill, Mischa was required to lead a meeting on "raising the fighting spirit of the party organizations in order to ensure the fulfillment of our contractual obligations." My husband refused, pointing out that no one, even in the embassy party committee, had been able to explain how the words *fighting spirit* could possibly apply to a Soviet party organization situated in a sovereign country.

When asked for clarification, the Russian-language teachers sent the questioner packing. They had their own hands full at the time, as they were trying to have the one Russian among them thrown out of Algeria. All the others—an Armenian, an Uzbek, a Ukrainian, and a Tatar— had used bribes and favors to get where they were, and each spoke with a pronounced non-Russian accent. They did not succeed, however; the Russian happened to be working for the KGB.

Finally one of the instructors did write a report about the "fighting spirit." No one stood up to yell "The emperor is wearing no clothes" during the two-hour meeting, but there was laughter and whispering in the hallways afterward.

The so-called political education was just another activity, like the choir, to distract the Soviet specialists from asking themselves why they were still so poor even though they had finally made it abroad. We might ask, for example, why we received only 40 percent of our pay in hard currency (and the rest in rubles), while the French, Poles, Chileans, and Yugoslavs working under similar contracts not only received their entire pay in hard currency but also enjoyed all sorts of freedoms, including that of traveling to other countries.

As soon as Soviet specialists arrived in Algeria, their passports were taken away, to be returned on the day of a flight back to the Soviet Union. "We want to make sure you don't lose it" was the explanation. If we had somehow managed to hold on to our passports, we still would not have been able to visit nearby Tunisia or Morocco, let alone France or Spain: any country's customs officials stamped a traveler's passport, and for a Soviet citizen these little marks in a passport would mean a complete ban on leaving the Soviet Union for ten years, even to travel to other countries in Eastern Europe.

Chapter Nineteen

THE YOUNGER GENERATION

Perhaps, one may speculate, at least the Soviet nouveaux riches were happy behind the tall fences they had built to set themselves apart from the "ordinary" people. A Russian adage says that "every cottage has its playthings," and the palaces of the *nomenklatura* did not lack for expensive toys. But where was their happiness? In their families?

Leonid Ilyich's greatest sorrows were prompted by his closest relatives. We know of many other political bosses whose children became a lifelong badge of shame, but Leonid's daughter, Galina, was unequaled. Eventually she was like an open sore, there for the whole world to see. From several of his statements, I know that in his old age Leonid felt nothing but sorrow for his daughter and annoyance with her behavior. It was only when he remembered Galina as a little girl, plump, pink, and funny, that tender feelings still stirred faintly in his heart.

During the perestroika period, after Leonid's death, the typewriters of sensation-hungry journalists rattled furiously with stories in which she was featured prominently—for good reason, of course. Her wild lifestyle had contributed to the complete discrediting of Leonid Brezhnev as a father and as a political leader. It had all begun years earlier.

Leonid's heart attack came several years after Galina's first marriage, in the 1950s, a union he never accepted. Her husband, Yevgeny Milaev, was only four years younger than her father and had been working in the circus since the age of eighteen. In 1950, he and his partners developed a unique act, involving tightrope walkers on a double ladder, which broke world records and brought fame to its creators. In 1951, he was in Kishinev, the capital of Moldavia, with a traveling show, and it was there that he met and married Galina.

Her father disliked Milaev's age and his occupation. When Leonid was first secretary of the Moldavian party, he would drop into his daughter's home on the way to work. Finding Galina still in bed, he would taunt her, holding a long pole above her head and saying, "Giddyup!" She responded by angrily throwing her pillow at him.

Like most Soviet citizens, Leonid was leary of the art world in general and the world of the performing arts in particular. He felt that Yevgeny's nomadic, haphazard existence would have a disruptive effect on young Galina, who already seemed somewhat unbalanced. He'd had a different future in mind for his daughter, hoping that after the university, she would marry within his own world. He had friends whose sons—military specialists and budding political careerists—would have made fine husbands for her, he thought. Her chances of finding a more suitable young man were good: she was not bad looking and not lacking in intelligence.

Leonid would have preferred almost any young man to Galina's choice. He used to tell his brother, "Yasha, she'd have been better off marrying some young tractor driver. What does she see in this Milaev fellow?"

Less and less, it appeared. After several years of married life, Galina grew bored and began to "wag her tail" again, as my father put it. Milaev was insanely jealous and tried to take her along whenever he went on tour. Once they both came to Magnitogorsk. Among the members of the troupe were Zoya and Sergey Naumov, two old friends of my mother's, and they dropped by our house.

Finally Milaev's jealousy caused him to break all the pieces in Galina's beloved crystal collection and then try out his fists on her face, for the first and final time. She ran to her father's house for protection; her first marriage had lasted eight years.

Afterward, Galina maintained friendly relations with her ex-husband and many other circus performers and continued to attend the circus. Leonid, on the other hand, virtually stopped going to the circus, convinced that it had ruined his daughter. Believing this at least gave him a focus for his hatred and disappointment.

In the late '70s, Milaev became the director of the circus in the Lenin Hills in Moscow. When I took my children there, as I often did, he would greet me cordially at the door or send someone to make sure that we were comfortable. He always found time to chat no matter how busy he was.

Galina, meanwhile, had been studying journalism and began to work in that field. In the early '60s, she worked as the editor of the department of the Novosti Press Agency that handled news from within the Soviet Union.

Ordinary journalists had no chance of being hired by the NPA; connections were the key. Not that good journalists were eager to work there: the main requirement was skill at following the party line, no matter how much distortion this required; initiative and talent were irrelevant.

From year to year, I observed Leonid being drained of strength in the losing battle with his children. He used to say of his daughter, "She has some kind of demon inside her. She's like a curse sent down on me."

Before his conflict with Viktoriya Petrovna, my father often visited Leonid at his dacha, spending the night there. He would watch as Leonid tried to give his recently divorced daughter some long-overdue discipline, alternately nagging and cajoling her, but all to no avail.

"One night she came home drunk, looking like something the cat dragged in," my father told me. "Lyonya stayed up until she came home and nearly dropped dead when he saw her. The next morning he began bawling her out over breakfast. It was like talking to a wall. She picked up her plate and stormed out of the dining room. I could see tears in Leonid's eyes. He had a full workday ahead. This is what his family had brought him to.

"All of his family treated me, Leonid's own brother, like a nobody. Good Lord, what a three-ring circus his family life was! How did he manage to survive it all? At the beginning, Leonid asked me to intervene. While scolding Galina, he would often say to me, 'Yasha, why don't you at least say something to her; you're her uncle after all!' Then that impudent little Galka would turn to me and say, 'Just you try!' and stalk out of the room. . . ."

Viktoriya and her daughter often had ugly, hysterical quarrels that ended with both of them turning to Leonid for comfort and support. He was near tears when this happened, too, and tried to unload his burdens on his brother: "What have I done to deserve this punishment, Yasha? I've been working like a mule all my life. I never take any time out to enjoy life. I've wanted to do the best for everyone around me, but I've always wound up doing more harm than good. Ever since Galina was a little girl, I let her have whatever her heart desired, but I never took part in raising her. As for Viktoriya, she has nothing but money on her mind; you know that."

Sometimes Leonid would go off to be alone in his study—and to weep. Back from a visit to his brother's dacha in the late '60s, my father said, "I went to Leonid's office to get a cigarette lighter. There was no answer to my knock on the door, so I figured no one was inside, and I went in. Leonid was alone at his desk, his eyes red. I asked him if he was sick. He was very distant. He pulled back slightly and said, 'All anyone is interested in is my health. No one cares what's happening with my soul.' "

In both my father's and my uncle's families, the upbringing of the children and grandchildren was firmly in the hands of the wives and grandmothers. Leonid Ilyich, who spent all his adult life in positions of leadership, often arrived home after midnight. He saw his children sporadically. Once when my father and I were in Leonid's office, talk turned to a subject near to the hearts of both men: their children and grandchildren. My uncle, referring to his wife and daughter, said, "What more do those dizzy broads want? They've grabbed everything they could lay their filthy paws on. They're both so wide that they can barely squeeze through the door, but they're not satisfied yet. It's my own fault, of course. Instead of racing from meeting to meeting, I should have been watching over my children—then I'd have a peaceful old age to look forward to. I practically never saw them. When I came home from work, they would already be sleeping. I would peek into the children's room and stroke them on the cheek. The next morning a car would be waiting outside the house, and off I went! I've spent my whole life running somewhere."

A little-known detail of Leonid's biography is that he had a third child, born at the end of the 1950s in either Moldavia or Kazakhstan. When the boy, whom Yakov Ilyich saw when he was four, grew up, his powerful father helped him, and he moved to Moscow. There he "misbehaved," as my father put it, and his life did not go well. Viktoriya Petrovna knew about her husband's illegitmate son, but my father was the only person I ever heard speak of him.

Yuri Churbanov, Galina's second husband, was a young militiaman. They married in April 1971, and he soon made a dizzying leap in his career. After their wedding, everyone heaved a deep sigh of relief: his second son-in-law was completely to Leonid's liking. I myself was somewhat shocked, because of the bad reputation that militiamen had among decent people in our country. The Russians called them *musor*, "trash."*

For a long time, the romance between Galina and Yuri had been the topic of detailed discussions. Handsome, standing tall and straight in his uniform, he impressed the Brezhnevs favorably. Here, they thought, is a forceful character. Even my father pinned high hopes on him, saying, "Finally there's a real man on the scene. He'll bring her into line!" My aunt Vera, an unsophisticated and unpretentious woman, was openly delighted with Galina's new husband. She had been mortified by tales of her niece's adventures and had scolded her more than once.

Galina was not a complete monster, not the hellcat sometimes portrayed in the press. She could be kind in her own condescending manner. She was temperamental but quick to forgive. She was well educated

*The Soviet militia functioned as a police force.

and, like her father, had a strong loyalty to friends. In her own circles, she was well loved. She was affectionate and reputed to know a thing or two about sex. And she lavished attention on Yuri.

Until he met Galina, his life had been lackluster. He was in no way outstanding: a young man who loved sports, his wife, and his son, Mischa. When he met the general secretary's daughter, everything changed. He was faced with a choice: either a stable, totally predictable and humdrum existence with his family or a life full of events, fame, flattery, and luxury at the side of a well-placed, unsettled, and spoiled woman. His friends advised him to choose the second: "You got lucky once; there will never be a second chance. . . ." All of a sudden Yuri Churbanov felt special, singled out by fate for fortune. He decided to divorce his wife and marry Galina.

They used the large new luxury apartment rapidly awarded them to indulge their shared passion—parties with an abundance of booze. They were quite happy, at the beginning.

One of Galina's close friends was Svetlana, the wife of Nikolay Shchelokov, head of the MVD, which was in charge of the militia. In exchange for his fawning loyalty, Leonid Brezhnev had pulled Shchelokov out of Dnepropetrovsk, brought him to Moscow, and given him the opportunity to rise to the post of minister. His wife was inordinately fond of diamonds and furs, as was Galina.

Watching the wives of the *nomenklatura* being chauffeured in their black automobiles to some presumably important gathering, I recalled what one historian has written about the czar's court at the end of the eighteenth century: "The luxury and extravagance of the aristocracy had grown, and exceedingly rich fur coats were worn." At the Soviet court, the *nomenklatura*'s wives rated one another by the quality and quantity of their coats, the number and price of one's furs serving as an indicator of social status rather than mere wealth. They created a definite hierarchy: Galina was the "first lady," Svetlana was the second, and some actress held third place, by virtue of her being the mistress of Grigory Romanov, secretary of the Leningrad Oblast party committee.

Churbanov rose swiftly in the ministry, having a father-in-law who was general secretary and a wife who was a close friend of his boss's wife. He received promotion after promotion, becoming successively colonel, major general, lieutenant general, and colonel general. For this, as for so many other things, my father had his own rather curious explanation: "Our Leonid always went in for pigeons, even as a kid. On Galka's advice, Yuri brought him the fanciest pigeons to be found in the whole country. Every time one of those birds craps, our Yuri Churbanov gets a new star on his uniform!" By 1980, he had ascended to the rank of Shchelokov's assistant, virtually the second militia boss in the country.

Leonid's lifelong friend, Kostya Grushevoy, himself a lieutenant general and chief of the political administration of the Moscow military district, was outraged: "I shed my blood for this rank. And now, Lyonya, you've gone and handed that punk, who's never fired a shot in his life, the same rank on a silver platter. Aren't you ashamed? You yourself were only a major general by the end of the war!" He insisted that no good would come of this promotion.

In the company of his son-in-law, Leonid began feeling uncomfortable for some reason, he said. He had had great hopes for Churbanov, expecting him to bring order to Galina's life. For a while, she did indeed quiet down: her infatuation with her new husband kept her busy for several years. But ultimately her husband turned out to be every bit as weak willed as the male members of the family he had married into.

At the beginning, he avidly sought out his father-in-law. In the evenings at the dacha, while Galina was arguing with her mother, he would drop by Leonid's study to talk. But Leonid did not react with great enthusiasm to these advances. He saw his own younger self in this handsome young opportunist, as though he were looking into a time-travel mirror.

In the late '70s, I went to a party given by the Brezhnev wives—something I almost never did—and was there when Galina came by with her husband. The men had been invited to show up later, after a preliminary "hen party," and Galina explained Yuri's presence by saying that they were planning to go to another gathering that evening. As always, she was outlandishly attired, in a light, fishnet dress, through which one could see her already sagging flesh. On her feet were gold-trimmed sandals that might have belonged to the wife of a Roman patrician, at least in some crazed designer's fancy. Her fingers boasted a dazzling number of rings.

Galina had a few drinks before the men arrived. When her brother, Yuri, dropped by with some male friends, Galina became even more buoyant and began to drape herself over one man after another. For some reason, Churbanov wasn't drinking that evening. He sat to one side looking gloomy. When Galina, hopping up and down like a little girl, approached him, swinging her hips and hanging from some man's neck, he grabbed her waist from behind and abruptly pulled her onto a chair: "Won't you ever sit down?" he said irately, his face livid. They left together soon afterward. It was obvious that their marriage was beginning to sour.

When drunk, Galina loved to prance about, cavorting and laughing—anything to be the center of attention. My father literally shook with frustration at the sight of her. After one of their many arguments, he told me, "I don't consider that nitwit my niece!"

Yakov Ilyich told me, too, of the traditional Russian wake held for his brother-in-law, Vera's husband, Zhora Grechkin. To keep Vera Ilyinichna from fainting, a nurse stood behind her, periodically giving her smelling salts.

Galina put in an appearance, dressed up for a night on the town and wearing the makeup of a streetwalker. Yet this was nothing more than what people had become accustomed to expect of her.

On her finger, Vera wore a diamond ring, a wedding-anniversary gift from her late husband. Galina, who had been eyeing it for years, sat next to the widow, slipped off the ring, and tried it on. "Aunt Vera," she said, "give it to me. I've adored it for such a long time."

Vera was speechless. My father, sitting nearby, took his niece to one side: "Galka, you're out of your mind. That was a gift from Grechkin!"

Galina, unruffled, said, "Oh well, he's dead now, and my aunt's an old woman; what does she need a ring for?" She didn't offer a word of condolence.

My uncle's trilogy includes the following passage: "In December 1947 a currency reform was carried out in the country, and there were individuals who . . . knew the exchange rates ahead of time and rushed to place their money in savings accounts. . . . I insisted that these people be expelled from the party."* Fine—expulsion from the party, I thought, reading this. But what about criminal prosecution?

In 1981, Galina was informed of an impending increase in the retail price of gold and jewelry, and she used this knowledge for personal gain: the day before the increase, she showed up with Svetlana Shchelokova in the biggest jewelry shop of Moscow's Arbat district. There they entered into a deal with the store's director: first they bought up all the largest items, and then the next morning they coolly returned the jewels to the stockroom, selling them at the new price. This was in blatant violation of Soviet law.

Semyon Tsvigun, a close friend of Leonid's, the husband of one of Vikoriya Petrovna's cousins and deputy chairman of the KGB, was hot on the trail of the general secretary's wayward daughter. When there was no longer any sense trying to conceal matters, Tsvigun paid Leonid a visit. Lying on the couch in his study, Brezhnev listened carefully as his friend told him of the jewelry-store caper and asked what should be done with Galina.

Saying "Prosecute her to the fullest extent of the law," Leonid turned toward the wall and wept. But Galina was never prosecuted.

Before long, Tsvigun shot himself. That day my father told me, "I may be her uncle, but I'd cast the first vote to send that bitch to the Butyrki.** I saw her a while back. She looked like a fishwife: glazed eyes, puffy mouth, and an ass bigger than her mother's. The hell with her, even if she is a doctor of science! All the grief she's put my brother through . . ."

When my father talked in this vein, I merely listened silently. Was Galina the only cause of my uncle's sorrows?

Leonid's son, Yuri, began his career modestly in the field of metallurgy. For two years after his graduation from the Dnepropetrovsk Met-

---

*Unlike cash, money in savings accounts was exchanged at its full value.
**A Moscow prison.

allurgy Institute, in 1955, he worked as a foreman of a tube-rolling shop at the Liebknecht Plant in the same city. Then he moved to Moscow with his young wife and entered the All-Union Foreign Trade Academy, where he specialized in the Scandinavian countries and learned English and Swedish.

The academy behind him, Yuri was shortly appointed engineer-in-chief and department head at the Soviet Trade Bureau in Sweden, and from 1966 to 1970 he was a deputy director of that bureau. He didn't distinguish himself, but in March 1979 he was appointed first deputy to the minister of foreign trade, a post known as a gold mine.

Bribery was pervasive in the ministry. The medium of exchange was not the ruble, cognac, or perfume but hard currency and electronic equipment. From Sweden came containers full of videocassette recorders. A great rarity in Russia in the late '70s, they cost fifteen to twenty thousand rubles—almost as much as a Volga in good condition.

Trips abroad were a special source of income for typical members of the *nomenklatura*, who, instead of conducting the business they had been sent abroad to do, stalked discount stores in search of the small consumer goods always in short supply in the Soviet Union. They bought up whatever they could find—cigarettes, lighters, souvenirs, handkerchiefs, paper napkins. . . .

Everyone who went abroad knew a black marketeer who would pick up the merchandise and leave the money—very discreetly, of course. You would never see the general secretary's son or grandson selling a tape recorder in an alley or haunting one of the consignment stores that bought used goods legally. The wives had their own buyers, who took dresses, cosmetics, socks, handbags, and brand-name diaphragms. The ultimate consumers were usually high-class prostitutes, the kind who could invest a thousand rubles in a Christian Dior jacket or five hundred in a skirt.

It's no secret that the trade agreements written by officials in the Ministry of Foreign Trade, including Yuri Brezhnev, provided little or no protection for the Soviet Union. Contracts for shipments of second-rate merchandise were sealed by bribes, gifts, and business and personal favors, including orgies that destroyed not only individual reputations but the prestige of the entire Soviet government as well. Our negotiators, remarkably compliant after being treated to lavish dinners, signed deals allowing foreign companies to dump wares on the Soviet masses that were deemed unfit for the West. Year after year the Yuri Brezhnevs purchased machinery with missing parts and products that had long been decaying or gathering rust in warehouses. Yes, butter and meat were sold to us at cut-rate prices—after their "sell by" dates had expired, that is. And such deals were hailed as favorable to the Soviet Union. The attitude was a sort of haughty "let them eat rancid butter."

Their disgraceful contracts signed, the diplomats returned, bringing their booty home by ship, plane, or train. The bribes, though not terribly large by Western standards, brought joy to many a wife and child and tidy profits to the black marketeers.

Diplomatic work was considered a sinecure even in the first years of the Soviet state, when an unhealthy atmosphere of intrigue, nepotism, and bribery began developing in the trade agencies. Many unqualified, illiterate people with no knowledge of economics or trade landed jobs in Soviet commerce and made gross blunders. In one well-known case, a contract to buy tin scythes, so weak that a child could bend them in two, was signed in exchange for a bribe and a smile.

I don't know a single case in which a Soviet trade official was punished for a deal that lost the government money. Such impunity signaled a green light. Honor and conscience, to these officials, were ballast to be discarded. Their sole concern was to keep making trips abroad.

Yuri Brezhnev was not an evil man, but he shared the weaknesses common to all the Brezhnevs. Like my father, he suffered from alcoholism and was treated for it unsuccessfully. To his credit, he always strove to maintain a proper façade and did not drink himself into oblivion, at least not in public.

He met his wife, Lyudmila Vladimirovna, or Lyusya as she was called in the family, during his final year at the institute. A pug-nosed blonde with delicate pink skin and barely visible eyebrows and eyelashes, she was rather pretty. They had two children: Leonid, who was named after his grandfather but resembled his mother, and Andrey, who looked somewhat like the general secretary.

For some reason, the Brezhnevs never considered Lyusya "good enough" for Yuri. Even my father, who usually shunned gossip, was of the opinion that Lyusya had "snared him." For that matter, Russian families are rarely happy with a son's bride. If she is made of purest gold, they will still find flaws in her.

Although there was no public display of the sheet at Yuri's marriage, virginity was still prized at the time. Rumor had it that Lyusya had got Yuri dead drunk at the wedding so that he wouldn't notice her dishonor. The Brezhnev relatives rehashed the story for years; behind her back, they used to say, "Lyusya really found a fool in Yuri." I found these insinuations tasteless and would cut them short.

Lyusya was a model wife and mother, from what I could gather. She built her life around her home and family, avoiding the intrigues so important to the other court wives. Of course, her situation was completely different from that of ordinary Soviet women: she had no need to work outside the home, and there was no shortage of money. She bought clothes and shoes in the Kremlin store or abroad; she certainly didn't stand in line for two hours at Detsky Mir (Children's World) to buy shoes for her sons. Leonid also helped them out and invited his grandsons to the Crimea for the summer. And with Yuri bringing back from Scandinavia whatever he could, Lyusya, swimming in abundance, soon lost touch with real life.

Lyusya's parents, like the majority of Leonid Ilyich's in-laws, made full use of their unexpected good fortune. Her mother, Antonina Petrovna, a longtime resident of Dnepropetrovsk, often came to Moscow to visit. A hardheaded, farsighted businesswoman, she used each trip to turn a profit. In the '60s, when Italian raincoats (the Russians liked to call them Bologna raincoats) were the rage, Antonina bought up large supplies to resell back home at inflated prices. She also brought back nylon shirts, "shirts by Brezhnev," as her clients dubbed them.

Along with foreign cars and hard currency, Yuri Brezhnev had a passion for collecting little porcelain dogs. Friends, acquaintances, and hangers-on often brought him new pieces. Even Leonid Ilyich bought his son porcelain dogs.

During the Andropov anti-corruption campaign that followed my uncle's death, Yuri Brezhnev was never touched, though the heads of many other *nomenklatura* figures rolled. Not until Gorbachev's presidency, when a special commission investigated the Brezhnev family, was he finally pensioned off.

Chapter Twenty

██████████████

"THEY LOST A GENERAL SECRETARY...."

O mortal man, you own nothing but your soul.

PYTHAGORAS

He made many errors, but no one can say that his career came easy, no one can accuse my uncle of laziness. Not at the beginning, at least: there was a time when he worked up to eighteen hours a day, leaving home in the early morning and coming home after midnight. During the first decades of Leonid's career, his life was a race between office, field, building site, factory shop, smoke-filled meeting room, train, and plane—a way of life that left him hardly a minute to stop and reflect.

While on business trips to metallurgy plants in the 1940s and '50s, Yakov would visit his brother in Zaporozhe, Kishinev, and Alma-Ata, as Leonid's party work took him to each of these cities in turn. A typical visit to Zaporozhe, where enormous efforts were being made to restore local industries devastated during the war, gives a sense of Leonid's pace in the early days.

Yakov and his sister-in-law, Viktoriya Petrovna, are sitting in the kitchen, waiting for Leonid, talking about their relatives back in Dneprodzerzhinsk. On the table are egg and cabbage pies and a bottle of the liqueur Yakov has brought from Natalya Denisovna. It is well after midnight when Leonid comes home. He enters the kitchen wearing his perennial smile, hugs his brothers, sits down in front of a cup of tea, and manages a few words before dropping his head into his hands and falling asleep. About fifteen minutes later, he wakes up, finishes his tea, and does some paperwork. Soon it is morning, time to return to work.

Thousands of functionaries lived out their lives this way, honorably discharging their solemn duty, as they saw it. They had no private life to speak of. They had chosen the sole, infallible God, and their descendants would remember them with pride and gratitude. As phones rang and express telegrams requesting urgent aid came in from the famine-stricken regions or the front lines, they worked tirelessly, giving scant thought to their own well-being. They clenched their fists, gritted their teeth, and swallowed their *validol*, washing it down with strong tea. For their efforts, they were rewarded with testimonials, pins, medals, and the joy of achievement. "We didn't get enough sleep or enough love," said Leonid Ilyich, referring to his whole generation.

Now he had arrived at the apex of power and fame. There was nothing left to aspire to. But where was the happiness that should have been his?

Viktoriya Petrovna used to say, not without a certain pride, that her husband "had been able to drink a whole barrel of vodka when he was young." Whether that was true or not, Leonid definitely enjoyed drinking. But his drinking came to an end for good in the mid-1970s, after a doctor at the Fourth Department decided to be candid. "Leonid," he said, "as far as alcohol goes, you've already had your lifetime's share. And if you start drinking what by right belongs to everyone else, then you can forget about living any longer. It's that simple."

Leonid had begun drinking as a teenager. To avoid his mother's wrath, he had always taken care to disguise his breath afterward, eating bread with lard and onions. "I smacked him with that stick so hard that sparks flew," Natalya Denisovna used to say in her old age, recalling a no-nonsense drubbing she once gave Leonid when she caught him drinking. But she never succeeded in beating the habit out of her favorite son. Only his doctor's words did the trick.

Smoking was another story. Leonid quit and started up and quit again and started up yet again. Once he joked, paraphrasing Mark Twain, "It's easy to stop smoking. I've done it forty times!" Viktoriya Petrovna, who kept close watch over her husband's health and realized that he was getting nowhere, decided to take matters into her own hands. She had all his cigarettes confiscated, his lighter and matches locked up. But one night the Soviet party chief, in undershorts and a T-shirt, wended his way to the kitchen, fished some cigarette butts out of the garbage pail, and crept into the toilet to light up. He was observed by one of the servants, who reported him promptly to his wife. She then forbade all smoking in the house and ordered the removal of every item connected to smoking.

I thought that the pressure from his wife and his doctors actually contributed to his degeneration, making him feel deprived of his manhood. I still think this, though I was practically accused of treason when I made my opinion known. Intimidated by the endless medical tests, the worried glances of his physicians, and the endless conversations about his health, my uncle came to believe in his own illnesses. He began thinking constantly about his aches and pains, only occasionally taking time out to think about affairs of state.

Leonid also began to be irritated by the constant questioning about his health. Once when his wife asked him how he felt, he replied angrily, "You people always ask how I feel; it's as though you can hardly wait for me to drop dead."

Viktoriya Petrovna's feelings were hurt. In reality, his death was the last thing in the world any of his relatives or in-laws wanted. Indeed, no one around him wanted to see him dead; he was necessary to them all. The only thing required of him was that he play the role of general secretary, and he did so splendidly for years, though in later years as little more than a figurehead.

During those last years, Leonid sought solitude ever more frequently, avoiding contact with everyone as much as possible; one of the few who enjoyed his full confidence was his chief bodyguard, a man who had been with him at the front lines during World War II.

Even when his walk began to betray the ravages of time, he never slouched; his shoulders were as broad as ever, his chin still jutted proudly from his unbowed face. But when I would look closer and see his dim, glassy eyes, the overall effect was a disconcerting mixture of youthful fire and touchingly defenseless frailty. Occasionally the characteristically broad, captivating Brezhnev smile would flash across my uncle's now doughy face, but his eyes did not light up as before. It seemed to me that he had little idea of what was happening around him. He often had an intent expression, as though he were listening closely to himself, trying to detect the sound of his diseases progressing.

One evening at the end of the 1970s when I was visiting my father in the Kremlin hospital, I saw the general secretary giving a televised speech. "He's a decrepit old man now," said my father after I kissed him on the cheek and sat down next to his bed. "I only thank God that our poor mother will never see him this way."

When my father heard Leonid say that the economy should be run economically, he grumbled, "Yeah, and oil should be oily."

He sat up in bed and turned the volume down. "Don't listen, honey. I don't think even he understands what he's talking about anymore." I looked closely at the screen. It was not a pretty sight. Leonid's skin was flabby, his eyes glassy and lifeless.

I recalled the time in 1976 when he had been revived after having been pronounced clinically dead. He remained seriously ill for about a half a year. His speech and his thinking were permanently impaired, and his memory began to fail; he remembered events quite well but forgot names. Predictions of his imminent demise circulated throughout the country, and people I didn't even know would ask me about his health.

After he returned to work, a new joke gained currency: "The general secretary has resumed his duties without regaining consciousness."

His barely comprehensible official addresses began to be taken as the whims of a senile old man; his speech impediments were copied by impersonators and ridiculed in anecdotes. What most people didn't know was that my uncle had lost his teeth at a young age and wore dentures and that his jaw had been blown out by a shell fragment during World War II. No wonder then that as the years passed, speaking and chewing became harder and harder for him. "You know, with false teeth and jaw it's harder to give patriotic speeches," my father would remind me.

Several members of the Brezhnev family, including me, were sure in 1976 that he would retire. Had he resigned then for health reasons, his memory might have been honored by future generations; at least, there would have been one less disgrace on his conscience, the war in Afghanistan. But he would remain in power another six years, long enough to lose every shred of the people's respect.

I remember clearly one of the times my father and I met with him for lunch in the Kremlin. At dessert, ice cream was served in small silver goblets. Leonid's hand trembled, and he splashed some of the ice cream onto his face. As I saw a white drop suspended indecorously from his nose, I was overcome with pity. There was something terribly childlike about him at that moment. I stroked his hand gently, and his eyes clouded over. I picked up a napkin and dried his nose. So this was what it meant to have limitless power and to be helpless. . . .

After 1976, it was decided that he needed a whole team of doctors to monitor his health. Medical stations were installed at his dacha, in his apartment, and wherever else he could be expected to spend a considerable length of time. The doctors found it necessary to examine him several times a day. But you didn't need a degree to see how ill he was.

As far as I know, not even his closest relatives were kept apprised of the true state of his health, though my father learned a bit from Leonid himself. On strolls together near Dalnyaya, he complained of a pain in the spine and revealed that he was being constantly tormented with shots and blood transfusions.

After these encounters, my father would tell me, "I wish he would retire. What good does it all do him? He can't even drink, smoke, or make love anymore. Viktoriya's relatives, that swarm of locusts, are the only ones that derive any pleasure from his power."

Leonid Ilyich, following doctors' advice, reduced his workload to several hours a day. He sometimes hinted to my father that he had a form of leukemia and that his doctors were keeping him alive "artificially."

"I can still see him now," my father would tell me after his brother's death, "walking down the path of the park at the dacha, drenched in sweat, taking short, mincing steps, almost shuffling with those sick legs of his. His gait was so uncertain that he reminded me of a child learning to walk. Why did the doctors have to put him through such an ordeal? To prove they were doing their job?"

What did my uncle have to comfort him in his last days? Was he a religious man? I don't think so, not in any serious way. Of course, when he was born, the peasant masses—and urbanized peasants like his parents—still prayed, attended church on Sundays, celebrated Russian Orthodox holidays, baptized their children, married in church, and held religious services for the dead. Religious rituals and the Ten Commandments were important parts of socialization. But this religiosity, imbibed like mother's milk, was kept in place by force of habit more than anything else.

Some of it persisted. Every year on the anniversaries of his parents' deaths, Leonid would ask his brother to drive to the Yelokhovsky Cathedral and light candles for the peace of their souls. For Easter, he would eat the traditional *paskha* cakes and decorated eggs; before he stopped drinking altogether, he would also take a drink to mark the occasion. In October 1964, two days before the culmination of the plot to unseat Khrushchev, my father suddenly remembered that Leonid had asked him to light a candle for luck. I went with him. He insisted that we go to a church near the Sokol subway station, which tradition holds favorable for those born under the sign of Sagittarius. Since many members of our family were born in early December, my father, my children, and I would go there often.

Unlike his predecessor—Khrushchev had thousands of churches destroyed and promised that by 1970 he would be able to display the last remaining priest in Russia—my uncle was not hostile to religion. One of the things that Leonid saw in Brezhnevo in 1923, on his way from Kamenskoye to Kursk, was the pilfering and desecration of the church where his grandmother had taken him for Communion as a boy.

He sometimes spoke to family members of this outrage and never forgot it.

The family in which Leonid and my father had grown up was religious, but no more so than was required for decency's sake. There was an icon on the wall in the corner, and Ilya Yakovlevich had the children say grace before supper and pray before going to sleep. But when I asked my father to recite the Our Father, he could remember only part of it.

At the age of seven, children took First Communion after a first confession. Only then, it was believed, did they have to answer before God for all their own deeds. Younger children were like angels: if they sinned, it was their mothers' fault.

My father told me about walking to his first confession and Communion. His grandmother Stepanida looked as nervous as he felt.

"You go up to the priest, Yashenka," she said. "You kiss his hand, and then you tell him you're a sinner. When I took that naughty Lyonya to confession, he refused to kiss the priest's hand. 'What next?' he said. I could have died for shame. I don't know how I managed to walk home."

It was traditional in the Brezhnev family for Natalya and Ilya to go with their children on the last day of Lent to Ilya's parents in Brezhnevo, to ask forgiveness for their misdeeds. Leonid, who caused more than his share of trouble, was readily forgiven by the adults; he had a charming smile and was usually considerate and generous. He was also known to be quick to cool off after anger, not prone to hold grudges. After Yakov and Stepanida graciously forgave their children and grandchildren, everyone kissed and happily said good-bye. The next morning might find the boys misbehaving all over again, shooting pebbles from a slingshot or chasing the neighbor's rooster, but little Vera would be crossing her arms on her chest. "Granny, see what a good little girl I am," she would say.

The two most cherished holidays in old Russia, Christmas and Easter, were preceded by a fast requiring abstention from meat and milk. People made do with potatoes, bread, sunflower oil, cabbage, and kvass. This regimen not only cleansed the body but trained the spirit as well. Natalaya observed the fast but did not ask the same of her children, demanding only that they not eat anything containing meat or lard.

One time Leonid and Yasha decided that they would fast along with their mother. They held out for one day, but on the first night Yasha's hunger pangs got the best of him. He got out of bed, tiptoed to the kitchen, and started eating. Leonid joined him. Their mother came in at the height of the feast.

"Look at you sinners; God will see you for sure," she said, laughing. "At night, the devil tries twice as hard."

During the first years after the 1917 revolution, squads of Young Communists, the predecessors of the Komsomol, marched with bugles and drums down the streets of Kamenskoye, singing anti-religious songs.

> Down with all the bourgeoisie
> And the priests as well,
> We'll climb up to heaven,
> And send the gods to hell.

Natalya would cross herself when she heard these songs. Leonid and Yasha did not join in, fearing their father's wrath.

In the *gimnaziya* that Leonid attended, he was exposed to anti-religious teachings that must have had an effect on him. One night he heard little Yasha, in bed near him, quietly asking God to forgive something he had done. "You dope," he said mockingly. "There's no God; the teacher told us so at school."

For many Russians, of course, poetry is the true religion. That and friendship.

Recalling his childhood, Leonid Ilyich loved to recite Yesenin's verses about the colt with the auburn mane:

> *That sweet and silly fool,*
> *Oh where is he racing to now?*

He was reminded of something he had seen as a boy in Brezhnevo: an auburn-maned colt kicking up his slender legs in sheer exuberance in a green glade, where he had been let loose to enjoy the spring sun, the smells, and the freedom.

I remember another phrase of Yesenin's that my uncle loved to repeat: "In my heart I never lie."

In his old age, in the intimate company of friends and loved ones, he would read Yesenin's poems with tears in his eyes. One of his favorites speaks of fleeting youth:

> *No regrets have I, no tears, no pleas,*
> *Fate has but one thing in store.*
> *Like apple blossoms, swept off the trees,*
> *Youth will be mine never more.*

> *My desires have waned. . . . Is it life I have led,*
> *Or a dream of a morning in spring,*
> *When, on a rose-colored pony, I sped,*
> *Through the dawn like a bird on the wing?*

Leonid sometimes said that he felt as close to the poet as to a brother. Once he remarked, "What a beautiful soul. He was a true Russian, his heart always restless. He wrote, 'I came to the Earth/To leave it as soon as I could.'" Leonid evidently knew that the poet's "suicide" in 1925 had been faked by the GPU (a predecessor of the KGB). As he said, "How could they have dared lay their hands on such a noble and defenseless human being! He left life before he could keep his promise—to 'pour out his heart to the last drop.'"

Leonid treasured Kostya Grushevoy, considering him his most loyal and devoted friend. Their friendship, which had begun when they were both young, was simple, profound, and close. There were short periods when they were separated, but their emotional bonds were permanent and only grew stronger with the passing years. During his last years, Leonid Ilyich reserved his greatest affection for Kostya and for the youngest members of the Brezhnev clan.

He had never had the time, by his own admission, to participate in his children's upbringing, nor were his grandchildren raised in his presence. So during his final years, he focused all his love on his great-grand-daughter Galochka, named for his own daughter. Everyone was always touched to see the tenderness with which he handled the girl. She adored her great-grandfather, who liked to sit next to her and kiss her little fingers one by one.

He worried about the kind of a life she would have: "Her parents are young and foolish. Galina has her own life, and Viktoriya and I are old now. What will become of her after we die?"

On November 7, 1982, I turned on the television and saw my uncle's face close up; he was standing on the rostrum, gazing at the colorful, noisy crowd, occasionally waving his gloved hand in a characteristic gesture. Disturbed by something I had seen in his face, I called my father the next day; when I inquired about his brother's health, he answered cheerfully that Leonid had spoken to him just the day before and hadn't complained of his health.

"Go visit him; I don't like the look of his eyes," I suggested.

"To drink tea with Viktoriya?"

"You could have tea with him alone in his study," I insisted. "Go see him."

On November 11, the Soviet mass media announced that Leonid Ilyich Brezhnev, outstanding political leader and general secretary of the Communist Party of the Soviet Union, had died at the age of seventy-five, after a protracted illness.

Nowadays few care whether or not he died a natural death. What my father told me, with great bitterness, was that after Leonid collapsed in his study on the morning of November 10, his wife was not allowed to see him. His life could have been saved at that time if medical assistance had been given, but none was; a physician was summoned, but only to write the death certificate.

I didn't encourage my father to speak in this vein, worried as I was about something entirely different: as death approached, did my uncle yearn for forgiveness, did he prepare his soul for the final test?

Later my father admitted that a few weeks before his death, Leonid had called him—something he did rarely, only when his wife was not around to know—and said, "Yasha, I can feel that the end is near. I'd like to be able to start everything again from the beginning, but my strength is gone. I'm so tired."

"Tired of what?" my father asked.

"I'm tired of living," answered Leonid and hung up.

When my father related this short conversation to me, I sensed immediately that my uncle had been reaching out for understanding and forgiveness. Who, besides his brother, was left for him to confide in? Earlier that year, his age-mate and best friend, Kostya Grushevoy, had died.

Paul Verlaine wrote, "I know of nothing more cheerful than a funeral," and my uncle's was a fine show, the spectacle of an entire nation in mourning. Factory whistles sounded, black flags sagged under the cold November rains, and Leonid Brezhnev was buried right on schedule. What was left of him was displayed in the Hall of Columns of the House of the Union, where for several hours the body of the general secretary was completely accessible, with no bodyguard ready to pounce on a would-be assassin.

Before emigrating, I saw it all on videotape: my father standing to the left of the coffin, hatless and wearing an overcoat; beside him, Leonid's wife, his grandchildren, other relatives. The guard of honor draws to a halt. Then the mortal remains of Leonid Brezhnev, the grandson of a peasant and the son of a worker, are wheeled down the "corpse way" to Red Square. I recalled how fond he had been of joking that he had "gone from Red Square to Red Square," referring to the days when he had worked in downtown Kursk in the 1920s.

After he was buried by the Kremlin wall, the final salute rang out, and the guests began leaving, heading in their black automobiles for the Russian-style wake. Once there, with vodka, caviar, crabs, and expensive candy, the mourners proposed toasts and offered condolences. It lasted for hours, though I could stand only thirty minutes of it. What a ridiculous, meaningless tradition. Many laudatory words were spoken. Someone pronounced the diagnosis that the Communists loved so much: "He burned out on the job."

To everyone's surprise, my father did not drink; steering clear of anyone who might express condolences, he mourned his brother as inconspicuously as he could. When several days later, he came to my home on Lenin Prospekt, his blood pressure had shot up; his eyes were still red, his face was flushed.

I invited him to stay for supper. He sat down on the bench in my kitchen and then, without saying a word, laid his head on the table and began to sob. "I'm like a dog without its master," he told me as he wiped his tears. "They lost a general secretary. I lost a brother. . . ."

He sat up. "I was sitting there at the wake and started thinking of our childhood. Seryozha was a mill operator who worked in the same shop as our father, and his family lived in the house next to ours. His wife, Taisia, tall and freckle-faced, as skinny as a rail, worked serving food in the cafeteria. Every year they had a new child, but each one died in infancy. There was always a little square-shaped crib hanging in a corner of their tiny room; Seryozha never lost hope that he would someday have an heir. Each time a child of theirs died, Taisia would hold a wake. The kids from the neighborhood would flock in and descend on the long table where the food was laid out: pickles, fluffy potatoes, lard, and sweet carrot pies, a real banquet in those days. Taisia would sit to one side on her bed and tell us, drying her tears with her apron, 'Little ones, say a few words about my Vanechka (or my Sashenka or my Petenka).' The children performed their duty well, offering a few kind words for the baby that had been looking up from its crib a few days before. My sister, Vera, and I were always among the mourners, but Leonid was too old to take part. He was associating with a whole other crowd by then. After the wake, we would wander off to our homes, sleepy eyed and contented. Once while I was climbing the steep staircase on my way home, I boasted that 'when our Lyonka dies, we'll throw a big wake for him, too!' The other children looked at Vera and me with such envy. . . ."

"He got his wake all right. As fine as anyone could hope for."

One evening on the anniversary of Leonid's death, my father told me a story from his childhood that he had been holding back for years. "It was nighttime and quiet in the house; Leonid and Vera had long since fallen asleep. Our parents were in the kitchen, drinking tea. I listened to their conversation.

" 'Ilyusha,' said my mother, 'a Gypsy woman came to the yard today. You know how they are; once they get your attention, nothing will shake them loose. She insisted on telling my fortune. She said our children will have unusual lives. Our eldest will fly high, so high that no one will be able to reach him. He'll have fame, fortune, and love—everything but happiness. And because of him, our other children will also be unhappy.'

" 'The higher he flies, the more it'll hurt when he falls,' said my father, standing up. Through the kitchen door, I saw him gently pat my mother's head, bend down, whisper something in her ear, and go off to bed. The workers had to leave early for the mill.

"My mother stayed in the kitchen for a long time, quietly drying tears and whispering prayers. I felt sorry for her and wanted to hug her, but I didn't dare: she liked things to be done a certain way. I just lay in the dark, wondering what the word *fame* meant. I couldn't figure it out, so I decided to ask my brother the next day. But when morning came, I had forgotten all about the Gypsy and my parents' late-night talk. Was it real? For years, I was sure it was a dream.

"Only in 1937, when Leonid was hiding from the NKVD in Sverdlovsk, did I ask my mother about the Gypsy, revealing what I had overheard as a little boy. She and I were on our way home from a series of grueling interrogations. 'Mama,' I said, straining to move my lips, painfully bruised by a hysterical interrogator. 'Nothing will happen to our Lyonka. He has to survive. After all, he hasn't lived to see fame yet.' . . . In the end, he saw it all right."

"Do you know what fame is now?" I asked.

He smiled sadly: "A painted lady that stalks the world, seducing the weak of heart, dropping her victims by the wayside when she's through with them."

"My brother was wrong to have climbed so high," he told me later. "No matter how high you rise, you can't sleep on more than one bed at a time or ride in more than one car or wear more than one suit. Viktoriya Petrovna already has one foot in the grave, and she won't be able to take anything with her when she goes. So what was the purpose of all those family feuds? You remember how many scenes she threw, how much yelling and screaming there was in their home—and all for nothing! How many frayed nerves did she cause Lyonya over the years? He was in the wrong place, Luba. Without political power he could have lived a fine life, given his talent and personality."

EPILOGUE

In the fall of 1990, my father and I went to the Church of the Holy Trinity and Sergiy Radonezhsky in the Lenin Hills, where our family had been going for years. It was crowded and stuffy. Father grew dizzy from the smell of incense but stayed on his feet during the entire service, as required. I lit candles for all my relatives, both living and dead. We took the priest's blessing.

As we were walking out, I had a sudden idea: I ordered a prayer service for my grandparents, all deceased. Taking a paper marked "for peace of their souls," I wrote in their names: *Ilya, Natalya, Nikolay, Anastasiya.*

After leaving, we passed the fountain by the main entrance to Moscow State University, site of so many painful memories. As we strolled under the trees, I showed my father the bench where Helmut had announced his departure.

"Do you still think of him even now, Daughter?"

"I will remember him as long as I live."

A few months later, I was on a plane bound for the United States.

Index

A

INDEX

ABOUT THE AUTHOR

LUBA BREZHNEVA was educated at the Moscow State Pedagogical Institute of Foreign Languages, where she earned the equivalent of a master of arts in French and German. She worked in the Soviet Union and in Algeria as a translator and teacher and then in Moscow as a journalist for the Znaniye publishing house. She emigrated to the United States in 1990. Ms. Brezhneva now lives in northern California.

ABOUT THE TRANSLATOR

GEOFFREY POLK, a native of New York City raised in California, studied Russian in high school and graduated from San Francisco State University. He met the author in the fall of 1991.

ABOUT THE TYPE

This book was set in Centaur, a typeface designed by the American typographer Bruce Rogers in 1929. Centaur was a typeface which Rogers adapted from the fifteenth-century type of Nicholas Jenson and modified in 1948 for a cutting by the Monotype Corporation.